HIGH SCHOOL FOOTBALL
RULES BY TOPIC
2016

ROBERT B. GARDNER, Publisher
Bob Colgate, Editor
NFHS Publications

To maintain the sound traditions of this sport, encourage sportsmanship and minimize the inherent risk of injury, the National Federation of State High School Associations (NFHS) writes playing rules for varsity competition among student-athletes of high school age. High school coaches, game officials and administrators who have knowledge and experience regarding this particular sport and age group volunteer their time to serve on the rules committee. Member associations of the NFHS independently make decisions regarding compliance with or modification of these playing rules for the student-athletes in their respective states.

NFHS rules are used by education-based and non-education-based organizations serving children of varying skill levels who are of high school age and younger. In order to make NFHS rules skill-level and age-level appropriate, the rules may be modified by any organization that chooses to use them. Except as may be specifically noted in the NFHS Football Rules Book, the NFHS makes no recommendation about the nature or extent of the modifications that may be appropriate for children who are younger or less skilled than high school varsity athletes.

Every individual using the NFHS football rules is responsible for prudent judgment with respect to each contest, athlete and facility, and each athlete is responsible for exercising caution and good sportsmanship. The NFHS football rules should be interpreted and applied so as to make reasonable accommodations for athletes, coaches and officials with disabilities.

2016 High School Football Rules By Topic

Produced by Referee Enterprises Inc., publishers of *Referee* magazine.

Published by the
NATIONAL FEDERATION OF STATE HIGH SCHOOL ASSOCIATIONS
PO Box 690
Indianapolis, IN 46206
Phone: 317-972-6900, Fax: 317-822-5700
www.nfhs.org

ISBN-13: 978-1-58208-315-5

Printed in the United States of America

Table of Contents

2016 NFHS Football Rules Changes

Rule Changed	Rule Change Description
1-5-1d(5)a	Completely clear or completely white tooth and mouth protectors are no longer prohibited.
1-5 NOTE; 1-5-2b	Football gloves are now required to meet either the new SFIA specification or the existing NOCSAE test standard at the time of manufacture.
2-17; 9-3-6; 9-3 PENALTY	Clipping in the free-blocking zone is now illegal.

2016 Editorial Changes

Diagram NOTE; 1-5-1b(1); 1-5-1b(2)a, (3)a;
1-5-3a(1)a; 2-38; 4-3-2; 5-1-1b; 7-5 PENALTY;
9-3-5; 9-4-3h; 9-4 PENALTY; 9-5-1a; 9-8-1a; 10-2-5; 10-5-1a; PENALTY SUMMARY.

New Case Plays for 2016

2016 Points of Emphasis

1. Risk Minimization

2. Legal and Illegal Blocks

3. Legal Jerseys, Pants and Pads

4. Unfair Acts

Introduction

Rules by Topic is a collection of information like no other.

Combining numerous NFHS educational elements into one collective resource will improve football rules understanding and retention.

Included in the book:

Rules — Official *NFHS Football Rules Book* language and references are linked, combining related items by topic. That way, all related items are found in one location, from definitions to penalties.

Case Plays — Taken right from the *NFHS Football Case Book*, related case plays are imbedded within the topic for easy reference. Some case plays are excerpted to show emphasis on special situations, but all rulings match the NFHS Football Case Book.

Rationales — The reasons behind the NFHS football rules are included, used from previous years' Comments on the Rules and rule change summaries. You not only see the rule, you learn the reason behind it.

Fundamentals — Related *NFHS Football Rules Book* fundamentals are connected to the specific topic.

In Simple Terms — Summary statements that take complex NFHS football rules and make them easier to understand are found throughout the book.

Did You Know? — Historical tidbits provide basis for the NFHS football rules as written today.

Signals — Thumbnail images of the correct NFHS football signals are connected to penalties for easy reference.

Rules by Topic is designed to complement the official NFHS publications. While not replacing the NFHS Football Rules Book and NFHS Football Case Book, *Rules by Topic* offers a different way to learn the rules. Some rules and case plays are repeated because they apply to more than one topic.

Rules by Topic will change the way you look at football rules and will greatly enhance your football rules knowledge.

Note: New or revised football rules language is indicated with gray shading. New football case book plays, or those with new language, are preceded by an asterisk (*).

Topic 1
Field and Equipment

PlayPic®

Key Terms

The goal is the vertical plane midway between the sidelines extending indefinitely above the inside of the uprights and the front edge of the crossbar and in the same vertical plane as the inside edge of the end line (1-2-5a).

The field is the area within the boundary lines and the end lines (2-10-1). The field of play is the area within the boundary lines and the goal lines (2-10-2). The side zones are the areas bounded by the sidelines, the hash marks and the goal lines (2-10-3).

The end zones are 10 yards in depth and are located at each end of the field between the goal line and the end line. The goal line is in the end zone and a team's end zone is the one it is defending (2-10-4).

The boundary lines are the end lines and sidelines and are out of bounds (2-26-1). The end line is the outer limit of each end zone (2-26-2). The goal line is the vertical plane which separates the field of play from the end zone. When related to a live ball in a runner's possession (touching inbounds) while the ball is over the out-of-bounds area, the goal line includes the extension beyond the sidelines. A team's own goal line is the one it is defending (2-26-3).

The hash marks are a series of marks parallel with the sidelines which divide the field of play longitudinally into thirds. The hash marks shall be marked so that they are bisected by the yard lines (2-26-4).

The line to gain is the yard line established when a new series (first down) is awarded. Unless there is a penalty following the ready-for-play signal, the line to gain is 10 yards in advance of the foremost point of the ball when placed for the first down of the series. If the line to gain extends into the end zone, the goal line is the line to gain (2-26-5).

The sideline is the lateral limit of the field of play and the end zones. It extends from one end line to the other (2-26-6).

A yard line is any line and its vertical plane parallel to the end lines. The yard lines, marked or unmarked, in the field of play are numbered in yards from a team's own goal line to the middle of the field (2-26-7).

Topic:
Field

The game of football is played on a rectangular field 360 by 160 feet (1-1-2). The field shall be a rectangular area with dimensions, lines, zones, goals and markers. There shall be two sidelines running the length of the field along each side line that serve as boundary lines for play. It is recommended there be a slope of 1/4 inch per foot from the center of the field to each sideline on a natural grass field. There shall be two goal lines, running parallel to each other and perpendicular to the sidelines. The field of play is the area within the boundary lines, and the goal lines. There shall be two endlines, running parallel to each other, parallel to the goal lines that serve as a boundary line or play (1-2-1). The rise from each sideline to the center of a natural grass field is 20 inches when the recommended slope is used (1-2-1 NOTE).

Lines and Markings

Yard-line markers, constructed of soft, pliable materials, if placed on the ground, should be no closer than 5 yards to the sideline (1-2-2).

Lines shall be marked with a noncaustic, nontoxic material designed for marking fields such as powdered gypsum, calcium carbonate and liquid aerosol paint. It is recommended that these lines be white. Neither lime, hydrated lime or other chemical derivatives of lime, nor caustic material of any kind may be used for marking football fields (1-2-3a).

Yard lines shall be marked with a continuous line every 5 yards beginning and ending 4 inches from each sideline (1-2-3b). Game administration may place on the field of play, 4 inches from each sideline, yard-line extensions that should be 24 inches in length and 4 inches in width (1-2-3b NOTE 1). If the field of play has a logo in the center or at any other part of the field of play, that logo shall not obstruct from the visibility of the required marks every five yards. A solid or shadow-bordered 4-inch-wide line is permissible. A shadow line is a line that designates the required 4-inch width by use of a border or outline lines, at least 1/4-inch wide which shall lie within the 4-inch width. Shadow lines that are the natural color of the field of play are permissible. The area within these lines need not be one color, but the continuous 4-inch-wide outline must be clearly visible to the game officials (1-2-3b NOTE 2).

End lines and sidelines shall be continuous lines at least 4 inches wide. All other field dimension lines should be marked 4 inches in width (1-2-3c).

A restraining line is a line placed around the outside of the field. No person, including but not limited to, spectators, game administrators or members of the media, shall be allowed within the restraining line. A maximum of three coaches as well as permitted nonplayers are allowed within the restraining line in front of the team box, as provided for in Rule 9-8-3 (2-26-8). A 4-inch-wide restraining line shall be placed around the outside of the field, at least 2 yards from the sidelines and end lines, as an extension of the line limiting the team box area, except in stadiums where the total playing enclosure does not permit the restraining line. It is recommended that the restraining line be marked by placing 12-inch long lines, separated by 24-inch intervals (1-2-3d). Game administration may place 4-inch wide and 12-inch long bisecting marks along the restraining line at each 5-yard line between the goal lines (1-2-3d NOTE).

A series of "hash marks" should be 24 inches in length and 4 inches in width and shall be located 53 feet, 4 inches from and parallel with each sideline dividing the field of play longitudinally in thirds. The lines shall be marked so that each 5-yard line bisects the hash mark (1-2-3e). Game administration may place on the field of play, with the inner edge of the extension in line with the outer edge of the hash mark, yard-line extensions that should be 24 inches in length and 4 inches in width (1-2-3e NOTE 1). It is permissible to use college or professional fields with hash marks marked at the distance specified by their respective codes, and with advertising and/or commercial markings placed on the field of play by home management that meet the requirements of Rule 1-2-3l (1-2-3e NOTE 2).

9-yard marks, 12 inches in length and 4 inches in width, shall be located 9 yards from each sideline. The 9-yard marks shall be marked so that at least each successive 10-yard line bisects the 9-yard marks. These marks shall not be required if the field of play is visibly numbered. If on-the-field numbers are used, the tops of those numbers shall be 9 yards from the sideline, should be 6 feet in height and 4 feet in width and may include directional arrows next to the yard-line numbers indicating the direction toward the nearest goal line (1-2-3f).

Team boxes shall be marked on each side of the field outside the coaches' area between the 25-yard lines for use of coaches, substitutes, athletic trainers, etc., affiliated with the team. The coaches' area is a minimum of a 2-yard belt between the front of the team box and the sideline, and becomes a restricted area when the ball is live (1-2-3g). It is permissible for both team boxes to be on the same side of the field, provided each team box is marked between respective 20- and 45-yard lines (1-2-3h NOTE 1). It is recommended goal lines and the team box boundaries be marked in a color which contrasts with other field markings and the area between the sidelines and the team box boundaries be solid white or marked with diagonal lines (1-2-3g NOTE 2).

Decorative markings in the end zones shall be no closer than 2 feet from the boundary and the goal lines (1-2-3h). Advertising and/or commercial markings shall not obstruct the yard lines, hash marks or

9-yard marks (7-yard marks for nine-, eight- and six-player) (1-2-3l).

Measurements shall be from the inside edges of the boundary marks, such marks being out of bounds (1-2-3i).

Each goal-line mark shall be entirely in its end zone so the edge toward the field of play and its vertical plane is the actual goal line. The goal line shall extend from sideline to sideline (1-2-3j).

A line, 4 inches wide and a minimum of 24 inches in length, shall be centered in the field of play, three yards from each goal line (1-2-3k).

Lines and Markings: Case Plays

1.2.3 SITUATION: The game officials inspect the playing field as a part of their pregame routine and determine that (a) the game field does not have the required markings such as a restraining line marked at all on the field from the sidelines and end lines or contains commercial logo art that obstructs the yard lines; or (b) the 3-yard line that is marked on the game field for the try is only 12 inches in length. **RULING:** In both (a) and (b), the field markings are not legal by rule, but the game will still be played. In (a), a 4-inch-wide restraining line shall be placed around the outside of the field, at least 2 yards from the sidelines and end lines, as an extension of the line limiting the team box area, except in stadiums where the total playing enclosure does not permit. In (b), a line 4 inches wide and a minimum of 24 inches in length shall be centered in the field of play, 3 yards from each goal line.

1.2.3 COMMENT: The game officials shall notify game management and the football administrator in their respective state association office to let them know that the football game field at this school was not properly marked as stated by NFHS football rules (1-2-3d; 1-2-3k; 1-2-3l).

9.4.8 SITUATION A: Third and five for A on B's 30-yard line when B1 intercepts A1's pass at B's 15-yard line. B1 returns the interception along A's sideline and is downed on A's 40-yard line. During B1's run the Head Linesman unintentionally runs into: (a) a cameraman between the restraining line and sideline at B's 20-yard line; (b) A's assistant coach in the restricted area at B's 45-yard line; or (c) A's head coach on the field of play at the 50-yard line. **RULING:** No foul in (a), but the game administrator must ensure the area between the playing field and the restraining line is clear of all non-authorized personnel. In (b) and (c) A's head coach is assessed a 15-yard non-player, illegal personal contact penalty at the succeeding spot. A second offense would result in a disqualification of the head coach.

9.4.8 SITUATION B: A1 throws a forward pass that is intercepted by B1 on B's 30-yard line and returned 70 yards along the B sideline for a B touchdown. During B1's run, the covering official is forced to change his course to run around an assistant team B coach who is in B's restricted area. The covering official drops his flag near B's restricted area. Later during the return, B12, a nonplayer, leaves the team box and runs alongside (yet out of bounds) B1 all the way to the goal line. B12 never enters the field of play during the down. The referee flags B12 for a nonplayer foul. **RULING:** Team B has committed two separate nonplayer fouls during this play, which cannot be combined to create a multiple foul. Team B's assistant coach has committed a violation of 9-8-3 for being in the restricted area while the ball is live while B12 has violated 9-8-1k and 9-8-3 by being outside his team box. Both fouls are administered. The first foul results in a sideline warning. The second violation is a 5-yard sideline interference foul for which the offended team may take the penalty on the try or the subsequent kickoff (8-2-4; 9-8-1k; 9-8-3; 10-2-4; 10-2-5).

9.4.8 SITUATION C: In the first quarter, the assistant coach for Team A accidentally collides with the line judge while the line judge is covering a play. Team A is penalized 15 yards for illegal personal contact by a nonplayer. In the second quarter, the back judge is covering a play near the sideline and observes an assistant in the restricted area during the play. **RULING:** This constitutes the first warning for Team A for violation of the restricted area and is not penalized in terms of yards. The occurrences of the new illegal personal contact foul and the restricted area violation are not combined for penalty enforcement purposes (9-4-8, 9-8-1k).

*9.8.1 SITUATION D: In the first quarter, the coach for Team A commits an illegal contact foul by accidentally bumping a game official while the coach was out of the team box. Team A is penalized 15 yards. In the second quarter, the coach of Team A is penalized 15 yards for an unsportsmanlike conduct foul for disagreeing with a foul called by one of the game officials. **RULING:** The first foul is for illegal personal contact and the second foul is for unsportsmanlike conduct. The penalties are not combined to force ejection of the head coach (9-4-8).

Pylons

A soft, flexible pylon, which is 4 inches square, 18 inches high, either orange, red or yellow in color, and does not create risk, shall be placed at the inside corner of each of the intersections of the sidelines with the goal lines and the end lines, as well as with each intersection of the hash marks extended and shall be placed either 3 feet beyond the end lines or on the end lines. When properly placed, the goal line pylon is out of bounds at the intersection of the sideline and the goal line extended (1-2-4).

◪ Rationale

Placing pylons off the end line prevents a situation in which a player may accidentally touch a pylon, thus placing him out-of-bounds.

Pylons: Case Play

8.2.1 SITUATION: Runner A10 dives into the pylon at the intersection of the goal line and sidelines and the ball breaks the plane of the goal line. **RULING:** Touchdown. Assuming the pylon was placed properly, the ball broke the plane of the goal line prior to the touching of the pylon.

Topic:
Coaches Field Equipment

Communication devices including but not limited to audio recorder, Local Area Network (LAN) phones and/or headsets, mobile phones, still photograph(s), film, analog or digital video(s) and/or Internet depictions, shall not be used to communicate with a player except during an outside 9-yard mark conference (7-yard marks in nine-, eight- and six-player competition) (1-6-1).

Communication devices including but not limited to audio recorder, Local Area Network (LAN) phones and/or headsets, mobile phones, still photograph(s), film, analog or digital video(s) and/or Internet depictions may be used by coaches and nonplayers (1-6-2).

Coaches Field Equipment: Case Plays

1.6.1 SITUATION A: During the game, the coach of B is observed talking into (a) a tape recorder; (b) tablet computer; or (c) a mobile phone. **RULING:** In (a), (b) and (c), legal for use during or after the game, provided these (or any other communication devices) are not used to communicate with a player during a between 9-yard marks conference. This precludes the use of any type of direct in-helmet communication with any player, and does not allow for the use of any communication devices during a between 9-yard marks conference, allowing for their use only during outside 9-yard mark conferences (1-6-2).

1.6.1 SITUATION B: During the game, the coach of Team B reports to the referee that (a) his wireless access has been interrupted and that he cannot use the software package he normally uses to record in-game details, or (b) Team B's headphones are not working. **RULING:** In (a) and (b), whether or not the headphones are working on either side does not come under the authority of the game officials, unless directed by the state association (1-6-2).

1.6.1 SITUATION C: The coach of Team A calls time-out and chooses a between 9-yard marks conference. As the coach heads out to the field, the wing official notices that he is carrying a tablet computer or other communication device that he has been using during the game. **RULING:** The game official covering that huddle should observe to ensure that the communication device is not used to communicate with any player during the conference (1-6-2).

1.6.1 SITUATION D: The quarterback of A: (a) after leaving the game and while in the team box, uses a headset to talk to a coach in the scouting booth; or (b) during a charged time-out, comes near the sideline to confer with two coaches who are wearing headphones; or (c) during a charged time-out, is handed the headset during a between 9-yard marks conference. **RULING:** Legal in (a) and (b) during an authorized conference. Illegal in (c) (1-6-2, 9-8-1e).

1.6.1 SITUATION E: Between plays during the first quarter, the game officials notice that one of the teams is using electronic signage to signal plays from the sideline or to signal information to the players during a between 9-yard marks conference. **RULING:** This would be considered to be communication with electronic communication devices and is not permitted. The game officials should stop play and direct the coach to immediately disable/disconnect the device. If such use persists, a foul should be called (9-8-1e).

1.6.1 SITUATION F: During the intermission between the third and fourth periods, A players come to the area in front of their team box to confer with their coaches. During the conference, the head coach talks via his headset to another coach in the press box and thereafter he: (a) discusses this conversation with his team; or (b) hands A1 his headset so that A1 may speak directly with the coach in the press box. RULING: Legal procedure in (a) and (b) as this is an authorized, sideline conference. The action in (b) would have been illegal during a between 9-yard marks conference (2-6; 9-8-1e).

1.6.1 SITUATION G: During the first period, an assistant coach of B takes: (a) individual photographs of each set or formation of A and makes these available to the head coach during the halftime intermission; or (b) digital or other instant developing sequence photographs of A and gives these to the coach during the game. RULING: Legal in (a) and (b) provided they are not shown to the players during a between 9-yard marks conference (1-6-1, 1-6-2, 9-8-1e).

1.6.1 SITUATION H: Team A has a computer at the game site and enters a record of offensive plays, defensive formations and other important data. This computer information is used: (a) after the game for evaluation of game performances; or (b) during the intermission between the first and second periods, the coach receives a computer printout of B's defensive alignments against various offensive formations; or (c) at halftime in the locker room, the coach views a computer screen displaying a summary of A's offensive play effectiveness. RULING: Legal in (a), (b) and (c) provided they are not shown to the players during a between 9-yard marks conference (1-6-1, 1-6-2, 9-8-1e).

In Simple Terms

It is legal for coaches to bring electronic tablets, phones or headsets onto the field during a between 9-yard mark conference and use them. However, only coaches may use them during that conference.

Topic:
Game Equipment

Ball

A legal ball has a tan-colored cover consisting of either pebbled-grain, cowhide or approved composition (leather or rubber) case without corrugations other than those formed by the natural seam grooves and the lace on one of the grooves (1-3-1a).

It has one set of either eight or 12 evenly spaced laces. The length of the lace shall be confined to within 3-3/4 inches from each end of the ball free from decorations or logos added during or after production (1-3-1b, c).

It features continuous 1-inch white or yellow stripe centered 3 to 3-1/4 inches from each end of the ball. The stripes shall be located only on the two panels adjacent to and perpendicular to the seam upon which the laces are stitched (1-3-1c) and, for ninth grade and above, shall include the NFHS Authenticating Mark (1-3-1g).

The ball weighs between 14 and 15 ounces (1-3-1e) and should be inflated to a pressure of 12-1/2 to 13-1/2 psi (pounds per square inch) or 878.8 to 949.1 grams per square centimeter (1-3-1f).

By state high school association adoption, the ball to be used in games involving only players below the 9th grade may conform to different specifications (1-3-1 NOTE). For 9th grade and above, the ball may weigh 14 to 15 ounces, have a long circumference between 27-3/4 and 28-1/2 inches and a long axis of 10-7/8 to 11-7/18 inches. The short circumference may be 20-3/4 to 21-1/4 inches. It may be inflated to 12-1/2 to 13-1/2 pounds (1-3-1 Table). For 8th grade and below, the ball may weigh 12 to 14 ounces, have a long circumference of 26 to 27 inches and a long axis of 10 to 11 inches. The short circumference may be 19 to 20 inches. It may be inflated to 12-1/2 to 13-1/2 pounds (1-3-1 Table).

When measuring a ball, all measurements shall be made after the ball is inflated to 13 pounds (1-3-1 NOTE 1). The long circumference should be measured 90 degrees from lace around the ends of the ball, over the groove but not in the groove (1-3-1 NOTE 2). The long axis should be measured from end to end but not in the nose indentation (1-3-1 NOTE 3). The short circumference should be measured around the ball, over the valve, over the lace, but not over a cross lace (1-3-1 NOTE 4).

Each team shall provide at least one legal game ball to the referee at the time the game officials assume authority for the contest. Only legal game balls approved by the referee may be used during the contest. Each team may use any referee-approved ball of its choice to free kick or start a new series of downs. If a touchdown occurs following a change of possession and the scoring team did not put the ball in play, any referee-approved ball may be used for the try (1-3-2). By state association adoption, a specific ball which meets specifications may be mandated for postseason or state playoff competition (1-3-2 NOTE, 1-7).

The referee shall decide whether the ball meets specifications. If the field is wet, the referee may order the ball changed between downs (1-3-3)

Ball: Case Plays

1.3.2 SITUATION A: A (a) requests a rubber ball on second down after using a leather ball on first down; or (b) on a dry day requests a different leather ball on fourth down; or (c) on the try requests a different leather ball than used during the touchdown play; or (d) recovers on the kickoff and requests a new ball. **RULING:** The request is denied in (a), (b) and (c), but approved in (d). A change from leather to rubber or vice versa, can only be made for a free kick or to start a series. If weather conditions warrant, a switch can be made by the game officials from leather to leather or rubber to rubber within a series.

 1.3.2 COMMENT: If a touchdown is scored during a down in which there is a change of possession, the scoring team may use a ball of its choice for the try (5-1-1a).

1.3.2 SITUATION B: During play in the fourth period, the quarterback of A (visitor) informs the referee that their ball is losing air pressure and is no longer usable. A does not have another legal ball. The home-team coach complains when the referee secures the Team B ball from the ball person for use by Team A. **RULING:** The visiting team may use the home-team ball if it wishes.

1.3.2 SITUATION C: Prior to the start of the game, A has provided two balls for the referee's examination, but B has not provided a ball. **RULING:** There is no penalty if a team does not provide a ball; however, in this case, B will have to use the ball(s) provided by A until such time B offers a legal ball for the referee's approval.

1.3.2 SITUATION D: The referee has examined and verified the legality of a number of balls provided by each team prior to the game. However, during the course of the game, the weather conditions change dramatically and the teams wish to have additional balls approved for use. **RULING:** This is permissible and is within the intent of the rule.

Game Clock

A timing device referred to as "the game clock" or "the clock" shall be provided by the game management. The operator(s) shall be approved by the referee (1-3-6).

Kicking Tee

A kicking tee shall be made of pliable material which elevates the lowest point of the ball no more than 2 inches above the ground (1-3-4).

No player shall use a kicking tee in violation of Rule 1-3-4. The penalty is not charged to the coach or player for the purpose of unsportsmanlike conduct disqualifications (9-10-4, NOTE).

Illegal Kicking Tee: Penalty

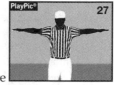

15 yards, basic spot. Signal 27.

Illegal Kicking Tee: Case Play

9.10.4 SITUATION: Team A scores: (a) on a try where the line of scrimmage was the 3-yard line and the tee was placed at the 10-yard line, or (b) on a field goal where the line of scrimmage was B's 20-yard line and the tee was placed at B's 27-yard line. In both cases, the referee determines during the kick that the kicker was using an illegal kicking tee. **RULING:** In (a), the basic spot is the previous spot and fouls by the offense behind the basic spot are enforced from the spot of the foul, therefore the penalty will be 15 yards marked from the 10-yard line, and if accepted, will result in a replay of the try from B's 25-yard line. In (b), the basic spot is the previous spot and fouls by the offense behind the basic spot are enforced from the spot of the foul, therefore the penalty will be 15 yards marked from the 27-yard line, and if accepted, will result in a replay of the down from B's 42-yard line.

Line-to-Gain Equipment

Either a yardage chain which joins two rods exactly 10 yards apart or any other 10-yard indicator with a visible line-to-gain indicator shall be used as the official line-to-gain equipment. This equipment and a down indicator shall be provided by game management (1-3-5).

The line-to-gain indicator shall be used to fix the line to gain, and the down indicator shall be used to mark the spot of the ball and indicate the number of the down in a series. The game officials shall check the line-to-gain indicator for accuracy prior to the start of the game (1-3-5a).

The official line-to-gain and down indicators shall be operated approximately 2 yards outside the sideline opposite the press box, except in stadiums where the total playing enclosure does not permit. If there is no press box, the location will be specified by game management at the request of the head linesman. The line-to-gain indicator shall be removed from the sideline when the line to gain is the goal line (1-3-5b).

Did You Know? The down marker is called "the box" because early markers consisted of a pole crowned with four rectangular wooden boards, nailed together to form a box. Each board had a number painted on it, one to four. The down was indicated by whichever numbered board faced the field.

Unofficial auxiliary line-to-gain and down indicators may be used on the sideline opposite the official line-to-gain and down indicators, and shall be operated approximately within 2 yards outside the sideline except in stadiums where the total playing enclosure does not permit (1-3-5c).

All line-to-gain and down-indicator rods shall have flat lower ends covered by protective caps (1-3-5d).

It is recommended that the members of the crew wear distinctive vests or jackets furnished by home or game management (1-3-5d NOTE).

Line-to-Gain Equipment: Case Play

1.3.5 SITUATION: The "chain crew" who has been "doing this for 25 years," wants to have the line-to-gain equipment on the sideline even though there is plenty of room to have the equipment two yards off the sideline on the restraining line. **RULING:** All "chain crews" must comply with Rule 1-3-5b. If the "chain crew" is insistent, the game officials should contact game administration to address the situation.

Topic:
The Goal

The top of the crossbar shall be 10 feet above the ground, measured from the base of each upright to the top of the crossbar at the intersection, or at each end of the crossbar perpendicular to the ground when a single pedestal is used (1-2-5b).

The crossbar shall be 23 feet, 4 inches long (1-2-5c).

The uprights shall be 23 feet, 4 inches apart inside to inside and each upright may not exceed 4 inches in width (1-2-5d). It is permissible to use college or professional fields with goal post uprights set at the width specified by their respective codes (1-2-5d NOTE). The uprights shall extend a minimum of 10 feet above the crossbar (1-2-5e).

Goal Posts

The goal posts shall be padded with resilient, shock absorbing material to a height of at least 6 feet above the ground (1-2-5f).

The horizontal crossbar and the uprights above it shall be free from any decorative material except paint which is recommended to be either silver, white or yellow in color. One wind directional streamer may be attached to the top of each upright. Wind directional streamers shall be 4 inches in width, 42 inches in length and either red, orange, or yellow in color (1-2-5g).

Goal Posts: Case Play

1.2.5 SITUATION: During the pregame meeting with the visiting coach, the coach complains to the referee that the distance between the goal posts is 18 feet, 6 inches as used at the college level. The college field is the home field for the host school: (a) The uprights are permanently set at 18 feet, 6 inches; or (b) the uprights are adjustable to 23 feet, 4 inches. **RULING:** In (a), it is permissible for the game to be played using the 18 feet, 6 inches goals. In (b), the adjustable goals shall be set at 23 feet, 4 inches.

Supplementary Equipment

Supplementary equipment to aid in game administration may be used if authorized by the state association (1-3-7, 1-7).

Supplementary Equipment: Case Play

1.3.7 SITUATION: The game officials are advised by the home-team management that supplementary equipment such as: (a) a ball-spotting device; (b) a ball-tracking device; or (c) a 25-second clock will be used during the game. **RULING:** None of the supplementary devices as described may be used unless the state association has given specific authorization.

 1.3.7 COMMENT: If responsibility for such supplementary equipment (such as the 25-second clock) is given to a non-official, the operator must be capable and approved.

Topic:
Auxiliary Player Equipment

Auxiliary equipment may be worn if sanctioned by the umpire as being soft, nonabrasive, nonhardening material. That includes:

- Forearm pads, which may be anchored on each end with athletic tape (1-5-2a).
- Gloves, which may be anchored with athletic tape, and even though modified, must meet the NOCSAE test standard or the SFIA specification at the time of manufacture, unless made of unaltered plain cloth. Gloves, unless made of unaltered plain cloth, must have a permanent, exact replica of the NOCSAE glove seal (Meets NOCSAE Standard) or SFIA glove seal (Meets SFIA Specification), that must be visible and appear legibly on the exterior wrist opening of the glove. A glove is a covering for the hand having separate sections for each finger. Pads worn on the hand, but not having separate sections encircling at least part of any finger are not gloves. The thumb is not considered a finger. Non-athletic gloves, worn solely for warmth and made of unaltered plain cloth, and which do not enhance contact with the ball, do not require a label or stamp indicating compliance (1-5-2b; 1-5-2b NOTE 1; 1-5-2b NOTE 2).

In Simple Terms

There is no penalty if a player's legal equipment is damaged to a point that it becomes illegal. However, the player may not participate until that equipment is replaced with legal equipment or is repaired so that it is again legal.

- Tape, bandage or support wrap on the hand or forearm to protect an existing injury (1-5-2c). Tape, bandage or support wrap(s) not to exceed three thicknesses are legal without inspection or approval (1-5-2c Exception) (1-5-2c).

Auxiliary Player Equipment: Case Plays

1.5.1 SITUATION F: During the pregame warm-ups, the umpire notices some of the players of Team A wearing (a) sweatbands on their biceps, (b) sweatbands on their calves, or (c) pants which clearly do not cover the knees. **RULING:** In (a) and (b), the uniform adornments must be removed prior to the individual becoming a player. In (c), the player may not participate without the pants covering the knees (1-5-1e; 1-5-3a(5)).

*1.5.2 SITUATION A: During the pregame conference, the home team's coach informs the umpire that all players' football gloves are new but none of the gloves have the required NOCSAE or SFIA label/stamp indicating compliance with the NOCSAE test standard or the SFIA

Specification. **RULING:** The gloves may not be worn; all gloves must have the required NOCSAE or SFIA label/stamp.

*1.5.2 SITUATION B: During the game, the umpire notices that a few of A's linemen have hand pads which do not have separate sections for each finger and do not have label/stamp indicating compliance with test specifications. **RULING:** These hand pads are legal. A NOCSAE or SFIA label/stamp is not required.

 *1.5.3 COMMENT: There are many items that would be considered to be illegal uniform adornments. Examples include but are not limited to: 1) Play cards designed for the wrist, but strapped to the belt as in 1-5-3c(8); 2) Eye shade as detailed in 1-5-3c(3) or that extends outside the eye socket or below the cheek bone; 3) Bandanas and other items if exposed from under the football helmet; and 4) Sweat bands not placed properly. Examples of items that have been determined to be legal are 1) Spats that properly cover the shoes as intended by the manufacturer; 2) Skull caps manufactured to be worn on the head that do not alter the fit of the football helmet and are not exposed outside of the football helmet; 3) Tinted eyewear worn on the face and under the face mask; 4) Hand warmers that do not enhance grip or create an advantage for a player.

1.5.3 SITUATION D: During the pregame visit with the head coach of A, the umpire notices that some squad members have eyeshields which are: (a) dark, or (b) clear with no tint. The head coach of A has a letter from a physician indicating that the dark shield is a necessity for the player. **RULING:** In (a), the umpire indicates to the head coach only eyeshields which are clear without the presence of any tint may be worn, a physician's statement cannot supersede this rule without expressed written consent of the state association. In (b), the eyeshield is legal if, in addition to being clear, it is also molded and rigid, and securely attached to the helmet (1-5-3c(4)).

9.8.1 SITUATION I: Near the end of the first period, A1 is discovered to be wearing a knee brace which has an unpadded strip of metal across the front of the leg. **RULING:** An unsportsmanlike penalty is assessed from the succeeding spot because the head coach has previously verified all players are legally equipped. The illegal item must be removed before A1 can participate further (1-5-4).

Topic:
Illegal Player Equipment

When any required player equipment is missing or when illegal equipment is found, correction shall be made before participation. An official's time-out shall be declared to permit prompt repair of equipment which becomes illegal or defective through use (1-5-5; 3-5-2b, 5b and 7f).

No player shall participate while wearing illegal equipment. This applies to any equipment, which in the opinion of the umpire is dangerous, confusing or inappropriate (1-5-3).

Game Uniform
The following items related to the Game Uniform are illegal:
- Jerseys and pants that have a visible manufacturer's logo/trademark or reference exceeding 2 1/4 square inches and exceeding 2 1/4 inches in any dimension (1-5-3a(1)a); more than one manufacturer's logo/trademark or reference on the outside of either item. (The same size restriction shall apply to either the manufacturer's logo/trademark or reference) (1-5-3a(1)b); or sizing, garment care or other nonlogo labels on the outside of either item (1-5-3a(1)c).
- Slippery or sticky substance of a foreign nature on equipment, towel, uniform, opponent or on an exposed part of the body which affects the ball or an opponent (1-5-3a (2)).
- Tear-away jerseys or jerseys that have been altered in any manner that produces a knot-like protrusion or creates a tear-away jersey (1-5-3a(3)).
- Any transverse stripe on the sleeve below the elbow (1-5-3a(4)).
- Uniform adornments, with the exception of one moisture-absorbing solid-colored towel that is not ball- or penalty flag-colored; is no less than 4 inches in width and 12 inches in length; no greater than 18 inches in width and 36 inches in length; has no more than one visible manufacturer's logo/trademark reference that does not exceed 2¼ square inches in any dimension; and if worn by any player, must be

the same solid color for all players wearing a towel (1-5-3a(5)a); or moisture-absorbing sweatbands, when worn on the wrist beginning at the base of the thumb and extending no more than 3 inches toward the elbow (1-5-3a(5)b).

Game Uniform: Case Plays

1.5.3 SITUATION A: During the pregame visits with both teams, the referee notices that Team B's jerseys have a series of symbols representing a company or the jersey has both a logo and a company reference, but it is not the company's logo/reference or trademark. The referee indicates that the jersey is illegal and that the symbols must be removed. **RULING:** The referee is correct. Jersey and pants may not have anything representing the manufacturer except for one logo/reference or trademark, and that mark must meet the size restrictions (1-5-3a(1)).

1.7 SITUATION B: A state association receives a request to allow a special uniform, patch or other insignia which is illegal by rule for a special purpose game (i.e., cancer awareness, military recognition, etc.). How should that be handled? **RULING:** Rule 1-7 allows for states to make special accommodations. However these accommodations should not fundamentally alter the sport, heighten risk to the athlete/others or place opponents at a disadvantage. Rather than allowing for illegal equipment, state associations should refer to other legal alternatives such as the allowances for commemorative or memorial patches, colors of sweatbands and other means of recognition that do not violate the rules. In the end, the state association must make the final determination.

9.8.1 SITUATION J: During the pregame inspection, the game officials note that one of the teams is wearing jerseys that do not comply with the NFHS football jersey rule by: (a) having color on sections of the white (visitor) jersey where color is restricted; (b) having white on sections of the non-white (home) jersey where white is not permitted; or (c) other illegal markings or violations of the rule. The team is unable to change jerseys prior to the start. **RULING:** In (a), (b) and (c), the team not in compliance is assessed an unsportsmanlike conduct foul against the head coach on the opening free kick for the team failing to wear legal equipment following verification. This is one of the two allowable unsportsmanlike fouls prior to ejection. The game officials should then report the incident to the state association for review as the state associations must ensure that this procedure is not used to circumvent the NFHS football rules (1-5-1b).

Pads and Padding

The following items related to pads and padding are illegal:
- Hard and unyielding items (guards, casts, braces, etc.) on the hand, wrist, forearm, elbow, or upper arm unless padded with a closed-cell, slow-recovery foam padding no less than 1/2-inch thick (1-5-3b(1)).
- Knee and ankle braces which are altered from the manufacturer's original design/production (1-5-3b(2)). Knee and ankle braces that are unaltered do not require any additional padding (1-5-3b(2) NOTE).
- Knee braces worn over the pants (1-5-3b(3)).
- Plastic material covering protective pads whose edges are not rounded with a radius equal to half the thickness of the plastic (1-5-3b(4)).
- Rib pads and back protectors unless fully covered by a jersey (1-5-3b(5)).
- Shin guards that do not meet NOCSAE specifications (1-5-3b(6)).

Pads and Padding: Case Play

9.8.1 SITUATION I: Near the end of the first period, A1 is discovered to be wearing a knee brace which has an unpadded strip of metal across the front of the leg. **RULING:** An unsportsmanlike penalty is assessed from the succeeding spot because the head coach has previously verified all players are legally equipped. The illegal item must be removed before A1 can participate further (1-5-4).

Other Illegal Equipment

The following other items are also considered illegal equipment:
- Ball-colored helmets, jerseys, patches, exterior arm covers/pads, undershirts or gloves (1-5-3c(1)).
- Communication devices used to communicate with a player except during an outside 9-yard mark conference (7-yard marks in nine-, eight- and six-player competition) (1-5-3c(2)).
- Eye shade (grease or no-glare strips or stickers) that is not a solid stroke or includes words, numbers, logos or other symbols within the eye shade (1-5-3c(3)).
- Eyeshield attached to the helmet that is not constructed of a molded rigid material (1-5-3c(4)a) or clear without the presence of any tint (1-5-3c(4)b). Tinted eyewear worn on the face and under the face mask is legal (1-5-3c(4) Note).

- Jerseys, undershirts or exterior arm covers/pads manufactured to enhance contact with the football or opponent (1-5-3c 5).
- Jewelry. Religious and medical alert medals are not considered jewelry. A religious medal must be taped and worn under the uniform. A medical-alert medal must be taped and may be visible (1-5-3c(6)).
- Metal which is projecting or other hard substance on clothes or person (1-5-3c(7)).
- Play cards not worn on the wrist or arm (1-5-3c(8)).
- Equipment not worn as intended by the manufacturer (1-5-3c(9)).

Other Illegal Equipment: Case Plays

9.8.1 SITUATION G: During the first period, B1 is detected wearing: (a) an earring; or (b) a necklace; or (c) a ring; or (d) a medical alert bracelet; or (e) a religious medallion. **RULING:** In (a), (b) and (c), an unsportsmanlike penalty is assessed to the head coach. B1 must comply with the rules before further participation. In (d), legal if securely attached to the body and visible, if necessary, and judged by the game official not to present a hazard to the wearer or other players. In (e), the medallion must be taped to the body (1-5-3c(6)).

9.8.1 SITUATION I: Near the end of the first period, A1 is discovered to be wearing: (a) shoes with cleats which are more than 1/2 inch in length; or (b) a slippery substance on his uniform, exposed body part or hands; or (c) a knee brace which has an unpadded strip of metal across the front of the leg; or (d) a multicolored towel or streamer attached at the waist; or (e) a helmet without an exterior warning label. **RULING:** In (a), (b), (c) and (d), an unsportsmanlike penalty is assessed from the succeeding spot because the head coach has previously verified all players are legally equipped. All illegal items must be removed before A1 can participate further. In (e) A1 will be given 25 seconds to comply. No penalty is assessed since it is assumed the label came off as a result of game action (1-5-4).

9.8.1 SITUATION K: In the first quarter, the umpire observes three linemen for Team A wearing towels. One towel is solid blue, and the other two are white. **RULING:** Illegal. If towels are worn by multiple players, they must all be of the same solid color, and must conform to the limitations on size and restrictions on manufacturers' logo/ trademark reference (1-5-3a(5)a).

*9.8.1 SITUATION N: A1 is discovered to have participated in a play with (a) a white unmarked towel hanging from his belt, which has a tacky substance on it, or (b) a piece of white unmarked plastic hanging from his belt. **RULING:** In both (a) and (b), the material does not meet the requirements of the rule and is illegal. Since the player was in the game while illegally equipped, a 15-yard penalty is assessed to Team A head coach and the illegal equipment must be removed for A1 to continue to play (9-8-1h).

Topic:
Mandatory Player Equipment

Each player shall properly wear the mandatory equipment while the ball is live (1-5-6). Each player shall participate while wearing legal and properly fitted equipment, which shall be professionally manufactured and not altered to decrease protection (1-5-1).

Prior to the start of the game, the head coach shall be responsible for verifying to the referee and umpire that all of his players are legally equipped and in compliance with these rules. Any questions regarding legality of a player's equipment shall be resolved by the umpire (1-5-4).

When any required player equipment is missing or when illegal equipment is found, correction shall be made before participation. An official's time-out shall be declared to permit prompt repair of equipment which becomes illegal or defective through use (1-5-5; 3-5-2b, 5b and 7e).

Failure of the head coach, following verification, to have his player(s) wear or use legal and/or required equipment results in a penalty for unsportsmanlike conduct charged to the head coach (9-8-1h).

No player shall fail to properly wear required equipment during a down (9-9).

 **Did You Know?** Chin straps did not become required equipment until 1973.

Helmet, Face Mask and Chin Strap

All players shall wear helmets that carry a warning label regarding the risk of injury and a manufacturer's or reconditioner's certification indicating satisfaction of NOCSAE test standards. The helmet and face mask must have met the NOCSAE test standard at the time of manufacture. All reconditioned helmets shall show recertification to indicate satisfaction with the NOCSAE test standard. The coach's pregame verification to the referee and umpire that all players are properly equipped in compliance with the rules includes the exterior warning label. The face mask shall have a surface covered with resilient material designed to prevent chipping, burrs or abrasiveness and be properly secured to the helmet as designed by the manufacturer. The helmet shall be secured by a properly fastened chin strap with at least four attachment points (1-5-1a 1-2, 1-5-1 NOTE).

> # Did You Know ?
> The rule requiring the home team to wear dark jerseys was approved in 1979.

Helmet, Face Mask and Chin Strap: Case Plays

*1.5.1 SITUATION A: B10 has (a) a two-attachment points chin strap or (b) a four-attachment points chin strap and the umpire notices that not all attachment points are secured. **RULING:** This is a foul in both situations. All available attachment points must be secured and all helmets must be secured with a four-attachment points system (1-5-1a(2); 1-5-6; 3-6-2d; 9-8-1h).

1.5.3 SITUATION D: During the pregame visit with the head coach of A, the umpire notices that some squad members have eyeshields which are: (a) dark, or (b) clear with no tint. The head coach of A has a letter from a physician indicating that the dark shield is a necessity for the player. **RULING:** In (a), the umpire indicates to the head coach only eyeshields which are clear without the presence of any tint may be worn, a physician's statement cannot supersede this rule without expressed written consent of the state association. In (b), the eyeshield is legal if, in addition to being clear, it is also molded and rigid, and securely attached to the helmet (1-5-3c(4)).

 9.9 COMMENT: Game officials must use good judgment when ruling on failure to properly wear required equipment during the down. Whenever a player is involved in contact during the down, it is possible for a tooth and mouth protectors, chin straps, shoes, helmets, etc., to come loose or be displaced. In such cases, it is not a foul (1-5-6).

9.4.3 SITUATION S: A1 is engaged with B1 in close line play. A1's helmet comes completely off as the play goes in another direction. He is beginning to put his helmet back on when B2 hits him from the side knocking him to the ground. **RULING:** B2 has committed a personal foul for contacting a player whose helmet has come completely off. However, since A1's helmet came off prior to the contact and the helmet coming off was not due to a foul by B, A1 must sit out the next play (9-4-3l, 3-5-10d).

9.6.4 SITUATION F: A1 is engaged with B1 in close line play. A1's helmet comes completely off as the play goes downfield without being caused by a foul by any member of B. A1, without his helmet, pursues the play downfield and (a) does or (b) doesn't make contact with a blocker. **RULING:** Illegal participation in both (a) and (b). Once the player's helmet comes completely off, he is to cease involvement with the play. He must also be removed for the next play if the helmet coming off was not caused by an opponent's foul (9-6-4, 3-5-10d).

9.8.1 SITUATION H: During the game: (a) A1 is discovered to be wearing an eye shield which is reflective, or (b) an entering substitute of B has a dark eye shield. **RULING:** In (a), the coach of A is charged with an unsportsmanlike foul and A1 must leave the game until he is legally equipped. In (b), the substitute of B will not be allowed to become a player, and he will be ordered to leave the field and not re-enter until he is legally equipped. There is no foul in (b) because the substitute did not become a player (1-5-3).

9.8.1 SITUATION I: Near the end of the first period, A1 is discovered to be wearing a helmet without an exterior warning label. **RULING:** A1 will be given 25 seconds to comply. No penalty is assessed since it is assumed the label came off as a result of game action (1-5-4).

9.9 SITUATION: Flanker A1 is detected with a chin strap hanging down: (a) while going downfield in his pass pattern; or (b) after being blocked by B1 downfield; or (c) after catching a pass and being hit by B1, he is continuing downfield. **RULING:** In (a), the covering official must determine if the chin strap came loose during a play or was not in place properly before determining that a foul occurred. No foul in (b) and (c) unless the covering official observes A1 unsnapping the strap which would then be enforced from the succeeding spot.

Jerseys and Pants

A jersey, unaltered from the manufacturer's original design/ production, with clearly visible and legible Arabic numbers 1-99 inclusive on the front and back and which shall be long enough to reach the top of the pants and shall be tucked in if longer. It must completely cover the shoulder pads and all pads worn above the waist on the torso (1-5-1b(1)).

Each player shall be numbered 1 through 99 inclusive (1-4-3, 7-2-5). The numbers shall be centered horizontally at least 8 inches and 10 inches high on front and back, respectively, and with bars or strokes approximately 1-1/2 inches wide (1-5-1c(2)). The color and style of the number shall be the same on the front and back (1-5-1c(3)). The body of the number shall be either a continuous color(s) contrasting with the jersey color, or the same solid color(s) as the jersey with a minimum of one border that is at least 1/4-inch in width of a single solid contrasting color (1-5-1c(4)).

Players of the opposing teams shall wear jerseys of contrasting colors. Players of the home team shall wear dark jerseys and players of the visiting team shall wear white jerseys. The visiting team is responsible for avoidance of similarity of colors, but if there is doubt, the referee may require players of the home team to change jerseys (1-5-1b(2)e, 1-5-1b(3)e).

One American flag, not to exceed 2 inches by 3 inches, may be worn or occupy space on each item of uniform apparel. By state association adoption, to allow for special occasions, commemorative or memorial patches, not to exceed 4 square inches, may be worn on the uniform without compromising its integrity (1-5-1b(2) NOTE, 1-5-1b(3) NOTE, Table 1-7 (6)).

Players of the visiting team shall wear jerseys, unaltered from the manufacturer's original design/production, that meet the following criteria: The body of the jersey (inside the shoulders, inclusive of the yoke of the jersey or the shoulders, below the collar, and to the bottom of the jersey) shall be white and shall contain only the listed allowable adornments and accessory patterns in a color(s) that contrasts to white: (a) as the jersey number(s) required in 1-5-1-c(1) or as the school's nickname, school logo, school name and/or player name within the body and/or on the shoulders; (b) either as a decorative stripe placed during production that follows the curve of the raglan sleeve or following the shoulder seam in traditional yoke construction, not to exceed 1 inch at any point within the body of the jersey; or as decorative stripe(s) added in the shoulder area after production, not to exceed 1 inch per stripe and total size of combined stripes not to exceed 3.5 inches; (c) within the collar, a maximum of 1 inch in width, and/or (d) as a side seam (insert connecting the back of the jersey to the front), a maximum of 4 inches in width but any non-white color may not appear within the body of the jersey (inside the shoulders, inclusive of the yoke of the jersey or the shoulders, below the collar, and to the bottom of the jersey). The exception to (d) would be what is stated in (b) above (1-5-

1b(2)d).

Players of the home team shall wear jerseys, unaltered from the manufacturer's original design/production, that meet the following criteria: The body of the jersey (inside the shoulders, inclusive of the yoke of the jersey or the shoulders, below the collar, and to the bottom of the jersey) may not include white, except as stated below.

If white appears in the body of the jersey of the home team, it may only appear: as the jersey number(s) required in 1-5-1c or as the school's nickname, school logo, school name and/or player name within the body and/or on the shoulders either as a decorative stripe placed during production that follows the curve of the raglan sleeve or following the shoulder seam in traditional yoke construction, not to exceed 1 inch at any point within the body of the jersey; or as decorative stripe(s) added in the shoulder area after production, not to exceed 1 inch per stripe and total size of combined stripes not to exceed 3.5 inches; (c) within the collar, a maximum of 1 inch in width, and/or (d) as a side seam (insert connecting the back of the jersey to the front), a maximum of 4 inches in width but any white color may not appear within the body of the jersey (inside the shoulders, inclusive of the yoke of the jersey or the shoulders, below the collar, and to the bottom of the jersey). The exception to (d) would be what is stated in (b) above (1-5-1b(3)d).

Every player must wear pants which completely cover the knees, thigh guards and knee pads and any portion of any knee brace that does not extend below the pants (1-5-1d).

Jerseys and Pants: Case Plays

1.4.3 SITUATION: After the ball has been marked ready for play, but prior to the snap, it is discovered: (a) A1 and A2 are both wearing number 81, or (b) B2 is wearing 00. **RULING:** In (a), it will become a foul at the snap for illegal numbering. In (b), it is a foul before the snap for illegal numbering and B2 will not be permitted to participate with that number, because 00 is not a legal number. If the illegal numbering is discovered during the down, it is a foul which occurred at the snap (1-5-1c(1); 7-2-5d).

*1.5.1 SITUATION B: Team A's players are wearing jerseys: (a) just covering the shoulder pads, and their midriffs are exposed; or (b) that extend below the top of their pants, but some players have them tucked in, while others have them outside their pants; or (c) that are waist length, but have tucked them up under the bottom of their shoulder pads. **RULING:** The jerseys in (a) and (c) are not legal. In (b), the jerseys of all players will have to be tucked inside the pants upon discovery (1-5-1b(1); 1-5-6; 3-6-2d; 9-8-1h).

1.5.1 SITUATION C: When the game officials arrive on the field they notice that both teams are wearing non-white jerseys. The visiting team's coach indicates that he was not informed prior to the game as to the color of the home-team's jerseys. **RULING:** It is the responsibility of the visiting team to wear its white jerseys when playing away from home. Whether the home team did or did not notify the visiting team of its school colors, the rules specify that the visiting team is to wear its white jerseys. The referee may require the home team to change to its white jerseys. This incident should be reported to the proper administrative authorities at the visiting-team's school and the state association office.

*1.5.1 SITUATION D: During the pregame visits with both teams, the referee and umpire note that the players are wearing brand new "throw back" jerseys with undersized and off-set numbers on the front of the jerseys. **RULING:** The referee shall require both teams to change to legal jerseys, if that is possible, and report the incident to the proper administrative authority of each school and the state association office (1-5-1c).

1.5.1 SITUATION F: During the pregame warm-ups, the umpire notices some of the players of Team A wearing (a) sweatbands on their biceps, (b) sweatbands on their calves, or (c) pants which clearly do not cover the knees. **RULING:** In (a) and (b), the uniform adornments must be removed prior to the individual becoming a player. In (c), the player may not participate without the pants covering the knees (1-5-1e; 1-5-3a(5)).

1.5.3 SITUATION A: During the pregame visits with both teams, the referee notices that Team B's jerseys have a series of symbols representing a company or the jersey has both a logo and a company reference, but it is not the company's logo/reference or trademark. The referee indicates that the jersey is illegal and that the symbols must be removed. **RULING:** The referee is correct. Jersey and pants may not have anything representing the manufacturer except for one logo/reference or trademark, and that mark must meet the size restrictions (1-5-3a5b).

9.8.1 SITUATION I: Near the end of the first period, A1 is discovered to be wearing a slippery substance on his uniform, exposed body part or hands. **RULING:** An unsportsmanlike penalty is assessed from the succeeding spot because the head coach has previously verified all players are legally equipped. All illegal items must be removed before A1 can participate further (1-5-4).

Pads and Protective Equipment

The following pads and protective equipment are required of all players:

• Hip pads and tailbone protector which are unaltered from the manufacturer's original design/production (1-5-3d(1)).
• Knee pads which are unaltered from the manufacturer's original design/production, which are worn over the knee and under the pants and shall be at least 1/2 inch thick or 3/8 inch thick if made of shock absorbing material (1-5-3d(2)).
• Shoulder pads and hard surface auxiliary attachments, which shall be fully covered by a jersey (1-5-3d(3)).
• Thigh guards which are unaltered from the manufacturer's original design/production (1-5-3c(4)).

Pads and Protective Equipment: Case Plays

*1.5.1 SITUATION G: The umpire notices that a player does not have protrusions indicating that hip pads and tailbone protector are being worn. Upon investigating, it is found that (a) the player is not wearing any padding or (b) the player is wearing a manufactured girdle with closed cell, "bubble type" protective padding that conforms and covers the hips and tailbone. **RULING:** (a) Hip pads and tailbone protector are required equipment. If required equipment is noted to be missing between downs, the player must be removed from the game. If the game officials are unable to detect the missing equipment and the player participates without the required equipment, a foul is to be called. In (b), there is no padding criteria listed for hip pads and tailbone protector and, therefore, the pads are legal (1-5-1d(1); 1-5-5; 1-5-6; 3-6-2d; 9-8-1h).

1.5.3 SITUATION B: A1 is wearing: (a) a biceps pad; or (b) a partially exposed hip pad; or (c) an ankle support. In all three cases a hard plastic surface on the outside of the pad/support is not covered, but all the edges are rounded and there are no cutting or abrasive surfaces. **RULING:** The items described in (a), (b) and (c) are legal. The exposed plastic does not require a covering on these specific items of equipment. However, if any of the plastic surface is cracked or has a cutting edge it would not be legal. If the biceps pad is connected to the shoulder pad, it must be fully covered by the jersey.

*1.5.3 SITUATION C: Prior to the game, the coach of B requests the umpire to examine a cast/splint on the forearm of a player. The protective item has "hard" material, but is padded with at least ½-inchthick, closed-cell, slow-recovery foam padding. The coach: (a)

provides; or (b) does not provide to the umpire prior to the start of the game, a written author ization from a licensed medical physician directing the use of the cast/splint as necessary to protect an injury. **RULING**: In (a) and (b), the cast/splint may be worn during the game. Written authorization is no longer required but the umpire must ensure the cast/split is properly padded (1-5-3b(1)).

Shoes

- Shoes which shall be made of a material which covers the foot (canvas, leather or synthetic) and attached to a firm sole of leather, rubber or composition material. Shoes may have cleats or may be cleatless. Among the items which do not meet these requirements are gymnastic slippers, tennis shoes cut so protection is reduced, ski and logger boots and other apparel not intended for football use (1-5-1f).

Removable cleats shall conform to the following specifications:

- Constructed of a material which does not chip or develop a cutting edge. Legal cleat material includes leather, nylon, rubber and non metallic polymers that will not chip or develop a cutting edge (1-5-1f (1)a). Cleats may be tipped with a steel material hardened to Rockwell hardness approximately C55 to a depth of .005-.008 while minimizing the risk of brittle failure of the tip component, in its entirety, including any shafts or threads that may be a part of the tip (1-5-1f (1)b).
- The base and the tip of the cleat shall be parallel (1-5-1f (1)c). The free end of the cleat may be rounded in an arc with a radius of not less than 7/16 inch provided the overall length is not more than 1/2 inch measured from the tip of the cleat to the sole of the shoe (1-5-1f (1)d). The cleat may be attached to a raised platform which is molded to the shoe. The platform may be no more than 5/32 inch in height and must be wider than the base of the cleat. The widest part of the cleat must be in direct contact with the platform. The 5/32-inch raised platform must be wider than the base of the cleat and must extend across the width of the sole to within 1/4 inch or less of the outer edges of the sole (1-5-1f (1)e). A single toe cleat does not require a raised platform that extends across the width of the sole. The raised platform of the toe cleat is limited to 5/32 inch or less (1-5-1f (1)f). The 5/32-inch platform is measured from the lowest point of the platform to the sole of the shoe (1-5-1f (1)g). An effective locking device which prevents the exposure of metal posts shall be incorporated (1-5-1f (1)h). The cleat wall shall be at least 3/16 inch in diameter (1-5-1f (1)i). The sides of the cleat shall taper uniformly from a minimum base of 3/4 inch in

diameter to a minimum tip of 3/8 inch in diameter (1-5-1f (1)j).
- Nonremovable cleats are limited to studs or projections that do not exceed 1/2 inch in length measured from the sole of the shoe to the tip of the cleat and which are made with nonabrasive rubber or rubber-type synthetic material that does not have or develop a cutting edge (1-5-1f (2)).

Shoes: Case Play

9.8.1 SITUATION I: Near the end of the first period, A1 is discovered to be wearing shoes with cleats which are more than 1/2 inch in length. **RULING:** An unsportsmanlike penalty is assessed from the succeeding spot because the head coach has previously verified all players are legally equipped. The illegal shoes must be changed before A1 can participate further (1-5-4).

Tooth and Mouth Protector

A tooth and mouth protector (intraoral) which shall include an occlusal (protecting and separating the biting surfaces) portion; include a labial (protecting the teeth and supporting structures) portion; and cover the posterior teeth with adequate thickness. It is recommended that the protector be properly fitted, protecting the anterior (leading) dental arch and: constructed from a model made from an impression of the individual's teeth, or constructed and fitted to the individual by impressing the teeth into the tooth and mouth protector itself (1-5-1d(5)a).

Tooth and Mouth Protector: Case Play

*1.5.1 SITUATION E: During the down, A4 is noticed to (a) have a clear tooth and mouth protector; or (b) have a tooth and mouth protector that is only covering the upper, front teeth. The umpire drops a flag for illegal equipment. **RULING:** The umpire is incorrect in (a), correct in (b). All tooth and mouth protectors shall cover the posterior teeth but have no color requirement. The game officials should, through normal observations, attempt to verify that each player is legally equipped prior to the ball becoming live, and if illegal equipment is detected, that player must fix the problem or leave the game (1-5-1d(5); 1-5-5). If the game officials are unable to detect the illegal equipment and the player is observed wearing a non-compliant tooth and mouth protector during a down, a foul is to be called 1-5-1d(5); 1-5-6; 3-6-2d; 9-8-1h).

Topic:
State Association Approval

Each state association may authorize the use of a drum by a team composed of deaf or partially deaf players, in order to establish a rhythmic cadence following the ready-for-play signal (1-6-1 NOTE).

Each state association may, in keeping with applicable laws, authorize exceptions to NFHS playing rules to provide reasonable accommodations to individual participants with disabilities and/or special needs, as well as those individuals with unique and extenuating circumstances. The accommodations should not fundamentally alter the sport, heighten risk to the athlete/others or place opponents at a disadvantage (1-7).

State associations may determine the number of game officials to be used in the game (Table 1-7 (1), 1-1-4 NOTE). Determine the time for game officials to assume authority if greater than 30 minutes (Table 1-7 (2), 1-1-7). Determine the size of ball to be used for games with players below 9th grade (Table 1-7 (3), 1-3-1 NOTE). Mandate the use of a specific ball for postseason or playoff competition (Table 1-7 (4), 1-3-2 NOTE). Authorize the use of supplementary equipment to aid in game administration (Table 1-7 (5), 1-3-7). Authorize the wearing of a commemorative/memorial patch (Table 1-7 (6), 1-5-1b(2-3 NOTE). Authorize the use of a drum for rhythmic cadence for deaf or partially deaf teams (Table 1-7 (7), 1-6-1 NOTE). Authorize exceptions to NFHS playing rules to provide reasonable accommodations to individual participants with disabilities or special needs (Table 1-7 (8), 1-7). Establish a procedure to resolve games tied following the fourth quarter (Table 1-7 (9), 3-1-1). Establish a point differential to terminate games or to use a running clock when the point differential is reached (Table 1-7 (10), 3-1-2). Establish rules regarding continuation of interrupted games (Table 1-7 (11), 3-1-4). Authorize the use of 10-minute periods for games involving combinations of 9th, 8th and/or 7th grade students (Table 1-7 (12), 3-1-5 NOTE 1). Determine the length of halftimes, provided it is not less than 10 minutes and not more than 20 minutes (Table 1-7 (13), 3-1-5 NOTE 2). Determine when the coin toss is to be held (Table 1-7 (14), 3-2-1). Authorize the use of TV/radio time-out (Table 1-7 (15), 3-5-7k). Designate the 11-player field dimensions as official for nine-, eight- or six-player competition (Table 1-7 (16).

State Association Approval: Case Play

1.7 SITUATION A: During the pregame visit with the visiting team, the head coach asks the umpire to examine an artificial: (a) arm; or (b) leg which is attached below the knee; or (c) leg which is attached above the knee. The coach has a letter or statement signed by the executive officer of the state association indicating approval of the artificial limb for football. **RULING:** The umpire has no decision to make as to whether it can be worn, unless required padding, etc., is missing. The artificial limbs in (a), (b) and (c) may be used since proper approval has been given as required by rule. Without the letter or statement of approval, the artificial limb could not be worn.

1.7 COMMENT: State associations are permitted to provide reasonable accommodations to individual participants with disabilities under the conditions of Rule 1-7. While the determination on the legality of this equipment, as well as the individual's ability to minimize risk, requires the judgment of medical authorities, it also requires the judgment of football administrators knowledgeable with the football rules and their purpose and philosophy. Each case must be handled on an individual basis, and each state association determines its own procedure for approval.

1.7 SITUATION B: A state association receives a request to allow a special uniform, patch or other insignia which is illegal by rule for a special purpose game (i.e., cancer awareness, military recognition, etc.). How should that be handled? **RULING:** Rule 1-7 allows for states to make special accommodations. However these accommodations should not fundamentally alter the sport, heighten risk to the athlete/others or place opponents at a disadvantage. Rather than allowing for illegal equipment, state associations should refer to other legal alternatives such as the allowances for commemorative or memorial patches, colors of sweatbands and other means of recognition that do not violate the rules. In the end, the state association must make the final determination.

Topic 2
Kicks

Key Terms

A kick is the intentional striking of the ball with the knee, lower leg or foot (2-24-1). A kick ends when a player gains possession or when the ball becomes dead while not in player possession (2-24-2).

A fumble is any loss of player possession other than by handing, passing or legal kick (2-18). A muff is the touching of a loose ball by a player in an unsuccessful attempt to secure possession (2-27). Touching refers to any contact with the ball, i.e., either by touching or being touched by it. Touching by a game official in the field of play or end zone is ignored (2-44).

A kicker is any player who legally punts, drop kicks or place kicks. A player becomes a kicker when his knee, lower leg or foot makes contact with the ball. He continues to be the kicker until he has had reasonable opportunity to regain his balance or until after a free kick, he has advanced 5 yards beyond his free-kick line or the kick has touched the ground or any other player (2-32-8).

A holder is a player who controls the ball on the ground or on a kicking tee for a kickoff or place kick (2-32-7).

A snapper is the player who is facing his opponent's goal line with his shoulders approximately parallel thereto and who snaps the ball. In a scrimmage-kick formation, the snapper remains a snapper until he has had a reasonable opportunity to regain his balance and protect himself or until he blocks or moves to otherwise participate in the play (2-32-14).

K is the team which legally kicks the ball during the down. The opponent is R (2-32-2, 2-43-3). Team designations (K and R) are retained until the ball is next marked ready for play (2-43-4).

A loose ball is a pass, fumble or a kick. The terms "pass," "fumble" and "kick" are sometimes used as abbreviations when the ball is loose following the acts of passing, fumbling or kicking the ball. A loose ball which has not yet touched the ground is in flight. A grounded loose ball is one which has touched the ground. Any loose ball continues to be a loose ball until a player secures possession of it or until it becomes dead by rule, whichever comes first (2-1-3). A loose ball is out of bounds when it touches anything, including a player or game official, that is out of bounds (2-29-3). The out-of-bounds spot is where the ball becomes dead because of going out of bounds (2-41-5).

A catch is the act of establishing player possession of a live ball which is in flight, and first contacting the ground inbounds while maintaining possession of the ball or having the forward progress of the player in possession stopped while the opponent is carrying the player who is in possession and inbounds (2-4-1). Catching is always preceded by touching the ball; thus, if touching causes the ball to become dead, securing possession of the ball has no significance (2-4-2). A simultaneous catch is a catch in which there is joint possession of a live ball by opposing players who are inbounds (2-4-3).

A recovery is gaining possession of a live ball after it strikes the ground. An airborne player has completed a recovery when he first contacts the ground inbounds with the ball in his possession (2-36-1). A simultaneous recovery is a recovery where there is joint possession of a live ball by opposing inbounds players (2-4-3, 2-36-2).

A runner is a player who is in possession of a live ball or is simulating possession of a live ball (2-32-13).

A captain of a team is a player designated to represent his team during ball placement on a try or after a touchback (2-32-5c).

The dead-ball spot is the spot under the foremost point of the ball when it becomes dead by rule (2-41-3). The inbounds spot is the intersection of the hash marks and the yard line through the foremost point of the ball when the ball becomes dead in a side zone; through the foremost point of the ball on the sideline between the goal lines when a loose ball goes out of bounds; or through the spot under the foremost point of the ball in possession of a runner when he crosses the plane of the sideline and goes out of bounds (2-41-4a through c; 4-3-3). The out-of-bounds spot is where the ball becomes dead because of going out of bounds (2-41-5).

Topic:
Styles of Kicks

Drop Kick
A drop kick is a legal kick by a player who drops the ball and kicks it when it touches the ground or as it is rising from the ground. A drop kick may be used for a scrimmage kick, including a field goal or try; a kickoff; a free kick following a safety; or for a free kick following a fair catch or awarded fair catch (2-24-6).

K may drop kick from in or behind the neutral zone before team possession has changed. It is not necessary to be in a scrimmage kick formation to execute a legal drop kick (6-2-1).

Place Kick

A place kick is a legal kick made while the ball is in a fixed position on the ground or on a kicking tee. No material or device may be placed on the ground to improve the kicker's footing (2-24-7).

The ball may be held in position on the ground or on a kicking tee by a place-kick holder who shall be a teammate of the kicker (1-3-4; 2-24-7; 2-32-7). A place kick may be used for a scrimmage kick, a kickoff, a free kick following a safety or for a free kick following a fair catch or awarded fair catch (2-24-7).

During a scrimmage down, K may place kick from in or behind the neutral zone before team possession has changed. It is not necessary to be in a scrimmage kick formation to execute a legal place kick (6-2-1).

Punt

A punt is a legal scrimmage kick by a player who drops the ball and kicks it before it has touched the ground. A punt may be used for a free kick following a safety or for a scrimmage kick (2-24-8).

K may punt from in or behind the neutral zone before team possession has changed. It is not necessary to be in a scrimmage kick formation to execute a legal punt (6-2-1).

In Simple Terms

Following a safety is the only time that a punt may be used as a free kick.

A punt may not be used for a free kick other than after a safety. When a punt is used following a safety, the ball must be kicked within one step behind K's free-kick line. In an emergency, such as a pool of water on K's free-kick line, the referee has authority to move the ball to a playable line, in which case, both free-kick lines are moved to compensate (6-1-2).

Topic:
Clock Starts

Each half of the game shall be started by a kickoff (3-2-1). The clock shall start when the kick is touched, other than first touching by K (3-4-1a; 3-4-3; 3-4-5). It is first touching if the ball is touched in the field of play by any K player before it crosses R's free-kick line and before it is touched there by any R player (2-12-1).

In Simple Terms

Any time a free kick is touched by a receiver, even illegally, the clock is started.

Rationale

The clock doesn't start when the kick is first touched by K so that R is not denied an opportunity to secure possession when there are only a few seconds remaining at the end of the second or fourth quarters. Without that aspect of the rule, K could run out the clock after a touchdown or safety by making one or more short free kicks.

Topic:
Clock Stops

The clock shall be stopped when the down ends following a foul; an official's time-out is taken; a charged or TV/radio time-out is granted; the period ends; the ball is out of bounds; a score or touchback occurs; a fair catch is made; an inadvertent whistle is sounded; or an airborne receiver is carried out of bounds, unless the receiver is carried backwards and his forward progress was stopped inbounds (3-4-4a-j).

Topic:
Ball Live and Dead

Ball Becomes Dead

The ball becomes dead and the down is ended when:

A runner goes out of bounds, is held so his forward progress is stopped or allows any part of his person other than hand or foot to touch the ground (4-2-2a).

When a live ball goes out of bounds (4-2-2b).

When any legal free kick which is not a scoring attempt or which is a grounded scoring attempt, breaks the plane of R's goal line (4-2-2d 1).

When any legal free kick which is a scoring attempt, while in flight touches a K player in R's end zone, or after breaking the plane of R's goal line has apparently failed (4-2-2d 2).

Fundamental IV-5

Any kick which is not a scoring attempt becomes dead when it breaks the plane of R's goal line.

When the ball is loose following a free kick and it is simultaneously caught or recovered by opposing players, is on the ground motionless and no player attempts to secure possession or touches, or is touched by, anything inbounds other than a player, substitute, replaced player, a game official, the ground or authorized equipment (4-2-2e 1-3).

When K catches or recovers any free kick anywhere, and when K catches or recovers a scrimmage kick beyond the neutral zone and when K is first (i.e., before any touching by R) to touch a scrimmage kick after it has come to rest beyond the neutral zone and between the goal lines (4-2-2f).

Following a valid or invalid fair-catch signal given by any member of the receiving team when a scrimmage kick or free kick is caught or recovered by any member of the receiving team beyond, in or behind the neutral zone (4-2-2g).

When a touchdown or field goal occurs (4-2-2h).

During a try if B secures possession or as soon as it is apparent that a kick has failed to score (4-2-2i).

When a game official sounds his whistle inadvertently (4-2-2j).

When the helmet comes completely off a player who is in possession of the ball (4-2-2k).

Ball Becomes Dead: Case Plays

4.2.3 SITUATION E: K's ball, fourth and 12, on R's 45-yard line. K8's punt is rolling on R's 16 when an inadvertent whistle sounds. R76 blocks K84 in the back on R's 22-yard line during the down prior to the whistle. **RULING:** By rule, an inadvertent whistle during the kick (loose-ball play) and declination of all fouls, stipulates a replay of the down. However, if the penalty for R's illegal block is accepted, the penalty is enforced from the previous spot and K will replay fourth down, fourth and 2 from R's 35-yard line (2-16-2h; 4-2-2j; 4-2-3a; 4-2-3d; 6-2-7; 10-4-3).

5.1.3 SITUATION A: K1's field-goal attempt is partially blocked behind the neutral zone, but deflects beyond the neutral zone and is then muffed by R1. The muffed ball is recovered: (a) behind, or (b) beyond the neutral zone by K2. **RULING:** In both (a) and (b), it is a first down for K. In (a), K2 could have advanced after recovering (5-1-3f).

6.2.3 SITUATION B: With third and 10 on K's 10-yard line, K1's punt is blocked and recovered on K's 4-yard line simultaneously by K2 and R1. RULING: The ball is dead immediately and is awarded to R because of the joint recovery.

7.4.3 SITUATION: An offensive and defensive player simultaneously gain possession of a live ball which is a: (a) legal forward pass and both players are touching inbounds; or (b) scrimmage kick muffed by R beyond the neutral zone; or (c) fumble by A1 on a running play. RULING: The down is ended in each situation. In (a), complete pass and the ball belongs to A at the spot of completion. In (b), the ball belongs to R at the spot of recovery, and in (c), the ball belongs to A at the spot of recovery (6-2-6; 7-5-4).

Ball Becomes Live

A ball becomes live when the ball has been legally free kicked and when a down is in progress (2-2-1) .

Ball Remains Live

After being put in play, the ball remains live until the down ends (4-1-5). No foul causes a live ball to become dead (2-16-4). The ball remains live if, at the snap, a place-kick holder with his knee(s) on the ground and with a teammate in kicking position:
1. Catches or recovers the snap while his knee(s) is on the ground and places the ball for a kick, or if he rises to advance, hand, kick or pass.
2. Rises and catches or recovers an errant snap and immediately returns his knee(s) to the ground and places the ball for a kick or again rises to advance, hand, kick or pass (4-2-2a Exception).
NOTE: The ball becomes dead if the place-kick holder muffs the snap or fumbles and recovers after his knees have been off the ground, and he then touches the ground with other than hand or foot while in possession of the ball.

Topic:
Free Kicks

A free kick is any kick which puts the ball in play to start a free-kick down. A free kick is used for a kickoff at the beginning of each half of the game; after a successful field goal and after any try; following a safety; and is used if a free kick is chosen following a fair catch or awarded fair catch (2-24-3; 2-24-5; 3-2-1; 4-1-1, 2a-c). A punt may not be used for a free kick other than after a safety (6-1-2).

Each team may use any referee-approved ball of its choice to free kick (1-3-2).

> # Did You Know ?
> In the early 1940s, a team could score a field goal if its free kick passed through the uprights and over the crossbar.

Ball Placement

A captain of a team is a player designated to represent his team during ball placement on a try, a kickoff, after a safety, and after a fair catch or awarded fair catch (2-32-5c).

When a team may designate the spot along the proper yard line from which the ball is to be put in play, it shall have the same privilege if the down is to be replayed or a dead-ball foul occurs (4-3-7).

A free kick shall be made from any point between the hash marks and on K's free-kick line (4-1-4; 6-1-2; 8-5-4). Once designated, K must kick from that spot (6-1-2).

Before the ready-for-play signal, A may designate the spot from which the ball is put in play anywhere between the hash marks for a kickoff (4-3-6b), following a safety (4-3-6c), following a fair catch (4-3-6d), following an awarded fair catch (4-3-6e).

When the ball becomes dead in a side zone or is awarded to a team there or is left there by a penalty, play is resumed at the nearest hash mark. This does not apply to the free kick or snap which follows a fair catch or awarded fair catch in a side zone (4-3-5d).

Ball Placement: Penalty

5 yards. Signals 7 and 19.

Ball Placement: Case Play

4.3.7 SITUATION: With the score tied near the end of the fourth period, R1 signals for a fair catch and catches the kick at K's 40. After a time-out, the captain of R advises the referee that he wishes to put the ball in play by snap. A1 throws a pass intended for A2. B1 interferes with A2 and the pass is incomplete. Following administration of the penalty, the captain of R decides to put the ball in play by free kick from K's 25 as a field-goal attempt. **RULING:** This is permissible and the clock will not start until the kick is touched, other than first touching by K. This is one of the times a field goal may be scored by a free kick. The captain may request a time-out prior to making the decision on whether to snap or free kick. In putting the ball in play in this situation, the captain of R is privileged to designate the point on K's 25, anywhere between the hash marks he wishes the ball to be placed (1-4-1; 5-2-4; 6-5-4).

Before the Ready
The ball remains dead and a down is not begun if a free kick is attempted before the ball is ready for play or a dead-ball foul occurs (3-6-2e; 4-1-6; 4-2-1).

Attempting a Kick Before the Ready: Penalty
5 yards. Signals 7 and 21.

Blocking by K
No member of the kicking team shall initiate contact to (block) an opponent on a free kick until the legal kick has traveled 10 yards; the kicking team is eligible to recover a free-kicked ball; or the receiving team initiates a block within the neutral zone (9-3-8a through c).

Illegal Block by K: Penalty
10 yards from the previous spot. Signal 43.

Blocking by K: Case Plays
9.3.8 SITUATION A: During a free kick (including an onside kick attempt), K1 initiates contact against R1 prior to the ball traveling past the receiving team's restraining line (10 yards). No member of R had initiated a block against K in the neutral zone. **RULING:** Live ball foul, illegal block. If the foul is accepted, the penalty is enforced from the previous spot.

9.3.8 SITUATION B: During a free kick (including an onside kick attempt): (a) R touches the ball prior to it traveling 10 yards after which K contacts R and recovers the ball; (b) after the ball travels 10 yards, K contacts R prior to R touching the ball; (c) after the ball touches the ground and travels 10 yards, K contacts R prior to recovering the ball; (d) after R initiates a block against K in the neutral zone, K recovers the ball; or (e) R and K contact each other approximately the same time prior to the ball traveling 10 yards. **RULING:** Legal recovery by K in (a), (b), (c) and (d). In (e), game officials should be guided by the thought that when in doubt, R initiated the contact and, therefore, this would be no foul.

Catch or Recovery by K

If any K player recovers or catches a free kick, the ball becomes dead (4-2-2f; 6-1-5). It belongs to K unless it is kick-catching interference and R chooses an awarded fair catch or unless it is first touching.

Fundamental IV-1

A kick always ends as soon as any player secures possession.

Any K player may catch or recover the ball before it goes beyond R's free-kick line if it is touched first by R. Such touching in the neutral zone by R is ignored if it is caused by K pushing or blocking R into contact with the ball or if any K player muffs or bats the ball into contact with R. Any K player may recover a free kick if it has both touched the ground and goes beyond the plane of R's free-kick line. The two requirements may occur in any order. If a free kick becomes dead inbounds between the goal lines while no player is in possession, or inbounds anywhere while opponents are in joint possession, the ball is awarded to R (6-1-5).

Catch or Recovery by K: Case Plays

6.1.6 SITUATION A: A kickoff by K1 from K's 40 is muffed by R1 near his 20-yard line. The muff is caught by K2 at the 18 and he advances into R's end zone. **RULING:** It will be K's ball first and 10 from R's 18. K2 may catch or recover the muffed kick, but may not advance. The ball is dead when K gains possession. The covering official should sound his whistle to stop play immediately when the ball becomes dead.

In Simple Terms

The receiving team cannot touch a free kick illegally, except by batting or kicking a loose ball.

6.1.6 SITUATION B: K's free kick is bouncing on the ground in the neutral zone where R1 and K1 are engaged in blocking one another. K2 muffs the ball and the ball touches R1 on the leg and K3 recovers the ball. **RULING:** The touching by R is ignored and R will be awarded possession of the ball at the spot of first touching or at the dead-ball spot.

6.1.7 SITUATION B: The ball is free kicked from K's 40-yard line and in flight, it crosses the 50-yard line before a strong wind blows it back to K's 45 where it: (a) is touched in flight by K1, or (b) touches the ground and is recovered by K2. **RULING:** Kick-catching interference in (a), first and 10 for K in (b).

6.1.7 COMMENT: The free-kick lines marking the neutral zone for K and R are vertical planes. When the free kick penetrates R's free-kick line in flight, it is considered to have gone the required 10 yards. If it also has touched the ground, before or after going 10 yards, it can be recovered, but not advanced by K (6-1-6).

◪ Rationale

The free-kick lines marking the neutral zone for K and R are vertical planes. When the free kick penetrates R's free-kick line in flight, it is considered to have gone the required 10 yards. If it also has touched the ground, before or after going 10 yards, it can be recovered, but not advanced by K.

Catch or Recovery by R

Any receiver may catch or recover a free kick in the field of play and advance, unless any R player has given a valid or invalid fair-catch signal. R may catch or recover a free kick in K's end zone (6-1-4, 6-5-1).

Catch or Recovery by R: Case Play

7.4.3 SITUATION: An offensive and defensive player simultaneously gain possession of a live ball which is a scrimmage kick muffed by R beyond the neutral zone. **RULING:** The down is ended. The ball belongs to R at the spot of recovery (6-2-6; 7-5-4).

Encroachment

After the ready-for-play signal and until the ball is kicked, each player other than the kicker and holder for a place kick must be behind his free-kick line (2-14-3; 2-24-3; 6-1-3).

Encroachment: Penalty

5 yards. Signals 7 and 18.

Forced Touching

Touching of a free kick by R in the neutral zone is ignored if it is caused by K pushing or blocking R into contact with the ball or it is caused by K legally batting or muffing the ball into R. Such catch or recovery by K beyond the neutral zone causes the ball to become dead (6-1-5). Touching of a free kick by K is ignored if it is caused by R pushing or blocking K into contact with the ball (6-1-6).

Fundamentals V-2

Free-kick lines are always 10 yards apart.

Forced Touching: Case Play

6.1.6 SITUATION B: K's free kick is bouncing on the ground in the neutral zone where R1 and K1 are engaged in blocking one another. K2 muffs the ball and the ball touches R1 on the leg and K3 recovers the ball. **RULING:** The touching by R is ignored and R will be awarded possession of the ball at the spot of first touching or at the dead-ball spot.

Formation

A free-kick formation is a formation used for a free-kick down. After the ball is marked ready for play and until the ball is kicked, the following formation requirements must be met: No player, other than the kicker and the holder for a place kick, may be beyond his free-kick line; and no K players, other than the kicker, may be more than five yards behind the kicking team's free-kick line. A player satisfies this rule when no foot is on or beyond the line 5 yards behind K's free kick line. If one K player is more than 5 yards behind the restraining line and any other player kicks the ball, it is a foul (2-14-3a through b; 6-1-3a through c). At the time the ball is kicked, at least four K players must be on each side of the kicker (6-1-4).

▧ Rationale

The provisions balance the kicking team's formation and restrict the distance of the run-up for the kicking team.

Formation: Case Plays

6.1.4 SITUATION: After the ready for play and as the ball is being kicked, Team K has three players to the left of the kicker and seven players to the right of the kicker. **RULING:** It is an encroachment foul by K. The ball shall be blown dead immediately and R given the option to accept the distance penalty of 5 yards for the dead-ball foul.

6.1.4 COMMENT: Communication between the game officials and both teams is critical and the referee shall ensure that all opportunities for assembling in a proper formation have been given before sounding the ready-for-play signal.

*6.1.3 SITUATION A: After the ready for play and prior to the ball being kicked, Team K has five players to the left of the kicker and five players to the right of the kicker with the ball spotted at the K40. The potential kicker, K1, is lined up at the K32 to begin his kick and all other K players are clearly outside of the K35. As K1 approaches the kick, he suddenly slows down and K2 then kicks an onside kick that is recovered by R1. **RULING:** Team K has committed a foul for encroachment and the ball shall be blown dead immediately. R is given the option to accept the distance penalty of 5 yards for the dead-ball foul.

6.1.3 SITUATION B: After the ready for play and prior to the ball being kicked, Team K has five players to the left of the kicker and five players to the right of the kicker with the ball spotted at the K40. Prior to the ball being kicked, player K2: (a) has both feet just beyond the K35 (toward midfield); (b) has a foot touching the K35; (c) has one foot touching beyond the K35 toward the K36 and one foot behind the K35; or (d) K has both feet clearly beyond the K35 (toward midfield) but his hand is touching behind the K35 (toward K's goal line). **RULING:** Legal in (a) and (d). Encroachment in (b) and (c).

Fouls During Free Kick Plays

Fouls that occur during free kicks are loose-ball fouls. A loose-ball play is action during a free kick (2-33-1a, d).

The basic spot is a point of reference for penalty enforcement. It is the previous spot for a loose-ball play (10-4-2b). The basic spot is the previous spot for a foul which occurs during a down in which a legal kick occurs and an inadvertent whistle ends the down prior to possession by either team (10-4-2c). The previous spot is where the ball was last free kicked (2-41-7).

Free-Kick Line

For any free kick, a free-kick line, corresponding to a scrimmage line, is established for each team. These lines are always 10 yards apart (2-28-1; 6-1-1). Unless moved by a penalty, K's free-kick line is its 40-yard line for a kickoff, its 20-yard line after a safety, or the yard line through the spot of the catch after a fair catch or an awarded fair catch (6-1-1a through d; 8-5-4).

Kick Out of Bounds

If a free kick goes out of bounds between the goal lines after it has been touched inbounds by R, the ball is put in play by R at the inbounds spot (5-1-5a; 6-1-9).

A free kick shall not be kicked out of bounds between the goal lines untouched inbounds by R (6-1-8a-c).

A player or other person is out of bounds when any part of the person is touching anything, other than another player or game official, who is on or outside the sideline or end line (2-29-1).

A ball in player possession is out of bounds when the runner or the ball touches anything, other than another player or game official, who is on or outside a sideline or end line (2-29-2).

A loose ball is out of bounds when it touches anything, including a player or game official, that is out of bounds (2-29-3).

When a loose ball goes out of bounds, the out-of-bounds spot is fixed by the yard line where the foremost point of the ball crossed the sideline. When the ball becomes dead in the field of play because of touching a person who is out of bounds, the out-of-bounds spot is fixed by the yard line through the foremost point of the ball (2-41-4c, 4-3-1).

When the out-of-bounds spot is between the goal lines, the ball shall be put in play at the nearest inbounds spot. If the out-of-bounds spot is behind a goal line, it is a safety, field goal or touchback. If the ball touches a pylon, it is out of bounds behind the goal line (2-41-4b, 4-3-2).

When the ball becomes dead between the hash marks, play is resumed at the dead-ball spot (4-3-4).

Kick Out of Bounds: Penalty

PlayPic® 19

If it is kicked out of bounds and R does not accept a penalty for kick-catch interference, 5 yards and re-kick, or put the ball in play 25 yards beyond the previous spot at the inbounds spot. Signal 19. Declining the penalty results in R taking the ball at the inbounds spot.

Kick Out of Bounds: Case Plays

2.29.3 SITUATION: A free kick by K1 is touched by R1 on his 15-yard line and then it: (a) rolls out of bounds at R's 5-yard line; or (b) contacts a game official in the field of play and thereafter rolls out of bounds at the 5-yard line; or (c) contacts a game official who is straddling the sideline at the 5-yard line; or (d) contacts a game official in the end zone. **RULING:** The ball will be put in play by R from its 5-yard line in (a), (b) and (c). In (a), R1 was the last to touch the kick before it went out of bounds. In (b), the fact that the ball touched a game official who was inbounds does not change its status. In fact, this touching is ignored and therefore R1, in effect, was the last to touch the ball before it went out of bounds. In (c), when the loose ball touches a game official who is straddling the sideline, it causes the ball to be out of bounds and R1 was the last to touch it. In (d), the ball is dead when it breaks the goal-line plane and a touchback results (6-1-9; 8-5-3a).

6.1.9 SITUATION A: The free kick by K1 is possessed by R1 who: (a) is airborne and alights with one foot in contact with the sideline at his 26, or (b) contacts the sideline on the 26 after completing the catch. **RULING:** In (a) and (b), R will put the ball in play, first and 10, from its 26-yard line because R1 caused the ball to go out of bounds at the 26 (2-4-1).

6.1.9 SITUATION B: The free kick by K1 from K's 40-yard line: (a) is touched by R1 at R's 5 and goes out of bounds at the 8-yard line; or (b) is muffed by R1 at his 15 and then touched by K2 before it rolls out of bounds at R's 10-yard line; or (c) bounces out of bounds on R's 30-yard line untouched by R or K. **RULING:** In (a) and (b) the ball belongs to R at the inbounds spot. In (c), it is a foul by K. The receivers may take the ball at the inbounds spot, take the ball at the inbounds spot at R's 35 which is 25 yards beyond the previous spot, or accept the 5-yard penalty and have K free kick from K's 35-yard line (6-1-10; 2-41-4).

6.1.9 SITUATION C: R1 is running near a sideline as he attempts to catch a free kick in flight. R1 has: (a) both feet inbounds; or (b) one foot on the sideline, when he reaches through the plane of the sideline. The ball bounces off his hands and lands out of bounds. **RULING:** In (a), the ball is not yet out of bounds until it hit the ground there. Since R1 touched it, he caused it to go out of bounds and R will have the ball at the inbounds spot. In (b), since R1 is out of bounds when the ball is touched, the kicker has caused the ball to be out of bounds.

6.1.9 SITUATION D: K1 tries an onside kick from K's 40, as the ball bounces near the sideline the ball is muffed out-of-bounds by K2 at R's 49. **RULING:** R could have K rekick after a five yard penalty, or take the ball 1st and 10 at the inbounds spot at R's 49, or take the ball 1st and 10 at the inbounds spot at R's 35.

6.1.9 SITUATION E: K1 squib kicks the kickoff to R's 30 where (a) R muffs the ball out-of-bounds at R's 28, (b) R muffs the ball toward the side lines where K2 muffs the ball out-of-bounds at R's 28. **RULING:** In both (a) and (b), R would put the ball in play at R's 28.

6.1.9 SITUATION F: K1 tries an onside kick from K's 40. K2 muffs the ball at K's 48, and the ball bounces off R and is muffed out of bounds by K3 at R's 45. K did not force the ball into R. **RULING:** R can either choose to take the ball at K's 48 at the spot of first touching or at R's 45 where the ball went out of bounds. The free kick was touched by R, so R has no re-kick option.

6.1.9 SITUATION G: Team K free kicks from its own 40-yard line. K1's onside kick is rolling at K's 46-yard line, when K2 muffs the ball, which then touches R3's leg and goes out of bounds at K's 48-yard line. **RULING:** Since R's touching is now ignored, this is a free kick that went out of bounds. R has the option of accepting the ball at the spot of first touching by K or having the penalty enforced for the free kick out of bounds with all these options: (a) re-kick following a 5-yard penalty; (b) awarded the ball at the inbounds spot at the yard line where the ball went out of bounds; or (c) accept the ball at the inbounds spot 25 yards from the yard line of the free kick (10-5-1a).

6.1.9 SITUATION H: Team K, after accepting the penalties for multiple R fouls, is now free kicking from R's 20-yard line. In attempting to onside kick, the ball goes out bounds untouched in the field of play. **RULING:** R may take the ball at the inbounds spot, or accept the 5-yard penalty and have K re-kick from R's 25-yard line.

9.6.2 SITUATION C: K1 free-kicks the ball toward the sideline. R1 runs to a sideline and intentionally steps out of bounds. While R1 is still out of bounds, he intentionally touches the ball as it nears the sideline. The ball is declared dead by the covering official. **RULING:** Illegal participation by R1 (4-3-1; 6-1-9).

Kick Not Repeated

A free kick is not repeated unless a foul occurs prior to a change of possession and the penalty acceptance requires a replay of the down; there is a double foul; or there is an inadvertent whistle during the kick (6-1-7a-c).

A free kick shall not be kicked out of bounds between the goal lines untouched inbounds by R (6-1-8a-c). If a free kick goes out of bounds between the goal lines touched inbounds by R, the ball is put in play by R at the inbounds spot (5-1-5a; 6-1-8a-c; 6-1-9; 10-5-1a).

◪ Rationale

Offering choices other than a re-kick to begin a new series speeds up the game.

Resuming Play After a Free Kick

When a free-kick down ends with the ball in the field of play between the goal lines, a new series is awarded to R at the spot of recovery if any K player recovers the kicked ball before it travels the 10 yards to R's free-kick line and before R has touched the ball (5-1-5c; 6-1-5); or if there is joint possession by R and K of a recovered kick (5-1-5d; 6-1-5). If any K player is the first to touch the kicked ball before it has gone 10 yards, a new series is awarded to R at the spot of first touching by K (5-1-5e, 5-1-6).

A new series is awarded to the team in possession of the ball when the down ends if the ball is recovered beyond R's free-kick line with no first touching by K (5-1-5b).

After a series of downs ends, a new series with first and 10 yards to gain is awarded unless one of the following is involved: a try; a field goal; or a free kick after a safety, fair catch or awarded fair catch (5-2-6).

When a loose ball goes out of bounds, the out-of-bounds spot is fixed by the yard line where the foremost point of the ball crossed the sideline. When the ball becomes dead in the field of play because of touching a person who is out of bounds, the out-of-bounds spot is fixed by the yard line through the foremost point of the ball (2-41-4b, 4-3-1).

When the out-of-bounds spot is between the goal lines, the ball shall be put in play at the nearest inbounds spot. If the out-of-bounds spot is behind a goal line, it is a safety, field goal or touchback. If the ball touches a pylon, it is out of bounds behind the goal line (4-3-2).

When the ball becomes dead between the hash marks, play is resumed at the dead-ball spot, unless it is a legal forward-pass incompletion in which case the ball is returned to the previous spot (4-3-4).

When the ball becomes dead in a side zone or is awarded to a team there or is left there by a penalty, play is resumed at the nearest hash mark.

This does not apply to a replayed try (4-3-5c), or the free kick or snap which follows a fair catch or awarded fair catch in a side zone (4-3-5d).

Before the ready-for-play signal, A may designate the spot from which the ball is put in play anywhere between the hash marks following a fair catch (4-3-6d), following an awarded fair catch (4-3-6e), following a touchback (4-3-6f).

When a scrimmage down ends with the ball in the field of play or out of bounds between the goal lines, a new series is awarded to R if K legally kicks during any scrimmage down and the ball is recovered by R, is in joint possession of opponents, goes out of bounds or becomes dead with no player in possession (5-1-3e).

Unless first touched by R beyond the neutral zone, if the kickers recover a scrimmage kick in or behind the neutral zone, the ball remains live and belongs to K and the down counts (5-1-4).

When a foul occurs prior to or during a free-kick down and before any change of team possession, the down which follows enforcement is a free-kick down, unless following a fair catch or an awarded fair catch, a scrimmage down is chosen for the replay (5-2-4).

Topic:
Scrimmage Kicks

A scrimmage kick is any kick from in or behind the neutral zone during a scrimmage down. Either a place kick, punt, or drop kick may be used. For a place kick, the ball must be controlled on the ground or on a legal kicking tee by a teammate (2-24-4). The kick must be made before team possession has changed. It is not necessary to be in a scrimmage kick formation to execute a legal scrimmage kick. K may not punt, drop kick or place kick from beyond the neutral zone. R may not punt, drop kick or place kick (6-2-1).

Ball Becomes Live

A ball becomes live when the ball has been legally snapped and a down is in progress. After being put in play, the ball remains live until the down ends (4-1-5). No foul causes a live ball to become dead (2-16-4).

Ball Becomes Dead

The ball becomes dead and the down is ended when K catches or recovers a scrimmage kick beyond the neutral zone; when K is first (i.e., before any touching by R) to touch a scrimmage kick after it has come to rest beyond the neutral zone and between the goal lines; or when a game official sounds his whistle inadvertently (4-2-2f, j; 6-2-4).

An inadvertent whistle ends the down. The down shall be replayed, if during a down, or during a down in which the penalty for a foul is declined, an inadvertent whistle is sounded during a legal kick (4-2-3a). The team last in possession may choose to either put the ball in play where possession was lost or replay the down if, during a down or during a down in which the penalty for a foul is declined, an inadvertent whistle is sounded while the ball is loose following an illegal kick(4-2-3b).

In Simple Terms

A kick does not end because of merely being touched, muffed or batted. It ends only if a player has gained possession; that is, he has momentarily held the ball in his hands or if declared dead by rule.

Batting a Scrimmage Kick

A K player may bat toward his own goal line a grounded scrimmage kick which is beyond the neutral zone and may also bat toward his own goal line a scrimmage kick in flight beyond the neutral zone, if no R player is in position to catch the ball (9-7-2 Exception).

Batting a Scrimmage Kick: Case Play

9.7.2 SITUATION A: With fourth and 4 from R's 40-yard line, K1 punts. The kick is bounding near R's goal line and K2, in an attempt to keep it from penetrating the plane of the goal line, bats the ball at the 2-yard line back toward his own goal line. **RULING:** The bat by K2 is legal because it occurred beyond the neutral zone.

Catch or Recovery by K

Any K player may catch or recover a scrimmage kick while it is in or behind the neutral zone and advance, unless it is during a try (6-2-3).

Any K player may catch or recover a scrimmage kick while it is beyond the neutral zone or the expanded neutral zone, provided such kick has been touched by a receiver who was clearly beyond the neutral zone at the time of touching (5-1-4; 6-2-4).

Catch or Recovery by K: Case Plays

5.1.3 SITUATION C: Fourth and 10 on K's 45-yard line. K1 punts the ball beyond the neutral zone. R1 muffs the ball back behind the neutral zone where K1 recovers and: (a) falls on the ball at K's 40-yard line; or (b) throws a forward pass to K3 which is complete at the 50-yard line and R1 interferes with K3; or (c) K1 punts the ball and R1 fair catches at his 30-yard line. **RULING:** Since R1 touched the kick beyond the neutral zone, it will be first down for the team in possession in (a), (b) and (c). In (a), it is a first down for K at K's 40-yard line. In (b), the pass is legal as there had been no change of team possession. If K accepts the penalty for pass interference, it will be K's ball at R's 40-yard line. In (c), the second punt is legal as there had been no change of team possession. The ball belongs to R first and 10 on its own 30-yard line (5-1-3f; 6-2-1; 7-5-1).

Fundamental VI-2

A scrimmage kick recovered in or behind the neutral zone may be advanced by K or R.

5.1.3 SITUATION D: K's ball, fourth and 2 at midfield. The scrimmage kick crosses the expanded neutral zone and is muffed by R at the R 40-yard line. The ball then bounds back behind the line of scrimmage and is recovered by K2 at K's 43-yard line. K2 advances to K's 49-yard line where he throws an incomplete pass to eligible receiver K80 at the R38. **RULING:** This is not an illegal forward pass as the ball was legally thrown behind the neutral zone. There has been no change of possession during the down. K is awarded a new series as the ball was touched by R beyond the expanded neutral zone and K is in possession at the end of the down. It will be K's ball, first and 10 at midfield due to the incomplete pass (7-5-2; 2-34-3; 5-1-3f; 7-5-5).

6.2.3 SITUATION B: With third and 10 on K's 10-yard line, K1's punt is blocked and recovered on K's 4-yard line: (a) simultaneously by K2 and R1, or (b) by K2 who advances to K's 15. **RULING:** In (a), the ball is dead immediately and is awarded to R because of the joint recovery. In (b), since K may recover in or behind the neutral zone and advance, it is fourth and 5 for K from its own 15-yard line. The series for K did not end because the kick was blocked (4-2-2e).

6.5.2 SITUATION B: K2's punt is high and a strong wind blows it back toward the neutral zone. R1 gives a valid signal while he is beyond the neutral zone. However, the ball comes down: (a) in, or (b) behind the neutral zone and K2 pushes R1 and then catches the kick and advances.

RULING: Since K may catch or recover a scrimmage kick in or behind the neutral zone and advance, the action in (a) and (b) is legal. Since R may not fair catch in or behind the neutral zone, he may be legally contacted there.

Catch or Recovery by R

Any receiver may catch or recover a scrimmage kick in the field of play and advance, unless it is during a try, or unless any R player has given a valid or invalid fair-catch signal. R may catch or recover a scrimmage kick in K's end zone (6-2-2, 6-5-1).

Catch or Recovery by R: Case Play

7.4.3 SITUATION: An offensive and defensive player simultaneously gain possession of a live ball which is a scrimmage kick muffed by R beyond the neutral zone. **RULING:** The down is ended. The ball belongs to R at the spot of recovery (6-2-6; 7-5-4).

Encroachment

Encroachment occurs when a player is illegally in the neutral zone during the time interval starting when the ball is marked ready for play and until the ball is snapped or free kicked as in 6-1-3a or 6-1-3b. For the purposes of enforcing encroachment restrictions, an entering substitute is not considered to be a player until he is on his team's side of the neutral zone. Encroachment also occurs when a player violates the free kick restrictions as in 6-1-4 (2-8).

Encroachment: Penalty

5 yards. Signals 7 and 18.

Encroachment: Case Plays

2.8 SITUATION B: After the ball is marked ready for play for a free kick, but before it is kicked: (a) place-kick holder K1 kneels so one leg and part of his body are beyond K's free-kick line; or (b) K2 who is near the kicker or the place-kick holder is beyond K's free-kick line before the ball is kicked. **RULING:** In (a), it is permissible for the place-kick holder or the kicker to be beyond the free-kick line prior to the time the ball is kicked. In (b), it is encroachment for any other player to be beyond his free-kick line prior to the time the ball is kicked.

2.8 SITUATION C: Following the ready-for-play signal, but before the free kick: (a) R1 advances to block the kicker/holder and is beyond the plane of R's free-kick line before the ball is kicked; or (b) R has only four players within 5 yards of its free-kick line; or (c) R2, who is one of several R players within 5 yards of his free-kick line, retreats from this area prior to the time the ball is kicked. **RULING:** In (a), it is encroachment. The covering official will sound his whistle to prevent the ball from being kicked when encroachment occurs. In (b) and (c), the action is legal, as there is no requirement for positioning of R players on their side of the neutral zone.

Forced Touching

Touching of a scrimmage kick by R is ignored if it is caused by K pushing or blocking R into contact with the ball or it is caused by K legally batting or muffing the ball into R. A catch or recovery by K beyond the neutral zone causes the ball to become dead (6-2-4). Touching of a scrimmage kick by K is ignored if it is caused by R pushing or blocking K into contact with the ball (6-2-5).

◪ Rationale

R should not be penalized if it is making no attempt to recover a kick and action by K causes the ball to contact R. Thus the contact with the ball is ignored if it is caused by K.

Forced Touching: Case Play

6.2.4 SITUATION: It is fourth and 10 and K11 punts the ball from K's 40-yard line. While R1 and K1 are engaged in blocking downfield at R's 30-yard line, K2 legally bats the ball at R's 28-yard line and the batted ball touches R1 on the leg. Then, K3 recovers the ball at the 30-yard line. **RULING:** This touching by R is ignored and R will have the choice of taking the ball at the spot of first touching or the dead-ball spot.

Formation

At the snap, at least seven K players shall be on their line of scrimmage (2-14-1, 7-2-5a). A scrimmage kick formation is one in which no player is in position to receive a hand-to-hand snap from between the snapper's legs, and at the snap, either a player is in position with a knee on the ground 7 yards or more behind the line of scrimmage, in position to be the holder and receive the long snap and with another player 3 yards or less behind that player in position to attempt a place kick, or a player is 10 yards or more behind the line of scrimmage and in position to receive the long snap (2-14-2a and b).

The players on each side of and next to the snapper may lock legs with the snapper, but any other A lineman must have each foot outside the closest foot of the player next to him at the snap. A's players may stand, crouch or kneel (7-2-2).

Formation: Case Plays

2.17.2 SITUATION E: A1 is in shotgun formation, lined up seven yards behind the line of scrimmage ready to receive the snap. Immediately after the snap to A1, (a) A2 immediately drops and blocks B1 below the waist or (b) A2 rises, and slightly retreats as if to go in traditional pass blocking protection, but then dives and blocks B1 below the waist. Both A2 and B1 were in the zone and on the line of scrimmage at the snap. The contact between A2 and B1 takes place in the free-blocking zone. **RULING:** It is a legal block in (a) and an illegal block below the waist in (b). It is legal for A2 to block B1 below the waist if the contact is made immediately following the snap. Any later, and the ball is considered to have left the free-blocking zone and the block is illegal.

In Simple Terms

There is not a time when a team can use the numbering exception without being in a scrimmage-kick formation.

7.2.5 SITUATION D: With fourth and 6 from the K20, Team K lines up with A21 as the left end; A34, A66, A25, A64 and A86 in the traditional five tackle-guard-center-guard-tackle spots; and A11 on the right end. All are on the line of scrimmage. Players A10, A20 and A5 are in the backfield with A79 lined up in the deep, position as a potential kicker. A25 places his hand on the ball. Prior to the snap, (a) A20 shifts to the line of scrimmage on the right of A86 and left of A11 and sets for one second before the ball is snapped; or (b) A11 steps back off of the line and A20 shifts to replace him as the end, where both are set for a second before the ball is snapped. Who are the eligible receivers prior to the ball being touched by B? **RULING:** Once A25 placed his hands on the ball, all players in between the ends (A34, A66, A25, A64 and A86) become ineligible and remain ineligible throughout the down. In (a), once A20 assumed a position on the line of scrimmage, A20 became ineligible as he was covered up by A11. A79 is ineligible by number. Only A21, A11, A10 and A5 are eligible on the play. In (b), because A11 stepped back off of the line first, A20 becomes eligible as he would be the end. A21, A20, A11, A10 and A5 are eligible (2-14-2; 2-32-9; 2-39; 7-2-5b(2); 7-5-6).

7.2.5 COMMENT: When A is in a scrimmage-kick formation, they do not have to kick and they may kick when they are not in this formation (2-14-2; 7-2-5b Exception).

7.2.5 SITUATION E: It is fourth and 6 for A from its own 40-yard line. A initially sets in a scrimmage-kick formation with Number 83 as an interior lineman and four other linemen numbered 50-79. Prior to the snap, B1 encroaches. The penalty is administered leaving A only 1 yard to go for a first down. A now lines up with Number 83 on the end of the line and through substitution has five interior linemen numbered 50-79. Number 83 goes downfield and catches a touchdown pass. **RULING:** A legal play. The dead-ball encroachment foul allowed A to cancel the use of the numbering exception and to use Number 83 as an eligible receiver. The numbering exception is canceled, or must be renewed, following a dead-ball foul, a charged time-out or TV/radio time-out, the end of a period or an official's time-out.

 7.2.5 COMMENT: If a place kick is used for a try, it is a scrimmage kick and the numbering exception may be used (7-2-5b Exception).

9.4.6 SITUATION D: A1 is lined up in a shotgun formation (5 yards behind the neutral zone) in position to take the snap and A4 is lined up at wingback and is 7 yards behind the neutral zone. Is this a scrimmage kick formation? **RULING:** No. A1 would have to be 10 yards or more behind the neutral zone on fourth down, or must meet the criteria in Rule 2-14-2a, in order to have a scrimmage kick formation.

Muffed Scrimmage Kicks
The ball remains live when a scrimmage kick is muffed (2-1-3).

Muffed Scrimmage Kicks: Case Plays
6.2.3 SITUATION A: A scrimmage kick by K1 is partially blocked in the neutral zone by R1. The kick goes beyond the neutral zone where R2 muffs it back behind the neutral zone. K2 recovers behind the neutral zone and advances across R's goal line. **RULING:** Touchdown for K.

6.2.7 SITUATION: Fourth and 3 for K from their own 10-yard line. A scrimmage kick by K1 is muffed in flight prior to being grounded beyond the neutral zone by R1 and rebounds back into K's end zone where it is simultaneously recovered by opposing players. **RULING:** Touchdown for R. If K is in possession in K's end zone at the end of the down, it is a safety. If R is in possession or if there is joint possession, it is a touchdown. The ball is awarded to R when any scrimmage kick is out of bounds between the goal lines, becomes dead inbounds between the goal lines while no player is in possession or becomes dead inbounds anywhere while opponents are in joint possession. Since the kick was muffed beyond the neutral zone and there has been no possession, it is still a kick into K's own end zone (4-2-2e; 8-2-1b).

8.5.1 SITUATION C: A scrimmage kick by K1 from his own end zone is muffed in flight beyond the neutral zone by R1 and rebounds into the end zone where it is recovered by K2. The ball becomes dead in the end zone when K2 is tackled there. **RULING:** This is a safety because the force which put the ball into the end zone was still the kick by K1. R will be awarded 2 points and K will free kick from K's 20-yard line (8-5-2b).

8.5.2 SITUATION B: With fourth and 3 from his own 10-yard line, the scrimmage kick by K1 is blocked so that it rebounds into K's end zone and is muffed out of bounds in the end zone by either K or R. **RULING:** It is a safety. R will be awarded 2 points and K will put the ball in play by a free kick from its 20-yard line 8-5-2b).

8.5.2 SITUATION C: K1's punt is blocked on K's 5-yard line and the ball is slowly rolling near the goal line. R1 attempts to recover and just barely touches the ball. The ball then rolls into the end zone where K2 falls on it. **RULING:** The covering official will have to judge whether or not a new force resulted from R1's touch. The covering official must decide whether the original force was such that the ball could have gone into the end zone regardless of the muff. If the covering official has doubt, he will rule that the force was supplied by the kick, thus resulting in a safety. If the covering official rules R1 supplied the force, it is a touchback (8-5-2b).

Neutral Zone

The neutral zone is the space between the two scrimmage lines during a scrimmage down (2-28-1). The neutral zone may be expanded following the snap up to a maximum of 2 yards behind the defensive line of scrimmage, in the field of play, during any scrimmage down (2-28-2). The neutral zone is expanded to allow offensive linemen to block and drive defensive linemen off the line of scrimmage. Low scrimmage kicks may touch or be touched by players of K or R, and such touching is ignored if the kick has not been beyond the expanded neutral zone. The zone disintegrates immediately when the kick has crossed the expanded zone or when the trajectory is such that it cannot be touched until it comes down. Once the zone disintegrates, touching of the kick by K in flight beyond the neutral zone is kick-catching interference if no R player is in position to catch the ball. If touched by R beyond the neutral zone, it establishes a new series (6.2.6 SITUATION).

The touching of a low scrimmage kick by any player is ignored if the touching is in or behind the expanded neutral zone. The neutral zone shall not be expanded into the end zone (6-2-6).

Rationale

The purpose of expanding the neutral zone during a scrimmage kick is to permit normal line play.

Neutral Zone: Case Plays

2.28.2 SITUATION B: B1 is on his defensive line of scrimmage when he is contacted by ineligible lineman A1 and driven back about 2 yards. **RULING:** If it is a low scrimmage kick and B1 touches it, the touching is ignored. B1 is considered to be on his line when he is within 1 yard of his line of scrimmage at the snap. The neutral zone may not be expanded into the end zone (2-25-3; 6-2-6; 7-5-12).

6.2.3 SITUATION A: A scrimmage kick by K1 is partially blocked in the neutral zone by R1. The kick goes beyond the neutral zone, where R2 muffs it back behind the neutral zone. K2 recovers behind the neutral zone and advances across R's goal line. **RULING:** Touchdown for K. The right of K to advance their recovered scrimmage kick depends entirely upon whether the kick is recovered in, behind or beyond the neutral zone. Whether the kick went beyond the neutral zone and then rebounded behind it is of no consequence. The spot of recovery is the only factor. If the recovery is in or behind the neutral zone, K may advance. If the recovery is beyond the neutral zone, K may recover, but may not advance.

In Simple Terms

If a place kick is used for a try, it is a scrimmage kick and the numbering exception may be used.

6.2.6 SITUATION: What is the reason for having an expanded neutral zone during scrimmage kicks and how does it affect the touching of a low kick in that area? **RULING:** The purpose of expanding the neutral zone during a scrimmage kick is to permit normal line play. The neutral zone is expanded up to a maximum of 2 yards behind the defensive line of scrimmage (beyond the neutral zone) to allow offensive linemen to block and drive defensive linemen off the line of scrimmage. Low scrimmage kicks may touch or be touched by players of K or R, and such touching is ignored if the kick has not been beyond the expanded neutral zone. The zone disintegrates immediately when the kick has crossed the expanded zone or when the trajectory is such that it cannot be touched until it comes down. Once the zone disintegrates, touching of the kick by K in flight beyond the neutral zone is kick-catching interference if an R player is in position to catch the ball. If touched by R beyond the neutral zone, it establishes a new series (2-28-2; 5-1-3f; 6-5-6).

Numbering Exception

On first, second or third down, when A sets or shifts into a scrimmage-kick formation as in 2-14-2a, the snapper may be a player numbered 1 to 49 or 80 to 99. If Team A has the snapper in the game under this exception, Team A shall have at least four players wearing numbers 50-79 on its line of scrimmage. The snapper in the game under this exception must be between the ends and is an ineligible forward pass receiver during that down unless the pass is touched by B (7-5-6b). On fourth down or during a kick try, when A sets or shifts into a scrimmage-kick formation, any A player numbered 1 to 49 or 80 to 99 may take the position of any A player numbered 50 to 79. A player in the game under this exception must assume an initial position on his line of scrimmage between the ends and he remains an ineligible forward-pass receiver during that down unless the pass is touched by B (7-2-5b Exceptions 1 and 2; 7-5-6b).

Rationale

The numbering exception allows K to put a player especially adept at long-snapping into the game, along with faster players to prevent long returns by R.

Illegal Numbering: Penalty

5 yards. Signal 19.

Resuming Play After a Scrimmage Kick

A new series is awarded to the team in possession at the end of the down if R is the first to touch a scrimmage kick while it is beyond the expanded neutral zone, unless the penalty is accepted for a non post-scrimmage kick foul which occurred before the kick ended or unless 6-2-7 applies (5-1-3f).

A new series is awarded to R at the spot of first touching by K if any K player is first to touch the kicked ball beyond the expanded neutral zone before it is touched beyond this zone by R and before it has come to rest (5-1-3g; 6-2-7).

A new series is awarded to R at the spot of recovery if there is joint possession by R and K of a recovered kick, unless there is first touching by K (5-1-5d).

When any scrimmage kick is out of bounds between the goal lines or becomes dead inbounds between the goal lines while no player is in possession, the ball is awarded to R (5-1-3e). Following an out-of-bounds kick, the ball is put in play at the inbounds spot unless R chooses a spot of first touching (5-1-3e, g).

Resuming Play After a Scrimmage Kick: Case Play

2.34.1 SITUATION: R1 muffs a scrimmage kick after making a valid fair-catch signal. The kick is near the sideline where K1 attempts to recover, but muffs it and it goes out of bounds. **RULING:** The ball belongs to R at the inbounds spot. The touching by K1 prior to the ball going out of bounds does not constitute possession (2-29-3; 2-41-4).

Roughing the Snapper

A defensive player shall not charge directly into the snapper when the offensive team is in a scrimmage-kick formation (9-4-6).

▨ Rationale

The snapper is unable to defend himself immediately upon snapping the ball in scrimmage-kick formation. The rule provides reaction time for the snapper.

Roughing the Snapper: Penalty

15 yards and first down from the previous spot. Signal 38. Disqualification also if any foul is flagrant. Signal 47.

Topic:
Post-Scrimmage Kick (PSK) Enforcement

Post-scrimmage kick penalty enforcement is used after a foul by R (other than illegal substitution or participation) when the foul occurs during scrimmage kick plays other than a try or successful field goal; during a scrimmage kick play in which the ball crosses the expanded neutral zone; beyond the expanded neutral zone; before the end of a kick; and K will not be next to put the ball in play (2-16-2h 1-5).

Post-scrimmage kick fouls are enforced from the basic spot. The basic spot is a point of reference for penalty enforcement. It is the previous spot for a loose-ball play unless the only accepted fouls meet the requirements of a post-scrimmage kick foul (2-16-2h; 10-4-2b; 10-4-3). The basic spot is the previous spot for a foul which occurs during a down in which a legal kick occurs and an inadvertent whistle ends the down prior to possession by either team (10-4-2c).

The post-scrimmage spot is the spot where the kick ends. R retains the ball after penalty enforcement from the post-scrimmage spot when a post-scrimmage foul occurs. Fouls by R behind the post-scrimmage spot are spot fouls (2-41-6).

▨ Rationale

By punting the ball, K has indicated it has ended its attempts to earn a series. PSK allows R to keep the ball after enforcement of a penalty for a foul committed under the correct circumstances.

PSK Fouls: Case Plays

10.2.1 SITUATION D: Fourth and five from K's 20-yard line, K is in an illegal formation at the snap. While K1's punt is in flight, beyond the expanded neutral zone, R2 blocks K8 in the back at the 50-yard line. R4 catches the kick at R's 36-yard line and returns it for a touchdown. **RULING:** This is a post-scrimmage kick foul by R. Therefore, R may decline the penalty for K's foul and keep the ball after enforcement of the 10-yard penalty for the block in the back, or it may accept the penalty against K, thereby creating a double foul in which case the down shall be replayed (10-2-1b).

10.4.3 SITUATION A: Fourth and 8 for K from its own 45-yard line. Prior to R2 catching the kick, R7 clips K5 at the 50-yard line and R2 catches the kick at his 20-yard line and is immediately tackled. **RULING:** The ball will belong to R, first and 10 at its 10-yard line. The basic spot is the 20-yard line as post-scrimmage kick enforcement applies (2-41-6).

10.4.3 SITUATION B: Fourth and 9 for K from its own 40-yard line. R10 holds K11 at K's 42-yard line. K11 catches the kick at R's 25-yard line and is tackled at R's 29-yard line. **RULING:** If K accepts the penalty for holding, it will be K's ball, first and 10 from the 50-yard line. Post-scrimmage kick enforcement applies only to R fouls committed beyond the expanded neutral zone (2-41-6).

In Simple Terms

It is not illegal for a player to shade his eyes, but if he does so, it must be so that it cannot be misinterpreted by an opponent or the covering official.

10.4.3 SITUATION C: Fourth and 11 from K's 36-yard line. While the ball was in flight, beyond the expanded neutral zone, R6 was guilty of holding K3 at R's 32-yard line. The kick goes into the end zone. **RULING:** Since the kick ended in R's end zone, the post-scrimmage kick enforcement spot is the 20-yard line. It will be R's ball, first and 10 from R's 10-yard line after the half-the-distance enforcement (2-41-6).

10.4.3 SITUATION D: K is in punt formation from the 50-yard line. Following the snap, but prior to the ball being kicked, R6 holds K4 at R's 46-yard line. The punt crosses the neutral zone, bounces at R's 25, and rolls to R's 18 where R4 recovers. **RULING:** This foul satisfies all the conditions for post-scrimmage kick enforcement as the foul occurred during the down and on R's side of the expanded neutral zone, so the basic spot is R's 18-yard line. Since R6's foul occurs beyond the basic spot, the penalty is enforced from the basic spot. R is penalized half the distance to the goal, making it R's ball first and 10 at R's 9-yard line (2-16-2h).

10.4.3 SITUATION E: K2 punts from the 50-yard line. The punt crosses the neutral zone, bounces at the R45 and then rebounds back to K's 48-yard line where R4 recovers. Prior to the end of the kick, R6 clips K11 at R's 40-yard line. **RULING:** This foul satisfies all the conditions for post-scrimmage kick enforcement, so the basic spot is K's 48-yard line. Since R6's foul occurs behind the basic spot, the penalty is enforced from the spot of the foul. R is penalized 15 yards, making it R's ball first and 10 at R's 25-yard line (2-16-2h).

10.4.4 SITUATION A: Fourth and 5 for K from R's 49-yard line. R9 catches the kick on the 15-yard line and returns the ball to R's 40-yard line, where he is downed. During the return, R3 holds K7 at R's 30-yard line. **RULING:** Following enforcement of R's holding penalty, it would be R's ball, first and 10 from R's 20-yard line. This is not a post-scrimmage kick enforcement, but a post-possession foul (2-41-6).

Topic:
Fair Catch

A fair catch is a catch by a receiver of a free kick in or beyond the neutral zone to the receiver's goal line, or of a scrimmage kick beyond the neutral zone to the receiver's goal line, after a valid signal, under conditions in which the receiver forfeits his right to advance the ball in return for protection from being blocked or tackled by an opponent. It is a fair catch and the ball is dead if any receiver gives a valid fair-catch signal and he catches a free kick in or beyond the neutral zone to R's goal line, or a scrimmage kick beyond the neutral zone to R's goal line (2-9-1; 6-5-2).

Fair Catch: Case Plays
6.5.1 SITUATION B: K1 attempts an onside kick from his own 40, but instead of causing the ball to strike the ground and bounce, he pops it up into the air. R1 signals for a fair catch while the kick is in flight and catches the ball: (a) before it crosses R's free-kick line; or (b) after it has gone beyond R's free-kick line. **RULING:** R1 has made a fair catch in both (a) and (b). A fair catch is permitted from in or beyond the neutral zone to R's goal line during a free kick (2-9-1).

6.5.2 SITUATION A: During a scrimmage kick beyond the expanded neutral zone, R1 gives a fair-catch signal. He muffs the kick into the air, where: (a) R1 catches it 5 yards in advance of his muff; or (b) K2 pushes R1 in an attempt to reach the ball; or (c) K3 tackles R1 following the muff, preventing R1 from catching the kick; or (d) R1 is blocked below the waist by K4 and K5 recovers. **RULING:** In (a), R1 has made a fair catch and the ball will be put in play at the spot where the catch was completed. In (b), the contact on R1 by K2 is legal because K may retain possession following the muff by R1. In (c), it is a holding foul for K3 to tackle R1 following the muff, thus preventing him from reaching the ball. The block by K4 is illegal in (d). The fouls in (c) and (d) are fouls during a loose-ball play and the penalty, if accepted, will be administered from the previous spot and the down replayed (2-3-5b; 6-2-4; 9-3-2).

Advancing a Dead Ball

No R player may advance the ball after a valid or invalid fair-catch signal has been given by any R player (3-6-2b; 6-5-5).

Advancing a Dead Ball: Penalty

5 yards. Signal 21.

PlayPic® 21

Awarded Fair Catch

An awarded fair catch occurs when the offended team chooses to take the ball after enforcement of a foul for kick-catching interference (2-9-2).

Blocking After Fair-Catch Signal

A receiver who has given a valid or invalid fair-catch signal shall not block an opponent until the kick has ended (6-5-1, 9-3-3).

◩ Rationale

The rule prohibits the receiver from signaling for a fair catch near his goal line, purposely making no attempt to catch the kick and then blocking an opponent to prevent the opponent from downing the ball before it goes into the end zone.

Blocking After Fair-Catch Signal: Penalty

15 yards. Signal 43. Disqualification also if any foul is flagrant. Signal 47.

Blocking After Fair-Catch Signal: Case Play

6.5.1 SITUATION A: R1 and R2 both signal for a fair catch and: (a) the punt is short and is caught by R3; or (b) the punt is over the head of R1, and R2 blocks K1 who is attempting to down the ball near the goal line; or (c) R2 muffs the punt which is then muffed by K2 and finally recovered by R1. **RULING:** R3 did not make a fair catch in (a), but the ball became dead when it was caught. In (b), it is an illegal block because R2 blocked before the kick ended after giving a signal and the penalty, if accepted, will be administered from the post-scrimmage kick spot. In (c), the ball became dead as soon as R1 recovered (4-2-2g; 6-5-5; 9-3-3)

Effect of a Fair-Catch Signal

The ball becomes dead following a valid or invalid fair-catch signal given by any member R player when a scrimmage kick or free kick is caught or recovered by any R player behind, in or beyond the neutral zone (4-2-2g).

Only the receiver who gives a valid signal is afforded protection. If, after a receiver signals, the catch is made by a teammate, it is not a fair catch but the ball becomes dead (6-5-3).

Contacting a receiver who did not give a fair-catch signal or contacting a receiver who has given a signal but is contacted where he cannot make a fair catch, is not a foul unless the contact is judged to be a personal foul. The receiver is not afforded special protection in such situations. Members of the kicking team have the responsibility for knowing when the ball is dead. If a K player could not have seen a fair-catch signal made by the teammate of the receiver, there is no foul. However, if he could have seen the signal, he does not have license to contact the receiver (6.5.3 SITUATION COMMENT).

Effect of a Fair-Catch Signal: Case Plays

3.4.3 SITUATION F: K11 punts on fourth and 10. R1 catches the kick after giving a legal fair catch signal. Prior to the snap, K2 was illegally in motion. R accepts the penalty for illegal motion. **RULING:** After enforcement, the clock shall start on the snap as both the down ending and clock stopping was due to the fair catch.

4.2.2 SITUATION F: K1 punts from midfield and R1 gives a fair-catch signal at R's 10-yard line. R1 muffs the catch and the ball bounces toward R's end zone (a) R2 recovers at the 1-yard line and his momentum takes him into the end zone where he is tackled; or (b) R3 recovers and is downed on R's 2-yard line; or (c) K2 recovers and is downed on R's 5. **RULING:** In (a), it is R's ball on the 1-yard line because the ball became dead when R2 recovered following the fair-catch signal. In (b), it is R's ball on the 2 and in (c) it is K's ball on the 5-yard line.

4.2.2 SITUATION G: K1's punt on fourth and 10 is from his own 20-yard line. The kick is high and short. R1 gives a valid signal beyond the neutral zone and muffs the kick. The ball rebounds behind the neutral zone where: (a) K1 recovers the ball and advances to his 18-yard line; or (b) K1 falls on the ball at his 15-yard line; or (c) R2 falls on the ball at K's 9-yard line; or (d) R2 recovers the ball at K's 9-yard line and is tackled immediately. **RULING:** Legal advance by K1 in (a). It will be an automatic first down for K in both (a) and (b) because R1 touched the kick beyond the neutral zone. In (c), it is R's ball first and goal at K's 9-yard line. In (d), the signal by R1 causes the ball to become dead at the spot of recovery. The covering official should sound his whistle as soon as R2 or any other receiver recovers the ball (4-2-2g; 6-1-5; 6-2-2,3; 6-5-5).

6.5.3 SITUATION: R1 signals for a fair catch of a scrimmage kick by K1. Teammate R2 catches the kick and is tackled immediately by K1 who did or did not have a chance to see the signal. The contact which was not a personal foul occurred before the covering official sounded his whistle. R2 fumbles when tackled and the ball is recovered by K2. **RULING:** The ball became dead when it was caught by R2. The contact by K1 was not a foul because R2 did not signal for a fair catch. R2 fumbled a dead ball and there could be no recovery by K2.

 6.5.3 COMMENT: Contacting a receiver who did not give a fair-catch signal or contacting a receiver who has given a signal but is contacted where he cannot make a fair catch, is not a foul unless the contact is judged by the game official to be a personal foul. The receiver is not afforded special protection in such situations. Members of the kicking team have the responsibility for knowing when the ball is dead. If a kicker could not have seen a fair-catch signal made by the teammate of the receiver, there is no foul. However, if he could have seen the signal, he does not have license to contact the receiver (4-2-2g).

◪ Rationale

By making a fair catch, R is trading the ability to advance the ball for protection from contact.

Invalid, Illegal or Valid Fair-Catch Signals

A valid fair-catch signal is the extending and lateral waving of one arm, at full arm's length above the head, by any R player (2-9-3).

An invalid fair-catch signal is any signal by a receiver before the kick is caught or recovered that does not meet the requirements of a valid signal; made after the kick has touched an R player; or made after the kick has touched the ground (2-9-4a-c; 6-5-7). An illegal fair-catch signal is any signal by a runner after the kick has been caught; or after the kick has been recovered (2-9-5a-b; 6-5-8).

Invalid or Illegal Fair-Catch Signals: Penalty

5 yards. Signal 32.

Invalid, Illegal or Valid Fair-Catch Signals: Case Plays

4.2.2 SITUATION H: R1 gives a fair-catch signal immediately following his catch of a kick. **RULING:** Illegal fair-catch signal, because it was given after the kick was caught and R1 had become a runner. The signal does not cause the down to end. If accepted, the 5-yard penalty is enforced under the all-but-one principle (2-9-5; 3-4-2c; 4-2-2g; 6-5-8).

*6.5.7 SITUATION A: During a scrimmage kick, R1 signals for a fair catch by: (a) extending and holding one arm above his head; or (b) partially extending and waving one hand in front of his face; or (c) fully extending and laterally waving both hands above his head or in front of the body without extending one hand at arm's length above his head; or (d) extending and laterally waving one arm at full length above his head. **RULING:** The signals in (a), (b) and (c) are invalid. In (d), the signal is valid. Giving an invalid signal is a foul for which the penalty is enforced under the post-scrimmage kick provision.

*6.5.7 SITUATION B: During a scrimmage kick, R1 signals for a fair catch by: (a) extending and holding one arm above his head; or (b) partially extending and waving one hand in front of his face; or (c) fully extending and laterally waving both hands above his head; or (d) extending and laterally waving one arm at full length above his head.

RULING: The signals in (a), (b) and (c) are invalid. In (d), the signal is valid. Giving an invalid signal is a foul for which the penalty is enforced under the post-scrimmage kick provision (2-9-3; 2-41-6; 6-5-1, 6).

 6.5.7 COMMENT: When a receiver shades his eyes during a legal kick, he must do so in a manner which is clearly not an invalid fair-catch signal. The responsibility of shading the eyes with a bent arm and not waving it is completely and entirely upon the receiver (2-9-3; 2-41-6; 6-5-1, 6).

6.5.8 SITUATION A: R1 catches K1's punt and then quickly gives a fair-catch signal after advancing a couple of steps. **RULING:** An illegal fair-catch signal by R1. The spot of the illegal signal is the spot of the foul for enforcement under the all-but-one principle (2-9-5).

6.5.8 SITUATION B: R2 gives a fair-catch signal just after R1 begins to advance after catching a punt. **RULING:** No foul, as only the runner can give an illegal fair-catch signal. Opponents must continue to play and not be deceived by a player waving an arm after a kick-catching situation (2-9-5).

Resuming Play After a Fair Catch

The team which next puts the ball in play by scrimmage following a fair catch is awarded a series of four consecutively numbered downs in which to advance the ball to the line to gain. Each awarded first down starts a new series of four consecutively numbered downs (5-1-1) unless R chooses a free kick after a fair catch or awarded fair catch (5-2-5c, f; 5-2-6).

The captain may choose to free kick or snap anywhere between the hash marks on the yard line through the spot of the catch when a fair catch is made; through the spot of interference, when a fair catch is awarded; or at the succeeding spot when the distance penalty for kick-catch interference is accepted following an awarded fair catch and the down is not replayed. These choices remain if a dead-ball foul occurs prior to the down, or a foul or an inadvertent whistle occurs during the down and the down is replayed (4-3-6d and e; 4-3-7; 6-5-4a through c).

When a foul occurs prior to or during a free-kick down and before any change of team possession, the down which follows enforcement is a free-kick down, unless following a fair catch or an awarded fair catch, a scrimmage down is chosen for the replay (5-2-4).

Resuming Play After a Fair Catch: Case Plays

4.2.3 SITUATION A: With fourth and 2 from K's 38-yard line, a scrimmage kick by K1 is muffed beyond the neutral zone by R1 following his signal for a fair catch. While the ball is loose following the muff, the covering official sounds his whistle inadvertently. **RULING:** Because the whistle was inadvertently sounded during a kick, the down will be replayed even though R1 was first to touch the scrimmage kick beyond the neutral zone. The clock will start on the ready-for-play signal (3-4-2c).

Fundamental IV-1

A kick always ends as soon as any player secures possession.

4.3.7 SITUATION: With the score tied near the end of the fourth period, R1 signals for a fair catch and catches the kick at K's 40. After a time-out, the captain of R advises the referee that he wishes to put the ball in play by snap. A1 throws a pass intended for A2. B1 interferes with A2 and the pass is incomplete. Following administration of the penalty, the captain of R decides to put the ball in play by free kick from K's 25 as a field-goal attempt. **RULING:** This is permissible and the clock will not start until the kick is touched, other than first touching by K. This is one of the times a field goal may be scored by a free kick. The captain may request a time-out prior to making the decision on whether to snap or free kick. In putting the ball in play in this situation, the captain of R is privileged to designate the point on K's 25, anywhere between the hash marks he wishes the ball to be placed (1-4-1; 5-2-4; 6-5-4).

6.5.4 SITUATION: R1 signals for a fair catch beyond the neutral zone on K's 40. K2 interferes with R1's opportunity to make the catch. R chooses an awarded catch and to put the ball in play with a snap. During the next down: (a) A1 gains 15 yards and the coach of B is charged with an unsportsmanlike foul; or (b) B2 commits pass interference; or (c) an inadvertent whistle sounds during A1's forward pass. **RULING:** In (a), the unsportsmanlike foul during the down does not give A another choice to snap or free kick. However in (b), A may snap or free kick following penalty enforcement. In (c), the down is replayed and A has the option to snap or free kick (10-4-5a).

Topic:
Field Goals/Trys

A field goal is worth 3 points (8-1). After a touchdown, the scoring team shall attempt a try during which the ball is snapped from a spot designated by A anywhere between the hash marks on B's 3-yard line, unless moved by penalty. This involves a scrimmage down which is neither numbered nor timed (8-3-1). However, if a touchdown is scored during the last down of the fourth period, the try shall not be attempted unless the point(s) would affect the outcome of the game or playoff qualifying (8-3-1 Exception).

During a try, A may score one point for a field goal under rules governing play at other times during the game. Only A may score during a try (8-3-3). If during a successful try, a loss of down foul by A occurs, there is no score and no replay (8-3-4). If during an unsuccessful try, a foul by A/K occurs, the penalty is obviously declined, the results of the play stand and there is no replay. If during an unsuccessful try, a foul by B/R occurs, and the penalty is accepted, the offended captain shall then choose to replay the down after enforcement, or to decline the distance penalty for the foul and replay the down from the previous spot. If a double foul occurs, the down shall be replayed (8-3-6, 8-3-7).

In order to score a field goal, the field-goal attempt shall be a place kick or a drop kick from scrimmage, or from a free kick following a fair catch, or an awarded fair catch. The kick shall not touch any player of K beyond the expanded neutral zone or the ground before passing through the goal. The kick shall pass between the vertical uprights or the inside of the uprights extended and above the crossbar of the opponent's goal (8-4-1a-c).

Field Goals/Trys: Case Plays

4.2.2 SITUATION B: During a try K1, who is apparently a place-kick holder, receives the snap with one knee on the ground and places the ball for a kick. Just as K2 comes forward to kick the ball, K1 lifts the ball, rises and: (a) throws a forward pass to K3 in the end zone; or (b) carries the ball into the end zone; or (c) starts to run, fumbles and the ball is recovered by K4 who advances into the end zone. **RULING:** Successful try in (a), (b) and (c). The ball remains live and may be advanced since the place-kick holder had his knee in contact with the ground at the time of the snap and a teammate was in position to kick.

4.3.6 SITUATION: Prior to the ready-for-play on a try, A's captain requests the ball be placed on the right side hash mark. A then deploys in a spread formation. (a) A1 does not like the defensive coverage and requests a time-out; or (b) a dead-ball foul occurs. The captain of A then asks the referee to move the ball to a position midway between the uprights. **RULING:** The request is denied in (a) and honored in (b). The captain may, in seven situations, ask that the ball be placed at a certain point between the hash marks. However, once spotted the ball may not be moved because of a second request. If a dead-ball foul occurs, or a foul occurs during the down and the penalty is accepted, the captain again will be given an opportunity to pick a spot for the replay. The request for placement of the ball is permissible for a try or kickoff, after a safety, fair catch, awarded fair catch, touchback, or the start of each series, using the 10-Yard Line Overtime Procedure (8-3-1).

8.4.1 SITUATION A: The field-goal attempt: (a) goes directly over an upright; or (b) is clearly over the crossbar between the uprights. In (a) and (b), the ball is blown back by the wind so that it drops into B's end zone. **RULING:** In (a), it is an unsuccessful attempt because the ball did not penetrate the plane of the goal between the inside of the uprights extended. It is a legal field goal in (b) and it doesn't matter if the ball comes back above or below the crossbar (8-4-1c).

8.4.3 SITUATION: With fourth and 5 from B's 18, K1's field-goal attempt is successful. B1 roughs the kicker/holder. **RULING:** K may accept the result of the play (3 points) and have the penalty enforced from the succeeding spot, or accept the penalty. If the penalty is accepted and K retains possession, it will be first and goal from R's 9-yard line (9-4-5; 10-5-1f).

Ball Becomes Live

A ball becomes live when the ball has been legally snapped or free kicked and a down is in progress. After being put in play, the ball remains live until the down ends (2-1-2; 4-1-5).

Ball Remains Live

The try begins when the ball is ready for play (8-3-2).

If a scoring attempt kick touches an upright, crossbar, a game official or R player in the end zone and caroms through the goal, the touching is ignored and the attempt is successful (4-2-2d 2 Exception).

The ball remains live if, at the snap, a place-kick holder with his knee(s) on the ground and with a teammate in kicking position catches or recovers the snap while his knee(s) is on the ground and places the ball for a kick, or if he rises to advance, hand, kick or pass; or rises and catches or recovers an errant snap and immediately returns his knee(s) to the ground and places the ball for a kick or again rises to advance, hand, kick or pass (4-2-2a Exception).

No foul causes a live ball to become dead (2-16-4).

Ball Remains Live: Case Plays

4.2.2 SITUATION A: K1 has one knee on the ground to hold for an apparent field-goal attempt. K2 is in position to kick. K1 catches the snap and: (a) places the ball which is kicked by K2; or (b) rises and either runs or passes. **RULING:** Legal in (a) and (b).

4.2.2 SITUATION B: During a try K1, who is apparently a place-kick holder, receives the snap with one knee on the ground and places the ball for a kick. Just as K2 comes forward to kick the ball, K1 lifts the ball, rises and: (a) throws a forward pass to K3 in the end zone; or (b) carries the ball into the end zone; or (c) starts to run, fumbles and the ball is recovered by K4 who advances into the end zone. **RULING:** Successful try in (a), (b) and (c). The ball remains live and may be advanced since the place-kick holder had his knee in contact with the ground at the time of the snap and a teammate was in position to kick.

4.2.2 SITUATION C: At the snap, K1 is in position to kick and K2 is in position to hold for a place kick with one knee on the ground. The snap is high and it is necessary for K2 to lift his knee off the ground in order to catch the ball, or is low and bounces along the ground. K2 catches or recovers the snap and: (a) immediately drops to one knee and places the ball for a kick; or (b) immediately drops to his knees and then rises and passes the ball; or (c) takes several steps and fumbles the ball which is subsequently recovered and advanced by K1 or K2. **RULING:** The ball remains live in (a), (b) and (c). In (c), the advance by K1 or K2 is legal.

4.2.2 SITUATION I: During a try, K1's place kick hits lineman K2 who is behind the neutral zone, and caroms between the uprights and above the crossbar. **RULING:** The try is successful. Touching a kick is ignored if the touching is in the neutral-zone expanded, or on K's side of it.

Ball Becomes Dead

The ball becomes dead and the down is ended when a runner allows any part of his person other than hand or foot to touch the ground (4-

2-2a). However, the ball remains live if, at the snap, a place-kick holder with his knee(s) on the ground and with a teammate in kicking position catches or recovers the snap while his knee(s) is on the ground and places the ball for a kick, or if he rises to advance, hand, kick or pass; or he rises and catches or recovers an errant snap and immediately returns his knee(s) to the ground and places the ball for a kick or again rises to advance, hand, kick or pass (4-2-2a Exception 1 and 2).

The ball becomes dead if the place-kick holder muffs the snap or fumbles and recovers after his knees have been off the ground, and he then touches the ground with other than hand or foot while in possession of the ball (4-2-2 NOTE).

The ball becomes dead and the down is ended when any legal free kick or scrimmage kick which is a scoring attempt, while in flight touches a K player in R's end zone, or after breaking the plane of R's goal line has apparently failed (4-2-2d 2). However, if a scoring attempt kick touches an upright, crossbar, a game official or R player in the end zone and caroms through the goal, the touching is ignored and the attempt is successful (4-2-2d 2 Exception).

The ball becomes dead and a try is ended when B secures possession; it is apparent a drop kick or place kick will not score; the try is successful; or the ball becomes dead for any other reason (8-3-2a-d).

Ball Becomes Dead: Case Plays

4.2.2 SITUATION E: With fourth and goal from R's 20-yard line, K1 attempts a field goal. The attempt is above the crossbar level, but is just wide of the left upright. **RULING:** The ball becomes dead immediately when the covering official determines the attempt is unsuccessful and the ball has broken the plane of R's goal line (4-2-2d(2)).

6.3.1 SITUATION B: During a field-goal attempt, R1, who is in the end zone, leaps up and blocks the ball away from the crossbar. **RULING:** Touchback. The touching by R1 in the end zone causes the ball to become dead, unless the ball caroms through the goal, thus scoring a field goal. This is not illegal batting. Touching by R1 in the field of play has no effect on the scoring of a field goal (4-2-2d; 6-2-6; 9-7-2).

8.3.2 SITUATION B: During a try by place-kick, the kick by K1 is blocked by R1 and recovered by K2, who advances across R's goal line. **RULING:** The try is unsuccessful. The try and down ended when the attempted place kick was blocked and it was obvious the kick would not score. The covering official should sound his whistle immediately when it is apparent the kick will not score (4-2-2i).

◪ Rationale

When a drop kick or place kick from scrimmage, or a free kick following a fair catch or awarded catch which touches a goal post, crossbar, or an R player and caroms through the goal, the ball remains live so the point(s) may be scored. That means an R player cannot prevent a score merely by touching the kicked ball in the end zone on its flight to the goal.

Penalties During a Successful Field Goal/Try

If during a successful field goal, a foul by R occurs, K is given the choice of accepting the penalty and replaying the down following enforcement; or accepting the result of the play and enforcement of the penalty from the succeeding spot (8-4-3; 10-5-1e).

If during a successful try, a foul by R occurs, K is given the choice of accepting the penalty and replaying the down following enforcement; or accepting the result of the play and enforcement of the penalty from the succeeding spot. The latter choice is available only if the next play is to be a kickoff (8-3-5a, b; 10-5-1d).

Penalties During a Successful Field Goal/Try: Case Plays

8.2.2 SITUATION A: During (a) A9's run for a touchdown, B2 holds A1, or (b) K1's field goal, R2 holds K1. **RULING:** In (a), A will likely keep the score and may choose to enforce the penalty on the try or enforce the penalty on the subsequent kickoff. In (b), K may keep the points and have the penalty enforced from the succeeding spot, or have the penalty enforced from the previous spot and replay the down (8-4-3).

8.2.2 SITUATION B: On the down in which time expired for the second period, Team A: (a) scores a field goal or (b) scores a touchdown. In both cases, the opponents of the scoring team commit a live-ball foul. **RULING:** In (a), the offended team has the option to keep the score, with the penalty assessed on the second half kickoff as this is the succeeding spot. In (b), the offended team has the option to keep the score, with penalty assessment on either the try or on the second half kickoff as this would be the subsequent kickoff.

8.3.5 SITUATION A: During a kick try: (a) B1 holds and the try is successful; or (b) A1 holds and the try is successful; or (c) B1 roughs the kicker/holder and the try is unsuccessful. **RULING:** In (a), A may accept the score and have the penalty enforced from the succeeding spot or enforce it from the previous spot and replay the down. In (b), B undoubtedly will accept the penalty and replay. In (c), A obviously would accept the penalty and replay (8-3-7; 10-5-2).

8.4.3 SITUATION: With fourth and 5 from B's 18, K1's field-goal attempt is successful. B1 roughs the kicker/holder. **RULING:** K may accept the result of the play (3 points) and have the penalty enforced from the succeeding spot, or accept the penalty. If the penalty is accepted and K retains possession, it will be first and goal from R's 9-yard line (9-4-d; 10-5-1f).

Resuming Play After a Field Goal/Try

After a successful try or field goal, the opponent of the scoring team shall designate which team will kick off (8-3-9; 8-4-2).

To resume play after a successful field goal or after any try, the ball shall be put in play by a kickoff (4-1-1; 5-2-6).

After an unsuccessful field goal, a new series is awarded to the team in possession at the end of the down if R is the first to touch a scrimmage kick while it is beyond the expanded neutral zone, unless the penalty is accepted for a non post-scrimmage kick foul which occurred before the kick ended or unless 6-2-7 applies (5-1-3f).

A new series is awarded to R at the spot of first touching by K if any K player is first to touch the kicked ball beyond the expanded neutral zone before it is touched beyond this zone by R and before it has come to rest (5-1-3g; 6-2-7).

A new series is awarded to R at the spot of recovery if there is joint possession by R and K of a recovered kick, unless there is first touching by K (5-1-5d).

When any scrimmage kick is out of bounds between the goal lines or becomes dead inbounds between the goal lines while no player is in possession, the ball is awarded to R (5-1-3e). Following an out-of-bounds kick, the ball is put in play at the inbounds spot unless R chooses a spot of first touching (5-1-3e, g; 6-2-7).

Did You Know? The rule regarding the first touching of free kicks was adopted in 1968. Before then, K could touch the ball any number of times without consequence, thus making it difficult for R to return the kick.

Resuming Play After a Field Goal/Try: Case Play

8.3.5 SITUATION A: During a kick try: (a) B1 holds and the try is successful; or (b) A1 holds and the try is successful; or (c) B1 roughs the kicker/holder and the try is unsuccessful. **RULING:** In (a), A may accept the score and have the penalty enforced from the succeeding spot or enforce it from the previous spot and replay the down. In (b), B undoubtedly will accept the penalty and replay. In (c), A obviously would accept the penalty and replay (8-3-7; 10-5-2).

Topic:
First Touching

Touching refers to any contact with the ball, i.e., either by touching or being touched by it (2-44).

If any K player touches a free kick before it crosses R's free-kick line and before it is touched there by any R player, or if any K player touches a scrimmage kick beyond the expanded neutral zone to R's goal line before it is touched beyond the neutral zone by R and before the ball has come to rest, it is referred to as "first touching of the kick" (2-12-1, 2; 6-1-6; 6-2-5). First touching is a game situation which produces results somewhat similar to a penalty, but is not classified as a foul (2-16-6).

Fundamental IV-1
First touching of a kick by K is always ignored if the penalty is accepted for a foul during the down.

When K first touches a scrimmage kick after it has come to rest beyond the neutral zone and between the goal lines, the ball becomes dead and the down has ended (4-2-2f).

The place where the touching occurs is the "spot of first touching" (6-2-5). Such touching is ignored if it is caused by R pushing or blocking K into contact with the ball (6-1-6; 6-2-5).

R may take the ball at the spot of first touching, or any spot if there is more than one spot of first touching, or they may choose to have the ball put in play as determined by the action which follows first touching. The right of R to take the ball at the spot of first touching by K is canceled if R touches the kick and thereafter during the down commits a foul or if the penalty is accepted for any foul committed during the down (6-1-6;

6-2-5). The touching of a low scrimmage kick by any player is ignored if the touching is in or behind the expanded neutral zone. The neutral zone shall not be expanded into the end zone (6-2-6).

Following an out-of-bounds scrimmage kick, the ball is put in play at the inbounds spot unless R chooses a spot of first touching (6-2-7).

◪ Rationale

The clock doesn't start when the kick is first touched by K so that R is not denied an opportunity to secure possession when there are only a few seconds remaining at the end of the second or fourth quarters. Without that aspect of the rule, K could run out the clock after a touchdown or safety by making one or more short free kicks.

First Touching: Case Plays

6.2.5 SITUATION A: K1 attempts to down a punt beyond the neutral zone, but his touching only slows it down. The bouncing ball is subsequently recovered by R1, who advances 25 yards but then fumbles and K2 recovers. K2 is immediately tackled. **RULING:** R may either take the results of the play or retain possession by taking the ball at the spot of K1's first touching. R can exercise this option, unless after R1 touches the ball, R commits a foul or the penalty is accepted for any foul committed during the down.

6.2.5 SITUATION B: K2, running toward R's end zone, leaps in the air to catch K1's punt which is in flight. K2 has the ball in his grasp over the 1-yard line, but first touches the ground in R's end zone. No player of R is in position to catch the punt. **RULING:** R can take the ball at the spot of first touching, his own 1-yard line, or take a touchback since K2 has not possessed the ball until he came to the ground in the end zone.

6.2.5 SITUATION C: With fourth and 5 from K's 30-yard line, K9 punts the ball downfield where it is grounded and touched by K88 (first touching) at R's 30. The ball continues rolling and is picked up by R35 at R's 25-yard line. R35 is subsequently hit and fumbles at R's 28. The loose ball is recovered by K88 on the ground at R's 26. During the kick, R55 is flagged for holding. **RULING:** If K accepts R's foul for holding, then it is enforced from the previous spot since post-scrimmage kick cannot apply as K is next to put the ball in play as a result of the recovered fumble. Also, if K accepts the foul, the awarded spot for illegal touching is not applied. If K declines R's foul, R will take the ball at the spot of first touching (2-12-1; 2; 2-16-2h).

Topic:
Illegal Kick

An illegal kick is any intentional striking of the ball with the knee, lower leg or foot which does not qualify as a free kick or scrimmage kick. When the ball is loose following an illegal kick, it retains the same status as prior to the illegal kick (2-24-9).

No player shall intentionally kick the ball other than as a free or scrimmage kick. R may not punt, drop kick or place kick after team possession has changed. The penalty for an illegal kick is 15 yards (6-2-1; 9-7-1).

Accidentally kicking a loose ball by a player in an unsuccessful attempt to secure possession is not illegal (2-27).

The team last in possession may choose to either put the ball in play where possession was lost or replay the down if, during a down or during a down in which the penalty for a foul is declined, an inadvertent whistle is sounded while the ball is loose following an illegal kick (4-2-3b). The penalty shall be administered as determined by the basic spot, and takes precedence over inadvertent whistle administration if, during a down a live-ball foul occurs prior to the inadvertent whistle and the penalty is accepted (4-2-3d).

Illegal Kick: Penalty
15 yards. Signal 31.

Illegal Kick: Case Plays
4.2.3 SITUATION F: A1 is in scrimmage kick formation with his back heel near the end line in the end zone. On a high snap, the potential kicker jumps and is able to keep the ball from going out of the end zone. It falls to the ground and is rolling around 5 yards into the end zone. In a panic, A1 then kicks the ball off the ground and it rolls to the A25 and is bounding around when there is an inadvertent whistle. The ball rolls dead at the A27. **RULING:** B has a choice of accepting the penalty for an illegal kick, which if accepted, results in a safety against A. If the penalty is declined, the inadvertent whistle rule allows for A to ask for a replay of the down since the ball was not in player possession at the time of the whistle.

8.5.1 SITUATION D: It is first down and 10 on A's 3. Runner A1 fumbles on his 2-yard line. B1 intentionally kicks the loose ball which is: (a) on A's 2; or (b) in the end zone. The ball then goes out of bounds behind the goal line. **RULING:** Undoubtedly, Team A will decline the penalty in (a)

and take the touchback. A will accept the penalty for the illegal kick in (b), because declining it would give B a safety (8-5-2b, 3c; 9-7-1).

8.5.3 Situation B: K1 kicks off to start the second half. The ball is rolling on R's 7-yard line when R1: (a) accidentally, or (b) intentionally kicks the ball into his own end zone where R2 recovers. Is the kick by R1 in either (a) or (b) a new force? If the action is a foul, where is it penalized from? **RULING:** It is not a new force in either (a) or (b), as force is not a consideration on kicks going into R's end zone. Even though the ball was kicked by R1, the kick had not ended. The contact in (a) is ignored, because it was not an intentional act. In (b), the kick is illegal, and if the penalty is accepted, it is enforced from the previous spot. If the penalty is declined, it is a touchback by rule. In both (a) and (b), the ball becomes dead when the kick breaks the plane of R's goal line (2-13-4; 9-7-1; 10-6).

9.7.1 SITUATION A: On a field-goal attempt, holder A2 muffs the snap and is attempting to gain possession of the ball on the ground when A1 kicks it between the uprights over the crossbar. **RULING:** An illegal kick by A1. If the penalty is declined, the result of the play is a touchback as the illegal kick cannot score a field goal (2-24-7).

9.7.1 SITUATION B: It is fourth and 10 for A from its own 15-yard line. A1 fakes a kick and runs beyond the neutral zone and kicks the ball at the 20. The kicked ball: (a) is caught by A2 at A's 30 and he is downed there; or (b) goes out of bounds at midfield; or (c) comes to rest on A's 45 and no player of either team will touch it, so the covering official sounds his whistle. **RULING:** The kick is illegal and the resulting loose ball is treated as a fumble. The normal kicking rules and restrictions are not in effect during an illegal kick. In (a), (b) and (c), if the penalty for the illegal kick is declined, it will be A's ball first and 10 from the yard line where the ball became dead. If the penalty is accepted, it is enforced from the end of the run which is the spot of the illegal kick (2-24-9; 2-33-1d; 4-2-2e(2); 6-2-1).

9.7.1 SITUATION C: A is in scrimmage-kick formation and the ball is snapped to A1 who is the potential punter. (a) A1 muffs the ball allowing it to hit the ground where he kicks it; or (b) A1 muffs the ball, but then picks it up and punts it. **RULING:** Illegal kicking in (a). If accepted, the penalty is 15 yards from the spot of the foul, because it is a foul by A behind the basic spot during a loose-ball play. It is a legal kick in (b) (2-24-4, 8; 2-33-1c; 10-3-1c).

Kicking Tee

A kicking tee may be used for a place kick when the place kick is a scrimmage kick (for a field goal), a kickoff, a free kick following a safety or for a free kick following a fair catch or awarded fair catch (2-24-4; 2-24-7). When rules allow a kicking tee to be used, a tee shall be made of pliable material which elevates the lowest point of the ball no more than 2 inches above the ground (1-3-4; 9-10-4).

Illegal Tee: Penalty

15 yards from the basic spot. Signal 27.

PlayPic® 27

Illegal Tee: Case Play

9.10.4 SITUATION: Team A scores: (a) on a try where the line of scrimmage was the 3-yard line and the tee was placed at the 10-yard line, or (b) on a field goal where the line of scrimmage was B's 20-yard line and the tee was placed at B's 27-yard line. In both cases, the referee determines during the kick that the kicker was using an illegal kicking tee. RULING: In (a), the basic spot is the previous spot and fouls by the offense behind the basic spot are enforced from the spot of the foul, therefore the penalty will be 15 yards marked from the 10-yard line, and if accepted, will result in a replay of the try from B's 25-yard line. In (b), the basic spot is the previous spot and fouls by the offense behind the basic spot are enforced from the spot of the foul, therefore the penalty will be 15 yards marked from the 27-yard line, and if accepted, will result in a replay of the down from B's 42-yard line.

Topic:
Kick-Catching Interference

While any free kick is in flight in or beyond the neutral zone to the receiver's goal line or any scrimmage kick is in flight beyond the neutral zone to the receiver's goal line, K shall not touch the ball or R, unless blocked into the ball or R or to ward off a blocker, nor obstruct R's path to the ball. This prohibition applies even when no fair-catch signal is given, but it does not apply after a free kick has been touched by an R player, or after a scrimmage kick has been touched by an R player who was clearly beyond the neutral zone at the time of touching (6-5-6).

K may catch, touch, muff or bat a scrimmage kick in flight beyond the neutral zone if no player of R is in position to catch the ball (6-5-6 Exception).

A K player may bat toward his own goal line a grounded scrimmage kick which is beyond the neutral zone and may also bat toward his own goal line a scrimmage kick in flight beyond the neutral zone, if no R player is in position to catch the ball (9-7-2 Exception).

Kick-Catching Interference: Penalty

R may accept the results of the play, an awarded fair catch after enforcement of a 15-yard penalty from the spot of the foul, or a 15-yard penalty from the previous spot and a replay of the down. Signal 33.

Kick-Catching Interference: Case Plays

6.1.7 SITUATION A: A free kick from K's 40 is high and comes down over K's 45 where it is muffed in flight by K2 after which it is recovered by K3 on R's 40. **RULING:** This is first touching and also kick-catching interference by K2. R may choose to take the ball at the spot of first touching, take the results of the play or accept the 15-yard penalty for kick-catching interference. If the distance penalty is accepted, it is R's choice to have the penalty enforced from the spot of the foul or to have it enforced from the previous spot and require K to rekick.

In Simple Terms

Interference is strictly a judgment call. There is no "halo" or hard and fast distance to be used as a guide.

6.1.6 SITUATION B: The ball is free kicked from K's 40-yard line and in flight, it crosses the 50-yard line before a strong wind blows it back to K's 45 where it is touched in flight by K1 and is recovered by K2. **RULING:** Kick-catching interference.

6.5.6 SITUATION A: K2's punt is partially blocked by R1 in or behind the neutral zone and it then travels beyond the neutral zone. R2 is in position to catch the ball, but it first touches K2's shoulder before hitting the ground, where it is recovered by R2. **RULING:** Since R1's touching is ignored, it is kick-catching interference by K2, because R2 was in position to catch the ball.

6.5.6 SITUATION B: K1's punt is coming down over R's 15-yard line and (a) R2 is in position to catch the ball, or (b) all R players have moved away from where the ball will land. In both (a) and (b), K3 catches the ball. **RULING:** In (a), it is kick-catching interference and R has the option to take the results of the play, or accept the 15-yard penalty for kick-catching interference. If the distance penalty is accepted, it is R's choice to have the penalty enforced from the spot of the foul or to have it enforced from the previous spot and require K to rekick. In (b), the play is legal and the ball is dead as soon as K3 catches it. The spot of the catch is also a spot of first touching and R will put the ball in play on that yard line, first and 10.

6.5.6 SITUATION C: K5, running down field under a punt, has the kick strike him on his helmet: (a) R1 is in a position to catch the kick if he so chooses; or (b) no R player is in position to be able to get to the ball and catch it. **RULING:** In (a), K5 has committed kick-catching interference. In (b), there is no foul.

6.5.6 SITUATION D: K1's punt is high but short. R2, from well down field, runs toward the ball to get in position to attempt to catch it. K2 is also moving toward the ball or just standing there when: (a) K2 is contacted by R2; or (b) K2 causes R2 to veer away from the ball but there is no contact by K2. The ball strikes the ground and is recovered by R3. **RULING:** K2 has committed kick-catching interference in both (a) and (b) since K2 did not provide R2 an unobstructed opportunity to catch the ball. R may choose to take the results of the play, or accept the 15-yard penalty for kick-catching interference. If the distance penalty is accepted, it is R's choice to have the penalty enforced from the spot of the foul or to have it enforced from the previous spot and require K to replay the down.

6.5.6 SITUATION E: While K1's punt is in flight beyond the neutral zone, R2 (a) gives a valid fair catch signal, or (b) does not give a signal. The ball strikes R2 on the shoulder and bounces high into the air. While the loose ball is still airborne, K4 pushes R2 in the chest and K4 catches the ball at that spot. **RULING:** In both cases, the ball is dead when K4 catches it. There is no foul for kick-catching interference since R2's protection ended when the kick was muffed.

9.7.2 SITUATION A: With fourth and 4 from R's 40-yard line, K1 punts. The kick is bounding near R's goal line and K2, in an attempt to keep it from penetrating the plane of the goal line, bats the ball at the 2-yard line back toward his own goal line. **RULING:** The bat by K2 is legal because it occurred beyond the neutral zone.

*9.7.2 SITUATION B: K1's punt is coming down over R's 10-yard line and: (a) R3 is in position to catch the ball; or (b) no R player is in position to catch the ball, when K2 bats the ball toward his own goal line while it is in flight, but the batted ball subsequently goes into R's end zone. **RULING:** In (a), it is a foul for kick-catching interference by K2 as well as first touching, and R may choose to take the result of the play, which is a touchback, or take an awarded fair catch at R's 25-yard line (15 yards in advance of the spot of interference after enforcement of the penalty) or the ball at the spot of first touching at the 10-yard line, or penalize K 15 yards from the previous spot and replay the down. In (b), there is no foul and the result of the play is a touchback. R will put the ball in play first and 10 from its own 20-yard line (6-5-6 Exception; 8-5-3; 9-7-2 Exception).

Topic:
The Kicker/Holder/Snapper

The kicker or place-kick holder of a free kick may not be blocked until after a free kick, he has advanced 5 yards beyond his free-kick line or the kick has touched the ground or any other player (2-32-8; 9-3-4a, b).

Blocking the Kicker/Holder: Penalty

15 yards. Signal 40. Disqualification also if any foul is flagrant. Signal 47.

Blocking the Kicker/Holder: Case Play

9.3.4 SITUATION: From his 40-yard line, K1 kicks the ball laterally and short on a kickoff, hoping his team can recover just beyond R's free-kick line. The ball bounces immediately after being kicked. K1 is blocked by R1: (a) on his 42-yard line; or (b) on his 43-yard line, 5 yards from the sideline. **RULING:** Legal block in both (a) and (b) if the contact is above the waist. As soon as the ball touches the ground, the kicker/holder may be contacted with a legal block.

In Simple Terms

It is legal for opponents to shoot the gaps between the center and the guards.

Roughing the Kicker/Holder/Snapper

A defensive player shall not block, tackle or charge into the kicker of a scrimmage kick, or the place-kick holder, other than when contact is unavoidable because it is not reasonably certain that a kick will be made; the defense touches the kick near the kicker and contact is unavoidable; contact is slight and is partially caused by movement of the kicker; or contact is caused by R being blocked into the kicker by K. That is roughing the kicker or holder (9-4-5a-d; 10-5-1h).

A defensive player shall not charge directly into the snapper when the offensive team is in a scrimmage-kick formation (9-4-6; 10-5-1i).

Rationale

The kicker is off balance, largely defenseless and vulnerable while in the act of kicking. Common sense demands the kicker and holder be given special protection.

Roughing the Kicker/Holder/Snapper: Penalty

Roughing the kicker, holder or snapper: 15 yards and first down from the previous spot. Signals 38 and 30. Disqualification also if any foul is flagrant. Signal 47.

Roughing the Kicker/Holder/Snapper: Case Plays

9.4.5 SITUATION A: K1 punts and R1 touches and partially blocks the kick. R2 does not touch the ball, but firmly contacts K1. **RULING:** If R1 partially blocked the kick near the kicker/holder and R2 was near the kicker/holder at the time R1 touched the ball and R2 had already started his charge at the time the kick was touched, there would be no foul as a result of the contact by R2, unless it was unnecessarily rough (9-4-5b).

9.4.5 SITUATION B: K1 in scrimmage-kick formation, muffs the snap, but quickly recovers and begins to run. However, K1 changes his mind and: (a) punts on the run; or (b) abruptly stops and punts. R1 is unable to stop his charge and forcibly contacts K1. R1 did not touch the kick.

RULING: No foul in either (a) or (b) because it was not reasonably certain K1 was going to punt the ball. It is always roughing the kicker if the contact could have been avoided regardless of whether or not it was apparent a kick would be made. Only unavoidable contact is ignored if it is not reasonably certain a kick will be made.

9.4.5 SITUATION C: R1, in an effort to block a place kick, charges through blocker K1 and without touching the ball, charges into the kicker/holder. **RULING:** The covering official must determine whether R1's charge would have taken him into the kicker/holder, regardless of the contact by the blocker. It is only when K1's block alters the course of R1's path and thus causes the contact with the kicker/holder that R1's contact is ignored and does not result in a foul.

9.4.5 SITUATION E: K10, the place kick holder, is contacted forcibly by R9, clearly after the kick is away. **RULING:** Roughing the kicker/holder is a personal foul. The penalty would be 15 yards and an automatic first down, if accepted.

9.4.5 SITUATION F: As R2 rushes punter K11 he: (a) brushes K11 who maintains his balance; (b) bumps K11 causing him to fall backwards or (c) runs over K11 knocking him to the ground. **RULING:** In (a), no penalty; (b) running into the kicker/holder, 5-yard penalty and replay the down; (c) roughing the kicker/holder, personal foul, 15-yard penalty and an automatic first down.

9.4.5 SITUATION G: A11 is in scrimmage kick formation. After taking the snap and attempting to kick the ball, he misjudges the distance and misses the ball. A11 is then contacted by B1 before he can regain his balance. B2 recovers the ball. **RULING:** Unless B1's contact is viewed as unnecessary roughness, there is no foul as A11 never became a kicker.

In Simple Terms

The period involved in roughing the kicker begins with his foot contacting the ball and continues until he regains his balance. The kicker is protected by rule and the responsibility in case of contact is on the opponent.

9.4.6 SITUATION A: From a scrimmage-kick formation, A1 snaps the ball to back A2 who is 3 yards behind the line and offset from the snapper by 1 yard. A2 runs for a 10-yard gain. Immediately after the snap started, B7 charges: (a) directly into the snapper; or (b) into the gap between the snapper and the adjacent A player making simultaneous contact with both the snapper and the other Team A player. The snapper had not had the opportunity to defend himself and was displaced by B7's charge. **RULING:** In (a), B7 has roughed the snapper. If accepted, it is a 15-yard penalty and an automatic first down. There is no requirement that the ball be kicked or that a deep back receive the snap. In (b), there is no foul. The snapper's protection does not include simultaneous contact with another A player, nor does it take away the "center-guard gap" from B. The roughing prohibition is only for a direct charge into the snapper (2-32-14).

9.4.6 SITUATION B: K is in scrimmage-kick formation on fourth and 17 from its own 20-yard line. Immediately following the snap, R1 charges directly into snapper A1. The kick is caught by R2 and he is downed on K's 40-yard line. **RULING:** R1 has roughed the snapper. In addition to the yardage, the penalty also includes an automatic first down. Following enforcement, it is K's ball first and 10 from its own 35-yard line.

9.4.6 SITUATION C: A is in a scrimmage kick formation with punter A2 standing twelve yards deep and four yards to the right of the snapper. The wind is blowing very strong and will probably move the ball to the right after it is snapped. Is the snapper afforded protection in this case? **RULING:** Yes, because the punter is in position to receive the snap.

Running Into the Kicker/Holder

A defensive player shall not run into the kicker nor holder, which is contact that displaces the kicker or holder without roughing (9-4-5; 10-5-1h).

Running Into the Kicker/Holder: Penalty

5 yards from the previous spot. Signal 30.

Running Into the Kicker/Holder: Case Play

9.4.5 SITUATION D: K11 is in scrimmage kick formation. After the kick is away, R10 is unable to stop his attempt to block the kick and R10 displaces the kicker/holder. **RULING:** The referee judges the infraction to be running into the kicker/holder. The penalty, if accepted, is 5 yards from the previous spot and a replay of the down.

Topic:
Force and Touchback

Force is the result of energy exerted by a player which provides movement of the ball. The term force is used only in connection with the goal line and in only one direction, i.e., from the field of play into the end zone. Initial force results from a kick. After a kick has been grounded, a new force may result from a bat, an illegal kick or a muff (2-13-1). Responsibility for forcing the ball from the field of play across a goal line is attributed to the player who carries, snaps, passes, fumbles or kicks the ball, unless a new force is applied to either a kick, fumble or backward pass that has been grounded (2-13-2). The muffing or batting of a kick in flight is not considered a new force (2-13-3, 8-5-1a). The accidental touching of a loose ball by a player who was blocked into the ball is ignored and does not constitute a new force (8-5-1b).

In Simple Terms

While a loose ball is still in flight, no touching, batting or muffing is considered a new force. Instead, the kick, pass or fumble is still considered the force if the ball goes from the field of play across a goal line.

Force is not a factor on kicks going into R's end zone, since these kicks are always a touchback regardless of who supplied the force (2-13-4a). It is a touchback if any free kick or scrimmage kick which is not a scoring attempt or which is a grounded three-point field-goal attempt, breaks the plane of R's goal line, unless R chooses a spot of first touching by K; if a three-point field-goal attempt in flight touches a K player in R's end zone, or after breaking the plane of R's goal line is unsuccessful; or if any scrimmage kick or free kick becomes dead on or behind K's goal line with the ball in possession of K (including when the ball is declared dead with no player in possession) and the new force is R's muff or bat of the kick after it has touched the ground (6-3-1, 2; 8-5-3).

Force and Touchback: Case Plays
4.2.2 SITUATION D: K1's free kick or scrimmage kick hits the ground at R's 10-yard line and bounces into R's end zone. **RULING:** The ball became dead immediately when it broke the plane of R's goal line and results in a touchback.

6.3.1 SITUATION A: A scrimmage kick by K1 comes to rest on R's 6-yard line. R1 attempts to recover and advance, but muffs the ball so that it rolls into the end zone where: (a) R2 downs the ball; or (b) R3 recovers and advances out of the end zone; or (c) K2 recovers and downs the ball in the end zone. **RULING:** The ball became dead as soon as it broke the plane of R's goal line. It is a touchback in (a), (b) and (c). The kick had not ended because muffing does not constitute possession, therefore, it is a kick into R's end zone which is an automatic touchback. The covering official should sound the whistle immediately when the ball becomes dead as a result of breaking the goal-line plane. Force is not a factor on kicks going into R's end zone. R will put the ball in play, first and 10, from their 20-yard line (2-24-2; 8-5-3a).

6.3.1 SITUATION B: During a field-goal attempt, R1, who is in the end zone, leaps up and blocks the ball away from the crossbar. **RULING:** Touchback. The touching by R1 in the end zone causes the ball to become dead, unless the ball caroms through the goal, thus scoring a field goal. This is not illegal batting, as the touching caused the kick to fail (4-2-2d2; 6-3-1b).

6.2.5 SITUATION B: K2, running toward R's end zone, leaps in the air to catch K1's punt which is in flight. K2 has the ball in his grasp over the 1-yard line, but first touches the ground in R's end zone. No player of R is in position to catch the punt. **RULING:** R can take the ball at the spot of first touching, his own 1-yard line, or take a touchback since K2 has not possessed the ball until he came to the ground in the end zone.

8.4.1 SITUATION B: K has the ball on R's 40-yard line for a free kick. The ball is in this position following a safety followed by a couple of dead-ball penalties. K1 place kicks the ball between the uprights and over the crossbar. **RULING:** Touchback (8-4-1, 2; 8-5-3a(1)).

8.5.1 SITUATION A: R1 returns the second half kickoff to K's 10 and fumbles: (a) the ball rolls into K's end zone; or (b) K1 attempts to recover and forces the ball into his own end zone. In both cases, the ball is in K's end zone and no player of either team attempts to recover. The referee, after waiting a few seconds, sounds his whistle. **RULING:** It is a touchdown for R both in (a) and (b) as the fumbling team retains possession (8-1-2c; 8-5-2b).

8.5.1 SITUATION D: It is first down and 10 on A's 3. Runner A1 fumbles on his 2-yard line. B1 intentionally kicks the loose ball which is: (a) on A's 2; or (b) in the end zone. The ball then goes out of bounds behind the goal line. **RULING:** Undoubtedly, Team A will decline the penalty in (a) and take the touchback. A will accept the penalty for the illegal kick in (b), because declining it would give B a safety (8-5-2b, 3c; 9-7-1).

8.5.2 SITUATION B: With fourth and 3 from his own 10-yard line, the scrimmage kick by K1 is blocked so that it rebounds into K's end zone and is simultaneously recovered in the end zone by K2 and R1. **RULING:** It is a touchdown for R (2-36-2; 8-5-2b).

8.5.2 SITUATION C: K1's punt is blocked on K's 5-yard line and the ball is slowly rolling near the goal line. R1 attempts to recover and just barely touches the ball. The ball then rolls into the end zone where K2 falls on it. **RULING:** The covering official will have to judge whether or not a new force resulted from R1's touch. The covering official must decide whether the original force was such that the ball could have gone into the end zone regardless of the muff. If the covering official has doubt, he will rule that the force was supplied by the kick, thus resulting in a safety. If the covering official rules R1 supplied the force, it is a touchback (8-5-2b).

8.5.3 SITUATION A: With fourth down and 7 from K's 10, K1 punts from the end zone. The kick is partially blocked and is just barely moving at K's 2-yard line when R1's muff provides a new force which moves the ball into, and out of, the end zone. **RULING:** Touchback. Because it was the new force by R1 which caused the ball to go out of K's end zone, the result is a touchback instead of a safety (2-13-1; 8-5-3b).

*9.7.2 SITUATION B: K1's punt is coming down over R's 10-yard line and: (a) R3 is in position to catch the ball; or (b) no R player is in position to catch the ball, when K2 bats the ball toward his own goal line while it is in flight, but the batted ball subsequently goes into R's end zone. **RULING:** In (a), it is a foul for kick-catching interference by K2 as well as first touching, and R may choose to take the result of the play, which is a touchback, or take an awarded fair catch at R's 25-yard line (15 yards in advance of the spot of interference after enforcement of the penalty) or the ball at the spot of first touching at the 10-yard line, or penalize K 15 yards from the previous spot and replay the down. In (b), there is no foul and the result of the play is a touchback. R will put the ball in play first and 10 from its own 20-yard line (6-5-6 Exception; 8-5-3; 9-7-2 Exception).

10.4.5 SITUATION I: K1's scrimmage kick is blocked on K's 5-yard line and is rolling away from K's goal line when R1 muffs the ball into K's end zone (applies a new force to a grounded kick). K2 recovers the ball and attempts to advance, but is downed in the end zone. During K2's run: (a) R1 holds K3 in the end zone; or (b) K3 holds R1 in the end zone. **RULING:** In (a), it is a touchback and the basic spot is the 20-yard line. In (b), since the foul is in the end zone, it is a safety.

Resuming Play After a Touchback

The team whose goal line is involved in a touchback shall put the ball in play anywhere between the hash marks on its 20-yard line by a snap (8-5-4).

Topic:
Momentum Exception

It is not a safety when an R player catches or recovers a scrimmage kick or free kick between his 5-yard line and the goal line, and his original momentum carries him into the end zone where the ball is declared dead in his team's possession or it goes out of bounds in the end zone. In that case, the ball belongs to the team in possession at the spot where the kick was caught or recovered (8-5-2a Exception).

When the momentum exception applies and the ball becomes dead behind the goal line, if the penalty for a foul by either team is accepted, the end of the run is the spot where the kick was caught or recovered. The penalty is enforced under the all-but-one principle. If momentum is not involved, the end of the run is the goal line (10.4.3 SITUATION C COMMENT).

▧ Rationale

The momentum exception allows R players to make positive plays close to their own goal line without fear of giving up a safety.

Momentum Exception: Case Plays

4.2.2 SITUATION F: K1 punts from midfield and R1 gives a fair-catch signal at R's 10-yard line. R1 muffs the catch and the ball bounces toward R's end zone. R2 recovers at the 1-yard line and his momentum takes him into the end zone where he is tackled. **RULING:** It is R's ball on the 1-yard line because the ball became dead when R2 recovered following the fair-catch signal. The momentum exception does not apply.

8.5.2 SITUATION A: R1 makes an over-the-shoulder catch of a scrimmage kick on his own 2-yard line, running full speed in the direction of his own goal line. His momentum carries him into the end zone with the ball. **RULING:** Since the momentum of R1 carried him into his own end zone, if the ball becomes dead in his possession in the end zone, it will be R's ball at the spot of the catch. This also would be true if the ball went out of bounds behind the goal line after R1's momentum carried him there and he was last in possession of the ball.

8.5.2 SITUATION H: R1, while in full stride at his 2-yard line (a) catches a punt over his shoulder; or (b) recovers a grounded punt. His momentum carries him into his end zone where he is downed. **RULING:** In (a) and (b) the ball would belong to R at the spot where the punt was caught or recovered as the momentum exception applies.

10.4.4 SITUATION E: R1 catches a punt on his 4-yard line and his momentum carries him behind his goal line where he is downed in the end zone. After the kick has ended, but before the ball becomes dead: (a) K1 holds in R's end zone; or (b) K1 holds at R's 5-yard line; or (c) R2 holds in the end zone. **RULING:** If R accepts the penalty in either (a) or (b), it will be R's ball first and 10 from its 14-yard line. R will put the ball in play by a snap. If R declines the penalty in either (a) or (b), the ball will be put in play by R at the 4-yard line since the kick was caught there. In (c), it is a safety since the foul occurred in the end zone.

 10.4.4 COMMENT: When the "momentum" exception applies and the ball becomes dead behind the goal line, if the penalty for a foul by either team is accepted, the end of the run is the spot where the kick, fumble or pass was caught or recovered. The penalty is enforced under the all-but-one principle. If "momentum" is not involved, the end of the run is the goal line (8-5-2a Exception; 10-3-3c).

Topic 3

Plays from Scrimmage

PlayPic®

Key Terms

Scrimmage is the action of the two teams during a down which begins with a legal snap (2-38). A snap shall, if elected, put the ball in play when a free kick is not specified (4-1-3).

The offense is the team which is in possession of the ball. The opponent is the defense (2-43-1). A is the team which puts the ball in play. The opponent is B (2-43-2). Team designations (A and B) are retained until the ball is next marked ready for play (2-32-2, 2-43-4).

The line of scrimmage for each team is a vertical plane through the point of the ball nearest the team's goal line. It is determined when the ball is ready for play and remains until the next ready-for-play signal (2-25-1).

An offensive player is on his line of scrimmage and is considered a lineman when he is facing his opponent's goal line with the line of his shoulders approximately parallel thereto and with his head or foot breaking an imaginary plane drawn parallel to the line of scrimmage through the waist of the snapper when the ball is snapped (2-25-2; 2-32-9). A back is any A player who has no part of his body breaking the plane of an imaginary line drawn parallel to the line of scrimmage through the waist of the nearest teammate who is legally on the line, except for the player under the snapper, who is also considered a back (2-32-3).

A defensive player is on his line of scrimmage when he is within 1 yard of his scrimmage line at the snap (2-25-3). B players may be anywhere on or behind their line of scrimmage (7-2-5d).

The neutral zone is the space between the two scrimmage lines during a scrimmage down (2-28-1). The neutral zone may be expanded following the snap up to a maximum of 2 yards behind the defensive line of scrimmage, in the field of play, during any scrimmage down (2-28-2).

A ball in player possession is a live ball held or controlled by a player after it has been handed or snapped to him, or after he has caught or recovered it (2-34-1). A ball in team possession is a live ball which is in player possession or one which is loose following loss of such player possession. A live ball is always in the possession of a team (2-34-2). A change of possession occurs when the opponent gains player possession during the down (2-34-3).

A fumble is any loss of player possession other than by handing, passing or legal kick (2-18). A muff is the touching of a loose ball by a player in an unsuccessful attempt to secure possession (2-27). Touching refers to any contact with the ball, i.e., either by touching or being touched by it. Touching by an official in the field of play or end zone is ignored (2-44).

While the ball is live, an interval called a down is in progress and the team in possession attempts to advance the ball by carrying, kicking or passing it. The team in possession has a series of four downs numbered 1, 2, 3 and 4 to advance the ball to the line to gain, which is usually 10 yards in advance of the spot where the series begins (1-1-2).

A runner is a player who is in possession of a live ball or is simulating possession of a live ball (2-32-13).

A captain of a team is a player designated to represent his team during ball placement on a try, after a touchback and to start an overtime (2-32-5c).

A loose ball is a pass, fumble or a kick. The terms "pass," "fumble" and "kick" are sometimes used as abbreviations when the ball is loose following the acts of passing, fumbling or kicking the ball. A loose ball which has not yet touched the ground is in flight. A grounded loose ball is one which has touched the ground. Any loose ball continues to be a loose ball until a player secures possession of it or until it becomes dead by rule, whichever comes first (2-1-3). An interception is the catch of an opponent's fumble or pass (2-23).

A recovery is gaining possession of a live ball after it strikes the ground. An airborne player has completed a recovery when he first contacts the ground inbounds with the ball in his possession (2-36-1). A simultaneous recovery is a recovery where there is joint possession of a live ball by opposing inbounds players (2-36-2).

A catch is the act of establishing player possession of a live ball which is in flight, and first contacting the ground inbounds while maintaining possession of the ball or having the forward progress of the player in possession stopped while the opponent is carrying the player who is in possession and inbounds (2-4-1). Catching is always preceded by touching the ball; thus, if touching causes the ball to become dead, securing possession of the ball has no significance (2-4-2). A simultaneous catch or recovery is a catch or recovery in which there is joint possession of a live ball by opposing players who are inbounds (2-4-3).

When an airborne player makes a catch, forward progress is the furthest point of advancement after he possesses the ball if contacted by a defender (2-15-2).

The dead-ball spot is the spot under the foremost point of the ball when it becomes dead by rule (2-41-3). The inbounds spot is the intersection of the hash marks and the yard line through the foremost point of the ball when the ball becomes dead in a side zone; through the foremost point of the ball on the sideline between the goal lines when a loose ball goes out of bounds; or through the spot under the foremost point of the ball in possession of a runner when he crosses the plane of the sideline and goes out of bounds (2-41-4a through c; 4-3-3).

The out-of-bounds spot is where the ball becomes dead because of going out of bounds (2-41-5).

Topic:
Downs and Series of Downs

The team in possession has a series of four downs numbered 1, 2, 3 and 4 to advance the ball to the line to gain, which is usually 10 yards in advance of the spot where the series begins (1-1-2). The team which next puts the ball in play by scrimmage following a free kick, touchback or fair catch is awarded a series of four consecutively numbered downs in which to advance the ball to the line to gain. Each awarded first down starts a new series of four consecutively numbered downs (5-1-1a).

The referee shall correct the number of the next down prior to the ball becoming live after a new series of downs is awarded and prior to the declaration of the end of any period (5-1-1b).

The team which next puts the ball in play by scrimmage following a free kick, touchback or fair catch is awarded a series of four consecutively numbered downs. To start a new series of downs, the inside edge of the rod nearest the goal of the team which is to snap the ball is set on the yard line through the ball's foremost point (5-3-3).

Loss of a down is the loss of the right to replay a down (2-7-2).

After a first, second or third down, a new series of downs is awarded only after considering the effect of any act during the down and any dead-ball foul by B (5-1-2a). After a fourth down, a new series of downs shall be awarded only after considering the effect of any act during the down, except a nonplayer or unsportsmanlike foul (5-1-2b).

Following a foul, a series of downs ends when there is acceptance or declination of the penalty for any foul which occurs after team possession changes during the down (5-2-5e), or R is first to touch a scrimmage kick while it is beyond the neutral zone, unless a non-post-scrimmage kick foul occurs before the kick ends and the penalty is accepted (5-2-5f).

After a series of downs ends, a new series with first and 10 yards to gain is awarded unless one of the following is involved: a try; a field goal; or a free kick after a safety, fair catch or awarded fair catch. The first down is awarded to the team in possession when the foul occurs unless, declining the penalty leaves the other team in possession, or as in 5-2-5c and 5-2-5f, accepting or declining the penalty leaves the other team in possession after fourth down (5-2-6).

No series can ever start on a down other than first (Fundamental II-6).

New Series Awarded to A

When a scrimmage down ends with the ball in the field of play or out of bounds between the goal lines, a new series is awarded to A, if the ball belongs to A on or beyond the line to gain (5-1-3a).

Following a foul, a series of downs ends and A is awarded a new series if the acceptance of the penalty includes the award of a first down (5-2-5a), or if acceptance or declination of any penalty leaves A in possession beyond the line-to-gain (5-2-5b).

New Series Awarded to B

When a scrimmage down ends with the ball in the field of play or out of bounds between the goal lines, a new series is awarded to B if the ball belongs to B at the end of any down (5-1-3b), or if at the end of the fourth down, the ball belongs to A behind the line to gain (5-1-3c).

Following a foul, a series of downs ends and B is awarded a new series when declination of any penalty leaves A in possession behind the line to gain after fourth down (5-2-5c), declination of any penalty leaves B in possession (5-2-5d), or acceptance of a penalty on fourth down which carries a loss of down leaves A in possession behind the line to gain (5-2-5g).

New Series Awarded to Team in Possession

When a scrimmage down ends with the ball in the field of play or out of bounds between the goal lines, a new series is awarded to the team in possession at the end of the down, if R is the first to touch a scrimmage kick while it is beyond the expanded neutral zone, unless the penalty is accepted for a non post-scrimmage kick foul which occurred before the kick ended (5-1-3f), or if there is a change of team possession during the down, unless the penalty is accepted for a non post-scrimmage kick foul which occurred before the change of possession (5-1-3d).

When a free-kick down ends with the ball in the field of play or out of bounds between the goal lines, a new series is awarded to the team in possession of the ball when the down ends if the ball is recovered beyond R's free-kick line with no first touching by K (5-1-5b).

Down After Penalty

When a penalty is declined, the number of the next down is the same as if the foul had not occurred. If a double foul occurs during a down, the number of the next down is the same as that of the down in which the foul occurred. After a distance penalty, the ball belongs to the team in possession at the time of the foul unless it is a post-scrimmage kick foul or kick-catching interference. Team possession may then change if a new series is awarded (5-2-1).

When a foul occurs during a scrimmage down and before any change of team possession, and before a receiver is first to touch a scrimmage kick while it is beyond the neutral zone, the ball belongs to A or K after enforcement unless it is a post-scrimmage kick foul or kick-catching interference. The number of the next down is the same as that of the down during which the foul occurred unless penalty acceptance includes a first down or loss of down, or the enforcement or the advance results in a first down. The loss of down aspect of a penalty has no significance following a change of possession or if the line to gain is reached after enforcement (5-2-2).

When a foul occurs prior to a scrimmage down, or simultaneously with the snap, the number of the next down after enforcement is the same as the number established before the foul occurred, unless enforcement for a foul by B results in a first down (5-2-3).

When a foul occurs prior to or during a free-kick down and before any change of team possession, the down which follows enforcement is a free-kick down, unless following a fair catch or an awarded fair catch, a scrimmage down is chosen for the replay (5-2-4).

Line to Gain and Measurements

The line to gain is the yard line established when a new series (first down) is awarded. Unless there is a penalty following the ready-for-play signal, the line to gain is 10 yards in advance of the foremost point of the ball when placed for the first down of the series (2-26-5, 5-3-1). The penalties for all fouls (including nonplayer and unsportsmanlike) committed prior to the ready-for-play signal shall be administered before the line to gain is established. The line to gain then remains fixed until the series ends and a new line to gain is established (5-3-1).

If the line to gain extends into the end zone, the goal line is the line to gain (2-26-5).

The referee may call for the head linesman to bring the yardage chain or other measuring device on the field for a measurement. Measurement shall be parallel with the sideline and from a convenient yard line to the yard line through the foremost point of the ball when it became dead. The ball shall be placed with its long axis parallel with the sideline before measurement. The inside edge of the foremost rod marks the line to gain when the traditional yardage chain is used (5-3-2).

A measurement may be requested by the captain prior to the ball being declared ready for play, but it may be denied if, in the referee's opinion, it is obvious the line to gain has or has not been reached (5-3-2 NOTE).

Line to Gain and Measurements: Case Plays

*5.1.1 SITUATION A: What procedure is used to correct an error if it is discovered: (a) a fifth down has been run and the discovery is prior to the ball becoming live after a new series of downs is awarded and prior to the declaration of the end of any period; or (b) A has not been given its allotted four downs and the discovery is prior to the ball becoming live after a new series of downs is awarded and prior to the declaration of the end of any period? **RULING:** In both cases, the number of the next down can be corrected by the referee. In (a), play will revert to where it was before the fifth down was run after the enforcement of any personal, dead ball or unsportsmanlike fouls that occurred during the down. In (b), the referee can declare the proper next down and resume play.

 *5.1.1 COMMENT: Even though play selection, etc., is determined by the down number displayed on the down marker, the official number of the down is determined by the referee.

*5.1.1 SITUATION B: Second down and six. On the last play of the third period, A38 gains three yards. After the play, the down-marker indicator is flipped to fourth down. Following a brief pause to ensure no reason to defer ending the quarter, the referee holds the ball over his head to signify the end of the period. Both teams change ends of the field and the chains are reversed. Before the ball is snapped for the first play of the fourth period, Team A's coach notifies the game officials that he believes there is an error in the down. **RULING:** The third period officially ended when the referee held the ball over his head, and therefore the down error may not be corrected.

*5.1.1 SITUATION C: During a fifth-down play, Team A is flagged for: (a) illegal formation; (b) holding; (c) twisting the face mask; (d) taunting; or (e) fighting. **RULING:** The penalties are not enforced in (a) or (b). In (c), (d) and (e), the penalty is enforced as a dead-ball foul before Team B snaps the ball. In (e), the offending player is also disqualified.

*5.1.1 SITUATION D: The ball is on the 50-yard line with 10 yards to go for a first down. The down-marker indicator erroneously indicates fourth down when Team K punts on what is actually: (a) third down or (b) fifth down. R6 returns the punt for an apparent touchdown. Prior to the try and without the period ending, it is brought to the attention of the game officials that the down-marker indicator was in error. **RULING:** In (a), the score is cancelled and the ball is returned to the 50-yard line, third down and 10 for A as Team A. In (b), the fifth down was run in error, the score is cancelled and the ball is returned to the 50-yard line, first down and 10 for R.

*5.1.1 SITUATION E: Erroneously, the chains are set before enforcement of a dead-ball foul instead of following enforcement. Up to what point can this be corrected? **RULING:** Until the ball is legally snapped. After that point, it is too late.

5.3.2 SITUATION A: With fourth and 1 from A's 47, quarterback A1 keeps the ball and is downed very near the line to gain. When the down ends, the ball in possession of A1 is: (a) positioned so that its long axis is diagonal to the sideline; or (b) positioned so that its long axis is parallel to the yard line. A measurement is requested. **RULING:** The ball must be aligned so the long axis is parallel to the sideline in both (a) and (b) prior to measurement. The referee will place his hand at the foremost point of the ball when it became dead and rotate the ball so that its long axis is parallel to the sideline and there is no gain or loss in distance. Following the rotation, measurement will be to the foremost point of the ball.

5.3.2 SITUATION B: Following a third-down play, the game officials do not measure as the referee judges the line to gain clearly has not been reached. A lines up in punt formation. Just before assuming his set position, the captain of A requests a measurement. **RULING:** The request is denied for two reasons. The captain must make a request for measurement before the ball is marked ready for play and no measurement is made if it is obvious the line to gain has not been reached.

5.3.2 COMMENT: In any situation where there is doubt, game officials should measure. Following measurement in a side zone, the chain should be used to place the ball at the hash mark (5-3-2 Note).

5.3.3 SITUATION: On fourth and goal from the 5-yard line, the ball is marked ready for play with the nose of the ball just touching the 5-yard line. Following A1's incomplete pass, B takes over and the referee places the ball in line with the down box as it was prior to A1's fourth-down incomplete forward pass, i.e., with the foremost point (nose) of the ball just touching the 5-yard line. **RULING:** This is incorrect. The ball shall be spotted in the same position it was at the start of the down. When a team fails to reach its line to gain on a fourth-down run, the foremost point of the ball at the time it became dead would become the rear point when direction of the offense is changed. After a fourth-down incomplete pass, the ball is placed "as it was at the start of the down" (or previous fourth-down play). Unless the fourth-down play resulted in a touchback or safety, or A reached its line to gain, B will gain approximately 11-1/2 inches (the length of the football) in field position, and the down box will have to be moved. Following a touchback or safety, the ball is placed with its foremost point touching the 20-yard line. Many game officials seem to find it convenient to merely reset the line-to-gain chains following an incomplete fourth-down pass by using the previous line of scrimmage (down marker) as the position for the rear rod when the direction is changed. This procedure is not correct.

5.3.4 SITUATION A: With first and 10 from A's 4-yard line, A1 is tackled and the ball is lying on the 5-inch line with its long axis parallel to the goal line. How is the ball to be spotted? **RULING:** The referee will, by rule, rotate and place the ball so that its rear point is not penetrating the plane of A's goal line. The ball is rotated with its rearmost point moved forward just enough so it isn't touching the goal line. A gains a few inches in the process.

Topic:
Before the Play

A captain of a team is a player designated to represent his team during ball placement on a try, a kickoff, after a safety, and after a fair catch or awarded fair catch (2-32-5c).

When a team may designate the spot along the proper yard line from which the ball is to be put in play, it shall have the same privilege if the down is to be replayed or a dead-ball foul occurs (4-3-7; 6-5-4).

To start a new series of downs after a change of team possession, which does not involve a fourth-down incomplete forward pass, a safety or touchback, the foremost point of the ball at the time it became dead becomes the rear point when the direction of the offense is changed (5-3-3a).

To start a new series of downs after a change of team possession after a fourth-down incomplete forward pass, the ball is placed at the previous spot so the rear point becomes the foremost point (5-3-3b).

To start a new series of downs after a change of team possession after a safety or touchback, the foremost point of the ball is placed on the 20-yard line (5-3-3c).

After a scrimmage kick, a new series is awarded to R at the spot of first touching by K, if K is first to touch the kicked ball beyond the expanded neutral zone before it is touched beyond this zone by R and before it has come to rest (5-1-3g). However, the right of R to take the ball at the spot of the first touching by K is canceled if R touches the kick and thereafter during the down commits a foul or if the penalty is accepted for any foul committed during the down.

When a free-kick down ends with the ball in the field of play or out of bounds between the goal lines, a new series is awarded to R at the inbounds spot if R touches the kicked ball before it goes out of bounds (5-1-5a).

When a free-kick down ends with the ball in the field of play or out of bounds between the goal lines, a new series is awarded to R at the spot of recovery if K recovers the kicked ball before it travels the 10 yards to R's free-kick line and before R has touched the ball (5-1-5c), or if there is joint possession by R and K of a recovered kick (5-1-5d).

When a free-kick down ends with the ball in the field of play or out of bounds between the goal lines, a new series is awarded to R at the spot of first touching by K if K is the first to touch the kicked ball before it has gone 10 yards (5-1-5e). However, the right of R to take the ball at the spot of the first touching by K is canceled if R touches the kick and thereafter during the down commits a foul or if the penalty is accepted for any foul committed during the down.

Encroachment

Encroachment occurs when a player is illegally in the neutral zone during the time interval starting when the ball is ready for play and until the ball is snapped. For the purposes of enforcing encroachment restrictions, an entering substitute is not considered to be a player until he is on his team's side of the neutral zone (2-8; 7-1-5, 6).

Encroachment: Penalty

5 yards. Signals 7 and 18.

Encroachment: Case Plays

2.8 SITUATION A: After the ball is ready for play for a scrimmage down: (a) B1 enters the neutral zone to give defensive signals; or (b) B2, the nose guard, places his hand on the ground so that it is in contact with the ball. After the ready-for-play signal and the snapper places hand(s) on the ball: (c) A1 or B3 break the plane of the neutral zone; or (d) B1 is conferring with his coach and is on A's side of the neutral zone. **RULING:** Encroachment in (a), (b), (c) and (d). Whenever a player is illegally in the neutral zone, it is encroachment (7-1, 2).

7.1.5 SITUATION: Following the ready-for-play signal, but before A has taken any positions on the line of scrimmage, B1 is either in or beyond the neutral zone facing his teammates while giving defensive signals. **RULING:** Encroachment by B1 (2-8).

7.1.6 SITUATION B: Snapper A1 is positioned over the ball following the ready signal, but has not yet placed his hand(s) on it. Either: (a) A2; or (b) B1, breaks the plane of the neutral zone. Both players adjust their position and get behind the neutral zone; or (c) A1 has a hand on the ground and then stands erect to call out a blocking assignment. **RULING:** No infraction in either (a), (b) or (c). In (c), the snapper is not restricted as are other linemen after placing a hand on or near the ground (7-1-7c).

In Simple Terms

Unless penetration of the neutral zone is simultaneous by both offensive and defensive players, it is not possible for both teams to encroach.

7.1.6 SITUATION C: A1 takes his position over the ball and places both hands on the ball. The ready-for-play signal has not been given. B1 breaks the plane of the neutral zone. **RULING:** No foul. Encroachment restrictions are not in effect before the ready-for-play signal has been given.

7.1.6 SITUATION D: Following the ready signal, snapper A1 positions over the ball and immediately places his hands on the ball and adjusts it. The rest of the team then take presnap positions. The coach of B realizes his team has only 10 players on the field and he sends B1 into the game. The ball is located at one end of the field so that B1 is on A's side of the neutral zone when he enters the field. He crosses through the neutral zone, but is onside prior to the snap. **RULING:** It is not encroachment for the substitute to cross through the neutral zone. An entering substitute cannot encroach until after he has established himself as a player on his team's side of the neutral zone. If B1 is unable to get onside prior to the snap, it will be a foul for illegal substitution. This foul occurs simultaneously with the snap and if penalized would be administered from the previous spot. Similarly, it is not encroachment when a replaced player crosses the neutral zone in leaving the field (2-32-15; 3-7-2, 6; 7-1-2; 10-4-2a).

Numbering Requirements

At the snap, at least five A players on the line of scrimmage must be numbered 50-79 (1-4-3; 7-2-5b). On first, second or third down, when A sets or shifts into a scrimmage-kick formation as in 2-14-2a, the snapper may be a player numbered 1 to 49 or 80 to 99. If Team A has the snapper in the game under this exception, Team A shall have at least four players wearing numbers 50-79 on its line of scrimmage. The snapper in the game under this exception must be between the ends and is an ineligible forward pass receiver during that down unless the pass is touched by B. On fourth down or during a kick try, when A sets or shifts into a scrimmage-kick formation, any A player numbered 1 to 49 or 80 to 99 may take the position of any A player numbered 50 to 79. A player in the game under this exception must assume an initial position on his line of scrimmage between the ends and he remains an ineligible forward-pass receiver during that down unless the pass is touched by B (7-2-5 Exceptions 1 and 2; 7-5-6b).

Players of the same team shall not participate during the same down while wearing identical numbers (7-2-5c).

Illegal Numbering: Penalty

5 yards. Signal 19.

◪ Rationale

The rules regarding numbering aid the game officials in determining the player's eligibility as a receiver.

Numbering Requirements: Case Plays

1.4.3 SITUATION: After the ball has been marked ready for play, but prior to the snap, it is discovered: (a) A1 and A2 are both wearing number 81, or (b) B2 is wearing 00. **RULING:** In (a), it will become a foul at the snap for illegal numbering. In (b), it is a foul before the snap for illegal numbering and B2 will not be permitted to participate with that number, because 00 is not a legal number. If the illegal numbering is discovered during the down, it is a foul which occurred at the snap (1-5-1c(1); 7-2-5d).

7.2.5 SITUATION A: Team A comes to its line of scrimmage with: (a) ends 80 and 71, tackles 70 and 81, guards 60 and 61, and center 50; or (b) ends 80 and 81, guards 72 and 75, tackles 62 and 63, and center 50 and one halfback numbered 76. **RULING:** The formations in both (a) and (b) are legal because there are at least five players numbered 50-79 on the offensive line. In (a), a player at tackle wearing 81 and the end wearing 71 are both ineligible receivers; 81 because of his position and 71 because of his number. In (b), number 76, a halfback, is not an eligible receiver because of the number he is wearing (7-5-6a).

7.2.5 SITUATION B: Team A sets with five players on its line numbered 50-79, while two teammates, both on the same side, are numbered 89 and 41. Number 41 is on the end and 89 is inside and next to him. Number 41 shifts to the backfield and Number 32, on the opposite side of the ball, shifts so he is on that end of the line. A touchdown pass is thrown to Number 89. **RULING:** The touchdown counts. The fact that A lined up with a player wearing an eligible receiver's number in the interior line does not eliminate the possibility of this player being eligible to receive a pass following a shift (7-5-6a).

7.2.5 SITUATION C: Substitute A1 comes in to replace A2. Both are wearing Number 88. **RULING:** No violation unless both participate at the same time (1-4-3; 7-2-5c).

7.2.5 SITUATION D: With fourth and 6 from the K20, Team K lines up with A21 as the left end; A34, A66, A25, A64 and A86 in the traditional five tackle-guard-center-guard-tackle spots; and A11 on the right end. All are on the line of scrimmage. Players A10, A20 and A5 are in the backfield with A79 lined up in the deep, position as a potential kicker. A25 places his hand on the ball. Prior to the snap, (a) A20 shifts to the line of scrimmage on the right of A86 and left of A11 and sets for one second before the ball is snapped; or (b) A11 steps back off of the line and A20 shifts to replace him as the end, where both are set for a second before the ball is snapped. Who are the eligible receivers prior to the ball being touched by B? **RULING:** Once A25 placed his hands on the ball, all players in between the ends (A34, A66, A25, A64 and A86) become ineligible and remain ineligible throughout the down. In (a), once A20 assumed a position on the line of scrimmage, A20 became ineligible as he was covered up by A11. A79 is ineligible by number. Only A21, A11, A10 and A5 are eligible on the play. In (b), because A11 stepped back off of the line first, A20 becomes eligible as he would be the end. A21, A20, A11, A10 and A5 are eligible (2-14-2; 2-32-9; 2-39; 7-2-5b(2); 7-5-6).

 7.2.5 COMMENT: When A is in a scrimmage-kick formation, they do not have to kick and they may kick when they are not in this formation (2-14-2; 7-2-5b Exceptions).

Planned Loose Ball

Any A player on his line of scrimmage may not advance a planned loose ball in the vicinity of the snapper (7-2-8).

Planned Loose Ball: Case Play

7.2.8 SITUATION: Between downs, quarterback A1 informs the referee via a "prearranged" confidential signal that during the next down A will run its trick play involving a planned loose ball. (a) Snapper A2 does not release the ball and guard A3 takes it and begins to advance; or (b) A1 takes the snap and places the ball on the ground after which guard A3, who has legally turned and faced his own goal line, scoops it up and advances; or (c) A1 takes the snap and hands the ball to guard A3, who has legally turned to face his own goal line. **RULING:** In (a), it is a snap-infraction, dead-ball foul whether or not the referee was informed. In (b), it is an illegal planned loose ball play even though the referee was notified (7-2-8). In (c), it is a legal play (7-2-4) Comment: In all cases, the referee should inform A1 immediately that a planned loose ball play is not legal and thus attempt to prevent a foul.

Requirements for Snapper

A snapper is the player who is facing his opponent's goal line with his shoulders approximately parallel thereto and who snaps the ball (2-32-14). The snapper may be over the ball but his feet must be behind the neutral zone and no part of his person, other than a hand(s) on the ball, may be beyond the foremost point of the ball (7-1-1). The snapper may lift the ball for lateral rotation but may not rotate end-for-end or change the location or fail to keep the long axis of the ball at right angles to the line of scrimmage (7-1-2).

Following the ready-for-play and after touching the ball, the snapper shall not remove both hands from the ball; make any movement that simulates a snap; fail to clearly pause before the snap; or following adjustment, lift or move the ball other than in a legal snap (7-1-3a through d; 7-1-4).

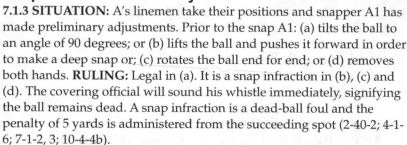

Snap Infraction: Penalty:
5 yards. Signals 7 and 19.

Snap Infraction: Case Plays
7.1.3 SITUATION: A's linemen take their positions and snapper A1 has made preliminary adjustments. Prior to the snap A1: (a) tilts the ball to an angle of 90 degrees; or (b) lifts the ball and pushes it forward in order to make a deep snap or; (c) rotates the ball end for end; or (d) removes both hands. **RULING:** Legal in (a). It is a snap infraction in (b), (c) and (d). The covering official will sound his whistle immediately, signifying the ball remains dead. A snap infraction is a dead-ball foul and the penalty of 5 yards is administered from the succeeding spot (2-40-2; 4-1-6; 7-1-2, 3; 10-4-4b).

7.1.6 SITUATION A: When A comes to the line of scrimmage, the linemen assume their final positions such that one interior lineman has his head penetrating the neutral zone while the other linemen are all penetrating the vertical plane of the snapper's waistline. **RULING:** It is encroachment for a player to have any part of his body penetrating the plane of the neutral zone after the ready and the snapper has placed his hand(s) on the ball. This is a dead-ball foul and the ball will not be permitted to become live (2-8; 2-25-2; 2-32-9; 7-1-5; 7-2-3).

Topic:
Formation

After the ball is ready for play, each player of A who participated in the previous down and each substitute for A must have been, momentarily, between the 9-yard marks, before the snap (7-2-1).

At the snap, at least seven A players shall be on their line of scrimmage (2-14-1, 7-2-5a).

The players on each side of and next to the snapper may lock legs with the snapper, but any other A lineman must have each foot outside the closest foot of the player next to him at the snap. A's players may stand, crouch or kneel (7-2-2).

Of the players of A who are not on their line at the snap only one may penetrate the vertical plane through the waistline of his nearest teammate who is on his line. He must have his hands in position to receive the ball if it is snapped between the snapper's legs but he is not required to receive the snap (7-2-3). Any other player(s) must be in legal position as a back (2-32-3; 7-2-3).

All A players eligible by position and number include those who, at the time of the snap, are on the ends of their scrimmage line or legally behind the line (possible total of six) and are numbered 1-49 or 80-99 (7-5-6a).

On first, second or third down, when A sets or shifts into a scrimmage-kick formation as in 2-14-2a, the snapper may be a player numbered 1 to 49 or 80 to 99. If Team A has the snapper in the game under this exception, Team A shall have at least four players wearing numbers 50-79 on its line of scrimmage. The snapper in the game under this exception must be between the ends and is an ineligible forward pass receiver during that down unless the pass is touched by B (7-5-6b). On fourth down or during a kick try, when A sets or shifts into a scrimmage-kick formation, any A player numbered 1 to 49 or 80 to 99 may take the position of any A player numbered 50 to 79. A player in the game under this exception must assume an initial position on his line of scrimmage between the ends and he remains an ineligible forward-pass receiver during that down unless the pass is touched by B (7-2-5b Exceptions 1 and 2; 7-5-6b).

B players may be anywhere on or behind their line of scrimmage (7-2-5d).

◪ Rationale

Allowing only one player under center eliminates potential confusion by the defense as to which player is receiving the snap.

Illegal Formation: Penalty

5 yards. Signal 19.

Illegal Formation: Case Plays

2.32.3 SITUATION: A players assume their pre-snap positions. A1 takes a position behind the line of scrimmage as a potential runner. A1 is standing and is turned so he is directly facing the quarterback. At the snap, A1's shoulder and elbow are breaking the plane through the waist of his nearest teammate who is on the line. **RULING:** Since A1 is not on the line and is not positioned as a back, it results in an illegal formation foul. To be a back, A1 cannot have any part of his body breaking the plane through the waist of his nearest teammate who is on the line (7-2-3; 7-2-7).

3.7.5 SITUATION A: Substitute (a) A1, or (b) B1, noticing his team has only 10 players on the field, comes onto the field just as the ball is about to be snapped. **RULING:** In (a), A1 must be on the field on A's side of the neutral zone, inside the 9-yard marks, and not violate the shift or motion provisions. Furthermore, the act of his coming onto the field must not deceive the defensive team. In (b), the substitution is legal as long as B1 is on the field on B's side of the neutral zone prior to the snap (3-7-6; 7-2-1,6,7; 9-6-4).

7.1.6 SITUATION A: When A comes to the line of scrimmage, the linemen assume their final positions such that five linemen penetrate the vertical plane through the waistline of the snapper while the head of the sixth penetrates the plane drawn through the waistline of the nearest teammate who is on his line of scrimmage. **RULING:** It is illegal formation which is a foul simultaneously with the snap. The offended team will be given the option of taking the result of the play or accepting the penalty and replaying the down (2-8; 2-25-2; 2-32-9; 7-1-5; 7-2-3).

7.2.1 SITUATION A: Following a second down play, A89 comes onto the field as a substitute for A93 but A89 stops 5 yards from the sideline as his team is ready to snap the ball. Following the snap, A89 goes down field and catches A1's legal forward pass for a first down. **RULING:** This is an illegal formation and if the penalty is accepted it would be marked off from the previous spot. Depending upon the situation (see 9-6-4d), this could also be illegal participation (9-6-4d).

7.2.1 SITUATION B: With fourth down and 8 from K's 20-yard line and K in scrimmage kick formation, K1 kicks the ball, but at the snap, K had only six players on the line of scrimmage. After the play is over, R1 throws K2 to the ground and swings at him. **RULING:** These fouls would be enforced separately and in order. R will likely decline the penalty for the K foul so that R will get the football, and then R's dead-ball personal foul is then enforced (and R1 is disqualified) with the ball being placed 15 yards behind the end of the run.

7.2.2 SITUATION: Following the snap on a kick try, the offensive linemen "step down" and interlock feet. **RULING:** Legal. However, prior to the snap only the linemen next to the snapper are permitted to lock legs with the snapper.

7.2.3 SITUATION A: Following the huddle, after A comes to its line of scrimmage, quarterback A1 is breaking the plane of the waistline of the snapper, and slot back A2 has a part of his body breaking the plane of the waistline of his nearest teammate who is on the line of scrimmage. **RULING:** This is an illegal formation foul at the snap. While quarterback A1 may be breaking the plane of the waistline of the snapper or nearest teammate legally on the line of scrimmage, it is illegal for any other back to break the plane of the waistline of his nearest teammate who is on the line of scrimmage (2-32-3).

7.2.3 SITUATION B: At the snap, A1 is in a position which is neither on the line of scrimmage nor clearly in the backfield. A1 is not on the line because neither his head nor his foot is breaking the plane through the waist of the snapper, and he is not a back because he is penetrating the plane through the waist of his nearest teammate, end A2, who is on the line. The position of A1 is inside that of end A2, who is clearly on the line of scrimmage. When the ball is snapped, both A1 and A2 go downfield and A1 catches a pass. **RULING:** The position of A1 is illegal when the ball is snapped. A1 is an ineligible receiver because he was not clearly a back. His advance beyond the neutral zone is illegal and when he touches the pass, it is illegal touching. This is a multiple foul and B has a choice of which penalty to accept (7-5-6a).

7.5.2 SITUATION F: In the last few seconds of a half, A1 completes a pass to A2 at B's 20-yard line. The ball is properly spotted and the referee marks it ready for play and signals the clock to start. In the rush and confusion to stop the clock, A's snapper and quarterback A1 are the only A players in legal position when the ball is snapped and legally "spiked" by A1. **RULING:** A foul for illegal formation occurs at the snap. The "spike" is legal. Since the spike is legal, the only applicable foul is for illegal formation.

 7.5.2 COMMENT: The determination by the referee as to whether or not the act was intended to illegally conserve time must be applied using Rule 3-4-6 (7-5-2 Exception).

Topic:
False Start

After the ball is ready for play and before the snap begins, no false start shall be made by any A player. It is a false start if a shift or feigned charge simulates action at the snap; any act is clearly intended to cause B to encroach; or any A player on his line between the snapper and the player on the end of his line, after having placed a hand(s) on or near the ground, moves his hand(s) or makes any quick movement (7-1-7a-c). If a false start causes B to encroach, only the false start is penalized (7-1-8).

False Start: Penalty

5 yards. Signals 7 and 19.

False Start: Case Plays

7.1.7 SITUATION A: A is on its line of scrimmage with A1 directly and immediately behind the snapper in a position to receive the ball. As the count is started, but before the ball is snapped: (a) A1 steps backward from the line of scrimmage and while so doing he fakes throwing a forward pass. B1 then charges across the neutral zone and contacts A2; or (b) A1 quickly withdraws his hands from under the snapper and goes in motion. Reaction on the part of B2 causes him to charge across the neutral zone and contact A3; or (c) A1 lifts the heel of one foot as a signal to start A2 in motion. **RULING:** False start by A1 in both (a) and (b). These are acts interpreted to cause an opponent to encroach and, therefore, are infractions. It is the intent of the rules to prohibit such acts. Whether or not the action by A1 draws B into the neutral zone should not be the determining factor in ruling a false-start foul. The action by A1 in (c) is legal (7-1-7b).

7.1.7 SITUATION B: On fourth and four from A's 35-yard line, K comes to the line in a scrimmage formation. After calling a few signals, A1 says "shift." All 11 players then make a movement. Some players move to a new position for a scrimmage-kick formation, while four interior linemen remain in place and move from a hands-on-thighs position to an upright position and finally to a three-point stance. **RULING:** This could be ruled a false start if the covering official(s) determine that it was designed to cause B to encroach. In judging the offensive team's intent, the game officials should consider whether players move to a new position, the speed and abruptness of movement, down and distance and if any player pretends to have the ball or otherwise simulate action at the snap with the start of a play (7-1-7; 7-2-6).

7.1.7 SITUATION C: On third and 10 from A's 40-yard line, all team A players are set. While quarterback A1 is calling signals, defensive back B1, starting from a position eight yards behind his line of scrimmage, runs toward the neutral zone. B1 stops directly in front of tackle A4 but does not enter the neutral zone. In response to B1's charge, A4 (a) does not move, or (b) flinches. **RULING:** No foul in (a). In (b), A4 is guilty of a dead-ball foul for false start. If in the covering official's judgment the action by B1 was for the purpose of disconcerting or hindering A, it is an unsportsmanlike conduct foul. In this case, the game official should sound the whistle before the snap (7-1-7; 9-5-1d).

Topic:
Shift/Motion

A shift is the action of one or more offensive players who, after a huddle or after taking set positions, move to a new set position before the ensuing snap (2-39).

A huddle is two or more players of the same team grouped together before a down (2-21).

After a huddle or shift all 11 players of A shall come to an absolute stop and shall remain stationary simultaneously without movement of hands, feet, head or body for at least one second before the snap (7-2-6).

Only one A player may be in motion at the snap and then only if such motion is not toward his opponent's goal line (7-2-7).

Only one A player may be off the line at the snap, with his hands in position to receive the ball if it is snapped. Any other A player in motion shall be at least 5 yards behind his line of scrimmage at the snap if he started from any position not clearly behind the line and did not establish himself as a back by stopping for at least one full second (7-2-7).

Illegal Shift/Motion: Penalty
5 yards. Signal 20.

Illegal Shift/Motion: Case Plays

Illegal motion: 1 hand
Illegal shift: 2 hands

2.38 SITUATION: Is it a shift if before the snap: (a) A's guards and tackles go from a hands-on-knees position to a three-point stance; or (b) back A1 misses the snap count and takes a half step forward while going from an upright position to a four-point stance; or (c) quarterback A1 takes a step forward and puts his hands under the center; or (d) quarterback A1 is in an upright position as he looks over the defense, but he then bends his knees and puts his hands under center? **RULING:** Yes, in (a), (b), (c) and (d). Each of these movements constitutes a shift. Normal shoulder and head movements by the quarterback are not considered a shift.

7.1.7 SITUATION D: Prior to the snap, A has eight players on the line of scrimmage. A1, who is on the end of the line, shifts and becomes a back. A2, who prior to A1's change of position was an interior lineman, is now on the end of the line. A2 rises from his three-point stance and moves to a new position 5 yards farther out on the line of scrimmage where he again assumes a three-point stance. **RULING:** A legal shift by A2. Restrictions that apply to interior linemen no longer apply to A2 after A1 moved off the line and assumed a position as a back, thus making A2 an end (2-39).

7.2.6 SITUATION A: A comes to its line of scrimmage with the quarterback A1 standing behind the snapper. Upon signal, A2 goes in motion and then A1 assumes his final position under the snapper. **RULING:** When the ball is snapped, it will be an illegal shift because A2 did not reset for one second along with the other A players after A1 shifted. Motion cannot be started legally until all 11 players of A have been set simultaneously for at least one second (2-39).

In Simple Terms

The only element in a shift which can make it illegal is the matter of time. A shift becomes illegal only if following the shift all 11 players fail to come to a complete stop for at least one second before the snap.

7.2.6 SITUATION B: Backs A1 and A2 simultaneously move to new backfield positions prior to the snap. In less than one second after both are stationary: (a) A3 goes in motion and is in motion at the snap; or (b) the ball is snapped. **RULING:** Illegal shift in both (a) and (b). Following a huddle or a shift, all 11 players of A must come to a complete stop and must remain stationary simultaneously for at least one second before the snap or before a player goes in motion (2-39).

7.2.6 SITUATION C: After A has been set for more than one second, back A1 goes in motion. While A1 is in motion, back A2 takes one step forward and then resets. A1 is still in motion when the ball is snapped two seconds after A2 reset. **RULING:** Illegal shift. A2's movement was a shift and the failure of the entire team to set for at least one second after the shift and before the snap is a foul at the snap (2-39).

7.2.7 SITUATION: The quarterback by voice command has signaled his teammates to assume a set position while he is standing upright behind the center. The quarterback steps forward and places his hands under the center to receive the snap: (a) at the instant the snap is made; or (b) which is made after he is motionless, but prior to one second having elapsed; or (c) which is made after he is motionless for one second; or (d) which is made after he is motionless for one second, but while he is stepping backward with one foot as the snap is made. **RULING:** In (a), it is illegal motion. In (b), it is an illegal shift. In (c), it is legal. In (d), it is legal unless a teammate is also in motion at the snap (2-39; 7-2-6).

Topic:
Batting

No player shall bat a loose ball other than a pass or a fumble in flight, or a low scrimmage kick in flight which he is attempting to block in or behind the expanded neutral zone. A K player may bat toward his own goal line a grounded scrimmage kick which is beyond the neutral zone and may also bat toward his own goal line a scrimmage kick in flight beyond the neutral zone, if no R player is in position to catch the ball (9-7-2 Exception).

Any pass in flight may be batted in any direction, by an eligible receiver unless it is a backward pass batted forward by the passing team (9-7-3).

A ball in player possession shall not be batted forward by a player of the team in possession (9-7-4).

Illegal Batting: Penalty
15 yards. Signal 31.

Batting: Case Plays
9.7.2 SITUATION A: With fourth and 4 from R's 40-yard line, K1 punts. The kick is bounding near R's goal line and K2, in an attempt to keep it from penetrating the plane of the goal line, bats the ball at the 2-yard line back toward his own goal line. In (a) it is recovered by R1 who advances to his 30; or (b) it is recovered by R2 who attempts to advance, but retreats and is downed in his own end zone. **RULING:** The bat by K2 is legal because it occurred beyond the neutral zone. In (a) R would obviously take the results of the play and put the ball in play first and 10 from its 30. In (b) since the result of the play is a safety, R would take the ball at the 2, which is the spot of first touching where K2 legally batted the kick (6-2-5; 8-5-2a; 9-7-2 Exception).

*9.7.2 SITUATION B: K1's punt is coming down over R's 10-yard line and: (a) R3 is in position to catch the ball; or (b) no R player is in position to catch the ball, when K2 bats the ball toward his own goal line while it is in flight, but the batted ball subsequently goes into R's end zone. **RULING:** In (a), it is a foul for kick-catching interference by K2 as well as first touching, and R may choose to take the result of the play, which is a touchback, or take an awarded fair catch at R's 25-yard line (15 yards in advance of the spot of interference after enforcement of the penalty) or the ball at the spot of first touching at the 10-yard line, or penalize K 15 yards from the previous spot and replay the down. In (b), there is no foul and the result of the play is a touchback. R will put the ball in play first and 10 from its own 20-yard line (6-5-6 Exception; 8-5-3; 9-7-2 Exception).

9.7.3 SITUATION: A is in punt formation and the ball is snapped to A1, who turns his back to the line of scrimmage and throws a backward pass into the air. A2 comes forward and bats the ball 20 yards downfield where: (a) A3 recovers it 5 yards beyond the line to gain; or (b) it is caught by A4 who advances for an additional 5 yards; or (c) it goes out of bounds in advance of the line to gain; or (d) B1 intercepts and returns it for an apparent touchdown. **RULING:** In (a), (b), (c) and (d), the batting by A2 is illegal. In (a), (b) and (c), it will be B's advantage to accept the penalty of 15 yards which will be administered from the spot of the foul because the batting occurred during the loose-ball play and behind the basic spot. In (d), because the foul was during a loose-ball play, before a change of possession, B may keep the touchdown by declining the penalty for A's foul. Otherwise, the penalty will be enforced from the spot of the foul and A will retain possession of the ball if B accepts the penalty (10-5-3).

*9.7.4 SITUATION: On fourth and 6 from B's 10-yard line, A1 is about to be hit short of the line to gain. While the ball is in A1's possession, either: (a) A2; or (b) B1, bats the ball forward into B's end zone where A3 recovers. **RULING:** It is an illegal bat in (a). The enforcement spot is the end of A1's run, which is where the bat occurred. In (b) the bat is legal and results in a touchdown for A (8-2-1).

Topic:
Handing

Handing the ball is transferring player possession from one player to a teammate in such a way that the ball is still in contact with the first player when it is touched by the teammate. Handing the ball is not a pass. Loss of player possession by unsuccessful execution of attempted handing is a fumble (2-19-1). A ball in player possession is a live ball held or controlled by a player after it has been handed to him (2-34-1).

Backward Handing
Backward handing occurs when the runner releases the ball when any part of the ball is on or behind the yard line where the runner is positioned (2-19-3). Any player may hand the ball backward at any time (7-3-1).

Forward Handing
Forward handing occurs when the runner releases the ball when the entire ball is beyond the yard line where the runner is positioned (2-19-2). No player may hand the ball forward except during a scrimmage down before a change of possession, provided both players are in or behind the neutral zone and it is to a lineman who has clearly faced his end line by moving both feet in a half-turn and is at least 1 yard behind his line when he receives the ball (7-3-2a, 7-3-3), or a back or a teammate who, at the snap, was on an end of his line and was not the snapper nor adjacent to the snapper (7-3-2b). During a scrimmage down after a change of team possession, no player may hand the ball forward to a teammate.

Illegal Forward Handing: Penalty
5 yards and loss of down. Signals 35 and 9.

Face pressbox

Illegal Forward Handing: Case Play
7.3.2 SITUATION: Quarterback A1 takes the snap and hands the ball forward to back A2. The handing is done: (a) behind; or (b) in; or (c) beyond the neutral zone. **RULING:** Legal in (a) and (b), but a foul in (c).

7.3.2 COMMENT: The position of the ball determines whether it is behind, in or beyond the neutral zone. If the entire ball is beyond the neutral zone when it is released, it is forward handing (2-19-2, 3).

Topic:
Passes

Passing the ball is throwing a ball that is in player possession. In a pass, the ball travels in flight (2-31-1).

A passer is a player who throws a legal forward pass. He continues to be a passer until the legal forward pass ends or until he moves to participate in the play (2-32-11).

Any pass in flight may be batted in any direction by an eligible receiver unless it is a backward pass batted forward by the passing team (9-7-3). Batting is intentionally slapping or striking the ball with the arm or hand (2-1-2).

Illegal Batting: Penalty
15 yards. Signal 31.

Topic:
Types of Passes

Backward Pass
A backward pass is a pass thrown with its initial direction parallel with or toward the runner's endline. A backward pass ends when it is caught or recovered or is out of bounds (2-31-5; 2-31-6).

During any down, any player in possession may make a backward pass or may lose player possession through a fumble (7-4-1). If a backward pass is caught or recovered by any player, he may advance (7-4-2). If a backward pass goes out of bounds between the goal lines or becomes dead inbounds while no player is in possession or while opponents are in joint possession, the ball belongs to the passing team unless lost after fourth down (7-4-3).

If a backward pass is out of bounds behind a goal line, the ball belongs to the team defending that goal and the result is either a touchback or a safety (7-4-4).

In Simple Terms

A pass is either forward or backward. Any pass that is not clearly forward is backward. There is no such thing as a "lateral."

Forward Pass

A forward pass is a pass thrown with its initial direction toward the opponent's endline (2-31-2). Prior to releasing the ball on a pass, if the potential passer is contacted, and the ball is released, it is a forward pass if his arm was moving forward on contact (2-31-2 NOTE).

A forward pass has gone beyond the neutral zone if at any time during the pass, the entire ball is beyond the neutral zone (2-31-3).

A forward pass ends when it is caught, touches the ground or is out of bounds (2-31-4).

The ball becomes dead when any forward pass (legal or illegal) is incomplete or is simultaneously caught by opposing players (4-2-2c).

Snap

A snap is a backward pass. A snap is the legal act of passing or handing the ball backward from its position on the ground (2-40-1). The snap begins when the snapper first moves the ball legally other than in adjustment. In a snap, the movement must be a quick and continuous backward motion of the ball during which the ball immediately leaves the hand(s) of the snapper and touches a back or the ground before it touches an A lineman (2-40-2). The snap ends when the ball touches the ground or any player (2-40-3).

A scrimmage down must start with a legal snap. An illegal snap or other snap infraction causes the ball to remain dead (7-2-4).

In Simple Terms

When the ball is snapped, the resulting action will either be a running play, a pass, or a scrimmage kick — like a punt or field-goal attempt.

Topic:
Legal Passes

It is a legal forward pass, if during a scrimmage down and before team possession has changed, a player of A throws the ball with both feet of the passer in or behind the neutral zone when the ball is released. Only one forward pass may be thrown during the down (7-5-1).

It is legal to conserve time by intentionally throwing the ball forward to the ground immediately after receiving a direct hand-to-hand snap (7-5-2e Exception).

Legal Passes: Case Plays

3.6.3 SITUATION A: With time expiring in the second or fourth period and A behind in the score, A1 intentionally throws the ball forward to the ground in order to stop the clock. A1's action took place immediately after receiving a direct hand-to-hand snap. **RULING:** The grounding is legal and the clock remains stopped until the subsequent snap.

5.1.3 SITUATION C: Fourth and 10 on K's 45-yard line. K1 punts the ball beyond the neutral zone. R1 muffs the ball back behind the neutral zone where K1 recovers and throws a forward pass to K3 which is complete at the 50-yard line and R1 interferes with K3. **RULING:** Since R1 touched the kick beyond the neutral zone, it will be first down for the team in possession. The pass is legal as there had been no change of team possession. If K accepts the penalty for pass interference, it will be K's ball at R's 40-yard line (5-1-3f; 6-2-1; 7-5-1).

In Simple Terms
The passer may cross the line of scrimmage, retreat behind the line and throw a pass as long as both feet are behind the line when the pass is thrown.

7.5.1 SITUATION: Quarterback A1 runs wide and while near the neutral zone, decides to throw a forward pass. As A1 releases the ball his foremost foot is touching the ground in the neutral zone. **RULING:** It is a legal forward pass (7-5-2b).

7.5.2 SITUATION G: In the last few seconds of a half, A1 completes a pass to A2 at B's 20-yard line. The ball is properly spotted and the referee marks it ready for play and signals the clock to start. In the rush and confusion to stop the clock, A's snapper and quarterback A1 are the only

A players in legal position when the ball is snapped and legally "spiked" by A1. **RULING:** A foul for illegal formation occurs at the snap. The "spike" is legal. Since the spike is legal, the only applicable foul is for illegal formation.

Fundamental X-5

The penalty for any one of the five illegal passes is 5 yards and loss of down, except for a forward pass following change of possession, which is 5 yards only.

Topic:
Illegal Passes

An illegal forward pass is a foul. Illegal forward passes include: a pass after team possession has changed during the down; a pass from beyond the neutral zone; a second and subsequent forward pass(es) thrown during a down; a pass intentionally thrown into an area not occupied by an eligible offensive receiver; or a pass intentionally thrown incomplete to save loss of yardage or to conserve time (7-5-2a-e, Table).

Some factors to look for in making an intentional-grounding decision are absence of eligible offensive receivers in the area and the "dumping" to avoid loss of distance. The ability and skill of the passer and the pressure of the defense are also factors to consider (7.5.2 SITUATION C Comment).

If the offended team declines the distance penalty for an illegal pass, it has the choice of having the down counted at the spot of the illegal incomplete forward pass or (if the illegal forward pass is caught or intercepted) of having the ball put in play as determined by the action which followed the catch (7-5-3).

If the offensive team throws an illegal forward pass from its end zone or commits any other foul for which the penalty is accepted and measurement is from on or behind its goal line, it is a safety (10-5-4).

Illegal Forward Pass: Penalty

5 yards measured from the spot of the pass and loss of down. Signals 35 and 9. 5 yards only if the illegal pass is thrown after team possession has changed during the down. Signal 35.

Rationale

When the defensive team forces a passer into a position from which he cannot safely deliver the ball to an eligible teammate and he is unable to escape the defensive confinement, the defensive team has accomplished its objective. The penalty prevents the defense from losing an advantage which was fairly earned.

Illegal Forward Pass: Case Plays

3.4.6 SITUATION A: With time expiring in the second or fourth period and A behind in the score, A1 intentionally throws the ball forward to the ground in order to stop the clock. A1's action took place: (a) immediately after receiving the snap while A1 was lined up 3 yards deep; or (b) after A1 delayed and took more than one step after receiving a direct hand-to-hand snap. **RULING:** Illegal forward pass in (a) and (b), the clock shall be started on the ready-for-play signal (7-5-2d Exception).

5.2.2 SITUATION B: With fourth down and 4 from the 50, A1 runs to B's 40 and then throws an incomplete forward pass. **RULING:** If B declines the penalty, it will be A's ball first and 10 from B's 40-yard line. If B accepts the 5-yard penalty for the illegal forward pass, it will still be a first down for A from B's 45-yard line. The loss of down part of the penalty has no significance since the succeeding spot is beyond the line to gain and a new series is awarded.

> ***7.5 COMMENT:** The following chart should help game officials distinguish between the various possible fouls that can occur when an ineligible receiver touches or is touched by the ball, including accidentally striking, muffing or catching, and with basic fouls regarding ineligibility. ENZ refers to expanded neutral zone. Answers are "Is it a foul if the act/touching occurs?"

Pass Interference (7-5-7; 7-5-10)	Behind Neutral Zone	In (including ENZ)	Beyond ENZ
Accidentally striking ineligible	No	No	If contact is made against an opponent that is deemed to be pass interference, or 7-5-10b occurs, yes, 15 yards. If no interference, No
Muff by ineligible	No	No	If contact is made against an opponent that is deemed to be pass interference, or 7-5-10b occurs, yes, 15 yards. If no pass interference, no.
Catch by ineligible	No	No	If contact is made against an opponent that is deemed to be pass interference, or 7-5-10b occurs, yes, 15 yards. If no pass interference, no.
Ineligible Downfield (7-5-12)	**Behind Neutral Zone**	**In (including ENZ)**	**Beyond ENZ**
Accidentally striking ineligible	No	No (see ENZ note)	If not yet touched, Yes, 5 yards
Muff by ineligible	No	No (see ENZ note)	If not yet touched, Yes, 5 yards
Catch by ineligible	No	No (see ENZ note)	If not yet touched, Yes, 5 yards
Illegal Touching (7-5-13)	**Behind Neutral Zone**	**In (including ENZ)**	**Beyond ENZ**
Accidentally striking ineligible	No	No	No
Muff by ineligible	Yes, 5 yard, loss of down	Yes, 5 yard, loss of down	Yes, 5 yard, loss of down
Catch by ineligible	Yes, 5 yard, loss of down	Yes, 5 yard, loss of down	Yes, 5 yard, loss of down

7.5.1 SITUATION: Quarterback A1 runs wide and while near the neutral zone, decides to throw a forward pass. As A1 releases the ball, his foremost foot is breaking the plane of B's side of the neutral zone. **RULING:** It is an illegal forward pass because the location of the passer's foremost foot was beyond the neutral zone (7-5-2b).

7.5.2 SITUATION A: Quarterback A1 drops back to pass, but is unable to find a receiver and: (a) throws the ball to the ground; or (b) throws the ball to the ground in an area occupied by only defensive players; or (c) deliberately throws the ball at the legs of onrushing defensive linemen. **RULING:** An illegal forward pass in (a), (b) and (c). Penalize A 5 yards from where the run ended and count the down in each situation (7-5-2b, c, d).

Did You Know? Before 1930, backward passes and fumbles going out of bounds were awarded to the team last touching the ball.

7.5.2 SITUATION B: Quarterback A1 is in position for a direct hand-to-hand snap: (a) A1 muffs the snap, but is able to take the ball from the ground and spike it forward; or (b) A1 receives the snap, but his spike attempt hits snapper A2's leg and ricochets into the air. A1 catches the ball and immediately spikes it forward. **RULING:** An illegal forward pass in both (a) and (b). Once the ball touches the ground, a player or a spike attempt is unsuccessful, it may not be grounded legally thereafter using this exception. In order to be a "direct snap" and therefore meet the allowance within the exception, the ball must go immediately from the snapper to the person in position to take the hand-to-hand snap without being muffed, fumbled or otherwise mishandled.

7.5.2 SITUATION C: Quarterback A1 drops back to pass and while under a good defensive rush, he throws the ball forward: (a) at the feet of two onrushing defensive linemen; or (b) 15 yards behind A3 who has run a deep post pattern; or (c) 5 to 10 feet over the head of eligible A3 who lined up near a sideline. **RULING:** Illegal forward pass in (a). In (b) and (c), the referee will have to judge whether the pass was intentionally thrown incomplete or whether A1 was simply unable to throw the ball close to A3 (7-5-2d).

7.5.2 SITUATION D: Runner A1 advances 5 yards beyond the neutral zone to B's 3-yard line where he is tackled. As he is going down, A1 simulates a fumble by tossing the ball forward into the end zone where A2 downs it. **RULING:** Illegal forward pass by A1. The penalty is 5 yards from the spot of the pass, plus loss of down. If A1 is contacted after releasing the ball, it is not roughing the passer since he lost that protection when he threw the pass from beyond the neutral zone (9-4-4).

7.5.2 SITUATION E: A1 throws a legal forward pass: (a) which is tipped by B1 behind the expanded neutral zone and A1 catches the pass and then throws a second pass which is completed to A8; or (b) to A5 who is behind the line of scrimmage and who then throws another forward pass to A11 who advances the ball for a first down. **RULING:** Illegal forward pass in (a) and (b) (7-5-2e).

7.5.6 SITUATION: Quarterback A1 drops back and throws a forward pass toward the sideline to A2 who is behind the neutral zone. A2 then throws a forward pass to A3 15 yards downfield. **RULING:** A2 has committed a foul for an illegal forward pass.

Topic:
Catch and Completed Pass

A catch is the act of establishing player possession of a live ball which is in flight, and first contacting the ground inbounds while maintaining possession of the ball or having the forward progress of the player in possession stopped while the opponent is carrying the player who is in possession and inbounds (2-4-1).

A forward pass, legal or illegal, is complete and the ball may be advanced when caught by any player of A or B (7-5-4).

Catching is always preceded by touching the ball; thus, if touching causes the ball to become dead, securing possession of the ball has no significance (2-4-2).

To make a catch, recovery or interception, the player must first come down inbounds (including possessing the ball and having forward progress being stopped inbounds). To make a catch, a player must return to the ground inbounds; have forward progress stopped inbounds prior to being carried out of bounds. To make an interception, the player must make a catch (7.5 NOTE).

Catch: Case Plays
2.15.2 SITUATION: It is first and 10 for A at B's 12-yard line. A1 sprints near the end line and then buttonhooks. He jumps and possesses a forward pass while in the air above the end zone. (a) A1's momentum carries him back into the field of play and he lands and is downed on the 1-yard line; or (b) while in the air in the end zone, he is contacted by B1 and he is carried out of the end zone and downed on B's 2-yard line. **RULING:** In (a), it is A's ball first and goal at B's 1-yard line. In (b), it is a touchdown because A1 was contacted in the end zone (2-4-1).

4.3.3 SITUATION B: A has third down and seven yards to gain at B's 30. A1 leaps near the sideline to attempt to catch a pass near B's 30-yard line. A1 is: (a) airborne trying to make the catch and is knocked backwards by B2 attempting to make the tackle and A1 lands outside the sideline at B's 32 or (b) airborne when he controls the ball attempting to complete the catch and is carried off the field by B2 landing out of bounds. **RULING:** In (a), the pass is incomplete and the clock should start on the snap. In (b), it is a catch and the clock should not stop. If the clock was stopped inadvertently by the covering official, it should be immediately restarted (2-15-1, 2; 4-3-2).

7.5.4 SITUATION B: A pass from A1 is possessed by A2 while he is in the air above B's end zone. A2 loses control when he is contacted by B1 while in the air. The ball: (a) falls to the ground; or (b) is caught by eligible A3 in B's end zone; or (c) is intercepted and downed by B2 in the end zone. **RULING:** In (a), the pass is incomplete. In (b), it is a touchdown and in (c), it is a touchback (8-2-1b; 8-5-3c).

7.5.4 SITUATION C: B1 attempts to intercept a pass while in the air and deflects the ball into the air, but is able to catch it after he comes down inbounds. **RULING:** Interception.

7.5.4 SITUATION G: A8, in B's end zone, leaps in the air to catch a pass and is contacted by B2 forcing A8 to come down inbounds on B's 1-yard line where he is downed. **RULING:** Touchdown, since A8's forward progress was stopped over B's end zone by B2's contact. Even though the catch was not made until A8 came down inbounds, his forward progress was stopped by B2's contact resulting in A possessing the live ball in its opponent's end zone, hence, a touchdown.

7.5.4 SITUATION I: Airborne A1 jumps high in an attempt to catch a legal forward pass. While still in the air, he is tackled by B1 and held momentarily without touching the ground before he is carried (a) backward toward A's goal line, or (b) forward toward B's goal line. He then lands out of bounds with the ball. **RULING:** In (a) and (b), completed pass as forward progress was stopped. The ball is dead at the yard line where the forward progress of the receiver was stopped (2-4-1, 4-2-2a).

Simultaneous Catch

A simultaneous catch or recovery is a catch or recovery in which there is joint possession of a live ball by opposing players who are inbounds (2-4-3).

If a forward pass is caught simultaneously by two opponents, the ball becomes dead and belongs to the passing team (7-5-4).

In order for there to be a simultaneous catch, opposing players must have simultaneous joint possession, and both must be in contact with the ground inbounds. The players' contact with the ground does not have to be exactly simultaneous. If A1 and B1 jointly possess a forward pass while airborne and both land inbounds, it is a completed pass, the ball is dead at that point and belongs to A. If there is simultaneous recovery of a fumble, the ball becomes dead and belongs to the team which last had possession (7-5 SITUATION COMMENT).

Simultaneous Catch: Case Plays

7.4.3 SITUATION: A1 and B1 simultaneously gain possession of a live ball which is a legal forward pass and both players are touching inbounds. **RULING:** The down is ended. It is a complete pass and the ball belongs to A at the spot of completion (7-5-4).

7.5.4 SITUATION A: Airborne A1 and B1 simultaneously gain possession of a legal forward pass near the goal line and return to the ground where: (a) they alight in the field of play inbounds; or (b) they alight in the end zone with the ball; or (c) A1 lands in the end zone and B1 in the field of play inbounds; or (d) B1 comes down in the end zone and A1 lands in the field of play. **RULING:** In (a), the ball is dead and belongs to A at the yard line through the foremost point of the ball when A1 and B1 contacted the ground inbounds. It is a touchdown in (b). In (c) and (d), the ball becomes dead and the pass is complete at the yard line through the foremost point of the ball when the players contacted the ground inbounds. If the ball has penetrated the plane of the goal line in either (c) or (d), it is a touchdown.

Topic:
Incomplete Pass

A forward pass, legal or illegal, is incomplete and the ball becomes dead when the pass touches the ground or goes out of bounds. It is also incomplete when a player in the air possesses the pass and alights so that his first contact with the ground or with anything other than a player or game official is on or outside a boundary (7-5-5).

When an incompletion occurs the down counts unless the pass is after a change of possession. If the pass is legal, the passing team next snaps the ball at the previous spot, unless lost after fourth down (7-5-5).

In the 1920s, it was a 5-yard penalty and loss of down to throw more than one incomplete forward pass in an offensive series.

Incomplete Pass: Case Plays

2.31.2 SITUATION: Quarterback A1 drops back to pass and is under a heavy rush. A1 is hit and the ball drops to the ground and B1 recovers. At the instant A1 was hit and lost possession, his passing arm was: (a) moving backward; or (b) was extended back, but not moving in either direction in relation to the line of scrimmage; or (c) was moving forward toward the line of scrimmage. **RULING:** In (a) and (b), it is a fumble and B gains possession. In (c), since A1's arm was moving forward toward the line of scrimmage, it is an incomplete forward pass and the ball becomes dead when it hits the ground (2-18).

7.5.4 SITUATION C: B1 attempts to intercept a pass while in the air and: (a) the ball touches one hand and then deflects to the other without securing possession, after which B1 lands with his first step inbounds and second out of bounds; or (b) is juggling the ball as he takes two steps inbounds and then out of bounds. **RULING:** Incomplete in (a) and (b).

In Simple Terms
If a player throws an incomplete pass after a change of possession, the ball is dead.

7.5.4 SITUATION A: Airborne A1 and B1 simultaneously gain possession of a legal forward pass near the goal line and return to the ground where A1 lands in the end zone and B1 lands out of bounds. **RULING:** Incomplete pass (4-2-2c; 7-5-4; 8-2-1). In order for there to be a simultaneous catch, opposing players must have simultaneous joint possession, and both must be in contact with the ground inbounds.

7.5.4 SITUATION H: A pass from A1 is thrown near the intersection of the sideline and the goal line. A2, running toward the goal line, leaps and possesses the pass at the 3-yard line and is forcibly: (a) contacted from the front by B1 (not carried) so that A2 contacts the ground out of bounds opposite B's 4-yard line; or (b) contacted from the side by B1 and A2 first contacts the ground out of bounds opposite the 3-yard line. **RULING:** In (a) and (b), it is an incomplete pass (2-4-1, 2-15-1, 2; 8-2-1).

Resuming Play After an Incomplete Pass

If a legal forward pass is incomplete, the ball is returned to the previous spot (4-3-2, 4-3-4, 4-3-5a).

Topic:
Receivers

Eligible Receivers

Pass eligibility rules apply only to a legal forward pass. All A players eligible by position and number include those who, at the time of the snap, are on the ends of their scrimmage line or legally behind the line (possible total of six) and are numbered 1-49 or 80-99 (7-5-6a).

All A players become eligible when B touches a legal forward pass. All B players are eligible. A player who is eligible at the start of the down remains eligible throughout the down (7-5-6d). All other players are ineligible receivers (7-5-6b-c).

Fundamental VII-1

A player who is eligible at the start of the down remains eligible throughout the down.

Eligible Receivers: Case Plays

7.2.5 SITUATION A: Team A comes to its line of scrimmage with: (a) ends 80 and 71, tackles 70 and 81, guards 60 and 61, and center 50; or (b) ends 80 and 81, guards 72 and 75, tackles 62 and 63, and center 50 and one halfback numbered 76. **RULING:** The formations in both (a) and (b) are legal because there are at least five players numbered 50-79 on the offensive line. In (a), a player at tackle wearing 81 and the end wearing 71 are both ineligible receivers; 81 because of his position and 71 because of his number. In (b), number 76, a halfback, is not an eligible receiver because of the number he is wearing (7-5-6a).

In Simple Terms

All 11 B players are eligible receivers.

Ineligible Receivers

All A players numbered 50-79 and those who are not on the ends of their scrimmage line or legally behind the line are ineligible receivers (7-5-6a). Ineligible A players may not advance beyond the expanded neutral zone on a legal forward pass play before a legal forward pass that crosses the neutral zone is in flight. If B touches the pass in or behind the neutral zone, this restriction is terminated. An ineligible is not illegally downfield if, at the snap, he immediately contacts a B lineman and the contact does not continue beyond the expanded neutral zone (7-5-12).

An ineligible A player has illegally touched a forward pass if he bats, muffs or catches a legal forward pass unless the pass has first been touched by B (7-5-13).

In Simple Terms

The most A players who can be eligible at the snap is six.

On first, second or third down, when A sets or shifts into a scrimmage-kick formation as in 2-14-2a, the snapper may be a player numbered 1 to 49 or 80 to 99. If Team A has the snapper in the game under this exception, Team A shall have at least four players wearing numbers 50-79 on its line of scrimmage. The snapper in the game under this exception must be between the ends and is an ineligible forward pass receiver during that down unless the pass is touched by B (7-5-6b). On fourth down or during a kick try, when A sets or shifts into a scrimmage-kick formation, any A player numbered 1 to 49 or 80 to 99 may take the position of any A player numbered 50 to 79. A player in the game under this exception must assume an initial position on his line of scrimmage between the ends and he remains an ineligible forward-pass receiver during that down unless the pass is touched by B (7-2-5b Exceptions 1 and 2; 7-5-6b).

Ineligible Downfield: Penalty
5 yards. Signal 37.

Ineligible Downfield: Case Plays
2.28.2 SITUATION A: B1 is on his defensive line of scrimmage when he is contacted by ineligible lineman A1 and driven back about 2 yards. **RULING:** A1 is not illegally downfield if a forward pass crosses the neutral zone, since he contacted B1 on the line and after driving him back did not go beyond the neutral zone expanded (2-25-3; 6-2-6; 7-5-12).

5.2.2 SITUATION A: With fourth and 5 from B's 30, A1 throws a forward pass that is intercepted by B1 on his 10-yard line and returned to B's 29. While the pass was in flight, ineligible A2 was illegally downfield, and the ball: (a) is muffed by A2 at the 12-yard line prior to being intercepted, or (b) did not touch A2 prior to the touching and interception by B1. **RULING:** In (a), A has committed two fouls —

illegal touching and ineligible downfield. B1 will decline the ineligible downfield penalty to keep the football, but will accept the penalty for illegal touching as the ball will be at B's 35 following enforcement, and will be B's ball due to the loss of down foul. In (b), the foul carries a 5-yard penalty and B would then likely decline the penalty and keep the ball first and 10 from its own 29-yard line.

7.5.7 SITUATION B: A1 drops back and throws a screen pass to flanker A2 who is behind the neutral zone. B2 has come across the line and deflects the pass so that its flight is altered and the pass goes beyond the neutral zone. Ineligible A8 has gone beyond the expanded neutral zone before the pass is released. **RULING:** Since B has touched the forward pass in or behind the neutral zone A8 is not downfield illegally.

7.5.7 SITUATION C: A1 throws a pass that is touched behind the neutral zone by B7. The pass touches ineligible A2 beyond the neutral zone and falls incomplete. **RULING:** Illegal touching has not occurred since B touched the ball in or behind the neutral zone.

7.5.10 SITUATION E: A1 throws a screen pass behind the neutral zone. The pass is touched by B1 and continues in flight beyond the neutral zone: (a) A2 has gone downfield and blocks B2 before the pass is touched; or (b) ineligible A3 is downfield beyond the neutral zone before A1's pass is in flight. **RULING:** Legal in both (a) and (b) because B1 touched the pass in or behind the neutral zone (2-31-3; 7-5-6b; 7-5-12).

7.5.12 SITUATION A: At the snap, interior lineman A1 moves about 3 yards downfield and finding no one to block, retreats behind the neutral zone and blocks for A2 who eventually throws a forward pass which crosses the neutral zone. **RULING:** A1 is an ineligible illegally downfield. The prohibition against ineligibles downfield for A starts at the snap, and the fact A1 was no longer downfield when the pass was thrown has no bearing on the ruling.

8.3.2 SITUATION C: During a try, A1 completes a pass to A2 in the end zone and ineligible A3 was illegally beyond the neutral zone. **RULING:** If the 5-yard penalty is accepted, the try will be repeated (7-5-10 Penalty; 7-5-12 Penalty; 8-3-5).

Topic:
Illegal Touching

An ineligible A player has illegally touched a forward pass if he bats, muffs or catches a legal forward pass unless the pass has first been touched by B (7-5-13).

Illegal Touching: Penalty

5 yards plus loss of down. Signals 16 and 9.

Illegal Touching: Case Plays

7.5.13 SITUATION A: Ineligible receiver A2 is behind, in or beyond his neutral zone and has committed no act against a defender that could be ruled pass interference when a forward pass by A1: (a) accidentally strikes him in the back; or (b) is muffed by him; or (c) is caught by him. **RULING:** In (a), there is no foul for illegal touching. In (b) and (c), it is illegal touching. The acts in both (b) and (c) are intentional and not accidental as in (a).

 7.5.13 COMMENT: Game officials should be very clear in explaining penalty options if the same act constitutes more than one foul as listed above, as each of the fouls has a different penalty.

7.5.13 SITUATION B: A1's forward pass is deflected by B1 and then caught by interior lineman A2 behind the neutral zone. **RULING:** No foul has occurred as A2 became an eligible receiver after B1 touched the pass.

9.2.1 SITUATION H: A1 throws a forward pass beyond the neutral zone which is touched by eligible A2 and is muffed high into the air. While the muffed ball is in the air: (a) ineligible A3 blocks B1 away from the ball, or (b) ineligible A3 touches the ball in an attempt to catch it. **RULING:** Legal action in (a), but illegal touching in (b). After A2 touches the ball, eligible offensive team players may use hands or arms. Pass interference restrictions for eligibles have ended. However, an ineligible Team A player may not touch the pass until after a Team B player has touched it. The ineligibles, however, may block an opponent to keep him from getting to the ball or to help a teammate secure possession (2-3-4c; 7-5-9b; 7-5-13).

Topic:
Interference by A

Pass interference restrictions only apply beyond the neutral zone and only if the legal forward pass, untouched by B in or behind the neutral zone, crosses the neutral zone. Pass interference restrictions are in effect for all A and B players until the ball is touched or the pass is incomplete (7-5-7).

Pass interference restrictions on a legal forward pass begin for A with the snap (7-5-8a).

Pass interference restrictions on a legal forward pass end for all eligible A players when the pass has been touched by any player and for all ineligible A players when B touches the pass, however it is not pass interference for ineligible A players to use hands and arms in a legal block to ward off an opponent. Pass interference restrictions on a legal forward pass end for all A players when the pass is incomplete (7-5-9a, b, d).

It is forward-pass interference if any player of A who is beyond the neutral zone interferes with an eligible opponent's opportunity to move toward, catch or bat the pass; or if any A player hinders an opponent's vision without making an attempt to catch, intercept or bat the ball, even though no contact was made (7-5-10a, b).

Interference by A: Penalty

15 yards. Signal 33. If the interference is intentional, A is penalized an additional 15 yards. Signal 27.

◪ Rationale

The interference restrictions on A players are more stringent because they know the play is a pass.

Interference by A: Case Plays

7.5.7 SITUATION A: A1 throws a screen pass behind the neutral zone. The pass is touched in or behind the neutral zone by B1 and continues in flight beyond the neutral zone: (a) A2 has gone downfield and blocks B2 before the pass is touched; or (b) ineligible A2 is downfield beyond the neutral zone before A1's pass is in flight. **RULING:** Legal in both (a) and (b) as B1 touched the pass in or behind the neutral zone.

7.5.7 COMMENT: The key to whether the action in (a) or (b) is legal is determined by the fact that the pass was touched by B in or behind the neutral zone, even though it went beyond the neutral zone. In both (a) and (b) A2's being downfield and blocking is not restricted because the pass was touched by B in or behind the neutral zone. Therefore, A2 is not an ineligible downfield illegally.

7.5.8 SITUATION: A81 goes downfield and pushes off B22 (pushes him away from A81 to help him make his cut) and cuts toward the sideline and catches A1's pass. A81's push occurred prior to B4 tipping the pass. **RULING:** This contact can be ruled pass interference as restrictions for Team A begin at the snap.

7.5.10 SITUATION B: Eligible receiver A1 blocks an opponent 10 yards downfield while the pass is in flight. The pass is completed to A2 who is: (a) beyond the neutral zone; or (b) behind the neutral zone when he catches the ball. When the covering official observes the block by A1 during a forward pass, he immediately drops a penalty marker to indicate an infraction. **RULING:** It is a foul for pass interference in (a), and a legal block in (b). It was proper for the covering official downfield in (b) to indicate a possible infraction because he had no way of knowing whether the pass was beyond the neutral zone (7-5-7).

7.5.10 SITUATION D: B3 gets in the path of a receiver, A4, without making contact. B3's presence results in A4 initiating contact in an effort to reach the ball. **RULING:** A foul by A4 for offensive pass interference (7-5-10a).

7.5.12 SITUATION B: Before A1 throws a pass beyond the neutral zone, A2 contacts lineman B1 on his line and drives him back 4 yards. **RULING:** Offensive pass interference by A2 because he has driven B1 beyond the expanded neutral zone (2-28-2).

8.3.2 SITUATION C: During a try, A1 completes a pass to A2 in the end zone and A4 interfered with B1. **RULING:** If the 15-yard penalty is accepted, the try will be repeated (7-5-10 Penalty; 7-5-12 Penalty; 8-3-5).

Not Interference

Pass interference restrictions only apply beyond the neutral zone and only if the legal forward pass, untouched by B in or beyond the neutral zone, crosses the neutral zone (7-5-7).

It is not forward-pass interference if unavoidable contact occurs when two or more eligibles are making a simultaneous, bona fide attempt to move toward, catch or bat the pass; contact by A is immediately made on a B lineman and the contact does not continue beyond the neutral zone; or if contact by B is obviously away from the direction of the pass (7-5-11a-c).

Rationale

The defense should not be penalized for interfering with a player who clearly cannot move close enough to the pass to be a receiver.

Not Interference: Case Plays

2.28.2 SITUATION A: B1 is on his defensive line of scrimmage when he is contacted by ineligible lineman A1 and driven back about 2 yards. **RULING:** A1 has not committed pass interference if a forward pass crosses the neutral zone, since he contacted B1 on the line and after driving him back did not go beyond the neutral zone expanded (2-25-3; 6-2-6; 7-5-12).

7.5.6 SITUATION: Quarterback A1 drops back and throws a forward pass toward the sideline to A2 who is behind the neutral zone. A2 then throws a forward pass to A3 15 yards downfield. (a) B1 blocks A2 behind the line prior to A2 touching the ball; or (b) B1 tackles A2 prior to A2 touching the pass; or (c) B1 pushes A3 prior to A3 touching the pass, and B1 intercepts. **RULING:** Legal block in (a) since pass interference restrictions for B do not apply to a forward pass that does not cross the neutral zone. In (b), it is a holding foul by B1. Legal contact in (c) since there are no pass interference restrictions on an illegal forward pass. It should be noted that A2 has also committed a foul for an illegal forward pass.

7.5.9 SITUATION: On second down, quarterback A1 drops back and throws an underhand shovel pass forward to back A2 who is behind the neutral zone. A2 throws the ball back to A1. A1 then throws the ball forward beyond the neutral zone to A3. B1 blocks A3 away from the ball and intercepts A1's pass. **RULING:** Legal contact by B1 and an illegal forward pass by A1. Pass interference restrictions for B players ended when the shovel pass was touched by any player. B will likely decline the penalty and keep the ball. If the foul for illegal forward pass is accepted.

7.5.10 SITUATION D: B3 gets in the path of a receiver, A4, without making contact. B3's presence results in A4 slowing down to avoid contact. **RULING:** No foul (7-5-10a).

Topic:
Interference by B

Pass interference restrictions on a legal forward pass begin for B when the ball leaves the passer's hand (7-5-8b). Pass interference restrictions are in effect for all B players until the ball is touched or the pass is incomplete (7-5-7). Pass interference restrictions on a legal forward pass end for all B players when the pass has been touched by any player or when the pass is incomplete (7-5-9c, d).

It is forward-pass interference if any player of B who is beyond the neutral zone interferes with an eligible opponent's opportunity to move toward, catch or bat the pass; or if any B player hinders an opponent's vision without making an attempt to catch, intercept or bat the ball, even though no contact was made (7-5-10a, b).

Interference by B: Penalty

15 yards. Signal 33. If the interference is intentional, B is penalized an additional 15 yards. Signal 27.

Interference by B: Case Plays

4.2.3 SITUATION B: While a legal forward pass is in flight: (a) B1 interferes with eligible A1 and then there is an inadvertent whistle; or (b) a whistle is inadvertently sounded after which B2 contacts A2 while the ball is still in flight. **Ruling:** In (a), if the captain accepts the penalty for a foul which occurred prior to the inadvertent whistle, the penalty takes precedence. It will be a new series for A, 15 yards in advance of the previous spot. In (b), the contact by B2 occurred during a dead-ball period and unless it is a personal foul, will be ignored. Because the whistle was inadvertently sounded while a legal forward pass was in flight, the down shall be replayed (7-5-10a).

7.5.10 SITUATION A: During a forward-pass play in which the ball crosses the neutral zone, A1, an ineligible receiver, is illegally downfield and: (a) B1 illegally contacts him with an elbow; or (b) A1 blocks B1. **RULING:** In (a), the personal foul by B1 and A1's foul for being downfield combine to make a double foul and the down will be replayed. The contact by B1 is not defensive pass interference because A1 was an ineligible receiver. Defensive pass interference may occur only against eligible receivers. Had there been no contact and had ineligible A1 touched such a pass, the result would have been illegal touching. In (b), it is a multiple foul for an ineligible illegally downfield and also offensive pass interference (7-5-6a; 7-5-13; 10-2-1, 10-2-3).

7.5.10 SITUATION C: A1 is in a position to catch a forward pass beyond the neutral zone. An opponent, who is in the vicinity, turns his back to the ball. The opponent directs his attention to A1 and waves his arms to block the vision of the potential receiver or interceptor. **RULING:** Hindering an opponent's vision without making an attempt to catch, intercept or bat the ball, is pass interference even though no contact was made.

7.5.11 SITUATION A: A11 is running a deep post pattern and B11 (a) contacts A11 knocking him off his intended path or (b) grabs A11's jersey. In both situations, the pass has already crossed the neutral zone and the pass is clearly away from the intended receiver. **RULING:** In (a) there is no foul for pass interference, and (b) there is a foul for illegal holding.

7.5.11 SITUATION B: A11 runs straight up the field and after the ball has left the passer's hand, B9 illegally blocks A11 and throws him off his pattern. The pass is completed to A10 who was clearly on the opposite side of the field. **RULING:** There is no pass interference call on B9; however, a flag should have been dropped for the illegal block.

8.3.2 SITUATION C: During a try, A1 completes a pass to A2 in the end zone and B2 interfered with A2. **RULING:** A undoubtedly will accept the result of the play and enforce the penalty from the succeeding spot (7-5-10 Penalty; 7-5-12 Penalty; 8-3-5).

9.2.3 SITUATION C: Quarterback A1 drops back 15 yards and throws a legal forward pass intended for A2, who is 5 yards behind the neutral zone. Before the pass reaches A2: (a) B1 tackles A2; or (b) B1 blocks A2. **RULING:** In (a), tackling A2 is a foul, as it is a form of holding. Defensive players are prohibited from grasping an opponent other than the runner. The foul in (a) occurs during a loose-ball play, and the 10-yard penalty will be administered from the previous spot. In (b), the contact by B1 is not pass interference and, if the block itself is legal, there is no infraction (7-5-10).

Topic:
Roughing the Passer

Defensive players must make a definite effort to avoid charging into a passer, who has thrown the ball from in or behind the neutral zone, after it is clear the ball has been thrown. No defensive player shall charge into the passer who is standing still or fading back, because he is considered out of the play after the pass (9-4-4; 10-1-7b; 10-5-4; 10-5-1g).

Roughing the Passer: Penalty

15 yards and a first down from the dead ball spot when the dead ball spot is beyond the neutral zone and A has possession of the ball at the end of the down and there has been no change of team possession and the foul is not for an incidental face mask as in 9-4-3h, or otherwise 15 yards and first down from previous spot. Signals 34 and 8.

Roughing the Passer: Case Plays

7.5.2 SITUATION D: Runner A1 advances 5 yards beyond the neutral zone to B's 3-yard line where he is tackled. As he is going down, A1 simulates a fumble by tossing the ball forward into the end zone where A2 downs it. **RULING:** Illegal forward pass by A1. The penalty is 5 yards from the spot of the pass, plus loss of down. If A1 is contacted after releasing the ball, it is not roughing the passer since he lost that protection when he threw the pass from beyond the neutral zone (9-4-4).

9.4.4 SITUATION A: A1 rolls out on a run-pass option (a) A1 passes from behind the neutral zone and is subsequently contacted by B1 who could have avoided the contact, but renewed his charge after the pass; or (b) A1 is 2 yards beyond the neutral zone when he passes and B1 continues his charge and contacts him. **RULING:** It is roughing the passer in (a), but cannot be roughing the passer in (b). However, in (b), though A1 lost his protection as a passer when he passed from beyond the neutral zone the contact could still be judged by the game official to be a personal foul.

9.4.4 SITUATION B: From A's 40-yard line, passer A1 is roughed by B1 and the pass is completed: (a) to A2 who is downed on A's 47-yard line; or (b) behind the neutral zone to A2 who is downed on A's 38; or (c)

completed to A2 behind the neutral zone and his fumble at A's 35 goes directly out of bounds. **RULING:** In (a), the roughing penalty is enforced from the 47-yard line and results in a first down for A at B's 38. In (b) and (c), if the penalty is accepted, enforcement is from the previous spot resulting in a first down for A from B's 45-yard line.

9.4.4 SITUATION C: 3rd down and 10 from B30. A1 passes to A2 who catches ball at B20. B1 roughs A1 following the legal forward pass. A2 advances to B15 where he fumbles (a) backward and the ball is recovered by A3 at the B 20; (b) forward and the ball is recovered by A3 at the B5; (c) forward and the ball is recovered by B2 at the B5; (d) forward and the ball is recovered by A3 in the end zone; (e) forward and the ball is recovered by B2 in B's end zone; (f) forward and the ball rolls through and out of the end zone; or (g) backward and the ball is recovered at the B31. **RULING:** In (a) the roughing penalty is enforced from the B20, half the distance with first and goal for A at the B10; in (b) the roughing penalty is enforced half the distance from the B5 yard line with first and goal for A at the B2 1/2-yard line; in (c), (e), (f) and (g) the roughing penalty is enforced from the B30 (previous spot) with first and 10 for A at the B15; in (d) touchdown for A and A is given the choice of enforcing the roughing penalty on the try or on the subsequent kickoff per 8-2-2.

Topic:
Live Ball

A live ball is a ball in play (2-1-2). A dead ball is a ball not in play. The ball is dead during the interval between downs (2-1-1). A down is action which starts with a legal snap (beginning a scrimmage down) or when the ball is kicked on a free kick (beginning a free-kick down). A down ends when the ball next becomes dead (2-7-1).

A ball becomes live when the ball has been legally snapped and a down is in progress. After being put in play, the ball remains live until the down ends (2-1-2; 4-1-5).

Fundamental I-1

A live ball is always in the possession of a team.

Live Ball: Case Plays

4.1.5 SITUATION: A forward pass strikes a game official standing inbounds, after which it rebounds into the air and is caught by A1 or B1. **RULING:** A1 or B1 has caught a live ball. Nothing has occurred to cause the ball to become dead (4-2-2e; 4-2-3a).

4.2.2 SITUATION A: K1 has one knee on the ground to hold for an apparent field-goal attempt. K2 is in position to kick. K1 catches the snap and: (a) places the ball which is kicked by K2; or (b) rises and either runs or passes. **RULING:** Legal in (a) and (b).

4.2.2 SITUATION B: During a try K1, who is apparently a place-kick holder, receives the snap with one knee on the ground and places the ball for a kick. Just as K2 comes forward to kick the ball, K1 lifts the ball, rises and: (a) throws a forward pass to K3 in the end zone; or (b) carries the ball into the end zone; or (c) starts to run, fumbles and the ball is recovered by K4 who advances into the end zone. **RULING:** Successful try in (a), (b) and (c). The ball remains live and may be advanced since the place-kick holder had his knee in contact with the ground at the time of the snap and a teammate was in position to kick.

4.2.2 SITUATION C: At the snap, K1 is in position to kick and K2 is in position to hold for a place kick with one knee on the ground. The snap is high and it is necessary for K2 to lift his knee off the ground in order to catch the ball, or is low and bounces along the ground. K2 catches or recovers the snap and: (a) immediately drops to one knee and places the ball for a kick; or (b) immediately drops to his knees and then rises and passes the ball; or (c) takes several steps and fumbles the ball which is subsequently recovered and advanced by K1 or K2. **RULING:** The ball remains live in (a), (b) and (c). In (c), the advance by K1 or K2 is legal.

4.2.2 SITUATION H: R1 gives a fair-catch signal immediately following his catch of a kick. **RULING:** Illegal fair-catch signal, because it was given after the kick was caught and R1 had become a runner. The signal does not cause the down to end.

4.2.2 SITUATION I: During a try, K1's place kick hits lineman K2 who is behind the neutral zone, and caroms between the uprights and above the crossbar. **RULING:** The try is successful. Touching a kick is ignored if the touching is in the neutral-zone expanded, or on K's side of it.

4.2.2 SITUATION J: With fourth down and 8 from the 50, A1 runs to B's 45-yard line where: (a) B1, in attempting to tackle A1, unsnaps A1's chin strap and play continues to the 40-yard line where A1 is finally downed; or (b) B1, in attempting to tackle A1, grasps the face mask/helmet opening and A1's helmet comes off; or (c) B1 contacts A1 at B's 46 and A1's helmet comes off and he subsequently fumbles the ball. **RULING:** In (a), play continues and it is a first down for A after enforcement of the face mask foul. In (b), the ball becomes dead at the spot A1's helmet came off and B is penalized for the face mask/helmet opening violation. In (c), the ball becomes dead at the spot where A1's helmet came off and because it was fourth down and the line to gain was not obtained, the ball goes over to B. The fumble is disregarded because it happened after the ball became dead and A1 must leave the field for one play (3-5-10d; 4-2-2k).

Topic:
Dead Ball

Ball In Possession Becomes Dead

The ball becomes dead and the down is ended when a runner goes out of bounds, is held so his forward progress is stopped or allows any part of his person other than hand or foot to touch the ground (4-2-2a); when the helmet comes completely off a player who is in possession of the ball (4-2-2k); when any score occurs (4-2-2h); when any loose ball is simultaneously caught or recovered by opposing players (4-2-2c, 4-2-2e 1); or when an inadvertent whistle is sounded (4-2-3a through c).

Ball In Possession Becomes Dead: Case Plays

2.26.3 SITUATION: Runner A1 is advancing towards B's goal line and is very near the sideline. A1 dives toward the end zone, but is hit by B1 which causes him to land out of bounds beyond the goal-line extended. A1's last contact with the ground was short of the goal line. The ball breaks the plane of B's goal-line extended. **RULING:** Since A1 was not touching inbounds and was short of the goal line when he was hit, it is not a touchdown even though the ball did break the goal-line plane extended. The ball is spotted at the inbounds spot on the yard line where the foremost point of the ball crossed the sideline plane when A1 was driven out of bounds.

4.2.2 SITUATION J: With fourth down and 8 from the 50, A1 runs to B's 45-yard line where: (a) B1, in attempting to tackle A1, unsnaps A1's chin strap and play continues to the 40-yard line where A1 is finally downed; or (b) B1, in attempting to tackle A1, grasps the face mask/helmet opening and A1's helmet comes off; or (c) B1 contacts A1 at B's 46 and A1's helmet comes off and he subsequently fumbles the ball. **RULING:** In (a), play continues and it is a first down for A after enforcement of the face mask foul. In (b), the ball becomes dead at the spot A1's helmet came off and B is penalized for the face mask/helmet opening violation. In (c), the ball becomes dead at the spot where A1's helmet came off and because it was fourth down and the line to gain was not obtained, the ball goes over to B. The fumble is disregarded because it happened after the ball became dead and A1 must leave the field for one play (3-5-10d; 4-2-2k).

4.2.2 SITUATION K: In attempting to tackle A1, B1's helmet comes completely off. A1 does not go down and he runs for a touchdown. **RULING:** The score stands. Play is not stopped and the ball does not become dead if the helmet comes off any player other than the player in possession of the ball. B1 must leave the field for one play (3-5-10d; 4-2-2k).

◢ Rationale
The runner is in a particularly vulnerable state when his helmet comes off. Thus ruling the ball dead in that situation reduces potential risk for the runner.

7.4.3 SITUATION: A1 and B1 simultaneously gain possession of a live ball which is a: (a) legal forward pass and both players are touching inbounds; or (b) fumble by A1 on a running play. **RULING:** The down is ended in each situation. In (a), complete pass and the ball belongs to A at the spot of completion. In (b), the ball belongs to A at the spot of recovery (6-2-6; 7-5-4).

Ball Remains Dead
The ball remains dead and a down is not begun if a snap is attempted before the ball is ready for play, there is an illegal snap or other snap infraction, or a dead-ball foul occurs before a snap or free kick (3-6-2e; 4-1-6; 4-2-1; 7-1-4; 7-2-4; 10-1-2); or a player fails to properly wear legal or required player equipment when the ball is about to become live (3-6-2d). In those cases, a game official shall indicate the ball remains dead by sounding his whistle immediately (4-2-1).

Rationale

The rules stipulating that the ball must remain dead following a dead-ball foul were for the purpose of eliminating many undesirable situations. Before the rule was implemented, situations developed into broken plays and, all too often, double or multiple fouls resulted. For example, when B encroached the ball was permitted to become live, and A then committed a foul, a double foul resulted. If the foul by A were a major infraction, the resulting penalties were of an unequal yardage and, theoretically at least, gave an advantage to the team that, under other circumstances, would be penalized.

Loose Ball Becomes Dead

The ball becomes dead and the down is ended when a live ball goes out of bounds (4-2-2b); when any forward pass (legal or illegal) is incomplete (4-2-2c); or when any loose ball is on the ground motionless and no player attempts to secure possession (4-2-1e 2).

If a legal forward pass or snap in flight touches or is touched by anything inbounds other than a player, substitute, replaced player, an official, the ground or authorized equipment, the ball is dead and the down will be replayed (4-2-2e 3).

If a backward pass, fumble or illegal forward pass touches or is touched by anything inbounds other than a player, substitute, replaced player, an official, the ground or authorized equipment, the ball is dead and the team last in possession may choose to put the ball in play where possession was lost or replay the down (4-2-2e 3; 4-2-3b).

Loose Ball Becomes Dead: Case Play

4.1.5 SITUATION: A forward pass strikes: (a) a game official standing inbounds, after which it rebounds into the air and is caught by A1 or B1; or (b) a dog or a spectator inbounds. **RULING:** In (a), A1 or B1 has caught a live ball. Nothing has occurred to cause the ball to become dead. In (b), the ball becomes dead immediately and is administered under the provisions of the inadvertent-whistle rule with a replay of the down (4-2-2e; 4-2-3a).

Out of Bounds

A player or other person is out of bounds when any part of the person is touching anything, other than another player or game official, who is on or outside the sideline or end line (2-29-1).

A ball in player possession is out of bounds when the runner or the ball touches anything, other than another player or game official, who is on or outside a sideline or end line (2-29-2).

A loose ball is out of bounds when it touches anything, including a player or game official, that is out of bounds (2-29-3).

Out of Bounds: Case Plays

2.29.3 SITUATION: A free kick by K1 is touched by R1 on his 15-yard line and then it: (a) rolls out of bounds at R's 5-yard line; or (b) contacts a game official in the field of play and thereafter rolls out of bounds at the 5-yard line; or (c) contacts a game official who is straddling the sideline at the 5-yard line; or (d) contacts a game official in the end zone. **RULING:** The ball will be put in play by R from its 5-yard line in (a), (b) and (c). In (a), R1 was the last to touch the kick before it went out of bounds. In (b), the fact that the ball touched a game official who was inbounds does not change its status. In fact, this touching is ignored and therefore R1, in effect, was the last to touch the ball before it went out of bounds. In (c), when the loose ball touches a game official who is straddling the sideline, it causes the ball to be out of bounds and R1 was the last to touch it. In (d), the ball is dead when it breaks the goal-line plane and a touchback results (6-1-9; 8-5-3a).

4.3.3 SITUATION A: It is fourth down and the line to gain is B's 45-yard line. A1, running near the sideline, is blocked by B1 on the 46 and he: (a) travels several feet in the air landing out of bounds opposite B's 44 1/2-yard line; or (b) lands inbounds on B's 44 and slides out of bounds. **RULING:** In (a), the covering official must locate the spot where the ball crossed the sideline and then determine whether the foremost point of the ball was behind or beyond the line to gain when A1 crossed the plane of the sideline. In (b), it is first down and 10 for A from B's 44-yard line.

7.5.4 SITUATION D: A passed or fumbled ball is near a sideline. B1 gets the ball in his hands while his foot is on the sideline. **RULING:** The ball becomes dead when touched. Since touching precedes player possession, there is no "catch" or "recovery" (2-36-2).

Topic:
Clock Starts

The ball is ready for play when, after it has been placed for a down, the referee gives the ready-for-play signal. The 25-second count is to begin (2-35; 3-6-1).

Clock Starts On Snap

The clock shall start with the snap if the clock was stopped because the ball goes out of bounds; B or R is awarded a new series; either team is awarded a new series following a legal kick; the ball becomes dead behind the goal line; a legal or illegal forward pass is incomplete; a request for a charged or TV/radio time-out is granted; a period ends; a team attempts to consume time illegally; the penalty for a delay of game foul is accepted; a fair catch is made; or if a period begins with a snap, when the ball is legally snapped (3-4-1b; 3-4-3a-j).

In Simple Terms

The determination by the referee as to whether or not the act was intended to illegally conserve time must be applied using Rule 3-4-6.

Clock Starts On Snap: Case Plays

3.4.3 SITUATION A: During a scrimmage kick: (a) R1 signals for and makes a fair catch; or (b) R2 is contacted by K1 before he can attempt to catch the kick. **RULING:** In (a), the clock was stopped because of the fair catch. It will start when the ball is snapped, or if put in play by a free kick, when the ball is touched other than first touching by K. In (b), the action which caused the clock to be stopped was the foul by K1. When there is kick-catching interference, the offended team has a number of choices. If an awarded fair catch is accepted, the clock will start as in (a) (3-4-2b).

3.4.3 SITUATION C: Receiver A1 controls a pass while airborne near A's sideline. B1 contacts A1 (but does not carry him) who then lands out of bounds in possession of the ball. B1 does not drive the receiver backward from his forward progress. The covering official rules an incomplete pass. **RULING:** The clock is stopped because of the receiver being out of bounds; therefore, the pass is incomplete. The clock will start with the snap.

3.4.3 SITUATION D: With third and 10: (a) A1 fumbles the ball and B recovers, or (b) A1's pass is intercepted by B. When will the clock be restarted? **RULING:** Since a change of possession has occurred in both (a) and (b) and B is awarded a new series of downs, the clock will start on the snap.

3.6.3 SITUATION B: With less than a minute remaining in the game, the score is 21-20 in favor of B. The clock is running and the ball is on B's 10-yard line. An option play on third down gains 5 yards, but is short of a first down. Following the tackle: (a) B players are slow unpiling and a penalty marker is dropped; or (b) the tackler B1 holds A1 down for a few moments, but the covering official does not judge the action to be illegal. **RULING:** In (a), the delay penalty is a situation which automatically dictates the clock will not be started until the snap. In (b), even though B1 held A1 down momentarily, the clock will continue to run because no foul was called (3-4-3h). In some situations there is a delay in unpiling and no individual player or team is to blame. In such situations the referee is authorized to stop the clock momentarily so no more clock time than normal is used in getting the ball ready for play.

4.3.3 SITUATION B: A has third down and seven yards to gain at B's 30. A1 leaps near the sideline to attempt to catch a pass near B's 30-yard line. A1 is: (a) airborne trying to make the catch and is knocked backwards by B2 attempting to make the tackle and A1 lands outside the sideline at B's 32 or (b) airborne when he controls the ball attempting to complete the catch and is carried off the field by B2 landing out of bounds. **RULING:** In (a), the pass is incomplete and the clock should start on the snap. In (b), it is a catch and the clock should not stop. If the clock was stopped inadvertently by the covering official, it should be immediately restarted (2-15-1, 2; 4-3-2).

7.5.2 SITUATION G: In the last few seconds of a half, A1 completes a pass to A2 at B's 20-yard line. The ball is properly spotted and the referee marks it ready for play and signals the clock to start. In the rush and confusion to stop the clock, A's snapper and quarterback A1 are the only A players in legal position when the ball is snapped and legally "spiked" by A1. A foul for illegal formation occurs at the snap. **RULING:** The "spike" is legal. Since the spike is legal, the only applicable foul is for illegal formation. The reason for the clock stoppage was the incomplete forward pass; therefore, the clock shall start on the snap. The determination by the referee as to whether or not the act was intended to illegally conserve time must be applied using Rule 3-4-6 (7-5-2 Exception).

Clock Starts On Ready-For-Play

The clock shall start with the ready-for-play signal on a down beginning with a snap if the clock was stopped for any reason other than because the ball goes out of bounds; B is awarded a new series; either team is awarded a new series following a legal kick; the ball becomes dead behind the goal line; a legal or illegal forward pass is incomplete; a request for a charged or TV/radio time-out is granted; a period ends; a team attempts to consume time illegally; the penalty for a delay of game foul is accepted; if a period begins with a snap, when the ball is legally snapped; or for an untimed down (3-4-2, 3-4-3).

Clock Starts On Ready-for-Play: Case Plays

3.4.2 SITUATION A: Near the end of the second period, there is a false start by A1 clearly for the purpose of stopping the clock. When will the clock be restarted? **RULING:** Because the foul was the only reason for stopping the clock, it will be restarted on the ready-for-play signal following the enforcement of the penalty.

3.4.2 SITUATION D: K11 punts the ball from a fourth and 10 situation. R1 catches the kick and returns 10 yards. During the down, but prior to the catch, K3 holds R2. R accepts the penalty. **RULING:** After enforcement, the clock starts on the ready-for-play signal (3-4-2b(3)).

4.3.3 SITUATION B: A has third down and seven yards to gain at B's 30. A1 leaps near the sideline to attempt to catch a pass near B's 30-yard line. A1 is: (a) airborne trying to make the catch and is knocked backwards by B2 attempting to make the tackle and A1 lands outside the sideline at B's 32 or (b) airborne when he controls the ball attempting to complete the catch and is carried off the field by B2 landing out of bounds. **RULING:** In (a), the pass is incomplete and the clock should start on the snap. In (b), it is a catch and the clock should not stop. If the clock was stopped inadvertently by the covering official, it should be immediately restarted (2-15-1, 2; 4-3-2).

Topic:
Clock Stops

The clock shall be stopped when the down ends following a foul; an official's time-out is taken; a charged or TV/radio time-out is granted; the period ends; the ball is out of bounds; a score or touchback occurs; a fair catch is made; an inadvertent whistle is sounded; or an airborne receiver is carried out of bounds, unless the receiver is carried backwards and his forward progress was stopped inbounds (3-4-4a-j).

Topic:
Delay of Game

Action or inaction which prevents promptness in putting the ball in play is delay of game. This includes failure to snap or free kick within 25 seconds after the ball is ready for play; unnecessarily carrying the ball after it has become dead; a coach-referee conference after all the permissible charged time-outs for the coach's team have been used, and during which the referee is requested to reconsider the application of a rule and no change in the ruling results; failure to properly wear legal or required player equipment when the ball is about to become live; snapping or free kicking the ball before it is marked ready for play; any other conduct which unduly prolongs the game or failure to unpile from an opponent in a timely manner (3-6-2a-g). A team shall play within two minutes after being ordered to do so by the referee (3-6-3). Game management is responsible for clearing the field of play and the end zones at the beginning of each half so play may begin at the scheduled time (3-6-4).

Delay of Game: Penalty

5 yards. Signals 7 and 21. Failure of a team to play within two minutes after being ordered to do so by the referee results in forfeiture (3-6-3).

Delay of Game: Case Plays

3.4.3 SITUATION B: There are 40 seconds to go in the first period when A is faced with a punting situation against a strong wind while deep in its own territory. After running 25 seconds off the clock, A is called for delay of game. **RULING:** If B accepts, A will be penalized 5 yards and the clock will not start until the snap (3-6-3).

3.6.2 SITUATION B: (a) A1's forward progress is stopped, but he continues to attempt to break free despite repeated blasts of the whistle by the covering official; or (b) B1 intercepts, is tackled, and then intentionally runs off the field with the ball. **RULING:** Delay of game in (a) and unsportsmanlike conduct in (b) (9-5-2).

> ## Fundamental I-8
>
> Possession of a live ball in the opponent's end zone is always a touchdown.

3.6.3 SITUATION B: With less than a minute remaining in the game, the score is 21-20 in favor of B. The clock is running and the ball is on B's 10-yard line. An option play on third down gains 5 yards, but is short of a first down. Following the tackle: (a) B players are slow unpiling and a penalty marker is dropped; or (b) the tackler B1 holds A1 down for a few moments, but the covering official does not judge the action to be illegal.

RULING: In (a), the delay penalty is a situation which automatically dictates the clock will not be started until the snap. In (b), even though B1 held A1 down momentarily, the clock will continue to run because no foul was called (3-4-3h). In some situations there is a delay in unpiling and no individual player or team is to blame. In such situations the referee is authorized to stop the clock momentarily so no more clock time than normal is used in getting the ball ready for play.

Topic:
Touchdown

It is the object of the game for one team to carry or pass the ball across the opponent's goal line or to kick the ball through the opponent's goal by a place kick or drop kick. The game is won by the team which accumulates the most points (1-1-1). Points are scored by touchdown, successful try, field goal or safety (1-1-2).

A touchdown is worth 6 points (8-1).

Possession of a live ball in the opponent's end zone is always a touchdown (8-2-1).

It is a touchdown when a runner advances from the field of play so that the ball penetrates the vertical plane of the opponent's goal line; a loose ball is caught or recovered by a player while the ball is on or behind his opponent's goal line; or when a backward pass or fumble is declared dead in the end zone of the opponent of the player who threw the backward pass or fumbled while no player is in possession (other than because of an inadvertent whistle) (8-2-1a-c).

Touchdown: Case Plays
2.26.3 SITUATION: Runner A1 is advancing towards B's goal line and is very near the sideline. A1 advances into B's end zone while holding the ball outside the sideline plane. The ball breaks the plane of B's goal-line extended. **RULING:** It is a touchdown because A1 was touching inbounds when the ball broke the plane of the goal-line extended.

7.5.4 SITUATION A: Airborne A1 and B1 simultaneously gain possession of a legal forward pass near the goal line and return to the ground where: (a) they alight in the end zone with the ball; or (b) A1 lands in the end zone and B1 in the field of play inbounds; or (c) B1 comes down in the end zone and A1 lands in the field of play. **RULING:** It is a touchdown in (a). In (b) and (c), the ball becomes dead and the pass is complete at the yard line through the foremost point of the ball when the players contacted the ground inbounds. If the ball has penetrated the plane of the goal line in either (b) or (c), it is a touchdown.

7.5.4 SITUATION B: A pass from A1 is possessed by A2 while he is in the air above B's end zone. A2 loses control when he is contacted by B1 while in the air. The ball: (a) falls to the ground; or (b) is caught by eligible A3 in B's end zone; or (c) is intercepted and downed by B2 in the end zone. **RULING:** In (a), the pass is incomplete. In (b), it is a touchdown and in (c), it is a touchback (8-2-1b; 8-5-3c).

7.5.4 SITUATION G: A8, in B's end zone, leaps in the air to catch a pass and is contacted by B2 forcing A8 to come down inbounds on B's 1-yard line where he is downed. **RULING:** Touchdown, since A8's forward progress was stopped over B's end zone by B2's contact. Even though the catch was not made until A8 came down inbounds, his forward progress was stopped by B2's contact resulting in A possessing the live ball in its opponent's end zone, hence, a touchdown.

7.5.4 SITUATION H: A pass from A1 is thrown near the intersection of the sideline and the goal line. A2, running toward the goal line, leaps and possesses the pass at the 3-yard line and is forcibly: (a) grasped from behind and carried by B1 so that first contact with the ground by A2 is out of bounds 1 yard beyond the goal line; or (b) tackled from behind by B1 so that A2 first contacts the ground in the end zone. **RULING:** In (a) and (b), it is a touchdown (2-4-1, 2-15-1, 2; 8-2-1).

8.2.1 SITUATION: Runner A10 dives into the pylon at the intersection of the goal line and sidelines and the ball breaks the plane of the goal line. **RULING:** Touchdown. Assuming the pylon was placed properly, the ball broke the plane of the goal line prior to the touching of the pylon.

8.5.1 SITUATION A: R1 returns the second half kickoff to K's 10 and fumbles: (a) the ball rolls into K's end zone; or (b) K1 attempts to recover and forces the ball into his own end zone. In both cases, the ball is in K's end zone and no player of either team attempts to recover. The referee, after waiting a few seconds, sounds his whistle. **RULING:** It is a touchdown for R both in (a) and (b) as the fumbling team retains possession (8-1-2c; 8-5-2b).
8.5.1 SITUATION B: It is first down and 10 on A's 12. A fumble by A1 is still rolling slowly on A's 4-yard line. During an attempt to recover the

ball, A2 pushes B1 into the ball causing the ball to roll across the goal line where it is recovered by B2 who is downed immediately. **RULING:** It is a touchdown (2-13-1; 7-4-2; 8-5-2b).

Topic:
Two-Point Try

After a touchdown, the scoring team shall attempt a try during which the ball is snapped from a spot designated by A anywhere between the hash marks on B's 3-yard line. This involves a scrimmage down which is neither numbered nor timed (8-3-1).

During a try, A may score two points from what would be a touchdown under rules governing play at other times during the game. Only A may score on a try (8-1; 8-3-3). If during a successful try, a loss of down foul by A occurs, there is no score and no replay (8-3-4). If during an unsuccessful try, a foul by A occurs, the penalty is obviously declined, the results of the play stand and there is no replay. If B fouls, and the penalty is accepted, the down is replayed after enforcement. If a double foul occurs, the down shall be replayed (8-3-6, 8-3-7).

If a touchdown is scored during the last down of the fourth period, the try shall not be attempted unless the point(s) would affect the outcome of the game or playoff qualifying (8-3-1 Exception).

The try begins when the ball is ready for play. It ends when B secures possession; the try is successful; or the ball becomes dead for any other reason (8-3-2a-d). When a try is replayed, the snap may be from any point between the inbounds lines on the yard line through the spot of the ball (8-3-8). After a successful try, the opponent of the scoring team shall designate which team will kick off (8-3-9).

Did You Know? The two-point try was adopted as a means of adding strategy and excitement to the game.

Two-Point Try: Case Plays
8.3.1 SITUATION: A has a huge lead and scores another touchdown in the third period, and the captain of A informs the referee that his team does not wish to attempt the try. **RULING:** There is no choice. A shall attempt a try, or at least snap the ball.

8.3.2 SITUATION C: During a try, A1 completes a pass to A2 in the end zone and: (a) ineligible A3 was illegally beyond the neutral zone; or (b) A4 interfered with B1; or (c) B2 interfered with A2. **RULING:** In (a), if the 5-yard penalty is accepted, the try will be repeated. In (b), if the 15-yard penalty is accepted, the try will be repeated. In (c), A undoubtedly will accept the result of the play and enforce the penalty from the succeeding spot (7-5-10 Penalty; 7-5-12 Penalty; 8-3-5).

8.3.5 SITUATION B: During a successful two-point try: (a) B1 roughs the passer; or (b) B2 holds tight end A8. **RULING:** In both (a) and (b), Team A may accept the score and have the penalty assessed from the succeeding spot.

8.3.5 SITUATION C: During a successful two-point try, B1 is flagged for pass interference against A1. After the untimed down is over, A1 taunts B1. **RULING:** Team A may accept the score and have the penalty enforced at the succeeding spot. However, B may accept the penalty for the dead ball foul by A, and have 15 yards marked off from the spot where the ball is placed after enforcement of B's penalty. The ball would then be free-kicked from K's 40-yard line.

Topic:
Safety

A safety results in two points being awarded to the opponent (8-1).

It is a safety when a runner carries the ball from the field of play to or across his own goal line and it becomes dead there in his team's possession; a player who is either in the field of play or in his end zone forces a loose ball from the field of play to or across his goal line by his pass, fumble, snap or by a new force to a grounded loose ball with his muff or bat or illegal kick (when the penalty is declined), provided the ball becomes dead there in his team's possession (including when the ball is declared dead with no player in possession), or the ball is out of bounds when it becomes dead on or behind their goal line (does not apply to a legal forward pass which becomes incomplete); a player on offense commits any foul for which the penalty is accepted and enforcement is from a spot in his end zone; or a player throws an illegal forward pass from his end zone and the penalty is declined in a situation which leaves him in possession at the spot of the illegal pass and with the ball having been forced into the end zone by the passing team (8-5-2a-c, 10-5-4).

A safety on a try results in one point being awarded to A (8-1).

After a safety, the team whose goal line is involved shall put the ball in play anywhere between the hash marks by a free kick. Unless moved by penalty, K's free-kick line is its 20-yard line (6-1-1b; 8-5-4).

Safety: Case Plays

4.2.3 SITUATION D: A1 throws a forward pass from his own 40-yard line. B1 intercepts on his 2-yard line and circles back into his end zone. While B1 is in the end zone, the covering official inadvertently sounds his whistle. **RULING:** Since B1 is in possession, B has the option of accepting the results of the play at the time of the whistle or asking for a replay of the down. Since the result of the play would be a safety, B would normally chose to replay the down (4-2-3c; 8-5-2a).

5.3.4 SITUATION B: A1 receives the snap behind his own goal line. A1 advances, but is tackled and the ball becomes dead with its foremost point in the field of play, but part of the ball is in the end zone. **RULING:** Safety. To avoid a safety, the ball must be advanced completely out of the end zone with no part of it touching the goal line (8-5-2).

8.3.3 SITUATION A: During a try, a fumble by A1 is nearly at rest on the 3-yard line when a muff by B1 is judged by the game official to be a new force causing the ball to go into B's end zone where B2 recovers and: (a) downs the ball in the end zone; or (b) advances to his 10-yard line. **RULING:** The try ends and the ball becomes dead when B2 recovers. In any ordinary down, such a dead ball in the end zone would be a safety, therefore, one point is scored for A in both (a) and (b) (4-2-2i; 8-1; 8-5-2b).

8.3.3 SITUATION B: During a non-kick try, A1 fumbles the ball, and in scrambling to recover the ball and avoid defenders, retreats into his own end zone where he is tackled. **RULING:** The ball is dead and no points are awarded. B cannot score on a try.

8.5.1 SITUATION B: It is first down and 10 on A's 12. A fumble by A1 is still rolling slowly on A's 4-yard line. During an attempt to recover the ball, A2 pushes B1 into the ball causing the ball to roll across the goal line where it is recovered by: (a) A3 who is downed there; or (b) A4 who advances to A's 15; or (c) B2 who is downed immediately. **RULING:** Safety in (a). In (b), it is A's ball on the 15 and the next down is second and 7. In (c), it is a touchdown (2-13-1; 7-4-2; 8-5-2b).

Did You Know? A safety has always been worth two points. It is the only scoring play for which the number of points awarded has never changed.

8.5.2 SITUATION D: Fourth and 15 for A from its own 8-yard line. A1 is in punt formation and receives the snap in his end zone, but fumbles the ball. A1 quickly recovers and throws a forward pass to ineligible A2, who is also in the end zone. A2 muffs the ball and it falls incomplete. **RULING:** If B accepts the penalty for A2's illegal touching, it results in a safety. If B declines the penalty for the foul by A2, the result is B's ball first and goal from A's 8-yard line (5-1-3c; 7-5-13 Penalty; 8-5-2c; 10-5-5).

8.5.2 SITUATION E: B1 intercepts a pass on B's 4-yard line with his momentum taking him directly toward his goal line: (a) B1 fumbles on the 1-yard line, or (b) B1 is contacted by A2 and the ball comes loose on the 2-yard line. In both cases B2 recovers the ball in B's end zone and is downed there. **RULING:** It is a safety in both (a) and (b). Once B1 gained possession in the field of play, he is responsible for the fumble which is the force which put the ball into the end zone. Had B1 not fumbled, the momentum exception would have been in effect.

8.5.2 SITUATION F: B1 intercepts on his own 4-yard line and his momentum takes him into B's end zone. (a) B1 advances out of the end zone and runs to his own 35-yard line; or (b) B1 runs out of the end zone then circles back into it and is downed there; or (c) B1 is hit and fumbles and A1 falls on the loose ball in the end zone; or (d) B2 holds A1 in the end zone as B1 is downed there. **RULING:** Legal advance in (a). In (b), it is a safety. Once B1 advances out of the end zone as in (a) or (b), the exception is canceled and action thereafter dictates the result of the play. Touchdown for A in (c). In (d), the foul by B2 occurred in the end zone behind the basic spot resulting in a safety (7-5-4; 8-2-1; 8-5-2a Exception; 10-4-3; 10-6).

10.5.2 SITUATION: A's ball second and 5 from its own 9-yard line. A2 muffs the handoff and the ball rolls into A's end zone. A1 picks up the ball and is immediately tackled by B3 in the end zone. B3 grasped A1 by the face mask/helmet opening in making the tackle. **RULING:** If A declines the penalty, this play would result in a safety. If the penalty is accepted, it will be enforced from the goal line, making it first and 10 for A from its 15-yard line (8-5-2b).

10.5.4 SITUATION A: A's ball second and 5 from its own 9-yard line. A2 fumbles the ball on his own 5-yard line and the ball rolls into the end zone. A1 recovers the ball in the end zone and is downed in the end zone, but B3 held A3 while the ball was loose. **RULING:** A undoubtedly will accept the penalty, because to decline would result in a safety. The foul occurred during a loose-ball play, therefore, the previous spot will be the enforcement spot, making it first and 10 for A from its own 19-yard line.

Topic:
Force and Touchbacks

Force is the result of energy exerted by a player which provides movement of the ball. The term force is used only in connection with the goal line and in only one direction, i.e., from the field of play into the end zone. Initial force results from a carry, fumble, pass or snap. After a fumble or backward pass has been grounded, a new force may result from a bat, or a muff (2-13-1). The muffing or batting of a pass or fumble in flight is not considered a new force (2-13-3).

Batting is intentionally slapping or striking the ball with the arm or hand (2-2). A muff is the touching of a loose ball by a player in an unsuccessful attempt to secure possession (2-27). A fumble is any loss of player possession other than by handing, passing or legal kick (2-18).

It is a touchback when a forward pass is intercepted in B's end zone and becomes dead there in B's possession (8-5-3d).

The team whose goal line is involved in a touchback shall put the ball in play anywhere between the hash marks on its 20-yard line by a snap (8-5-4).

Touchbacks on Forward Passes: Case Plays

7.5.4 SITUATION B: A pass from A1 is possessed by A2 while he is in the air above B's end zone. A2 loses control when he is contacted by B1 while in the air. The ball is intercepted and downed by B2 in the end zone. **RULING:** It is a touchback (8-2-1b; 8-5-3c).

7.5.4 SITUATION E: B1 leaps in the air over his 2-yard line and has A's pass in his grasp. He returns to the ground in his end zone inbounds. **RULING:** B1's interception was not completed until he returned to the ground inbounds. He now possesses a live ball in his own end zone and may attempt to run it out or down it in the end zone for a touchback. Momentum is not involved.

8.5.1 SITUATION E: A1's forward pass is intercepted in B's end zone by B1 who attempts to advance, but is downed there. B2 clips at B's 3: (a) during B1's run, or (b) after B1 is downed. **RULING:** It is a touchback in both (a)

and (b) and the basic spot is the succeeding spot. In (a), it is first and 10 for B from B's 11/2 yard line. In (b), the dead-ball foul will be penalized from B's 20 resulting in first and 10 from B's 10-yard line (8-5-3d; 10-4-4d).

10.4.4 SITUATION B: A1 throws a pass from B's 22-yard line. B1 intercepts the pass in his own end zone and is tackled prior to leaving the end zone. During the run, B2 holds A2 at B's 10-yard line. **RULING:** The basic enforcement spot is the 20-yard line. If the penalty is accepted, it will be enforced from the spot of the foul. B will have a first and 10 from its own 5-yard line. If the penalty is declined, it will be B's first and 10 from B's 20-yard line.

Touchbacks on Bats, Fumbles, Muffs and Backward Passes

It is a touchback when a fumble is the force, or a muff or bat of a backward pass or a fumble after either has touched the ground is the new force, which sends the ball to or across the opponent's goal line and provided such opponent is in team possession or the ball is out of bounds when it becomes dead on or behind its goal line (8-5-3c).

If a player provides the force to a fumble or a backward pass that goes out of bounds behind the opponent's goal line, the result is a touchback (7-4-4).

The team whose goal line is involved in a touchback shall put the ball in play anywhere between the hash marks on its 20-yard line by a snap (8-5-4).

Touchbacks on Bats, Fumbles, Muffs and Backward Passes: Case Plays

8.5.2 SITUATION C: K1's punt is blocked on K's 5-yard line and the ball is slowly rolling near the goal line. R1 attempts to recover and just barely touches the ball. The ball then rolls into the end zone where K2 falls on it. **RULING:** The covering official will have to judge whether or not a new force resulted from R1's touch. The covering official must decide whether the original force was such that the ball could have gone into the end zone regardless of the muff. If the covering official has doubt, he will rule that the force was supplied by the kick, thus resulting in a safety. If the covering official rules R1 supplied the force, it is a touchback (8-5-2b).
8.5.3 SITUATION A: With fourth down and 7 from K's 10, K1 punts from the end zone. The kick is partially blocked and is just barely moving at K's 2-yard line when R1's muff provides a new force which moves the ball into, and out of, the end zone. **RULING:** Touchback. Because it was the new force by R1 which caused the ball to go out of K's end zone, the result is a touchback instead of a safety (2-13-1; 8-5-3b).

8.5.3 SITUATION C: B1 intercepts a forward pass in his end zone and then passes backward to B2 who: (a) muffs the ball so that it goes out of bounds across the sideline behind the goal line; or (b) bats the ball over the end line. **RULING:** In both (a) and (b), the force which put the ball into the end zone was the pass by A1. When B2 muffed the backward pass out of bounds in the end zone or batted the backward pass in flight so that it went over the end line, the result is a touchback. It will be first and 10 for B from its 20-yard line (8-5-3c, 9-7-2).

10.4.5 SITUATION I: K1's scrimmage kick is blocked on K's 5-yard line and is rolling away from K's goal line when R1 muffs the ball into K's end zone (applies a new force to a grounded kick). K2 recovers the ball and attempts to advance, but is downed in the end zone. During K2's run: (a) R1 holds K3 in the end zone; or (b) K3 holds R1 in the end zone. **RULING:** In (a), it is a touchback and the basic spot is the 20-yard line. In (b), since the foul is in the end zone, it is a safety.

Topic:
Momentum Exception

It is not a safety when a defensive player intercepts an opponent's forward pass; intercepts or recovers an opponent's fumble or backward pass between his 5-yard line and the goal line, and his original momentum carries him into the end zone where the ball is declared dead in his team's possession or it goes out of bounds in the end zone. In that case, the ball belongs to the team in possession at the spot where the pass or fumble was intercepted or recovered (8-5-2a Exception).

When the momentum exception applies and the ball becomes dead behind the goal line, if the penalty for a foul by either team is accepted, the end of the run is the spot where the kick, fumble or pass was caught or recovered. The penalty is enforced under the all-but-one principle. If momentum is not involved, the end of the run is the goal line.

Momentum Exception: Case Plays
7.5.4 SITUATION E: B1 leaps in the air over his 2-yard line and has A's pass in his grasp. He returns to the ground in his end zone inbounds. **RULING:** B1's interception was not completed until he returned to the ground inbounds. He now possesses a live ball in his own end zone and may attempt to run it out or down it in the end zone for a touchdown. Momentum is not involved.

7.5.4 SITUATION F: B1 leaps in the air over his 2-yard line and has A's pass in his grasp. He returns to the ground on his 1-yard line and his momentum carries him back into his end zone where he is downed. **RULING:** Since B's interception was made in the field of play and his momentum carried him into his end zone where he is downed, the momentum exception is in effect and the spot of the interception, B's 1-yard line, is the spot from which B will start its series.

8.5.2 SITUATION F: B1 intercepts on his own 4-yard line and his momentum takes him into B's end zone. (a) B1 advances out of the end zone and runs to his own 35-yard line; or (b) B1 runs out of the end zone then circles back into it and is downed there; or (c) B1 is hit and fumbles and A1 falls on the loose ball in the end zone; or (d) B2 holds A1 in the end zone as B1 is downed there. **RULING:** Legal advance in (a). In (b), it is a safety. Once B1 advances out of the end zone as in (a) or (b), the exception is canceled and action thereafter dictates the result of the play. Touchdown for A in (c). In (d), the foul by B2 occurred in the end zone behind the basic spot resulting in a safety (7-5-4; 8-2-1; 8-5-2a Exception; 10-4-3; 10-6).

8.5.2 SITUATION G: B1, while in full stride at B's 2-yard line (a) intercepts a backward pass; (b) intercepts a fumble; or (c) recovers a grounded fumble or backward pass and his momentum carries him into his end zone where he is downed. **RULING:** In (a), (b) and (c) the ball would belong to B at the spot where the backward pass or fumble was intercepted or recovered as the momentum exception applies.

Rationale

For simplicity, the momentum exception applies to all types of loose balls. Also, backward passes, fumbles and muffs need only be recovered — not necessarily caught — for the rule to apply.

Topic:
Forward Progress

Forward progress is the end of advancement of the ball, toward the opponent's goal, in a runner's possession or the forward-most point of the ball when it is fumbled out of bounds and it determines the dead-ball spot (2-15-1).

When an airborne player makes a catch, forward progress is the furthest point of advancement after he possesses the ball if contacted by a defender (2-15-2).

The ball becomes dead and the down is ended when a runner goes out of bounds, is held so his forward progress is stopped or allows any part of his person other than hand or foot to touch the ground (4-2-2a).

An offensive player shall not push, pull or lift the runner to assist his forward progress (9-1).

Forward Progress: Case Plays

2.41.3 SITUATION: Runner A1 is tackled and one knee contacts the ground, but he holds the ball several feet forward. **RULING:** The dead-ball spot is below the ball's foremost point in the direction of the opponent's end line the instant the ball becomes dead by rule (because knee touched the ground), or is declared dead by a game official.

3.4.3 SITUATION C: Receiver A1 controls a pass while airborne near A's sideline. B1 contacts A1 (but does not carry him) who then lands out of bounds in possession of the ball. B1 does not drive the receiver backward from his forward progress. The covering official rules an incomplete pass. **RULING:** The clock is stopped because of the receiver being out of bounds; therefore, the pass is incomplete. The clock will start with the snap.

7.5.4 SITUATION G: A8, in B's end zone, leaps in the air to catch a pass and is contacted by B2 forcing A8 to come down inbounds on B's 1-yard line where he is downed. **RULING:** Touchdown, since A8's forward progress was stopped over B's end zone by B2's contact. Even though the catch was not made until A8 came down inbounds, his forward progress was stopped by B2's contact resulting in A possessing the live ball in its opponent's end zone, hence, a touchdown.

7.5.4 SITUATION I: Airborne A1 jumps high in an attempt to catch a legal forward pass. While still in the air, he is tackled by B1 and held momentarily without touching the ground before he is carried (a) backward toward A's goal line, or (b) forward toward B's goal line. He then lands out of bounds with the ball. **RULING:** In (a) and (b), completed pass as forward progress was stopped. The ball is dead at the yard line where the forward progress of the receiver was stopped (2-4-1, 4-2-2a).

Topic 4
Contact

PlayPic®

Key Terms

Blocking is obstructing an opponent by contacting him with any part of the blocker's body (2-3-1).

An offensive blocker is a player who is blocking or in position to block by being between the potential tackler and the runner (2-32-4).

The frame of the blocker's body is the front of the body at or below the shoulders (2-3-2b 2). The frame of the opponent's body is at the shoulders or below other than the back (2-3-2b 3).

A runner is a player who is in possession of a live ball or is simulating possession of a live ball (2-32-13). When a player simulates possession of the ball, reasonable allowance may be made for failure of the defense to discover the deception. This does not cancel the responsibility of any defensive player to exercise reasonable caution in avoiding any unnecessary contact (2-3-5 NOTE).

A passer is a player who throws a legal forward pass. He continues to be a passer until the legal forward pass ends or until he moves to participate in the play (2-32-11).

A kicker is any player who legally punts, drop kicks or place kicks. A player becomes a kicker when his knee, lower leg or foot makes contact with the ball. He continues to be the kicker until he has had reasonable opportunity to regain his balance (2-32-8). A holder is a player who controls the ball on the ground or on a kicking tee for a kickoff or place kick (2-32-7).

A snapper is the player who is facing his opponent's goal line with his shoulders approximately parallel thereto and who snaps the ball. In a scrimmage-kick formation, the snapper remains a snapper until he has had a reasonable opportunity to regain his balance and protect himself or until he blocks or moves to otherwise participate in the play (2-32-14).

Topic:
Blocking During a Free Kick

No member of the kicking team shall initiate contact to (block) an opponent on a free kick until the legal kick has traveled 10 yards; the kicking team is eligible to recover a free-kicked ball; or the receiving team initiates a block within the neutral zone (9-3-8a through c).

Illegal Block by K: Penalty

10 yards from the previous spot. Signal 43.

Blocking by K: Case Plays

9.3.8 SITUATION A: During a free kick (including an onside kick attempt), K1 initiates contact against R1 prior to the ball traveling past the receiving team's restraining line (10 yards). No member of R had initiated a block against K in the neutral zone. **RULING:** Live ball foul, illegal block. If the foul is accepted, the penalty is enforced from the previous spot.

9.3.8 SITUATION B: During a free kick (including an onside kick attempt): (a) R touches the ball prior to it traveling 10 yards after which K contacts R and recovers the ball; (b) after the ball travels 10 yards, K contacts R prior to R touching the ball; (c) after the ball touches the ground and travels 10 yards, K contacts R prior to recovering the ball; (d) after R initiates a block against K in the neutral zone, K recovers the ball; or (e) R and K contact each other approximately the same time prior to the ball traveling 10 yards. **RULING:** Legal recovery by K in (a), (b), (c) and (d). In (e), game officials should be guided by the thought that when in doubt, R initiated the contact and, therefore, this would be no foul.

Topic:
Defenseless Player

A defenseless player is a player who, because of his physical position and focus of concentration, is especially vulnerable to injury (2-32-16).

9.4.3 COMMENT Is there suggested guidance or rules coverage on a "defenseless player" who should be protected from unnecessary roughness? Yes, defenseless players are especially vulnerable to potential injury. Game officials must diligently observe all action and watch for contact against players who are deemed defenseless. Examples include, but are not limited to: (a) A quarterback moving down the line of scrimmage who has handed or pitched the ball to a teammate, and then makes no attempt to participate further in the play; (b) A kicker who is in the act of kicking the ball, or who has not had a reasonable amount of time to regain his balance after the kick; (c) A passer who is in the act of throwing the ball, or who has not had a reasonable length of time to participate in the play again after releasing the ball; (d) A pass receiver whose concentration is on the ball and the contact by the defender is unrelated to attempting to catch the ball; (e)

A pass receiver who has clearly relaxed when he has missed the pass or feels he can no longer catch the pass; (f) A kick returner attempting to catch a kick; (g) A kick receiver who is immediately contacted after touching the ball; (h) A player on the ground; (i) Any player who has relaxed once the ball has become dead; (j) A player who receives a blind side block; (k) A ball carrier already in the grasp of an opponent and whose forward progress has been stopped; and (l) Any player who is obviously out of the play. The game official must draw distinction between contact necessary to make a legal block or tackle, making unnecessary contact on a defenseless player and targeting any player at any time (2-32-16; 9-4-3i(3)).

◪ Rationale

The committee added the definition of a defenseless player in an attempt to continue concentrating on risk minimization. A defenseless player is a player who, because of his physical position and focus of concentration, is especially vulnerable to injury.

Topic:
Free-Blocking Zone

The free-blocking zone is a rectangular area extending laterally 4 yards either side of the spot of the snap and 3 yards behind each line of scrimmage. A player is in the free-blocking zone when any part of his body is in the zone at the snap (2-17-1).

The free-blocking zone disintegrates and the exception for a player to block below the waist and/or the exception for an offensive lineman to block in the back is not to continue after the ball has left the zone (2-17-2, 3).

Blocking below the waist is making initial contact below the waist from the front or side against an opponent other than a runner. Contact with an opponent's hand(s) below the waist that continues into the body below the waist is considered blocking below the waist. Blocking below the waist applies only when the opponent has one or both feet on the ground (2-3-7). Blocking below the waist is permitted in the free-blocking zone when all players involved in the blocking are on the line of scrimmage and in the zone at the snap and the contact is in the zone (2-17-2a-b).

Clipping is a block against an opponent when the initial contact is from behind, at or below the waist, and not against a player who is a runner or pretending to be a runner (2-5-1; 9-3-6).

Blocking in the back is a block against an opponent when the initial contact is in the opponent's back, inside the shoulders and below the helmet and above the waist, and not against a player who is a runner or pretending to be a runner. Blocking in the back is permitted in the free-blocking zone by offensive linemen who are on the line of scrimmage and in the zone at the snap, against defensive players who are in the zone at the snap and the contact is in the zone (2-5-2; 2-17-3a-c).

◪ Rationale

Limiting the amount of a time players may block below the waist minimizes risk.

Free-Blocking Zone: Case Plays

*2.17.2 SITUATION A: A1 is legally in motion at the snap: (a) within the free-blocking zone, or (b) outside the free-blocking zone. In (a), A1 blocks B1 below the waist within the free-blocking zone. In (b), A1 comes into the free-blocking zone and blocks B1 above the waist and in the back. **RULING:** It is an illegal block in both (a) and (b). In (a), this is blocking below the waist and in (b) it is blocking in the back. The offensive blocker must be on the line of scrimmage at the snap to be able to legally block below the waist (2-17-3, 9-3-2, 5 Penalty).

2.17.2 SITUATION B: After the snap A1, an offensive lineman in the free-blocking zone at the snap, blocks B1 then disengages and blocks B2 below the waist before the ball has left the zone. Both B1 and B2 were in the zone and on the line of scrimmage at the snap. The contact takes place in the free-blocking zone. **RULING:** It is legal for A1 to block below the waist on his second block since the ball is still in the zone (9-3-2).

2.17.2 SITUATION C: Back A9 is lined up behind quarterback A8 within the free-blocking zone. As A8 drops back to pass, A9 blocks B7, who was in the free-blocking zone at the snap, below the waist. **RULING:** Illegal block by A9. An offensive player must be on the line of scrimmage and in the free-blocking zone at the snap in order to block a defensive player below the waist who was also on the line of scrimmage and in the free-blocking zone at the snap (9-3-2).

2.17.2 SITUATION D: Linebacker B7 is in the free-blocking zone, but off the line of scrimmage. B7 blocks A8 below the waist. **RULING:** Illegal block. In order for a block below the waist to be legal, both the blocker and the person being blocked must be on the line of scrimmage and in the free-blocking zone.

2.17.2 SITUATION E: A1 is in shotgun formation, lined up seven yards behind the line of scrimmage ready to receive the snap. Immediately after the snap to A1, (a) A2 immediately drops and blocks B1 below the waist or (b) A2 rises, and slightly retreats as if to go in traditional pass blocking protection, but then dives and blocks B1 below the waist. Both A2 and B1 were in the zone and on the line of scrimmage at the snap. The contact between A2 and B1 takes place in the free-blocking zone. **RULING:** It is a legal block in (a) and an illegal block below the waist in (b). It is legal for A2 to block B1 below the waist if the contact is made immediately following the snap. Any later, and the ball is considered to have left the free-blocking zone and the block is illegal.

*9.3.6 SITUATION A: A1 is on the line of scrimmage and in the free-blocking zone at the snap. Immediately following the snap, he drops back one step, moves three steps inside and while still in the free-blocking zone, clips B2 who was on the line of scrimmage, in the free-blocking zone at the snap and the ball had not left the free-blocking zone. **RULING:** Illegal block (clipping).

Topic:
Legal Blocking

Blocking by a player either on offense or defense is legal unless it is kick-catching interference as in 6-5-6, forward-pass interference as in 7-5-10 or a personal foul as in 9-4 (9-3-1).

Any player may push, pull or ward off an opponent in an actual attempt to get at the runner or a loose ball if such contact is not pass interference, a personal foul or illegal use of hands (2-3-4c; 2-3-5b).

The closed- or cupped-hand technique is a legal method of blocking. In that technique, the elbows may be inside or outside the shoulders, the hands must be closed or cupped with the palms not facing the opponent and the forearms are extended no more than 45 degrees from the body (2-3-2a 1-3).

Fundamental VIII-1

Blocking by either team is permissible, unless it is kick-catching interference, a personal foul, or an illegal block.

The open-hand technique is also a legal method of blocking. In that technique, the hand(s) shall be in advance of the elbow, inside the frame of the blocker's body and inside the frame of the opponent's body, except when the opponent turns his back to the blocker during the block or after the blocker is committed to his charge; at or below the shoulders of the blocker and the opponent, except when the opponent squats, ducks or submarines during the block or after the blocker is committed to his charge; and the hands shall be open, when the palm(s) are facing the frame of the opponent or when the forearms are extended beyond the 45 degree angle from the body (2-3-2b 1-5).

A defensive player may also use unlocked hands, hand or arm to ward off an opponent who is blocking him or is attempting to block him (2-3-5a).

When a player simulates possession of the ball, reasonable allowance may be made for failure of the defense to discover the deception (2-3-5 NOTE).

A runner may use hands or arms to ward off or push any player (2-3-4a). An offensive player may also use his hands or arms during a kick, to ward off an opponent who is attempting to block him (2-3-4b; 9-3-5).

When a player on defense uses a hand or arm, the hand must be in advance of the elbow at the time of the contact and at the shoulder or below unless the opponent squats, ducks or submarines (2-3-6).

Legal Blocking: Case Plays

*2.17.3 SITUATION A: Offensive lineman A1 is on his scrimmage line and in the free-blocking zone at the snap. Immediately after the snap he drops back one step, then moves quickly three steps to the inside and while still in the free-blocking zone, contacts B1 in the back. The ball has not left the free-blocking zone prior to A1's block. B1 was in the free-blocking zone at the snap. **RULING:** Legal block by A1.

*2.17.3 SITUATION B: Quarterback A1 takes the snap and hands off to back A2 who takes a few steps left and then hands off to back A3 who attempts to run wide to the right. Linemen A4 and A5 pull and block opponents from behind in the back while the ball is still in the zone. The defenders and linemen were in the zone at the snap and the contact occurred in the free-blocking zone. **RULING:** Legal contact.

9.2.1 SITUATION C: During a scrimmage down, blocker A1 contacts B1 with open hands: (a) while his forearms are extended more than 45 degrees from his body and the palms of his hands are toward the defender; or (b) in a pushing action when extending his arms beyond 45 degrees from his body. **RULING:** It is a legal blocking technique in both (a) or (b) (2-3-2).

*9.2.1 SITUATION D: Lineman A1 and B1 are both inside the free-blocking zone at the snap. Before the zone disintegrates, A1 blocks B1 with open hands from behind pushing B1 with his arms fully extended. **RULING:** Legal block (2-17-3).

9.2.3 SITUATION B: As the offensive linemen charge on the snap of the ball, B1: (a) contacts A1 with one hand on his shoulder pad and the other hand on his helmet in fighting off the block; or (b) pulls A1's shoulders to one side and charges through in an effort to get to the runner. **RULING:** The action by B1 in (a) and (b) is legal.

9.2.3 SITUATION C: Quarterback A1 drops back 15 yards and throws a legal forward pass intended for A2, who is 5 yards behind the neutral zone. Before the pass reaches A2, B1 blocks A2. **RULING:** The contact by B1 is not pass interference and, if the block itself is legal, there is no infraction (7-5-10).

*9.3.2 SITUATION B: A1 and A2 combine in blocking B1 as follows: (a) A1 blocks B1 above the waist and at the same time or thereafter, A2 blocks B1 below the waist and above the knees; or (b) both A1 and A2 block B1 below the knees from the front of B1 while in the free-blocking zone. **RULING:** In (a) the block by A2 is legal if the block and both blockers were on the line of scrimmage and in the free-blocking zone at the snap; in (b) this combination or multiple block is legal if the block and both blockers were in the free-blocking zone at the snap (9-3-6).

9.3.2 SITUATION C: A sets in a formation with the split end A1 outside the defensive end and outside the linebacker. Following the snap, A1 blocks toward the ball on either B1, the defensive end, or B2, the linebacker, who is 2 yards behind the neutral zone. A1 blocks: (a) B1 above the waist from the front; or (b) B1 with his hands on the side of B1's shoulder pads. **RULING:** Legal block in (a) and (b).

9.3.2 SITUATION D: A1 is leading interference on a sweep play and is outside the free-blocking zone when he blocks B1. Initial contact on B1 is at waist level, but as he continues contact he does block on B1's legs. **RULING:** If the initial contact is with the opponent's body, hands or arms, at the waist or above, and in continuation the contact is below the waist, it is a legal block (2-3-7).

9.3.2 SITUATION E: R1 rushes in to block a punt by K1. K2 attempts to block R1. The direction of K2's block is above the waist; however, just before contact R1 jumps in the air attempting to block the punt and contact by K2 is below R1's waist. **RULING:** K2's block is legal since the initial direction was legal and the below-the-waist contact was as a result of R1's movement. When R1 jumped in the air, it absolved K2 of responsibility for the low block. This would not be true if R1 changed direction laterally; in that case initial blocking contact must be above the opponent's waist (2-3-7).

9.3.2 SITUATION F: A1 contacts B1 with a legal block above the waist. The contact causes both players to stop or to bounce backward slightly and A1 immediately continues his charge and blocks B1 below the waist. **RULING:** Legal block. It is permissible for A1's block to be below the waist if it is part of a continuous block or continuous charge after first contact was above the waist.

9.3.4 SITUATION: From his 40-yard line, K1 kicks the ball laterally and short on a kickoff, hoping his team can recover just beyond R's free-kick line. The ball bounces immediately after being kicked. K1 is blocked by R1: (a) on his 42-yard line; or (b) on his 43-yard line, 5 yards from the sideline. **RULING:** Legal block in both (a) and (b) if the contact is above the waist. As soon as the ball touches the ground, the kicker/holder may be contacted with a legal block.

9.3.5 SITUATION A: Runner A1 is hit behind the line. The ball pops free and: (a) is in the air; or (b) is rolling on the ground, when B1 pushes A2 in the back above the waist to get to the loose ball. **RULING:** Legal in both (a) and (b) (2-3-4c; 2-3-5b).

9.3.5 SITUATION B: Runner A1 breaks free beyond the neutral zone at midfield. A2 is running between A1 and safety B1, who is gaining fast on both of them. As B1 nears A2 he pushes him from behind above the waist to clear the way to A1. B1 subsequently tackles A1 at B's 10-yard line. **RULING:** B1's contact on blocker A2 is legal when attempting to get to the runner or to catch or recover a loose ball which he may possess (2-3-5b).

Topic:
Illegal Blocking

Blocking Below the Waist

Blocking below the waist is making initial contact below the waist from the front or side against an opponent other than a runner. Blocking below the waist applies only when the opponent has one or both feet on the ground (2-3-7). A player shall not block an opponent below the waist except when rules regarding the free-blocking zone apply; or to tackle a runner or player pretending to be a runner (9-3-2).

Blocking Below the Waist: Penalty

15 yards. Signal 40.

PlayPic® 40

Blocking Below the Waist: Case Plays

2.17.2 SITUATION E: A1 is in shotgun formation, lined up seven yards behind the line of scrimmage ready to receive the snap. Immediately after the snap to A1, (a) A2 immediately drops and blocks B1 below the waist or (b) A2 rises, and slightly retreats as if to go in traditional pass blocking protection, but then dives and blocks B1 below the waist. Both A2 and B1 were in the zone and on the line of scrimmage at the snap. The contact between A2 and B1 takes place in the free-blocking zone. **RULING:** It is a legal block in (a) and an illegal block below the waist in (b). It is legal for A2 to block B1 below the waist if the contact is made immediately following the snap. Any later, and the ball is considered to have left the free-blocking zone and the block is illegal.

6.5.2 SITUATION A: During a scrimmage kick beyond the expanded neutral zone, R1 gives a fair-catch signal. He muffs the kick into the air, where R1 is blocked below the waist by K4 and K5 recovers. **RULING:** It is an illegal block below the waist by K4 (2-3-5b; 6-2-4; 9-3-2).

9.3.2 SITUATION A: During a running play to the left, lineman A1, who was in the free-blocking zone, crosses through the zone and blocks B1 from the side below the waist, and away from the spot of the snap, as the lead blocker for a reverse. B1 was also in the zone at the snap. **RULING:** Illegal block by A1 because the block was below the waist outside the free-blocking zone (2-17-2).

*9.3.2 SITUATION B: A1 and A2 combine in blocking B1. Both block B1 downfield with A1 making contact above the waist and A2

simultaneously making contact below the waist but above the knees.
RULING: Illegal block below the waist by A2 since the block is not in
the free-blocking zone (9-3-6).

9.3.2 SITUATION C: A sets in a formation with the split end A1 outside
the defensive end and outside the linebacker. Following the snap,
A1 blocks toward the ball on either B1, the defensive end, or B2, the
linebacker, who is 2 yards behind the neutral zone. A1 blocks B2 below
the waist from the front. **RULING:** Illegal block below the waist. A1 may
block this player, but the block must be above the waist and on the front
or side of the opponent.

9.3.2 SITUATION D: A1 is the lead blocker on a sweep play and is
outside the free-blocking zone when he blocks B1: (a) and initial contact
is below B1's waist; or (b) as A1 moves in to block, initial contact is with
B1's hands that are below the waist and, thereafter, contact is at B's
knees; or (c) initial contact on B1 is at waist level, but as he continues
contact he does block on B1's legs. **RULING:** Illegal block below the
waist in (a) and (b) and legal contact in (c). If the initial contact is with
the opponent's body, hands or arms, at the waist or above, and in
continuation the contact is below the waist, it is a legal block (2-3-7).

9.3.2 SITUATION F: A1 contacts B1 with a legal block above the waist.
The contact causes both players to stop or to bounce backward slightly
and A1 immediately continues his charge and blocks B1 below the waist.
RULING: Legal block. It is permissible for A1's block to be below the
waist if it is part of a continuous block or continuous charge after first
contact was above the waist.

Block In the Back

Blocking in the back is a block against an opponent when the initial
contact is in the opponent's back, inside the shoulders and below the
helmet and above the waist and not against a player who is a runner or
pretending to be a runner. Blocking an opponent in the back is illegal
when: it is not in the free-blocking zone; is not an attempt to ward off a
blocker, reach a runner or catch or recover a loose ball which the blocker
may legally touch or possess; or is not against a player who is a runner
or pretending to be a runner (2-5-2; 9-3-5a-c). When in doubt, the contact
is legal and not from behind.

Block In the Back: Penalty

10 yards. Signal 43.

▧ Rationale

Blocking in the back above the waist is less dangerous than clipping, which is blocking in the back below the waist. That's why the penalty for blocking in the back is less severe.

In 2002, a 10-yard "block in the back" foul was separated from the 15-yard "clipping" foul. Before then, any block in the back — above or below the waist — was considered clipping. Now, clipping only occurs if the block from behind is at or below the waist.

Block In the Back: Case Plays

*2.17.4 SITUATION C: A9 is approaching B10 in the open field and at an angle. A9 pushes B10 in the back with one hand and with the other hand on the shoulder. **RULING:** This is an illegal block in the back (9-3-5).

9.3.5 SITUATION B: Runner A1 breaks free beyond the neutral zone at midfield. A2 is running between A1 and safety B1, who is gaining fast on both of them. As B1 nears A2 he pushes him from behind above the waist to clear the way to A1. B1 subsequently tackles A1 at B's 10-yard line. **RULING:** B1's contact on blocker A2 is legal when attempting to get to the runner or to catch or recover a loose ball which he may possess (2-3-5b).

Blocking the Kicker/Holder

The kicker or place-kick holder of a free kick may not be blocked before he has advanced 5 yards beyond his free-kick line or the kick has touched the ground or any other player (2-32-7, 8; 9-3-4a, b).

Blocking the Kicker/Holder: Penalty

15 yards. Signal 40. Disqualification also if any foul is flagrant. Signal 47.

Blocking the Kicker/Holder: Case Play

9.3.4 SITUATION: From his 40-yard line, K1 kicks the ball laterally and short on a kickoff, hoping his team can recover just beyond R's free-kick line. The ball bounces immediately after being kicked. K1 is blocked by R1: (a) on his 42-yard line; or (b) on his 43-yard line, 5 yards from the sideline. **RULING:** Legal block in both (a) and (b) if the contact is above the waist. As soon as the ball touches the ground, the kicker/holder may be contacted with a legal block.

◪ Rationale

The rule restricting blocking the kicker of a free kick was instituted to prevent opponents from "taking out" an opponent with potentially great scoring capability.

Chop Block

Chop block is a combination block by two or more teammates against an opponent other than the runner, with or without delay, where one of the blocks is low (at the knee or below) and one of the blocks is high (above the knee) (2-3-8; 9-3-6 Table).

Chop Block: Penalty

15 yards. Signal 41.

Chop Block: Case Play

*9.3.2 **SITUATION B:** A1 and A2 combine in blocking B1. Both block B1 in the free blocking zone with A1's block above the waist and A2's block at the knees or below. **RULING:** Illegal chop block by A2.

Clipping

Clipping is a block against an opponent when the initial contact is from behind, at or below the waist, and not against a player who is a runner or pretending to be a runner. When the contact is ruled to be from behind, and the game official has question as to the initial point of contact, it shall be ruled clipping (2-5-1; 2-5-3; 9-3-5c).

Clipping: Penalty

15 yards. Signal 39.

◪ Rationale

Clipping is an extremely dangerous block because it is directed at an especially vulnerable part of the opponent's body and in a manner that prevents the blocked player from anticipating or avoiding it.

Clipping: Case Play

*9.3.6 SITUATION B: Linebacker B1 is lined up three yards from the line of scrimmage and in the free-blocking zone. A2, who is on the line of scrimmage and in the free-blocking zone, when the ball is snapped, blocks B1 below the waist, from behind. The contact is in the zone and the ball is in the zone when the contact occurs. **RULING:** It is clipping and a 15-yard penalty would be assessed from the basic spot.

Helping the Runner

An offensive player shall not push, pull or lift the runner to assist his forward progress (9-1).

Helping the Runner: Penalty

5 yards. Signal 44.

Helping the Runner: Case Play

9.1 SITUATION: With fourth and goal from B's 1-yard line, runner A1 is pushed at the line of scrimmage from behind by A2 in an effort by A2 to get him into the end zone. **RULING:** A2 has fouled by helping the runner. The foul carries a 5-yard penalty. Therefore it will be fourth and goal from B's 6-yard line if the penalty is accepted.

Holding

An offensive player (except the runner) shall not use his hands, arms or legs to hook, lock, clamp, grasp, encircle or hold in an effort to restrain an opponent. A defensive player shall not use his hands, arms or legs to hook, lock, clamp, grasp, encircle or hold in an effort to restrain an opponent other than the runner (9-2-1c; 9-2-3c).

Holding: Penalty

10 yards. Signal 42.

Holding: Case Plays

6.5.2 SITUATION A: During a scrimmage kick beyond the expanded neutral zone, R1 gives a fair-catch signal. He muffs the kick into the air, where K3 tackles R1 following the muff, preventing R1 from catching the kick. **RULING:** It is a holding foul for K3 to tackle R1 following the muff, thus preventing him from reaching the ball.

7.5.6 SITUATION: Quarterback A1 drops back and throws a forward pass toward the sideline to A2 who is behind the neutral zone. A2 then throws a forward pass to A3 15 yards downfield. B1 tackles A2 prior to A2 touching the pass. **RULING:** It is a holding foul by B1. It should be noted that A2 has also committed a foul for an illegal forward pass.

7.5.11 SITUATION A: A11 is running a deep post pattern and B11 grabs A11's jersey. The pass has already crossed the neutral zone and the pass is clearly away from the intended receiver. **RULING:** That is a foul for illegal holding.

9.2.1 SITUATION F: A1 is blocking with open hands: (a) outside his own frame; or (b) outside B1's frame, during contact. **RULING:** A1 is using an illegal blocking technique in both (a) and (b). When the hands are outside the frame, as described above and grasps the opponent or his equipment, it is a holding foul instead of illegal use of hands.

9.2.3 SITUATION B: As the offensive linemen charge on the snap of the ball, B1 grasps guard A1 by the jersey and controls him until he sees where the ball is going. **RULING:** It is holding, which will result in a 10-yard penalty administered in accordance with the all-but-one principle, if accepted.

9.2.3 SITUATION C: Quarterback A1 drops back 15 yards and throws a legal forward pass intended for A2, who is 5 yards behind the neutral zone. Before the pass reaches A2, B1 tackles A2. **RULING:** Tackling A2 is a foul, as it is a form of holding. Defensive players are prohibited from grasping an opponent other than the runner. The foul occurs during a loose-ball play, and the 10-yard penalty will be administered from the previous spot.

Illegal Use of Hands or Arms

The runner may not grasp a teammate (9-2-2).

A defensive player shall not use his hands to add momentum to the charge of a teammate who is on the line of scrimmage; use his hands or arms to hook, lock, clamp, grasp, encircle or hold in an effort to restrain an opponent other than the runner; or contact an eligible receiver who is no longer a potential blocker (9-2-3a-d).

The blocker's hand(s) may not be locked nor may he swing, throw or flip the elbow or forearm so that it is moving faster than the blocker's shoulders at the time the elbow, forearm or shoulder contacts the opponent. The blocker may not initiate contact with his arm or hand against an opponent above the opponent's shoulder, but he may use his hand or arm to break a fall or maintain his balance (2-3-3; 9-2-1a).

Illegal Use of Hands or Arms: Penalty

10 yards. Signal 42.

Illegal Use of Hands or Arms: Case Plays

9.2.1 SITUATION A: During a running play, blocker A1 has his hands cupped and together in front of his body with his elbows outside his shoulders. As he approaches his opponent, he raises his hands and forearms perpendicular to the ground to contact his opponent. **RULING:** If the blocker's palms are facing the opponent, or if his forearms are extended more than 45 degrees from his body, the hands must be open at and during contact (2-3-2).

Did You Know?

The rules of 1888 prohibited blocking with extended arms, and tackling was restricted to contact above the knees.

9.2.1 SITUATION B: Blocker A1 has his hands and arms in legal position with the elbows outside the body and: (a) when B1 attempts to penetrate his block in an upright position, he contacts B1 above the shoulders with his forearm; or (b) as B2 ducks or submarines, A1 contacts him above the shoulder with his cupped hands. **RULING:** In (a), it is an illegal blocking technique because contact was made above the defensive player's shoulders while he was in a normal upright position. In (b), the responsibility for the contact on the head of B2 is that of B2, because he has taken evasive action to avoid the block. It is assumed contact by A1 in (b) does not violate the provision of striking or contacting above the shoulders (2-3-2).

9.2.1 SITUATION E: In blocking B1, A1's forearms are almost fully extended from his body and he contacts B1 with the side of his closed hands. The palms of A1's hands are not directly facing B1. **RULING:** An illegal blocking technique by A1. The hands may not be closed or cupped when the arms are extended more than 45 degrees from the blocker's body (2-3-2).

9.2.1 SITUATION F: A1 is blocking with open hands: (a) outside his own frame; or (b) outside B1's frame, during contact. **RULING:** A1 is using an illegal blocking technique in both (a) and (b). When the hands are outside the frame, as described above and grasps the opponent or his equipment, it is a holding foul instead of illegal use of hands.

9.2.1 SITUATION G: A1 makes legal contact on B1's chest using extended arms with open hands. B1 spins in an effort to evade A1 and get to the passer. A1 effectively maintains contact while shifting his hands to B1's upper arm and then directly on his back as B1 turns. A1 continues the contact and finishes the block by forcing B1 beyond the passer. **RULING:** The described blocking technique is legal. In order to legally contact the back of the opponent in this situation it must either be a continuation of contact that was legal originally, or because the opponent turned so quickly the blocker could not stop his charge in time to avoid contact on the back. When the extended-arms technique is used, the hands must be open on contact and remain open during the contact. The open-hand blocking technique may be used in any situation where blocking is legal for A.

9.2.3 SITUATION A: End A1 sprints from the line and then cuts sharply toward the middle of the field. A1 makes no attempt to block defensive back B1. B1 pursues A1 and pushes him from the side using his open hands. Contact is made on A1's upper arm before the pass is thrown. A1 was moving away from B1 when the contact occurred. **RULING:** Illegal use of hands by B1. A defender may legally contact an eligible receiver beyond the neutral zone before the pass is in flight provided the receiver is a potential blocker. The contact may be a block or warding off the opponent who is attempting to block by pushing or pulling him. However, if the receiver is not attempting to block or has gone past the yard line occupied by the defender or is moving away, it is illegal for the defender to use hands in the manner described. In this situation, it is clear that A1 is no longer a potential blocker on B1 (2-3-5a; 7-5-7).

9.2.3 SITUATION B: As the offensive linemen charge on the snap of the ball, B1: (a) grasps guard A1 by the jersey and controls him until he sees where the ball is going; or (b) slaps A1 on the side of the helmet with an open hand and forces his head to the side with what is commonly called the "bell ringer;" or (c) contacts A1 with one hand on his shoulder pad and the other hand on his helmet in fighting off the block; or (d) pulls A1's shoulders to one side and charges through in an effort to get to the runner; or (e) pulls A1's shoulders to one side so B2 may charge through to the runner. **RULING:** It is holding in (a), which will result in a 10-yard penalty administered in accordance with the all-but-one principle, if accepted. In (b), it is illegal personal contact, and (e), it is illegal use of hands by B1, which also carries a 10-yard penalty. The action by B1 in (c) and (d) is legal.

Interlocked Blocking

An offensive player (except the runner) shall not grasp or encircle any teammate to form interlocked blocking (2-3-9; 9-2-1b).

Interlocked Blocking: Penalty

10 yards. Signal 44.

Interlocked Blocking: Case Plays

7.2.2 SITUATION: Following the snap on a kick try, the offensive linemen "step down" and interlock feet. **RULING:** Legal. However, prior to the snap only the linemen next to the snapper are permitted to lock legs with the snapper.

9.2.1 SITUATION I: K is attempting a try by kick. After the ball is snapped, the offensive guards and tackles each grab the jersey of an adjacent teammate. The kick by K1 is successful. **RULING:** Grabbing the jersey of an offensive teammate is considered to be the same as grasping the teammate and it is interlocked blocking, which is a form of illegal use of hands and carries a 10-yard penalty. Any time offensive players grasp teammates in this manner, it would have to be considered interlocked blocking whether they grab each other at the shoulders, arms, legs, ankles, etc.

> The rule banning interlocked blocking eliminated the flying wedge, one of the earliest ploys in the football playbook.

9.2.1 SITUATION J: On a successful try for point by kick, the interior linemen of K all reached across and grasped the teammate immediately to their inside after the snap. **RULING:** Interlocked blocking, 10-yard penalty from the spot of the foul since this spot is probably behind the basic spot.

Tripping

A player shall not trip an opponent who is not a runner. Tripping is the use of the lower leg or foot to obstruct an opponent, who is not the runner, below the knee (2-45; 9-3-7).

Tripping: Penalty

15 yards. Signal 46.

Tripping: Case Play

2.42.1 SITUATION: B1 tackles runner A1 with a trip with his foot. **RULING:** That is a legal method of tackling the runner (9-3-5c).

Topic:
Legal Tackling

Tackling is the use of hands, arms, legs or body by a defensive player in his attempt to hold a runner or to bring him to the ground (2-42-1).

Legal Tackling: Case Plays

2.20.1 SITUATION C: During a running play beyond the neutral zone, A1 is momentarily in the clear and B1 comes up to make the tackle. B1 keeps his head in an upright position with his eyes on the numbers of A1 and: (a) moves his head at the last moment so that he contacts A1 with his shoulder; or (b) moves his head to attempt a shoulder tackle, but because of a sharp cut by A1, there is some contact with the side of the helmet of B1. **RULING:** A legal tackle in both (a) and (b).

2.42.1 SITUATION: B1 tackles runner A1 with: (a) a cross-body block at the knees; or (b) a block from behind and below the waist; or (c) a trip with his foot; or (d) his arms and shoulder. **RULING:** The techniques in (a), (b), (c) and (d) are all legal methods of tackling the runner (9-3-5c).

Topic:
Illegal Helmet Contact

Illegal helmet contact is an act of initiating contact with the helmet against an opponent. Butt blocking, face tackling and spearing are examples of illegal helmet contact. Illegal helmet contact may be judged by the game official a flagrant act (2-20-1a-c; 9-4-3i).

Butt Blocking/Face Tackling/Spearing

Butt blocking is any act by an offensive or defensive player who initiates contact against an opponent who is not a runner with the front of his helmet (2-20-1a, 9-4-3i).

Face tackling is an act by a defensive player who initiates contact against a runner with the front of his helmet (2-20-1b, 9-4-3i).

Spearing is an act by any player who initiates contact against an opponent at the shoulders or below with the crown (top portion) of his helmet (2-20-1c, 9-4-3i).

Butt Blocking/Face Tackling/Spearing: Penalty

15 yards. Signal 24. Disqualification if flagrant. Signal 47.

Butt Blocking/Face Tackling/Spearing: Case Plays

2.20.1 SITUATION A: From a four-point stance on the offensive line, interior lineman A1: (a) initially contacts an opponent by driving his face mask directly into the opponent's chest who is not the runner; or (b) contacts an opponent with his shoulder so that his head is to the side of the opponent's body and the helmet does not make initial contact; or (c) attempts to block an opponent with a shoulder, but because of a defensive slant, primary contact with the opponent is made with A1's helmet. **RULING:** The block in (a) is illegal butt blocking. In (b), even though there was some contact with the helmet, the block is legal because the helmet or face mask was not used to deliver the blow. In (c), the covering official will have to judge whether or not it is a foul. Because of defensive slants and stunts, there will be instances in which the blocker attempts to make a legal shoulder block, but inadvertently contacts an opponent with either his face mask or helmet. When this is the case, contact does not result in a direct blow and is legal (9-4-3i).

2.20.1 SITUATION B: A1 is a flanker outside the free-blocking zone. Immediately following the snap, he comes back toward the ball and contacts B1 from the front above the waist in delivering a blow with his face mask. **RULING:** Even though the contact with B1 was above the waist, it is butt blocking because the face mask was used to make initial contact (2-20).

9.4.3 SITUATION B: Wide receiver A1 goes downfield 15 yards, cuts sharply to the outside and stops near the sideline and catches the pass. B1 drives the crown (top portion) of his helmet into A1. **RULING:** This use of the helmet is spearing by B1.

 9.4.3 COMMENT: Face tackling, butt blocking and spearing are somewhat related fouls. All are illegal and each carries a 15-yard penalty. Butt blocking is initiating contact with front of the helmet against an opponent who is not the runner. It may be committed by any player. Face tackling is the same act against the runner and can only be committed by the defense. Both fouls may result from inadvertent acts. Spearing is initiating contact at the shoulders or below against an opponent with the crown (top portion) of the helmet and may be committed by any player. Any tactic which involves the illegal use of the helmet is condemned by all who are concerned with the well-being of players and the perpetuation of the game (2-20-1c).

9.4.3 SITUATION D: Runner A1 breaks free beyond the neutral zone (a) As B1 and B2 are closing in to tackle him, A1 veers into B1 and deliberately drives the crown (top portion) of his helmet into B1's chest; or (b) as B1 and B2 attempt to bring him down, A1 lowers his head and drives forward for yardage and he contacts B1 and/or B2 with his helmet. **RULING:** Spearing by A1 in (a) as he uses the crown (top portion) of his helmet to punish B1. It is a 15-yard penalty. If the spearing is judged by the game official to be flagrant, A1 must be disqualified. In (b), the lowering of the head to pick up additional yardage is not illegal unless it is done to punish an opponent, if he uses his helmet to butt or ram, or the runner commits spearing or butt blocking or targeting. The runner's normal reaction is to attempt to gain yardage when being tackled. The reason for including the runner in the illegal helmet contact and targeting prohibition is to prevent him from using his helmet to abuse an opponent as well as protection of the player. The illegal helmet contact rules apply equally to all players (2-20-1; 2-20-2).

9.4.3 SITUATION L: During a running play, A1 breaks into the secondary. Safety B1 comes up quickly and drives his face mask or helmet directly into the chest of A1. B1 simultaneously wraps his arms around A1 bringing him to the ground. **RULING:** This is a face tackling foul by B1 (2-20).

9.4.3 SITUATION M: A1 is running in the open field and B1 grabs A1's shoulder pad opening from behind and: (a) pulls A1 down abruptly; (b) pulls A1 down to the ground from the side; (c) rides A1 for several yards before pulling A1 backwards to the ground; or (d) rides A1 for several yards before A1 falls forward. **RULING:** Illegal horse-collar foul in (a), (b) and (c), legal in (d).

Topic:
Illegal Personal Contact

Fighting

No player or nonplayer shall fight. Fighting is any attempt by a player or nonplayer to strike or engage a player or nonplayer in a combative manner unrelated to football. Such acts include, but are not limited to, attempts to strike an opponent(s) with the arm(s), hand(s), leg(s) or foot (feet), whether or not there is contact (2-11; 9-4-1).

Fighting: Penalty

15 yards and disqualification. Signals 38 and 47.

Fighting: Case Plays

9.4.1 SITUATION A: With the ball on B's 2-yard line and between downs, a fight starts between A1 and B1. The game officials do not know which player struck the first blow. **RULING:** Disqualify both A1 and B1 and signal personal fouls against each team, but the penalties cancel (2-11; 10-2-5b, c).

*9.4.1 SITUATION B: It is A's ball, third down and 1, on A's 10-yard line. B1 tackles A1 with a hard legal tackle at the line of scrimmage. A1, feeling the tackle was unjustly harsh, jumps to his feet and attacks B1, delivering blows with his fist. In response, B1 directs a profanity toward A1. **RULING:** The penalties for A1's dead-ball personal foul and B1's unsportsmanlike conduct foul would cancel. A1 shall be disqualified for fighting; B1 would remain in the game unless the game officials judged that his reaction was flagrant or it was his second unsportsmanlike conduct foul. It's A's ball fourth down and on its own 10-yard line (2-11; 9-8-1 Penalty; 10-2-5b, c).

9.4.1 SITUATION C: During B1's tackling of runner A1, he delivers a blow toward the ball in an attempt to dislodge it, but instead strikes A1 with his fist. **RULING:** B1 is charged with a personal foul and disqualified for fighting. B will be assessed a 15-yard penalty.

9.4.1 COMMENT: This specific situation is intended to depict an act which is clearly a personal foul and not inadvertent contact resulting from an attempt to dislodge the football. Game officials must continually use prudent judgment and see the entire play in order to view these types of acts in the proper context. If it is judged by the game official that this contact is excessive, but is not an act to be construed as fighting, the personal foul would result in an ejection for striking, but would not be fighting by rule (2-11).

9.4.1 SITUATION D: After completing the catch, receiver A12's momentum carries him into B's team box, where nonplayer B44 pushes A12 into a bench. **RULING:** Nonplayer B44 is disqualified and a 15-yard penalty is assessed from the succeeding spot.

9.8.1 SITUATION M: A fight breaks out between several opposing players and: (a) two substitutes from each team come onto the field; or (b) one substitute of A enters and three enter from B's team box. **RULING:** In (a), the substitutes are disqualified and the penalties cancel. In (b), since all fouls are dead-ball fouls, the one 15-yard penalty on A will cancel one by B resulting in two 15-yard penalties on B. In both cases, those who were fighting will be disqualified (2-11; 9-4-1; 10-1-1; 10-2-5a, b).

Hurdling
No player or nonplayer shall hurdle an opponent. Hurdling is an attempt by a player to jump (hurdle) with one or both feet or knees foremost over an opponent who is contacting the ground with no part of his body except one or both feet (2-22; 9-4-3d).

Hurdling: Penalty
15 yards. Signal 38.

Personal Fouls
No player or nonplayer shall charge into or throw an opponent to the ground after he is obviously out of the play or after the ball is clearly dead either in or out of bounds; pile on any player who is lying on the ground; position himself on the shoulders or body of a teammate or opponent to gain an advantage; throw a helmet to trip an opponent; or make any other contact with an opponent, including a defenseless player, which is deemed unnecessary or excessive and which incites roughness (9-4-3a-g).

No defensive player may use the hand(s) to slap the blocker's head (9-4-7).

The blocker may not initiate contact with his arm or hand against an opponent above the opponent's shoulder (2-3-3).

Personal Fouls: Penalty

15 yards. Signal 38. Disqualification also if any foul is flagrant. Signal 47.

Personal Fouls: Case Plays

9.2.3 SITUATION B: As the offensive linemen charge on the snap of the ball, B1 slaps A1 on the side of the helmet with an open hand and forces his head to the side with what is commonly called the "bell ringer." **RULING:** It is illegal personal contact.

9.2.3 COMMENT: Is there suggested guidance or rules coverage on a "defenseless player" who should be protected from unnecessary roughness? Yes, defenseless players are especially vulnerable to potential injury. Game officials must diligently observe all action and watch for contact against players who are deemed defenseless. Examples include, but are not limited to: (a) A quarterback moving down the line of scrimmage who has handed or pitched the ball to a teammate, and then makes no attempt to participate further in the play; (b) A kicker who is in the act of kicking the ball, or who has not had a reasonable amount of time to regain his balance after the kick; (c) A passer who is in the act of throwing the ball, or who has not had a reasonable length of time to participate in the play again after releasing the ball; (d) A pass receiver whose concentration is on the ball and the contact by the defender is unrelated to attempting to catch the ball; (e) A pass receiver who has clearly relaxed when he has missed the pass or feels he can no longer catch the pass; (f) A kick returner attempting to catch a kick; (g) A kick receiver who is immediately contacted after touching the ball; (h) A player on the ground; (i) Any player who has relaxed once the ball has become dead; (j) A player who receives a blind side block; (k) A ball carrier already in the grasp of an opponent and whose forward progress has been stopped; and (l) Any player who is obviously out of the play. The game official must draw distinction between contact necessary to make a legal block or tackle, making unnecessary contact on a defenseless player and targeting any player at any time (2-32-16; 9-4-3i(3)).

9.4.3 SITUATION C: Quarterback A1 has: (a) handed off to A2 and is walking away observing the progress of the play; or (b) thrown a legal forward pass and is moving away from the play after the pass was caught. In (a) and (b), B1 tackles A1. **RULING:** Illegal personal contact by B1 in both (a) and (b). It is a foul for illegal personal contact when a player charges into or throws an opponent to the ground after he is obviously out of the play. The 15-yard penalty is administered in accordance with the all-but-one principle. If the act is judged by the game official to be flagrant, B1 must be disqualified (2-40).

9.4.3 SITUATION E: (a) End A1 goes 5 yards downfield and stops. Wide receiver A2 jumps on his back and catches a pass; or (b) B1 steps on the back of snapper A1 immediately after the snap as he propels himself into the air to block a punt; or (c) B1 jumps on B2's shoulders in an effort to block a field-goal attempt. **RULING:** A personal foul in (a), (b) and (c). In all cases, an advantage has been gained illegally.

9.4.3 SITUATION F: During a forward-pass play, eligible receiver A1 runs a pass pattern and it is obvious he will be unable to catch the pass from A2 because: (a) the pass is incomplete, striking the ground; or (b) it is well overthrown but in the general area of A1. In both (a) and (b), when it is obvious the pass will not be caught by A1, B1 aggressively contacts A1. **RULING:** In (a), because this contact is following the incomplete pass, it is a dead-ball foul and would be penalized 15 yards from the succeeding spot. In (b), because the pass was still in flight when B1 contacted A1, it was pass interference even though it is obvious the pass was overthrown. The penalty is 15 yards from the previous spot. If the pass had been touched by a teammate of A1, prior to the contact by B1, the result would be a personal foul by B1, because A1 was obviously out of the play (7-5-10a).

In Simple Terms

Helmet openings are the back of the helmet near the neck, the ear holes and the edges on the front at the top and around the sides of the helmet.

9.4.3 SITUATION P: A1 is carrying the ball when B1 grabs him by the back or side of the collar of the shoulder pads (or jersey). A1 then: (a) fumbles the ball and is subsequently brought to the ground by B1; (b) crosses the goal line to score a touchdown and is then brought down by B1; or (c) crosses the sideline and is then brought down by B1. **RULING:** In (a), (b) and (c), a horse-collar foul should be called.

9.4.3 SITUATION S: A1 is engaged with B1 in close line play. A1's helmet comes completely off as the play goes in another direction. He is beginning to put his helmet back on when B2 hits him from the side knocking him to the ground. **RULING:** B2 has committed a personal foul for contacting a player whose helmet has come completely off. However, since A1's helmet came off prior to the contact and the helmet coming off was not due to a foul by B, A1 must sit out the next play (9-4-3l, 3-5-10d).

9.4.3 SITUATION T: B54's helmet comes completely off during an attempt to tackle A32. A32 drags B54 for a few yards, and A76, in an attempt to keep A32 from being tackled, blocks B54. **RULING:** A76 contacted a helmetless player; therefore, illegal personal contact has occurred and a personal foul shall be called. B54 must leave the field for at least one play (3-5-10d; 9-4-3l; 9-6-4g).

9.4.3 SITUATION U: B54's helmet comes completely off during an attempt to tackle A32. After disengaging, B54 puts his helmet back on, then resumes his pursuit of runner A32. B54 is then blocked by A76. **RULING:** B54 has committed illegal participation by continuing to play after his helmet came completely off. A76 has not fouled. B54 must leave the field for at least one play (3-5-10d; 9-4-3l; 9-6-4g).

9.4.7 SITUATION A: Wide receiver A9 goes down field 10 yards and starts to block B10. B10 slaps A9 on the side of the helmet in an effort to avoid the block. **RULING:** Illegal personal contact. The 15-yard penalty is administered in accordance with the all-but-one principle. Disqualification also if the foul is judged by the game official to be flagrant.

9.4.7 SITUATION B: In an attempt to tackle the quarterback, B1 (a) contacts offensive blocker A1 with an open hand on the head or (b) strikes A1 with a closed fist. **RULING:** In (a), 15-yard penalty from the end of the run. In (b), B1 is disqualified for fighting.

9.4.7 SITUATION C: It is third and five from B's 40-yard line. On the snap, B1 slaps offensive guard A1 on the helmet. The quarterback then hands off to A2, who is tackled at B's 20-yard line. **RULING:** Illegal personal contact foul on B1. First and 10 from B's 10-yard line.

Face Mask, Chin Strap, Helmet Opening, Tooth and Mouth Protector Fouls

No player or nonplayer shall grasp an opponent's face mask, any edge of a helmet opening, chin strap, or a tooth and mouth protector attached to the face mask and twist, turn or pull the face mask, helmet opening, chin strap or a tooth and mouth protector attached to the face mask; or incidentally grasp an opponent's face mask, helmet opening, chin strap or a tooth and mouth protector attached to the face mask (9-4-3h).

Face Mask, Chin Strap, Helmet Opening, Tooth and Mouth Protector Fouls: Penalty

5 yards for incidental grasping. Signal 45 only. 15 yards for grasping and twisting, turning or pulling the face mask, helmet opening, chin strap or tooth and mouth protector. Signals 38 and 45. Disqualification also if flagrant. Signal 47.

◪ Rationale

It is illegal to grasp the helmet opening, tooth and mouth protector attached to the helmet or chin strap as well as the face mask because it is just as dangerous to use those to wrench the neck of an opponent as it to grasp the face mask. Neither the helmet, tooth and mouth protector attached to the helmet, the face mask nor chin strap were intended to provide a handle for the tackler. The rule does not prohibit tackling a runner around the head, or even grabbing the helmet, as long as the tackler's hands do not grasp the face mask, any edge of the helmet opening, the tooth and mouth protector attached to the helmet or any part of the chin strap.

Face Mask, Chin Strap, Helmet Opening, Tooth and Mouth Protector: Case Plays

4.2.2 SITUATION J: With fourth down and 8 from the 50, A1 runs to B's 45-yard line where: (a) B1, in attempting to tackle A1, unsnaps A1's chin strap and play continues to the 40-yard line where A1 is finally downed; or (b) B1, in attempting to tackle A1, grasps the face mask/helmet opening and A1's helmet comes off; or (c) B1 contacts A1 at B's 46 and A1's helmet comes off and he subsequently fumbles the ball. **RULING:** In (a), play continues and it is a first down for A after enforcement of the face mask foul. In (b), the ball becomes dead at the spot A1's helmet came off and B is penalized for the face mask/helmet opening violation. In (c), the ball becomes dead at the spot where A1's helmet came off and because it was fourth down and the line to gain was not obtained, the ball goes over to B. The fumble is disregarded because it happened after the ball became dead and A1 must leave the field for one play (3-5-10d; 4-2-2k).

9.4.3 SITUATION G: With second down and five yards to go from B's 30-yard line, A1 throws a pass to eligible A2. Following the reception, A2 inadvertently grasps B1's face mask/helmet opening, chin strap or attached tooth and mouth protector at B's 15-yard line as B1 attempts to tackle A2 who scores a touchdown. **RULING:** If B accepts the penalty for the inadvertent grasping of the face mask/helmet opening, chin strap or attached tooth and mouth protector by A2, the score is nullified. Following the penalty enforcement, it will be A's ball first and 10 at B's 20-yard line.

9.4.3 SITUATION H: A1 is tackled by B1 who: (a) grasps A1's face mask/helmet opening, chin strap or attached tooth and mouth protector momentarily and lets go; (b) has his hand brush across A1's face mask; (c) pulls A1 to the ground by grasping A1's face mask/helmet opening, chin strap or attached tooth and mouth protector. **RULING:** There is no penalty in (b). There is a five-yard penalty in (a) and a 15-yard penalty in (c).

9.4.3 SITUATION I: As B1 attempts to tackle A1 he: (a) grasps A1's face mask/helmet opening, chin strap or attached tooth and mouth protector which turns the head of A1; or (b) grasps A1's face mask/ helmet opening, chin strap or attached tooth and mouth protector and immediately releases it without twisting, turning, or pulling. **RULING:** It is a personal foul in (a) that results in a 15-yard penalty from the end of the run. In (b) B will be assessed a 5-yard penalty from the end of the run because of the incidental face mask.

9.4.3 SITUATION J: As B5 attempts to tackle A6, he has his hand on the helmet but does not have his fingers in the face mask or inside the helmet. **RULING:** No foul as B5 did not grasp the face mask/helmet opening or attached tooth and mouth protector.

Horse-Collar

No player or nonplayer shall grab the inside back or side collar of the shoulder pads or jersey of the runner and subsequently pull (backward or sideward) that opponent to the ground (Horse-collar), even if possession is lost. The horse-collar foul is enforced as a live ball foul (9-4-3k).

Horse-Collar: Penalty

15 yards. Signals 38 and 25.
Disqualification also if any foul is
flagrant. Signal 47.

Horse-Collar: Case Plays

9.4.3 SITUATION M: A1 is running in the open field and B1 grabs A1's shoulder pad opening from behind and: (a) pulls A1 down abruptly; (b) pulls A1 down to the ground from the side; (c) rides A1 for several yards before pulling A1 backwards to the ground; or (d) rides A1 for several yards before A1 falls forward. **RULING:** Illegal horse-collar foul in (a), (b) and (c), legal in (d).

9.4.3 SITUATION N: A1 is running in the open field and B1 grabs A1's shoulder pad opening from behind and pulls and: (a) A1 does not go down from the contact; (b) B2 comes in and tackles A1 while still in B1's grasp; or (c) A1 runs four more yards before being pulled down. **RULING:** Legal in (a) and (b); illegal horse-collar foul in (c) because runner subsequently went down because of the horse-collar foul.

9.4.3 SITUATION O: A1 is running in the free blocking zone and (a) B1 grabs A1's jersey collar opening from behind and pulls him down; (b) B1 grabs the front of A1's jersey collar opening and pulls him down; (c) B1 grabs A1's jersey at the top of the shoulder area and pulls him down. **RULING:** Illegal horse-collar foul in (a); legal in (b) and (c).

9.4.3 SITUATION P: A1 is carrying the ball when B1 grabs him by the back or side of the collar of the shoulder pads (or jersey). A1 then: (a) fumbles the ball and is subsequently brought to the ground by B1; (b) crosses the goal line to score a touchdown and is then brought down by B1; or (c) crosses the sideline and is then brought down by B1. **RULING:** In (a), (b) and (c), a horse-collar foul should be called.

9.4.3 SITUATION Q: A has possession, 3rd and 10 from the A10. A25 is running in the open field and B1 uses an illegal horse collar to bring him down (a) at the 50 after he was grabbed by the collar at the A45; or (b) at the A25 after he was initially grabbed by the collar at the A30 but the runner had retreated on his own to the A25; or (c) on B's 4 yard line and A25 drags B1 into B's end zone. **RULING:** Each of these plays are running plays, so the foul is enforced from the end of the run. In (a) it will be enforced from the 50, making it first and 10 for A at the B35; in (b) the foul is enforced from the A25, making it first and 10 for A at the A40; in (c) the touchdown is scored and A has the option of enforcing the foul on the try or the subsequent kickoff.

9.4.3 SITUATION R: A has possession 4th and 8 from the B40. A1 advances 7 yards where B1 grabs him and commits an illegal horse collar foul. The jersey/collar is grabbed one yard inbounds and B1 pulls him down a) inbounds at the B33 or 2) just out of bounds with A1 crossing the sideline at the B33. **RULING:** In both (a) and (b), the penalty for illegal horse collar is penalized from the end of the run and A is award a new series as the horse collar foul is to be enforced as a live ball foul, it will be first and 10 for A at the B18.

Roughing the Kicker/Holder/Snapper

A defensive player shall not block, tackle or charge into the kicker of a scrimmage kick, or the place-kick holder, other than when contact is unavoidable because it is not reasonably certain that a kick will be made; the defense touches the kick near the kicker and contact is unavoidable; contact is slight and is partially caused by movement of the kicker; or contact is caused by R being blocked into the kicker by K (9-4-5a-d; 10-5-1h).

A defensive player shall not charge directly into the snapper when the offensive team is in a scrimmage-kick formation (9-4-6; 10-5-1h).

Roughing the Kicker/Holder/Snapper: Penalty

15 yards and first down from the previous spot. Signals 38 and 30. Disqualification also if any foul is flagrant. Signal 47.

▨ Rationale

The kicker is off balance, largely defenseless and vulnerable while in the act of kicking. Common sense demands the kicker and holder be given special protection.

Roughing the Kicker/Holder/Snapper: Case Plays

9.4.5 SITUATION A: K1 punts and R1 touches and partially blocks the kick. R2 does not touch the ball, but firmly contacts K1. **RULING:** If R1 partially blocked the kick near the kicker/holder and R2 was near the kicker/holder at the time R1 touched the ball and R2 had already started his charge at the time the kick was touched, there would be no foul as a result of the contact by R2, unless it was unnecessarily rough (9-4-5b).

9.4.5 SITUATION B: K1 in scrimmage-kick formation, muffs the snap, but quickly recovers and begins to run. However, K1 changes his mind and: (a) punts on the run; or (b) abruptly stops and punts. R1 is unable to stop his charge and forcibly contacts K1. R1 did not touch the kick. **RULING:** No foul in either (a) or (b) because it was not reasonably certain K1 was going to punt the ball. It is always roughing the kicker if the contact could have been avoided regardless of whether or not it was apparent a kick would be made. Only unavoidable contact is ignored if it is not reasonably certain a kick will be made.

9.4.5 SITUATION C: R1, in an effort to block a place kick, charges through blocker K1 and without touching the ball, charges into the kicker/holder. **RULING:** The covering official must determine whether R1's charge would have taken him into the kicker/holder, regardless of the contact by the blocker. It is only when K1's block alters the course of R1's path and thus causes the contact with the kicker/holder that R1's contact is ignored and does not result in a foul.

9.4.5 SITUATION E: K10, the place kick holder, is contacted forcibly by R9, clearly after the kick is away. **RULING:** Roughing the kicker/holder is a personal foul. The penalty would be 15 yards and an automatic first down, if accepted.

9.4.5 SITUATION F: As R2 rushes punter K11 he: (a) brushes K11 who maintains his balance; (b) bumps K11 causing him to fall backwards or (c) runs over K11 knocking him to the ground. **RULING:** In (a), no penalty; (b) running into the kicker/holder, 5-yard penalty and replay the down; (c) roughing the kicker/holder, personal foul, 15-yard penalty and an automatic first down.

9.4.5 SITUATION G: A11 is in scrimmage kick formation. After taking the snap and attempting to kick the ball, he misjudges the distance and misses the ball. A11 is then contacted by B1 before he can regain his balance. B2 recovers the ball. **RULING:** Unless B1's contact is viewed as unnecessary roughness, there is no foul as A11 never became a kicker.

9.4.6 SITUATION A: From a scrimmage-kick formation, A1 snaps the ball to up-back A2 who is 3 yards behind the line and offset from the snapper by 1 yard. A2 runs for a 10-yard gain. Immediately after the snap started, B7 charges: (a) directly into the snapper; or (b) into the gap between the snapper and the adjacent A player making simultaneous contact with both the snapper and the other Team A player. The snapper had not had the opportunity to defend himself and was displaced by B7's charge.

RULING: In (a), B7 has roughed the snapper. If accepted, the loose ball foul is enforced with a 15-yard penalty from the previous spot and an automatic first down. There is no requirement that the ball be kicked or that a deep back receive the snap. In (b), there is no foul. The snapper's protection does not include simultaneous contact with another A player, nor does it take away the "center-guard gap" from B. The roughing prohibition is only for a direct charge into the snapper (2-32-14).

9.4.6 SITUATION B: K is in scrimmage-kick formation on fourth and 17 from its own 20-yard line. Immediately following the snap, R1 charges directly into snapper A1. The kick is caught by R2 and he is downed on K's 40-yard line. **RULING:** R1 has roughed the snapper. In addition to the yardage, the penalty also includes an automatic first down. Following enforcement, it is K's ball first and 10 from its own 35-yard line.

9.4.6 SITUATION C: A is in a scrimmage kick formation with punter A2 standing twelve yards deep and four yards to the right of the snapper. The wind is blowing very strong and will probably move the ball to the right after it is snapped. Is the snapper afforded protection in this case? **RULING:** Yes, because the punter is in position to receive the snap.

Roughing the Passer

A passer is a player who throws a legal forward pass. He continues to be a passer until the legal forward pass ends or until he moves to participate in the play (2-32-11).

Defensive players must make a definite effort to avoid charging into a passer, who has thrown the ball from in or behind the neutral zone, after it is clear the ball has been thrown. No defensive player shall commit any illegal personal contact foul against the passer (9-4-4; 10-1-7b; 10-5-4; 10-5-1g).

Roughing the Passer: Penalty

15 yards and a first down from the dead ball spot when the dead ball spot is beyond the neutral zone and A has possession of the ball at the end of the down and there has been no change of team possession and the foul is not for an incidental face mask as in 9-4-3h, or otherwise 15 yards and first down from previous spot. Signals 34 and 8. Disqualification also if any foul is flagrant. Signal 47.

Roughing the Passer: Case Plays

7.5.2 SITUATION D: Runner A1 advances 5 yards beyond the neutral zone to B's 3-yard line where he is tackled. As he is going down, A1 simulates a fumble by tossing the ball forward into the end zone where A2 downs it. **RULING:** Illegal forward pass by A1. The penalty is 5 yards from the spot of the pass, plus loss of down. If A1 is contacted after releasing the ball, it is not roughing the passer since he lost that protection when he threw the pass from beyond the neutral zone (9-4-4).

8.3.5 SITUATION B: During a successful two-point try, B1 roughs the passer. **RULING:** Team A may accept the score and have the penalty assessed from the succeeding spot.

9.4.4 SITUATION A: A1 rolls out on a run-pass option (a) A1 passes from behind the neutral zone and is subsequently contacted by B1 who could have avoided the contact, but renewed his charge after the pass; or (b) A1 is 2 yards beyond the neutral zone when he passes and B1 continues his charge and contacts him. **RULING:** It is roughing the passer in (a), but cannot be roughing the passer in (b). However, in (b), though A1 lost his protection as a passer when he passed from beyond the neutral zone the contact could still be judged by the game official to be a personal foul.

9.4.4 SITUATION B: From A's 40-yard line, passer A1 is roughed by B1 and the pass is completed: (a) to A2 who is downed on A's 47-yard line; or (b) behind the neutral zone to A2 who is downed on A's 38; or (c) completed to A2 behind the neutral zone and his fumble at A's 35 goes directly out of bounds. **RULING:** In (a), the roughing penalty is enforced from the 47-yard line and results in a first down for A at B's 38. In (b) and (c), if the penalty is accepted, enforcement is from the previous spot resulting in a first down for A from B's 45-yard line.

9.4.4 SITUATION C: 3rd down and 10 from B30. A1 passes to A2 who catches ball at B20. B1 roughs A1 following the legal forward pass. A2 advances to B15 where he fumbles (a) backward and the ball is recovered by A3 at the B 20; (b) forward and the ball is recovered by A3 at the B5; (c) forward and the ball is recovered by B2 at the B5; (d) forward and the ball is recovered by A3 in the end zone; (e) forward and the ball is recovered by B2 in B's end zone; (f) forward and the ball rolls through and out of the end zone; or (g) backward and the ball is recovered at the B31. **RULING:** In (a) the roughing penalty is enforced from the B20, half the distance with first and goal for A at the B10; in (b) the roughing penalty is enforced half the distance from the B5 yard line with first and goal for A at the B2 1/2-yard line; in (c), (e), (f) and (g) the roughing penalty is enforced from the

B30 (previous spot) with first and 10 for A at the B15; in (d) touchdown for A and A is given the choice of enforcing the roughing penalty on the try or on the subsequent kickoff per 8-2-2.

9.4.4 SITUATION D: B1 is attempting to tackle the passer when: (a) B1 lunges at the passer and commits an illegal helmet contact foul by hitting the passer with his helmet; (b) B1 grasps the passer's face mask attempting to complete the tackle; or (c) as the ball is being released, B1 grabs the passer by the inside back or side collar of the shoulder pads and brings him to the ground. In (a), (b) and (c), the pass is thrown toward A2. **RULING:** In (a), (b) and (c), an illegal personal contact foul has occurred, and roughing the passer has occurred. The referee shall ensure that the captain of Team A is aware of all penalty options as roughing the passer also carries an automatic first down.

Running Into the Kicker/Holder

A defensive player shall not run into the kicker nor holder, which is contact that displaces the kicker or holder without roughing (9-4-5).

Running Into the Kicker/Holder: Penalty

5 yards from the previous spot. Signal 30.

Running Into the Kicker/Holder: Case Play

9.4.5 SITUATION D: K11 is in scrimmage kick formation. After the kick is away, R10 is unable to stop his attempt to block the kick and R10 displaces the kicker/holder. **RULING:** The referee judges the infraction to be running into the kicker/holder. The penalty, if accepted, is 5 yards from the previous spot and a replay of the down.

Striking, Kicking, Kneeing an Opponent, or Intentionally Contacting a Game Official

No player or nonplayer shall intentionally contact a game official; swing the foot, shin or knee into an opponent, nor extend the knee to meet a blocker; or strike an opponent with his fist, locked hands, forearm or elbow, nor kick or knee him (9-4-2; 9-4-3j).

Striking, Kicking, Kneeing an Opponent, or Intentionally Contacting a Game Official: Penalty

15 yards and disqualification. Signal 47.

Targeting

Targeting is an act by any player who takes aim and initiates contact against an opponent above the shoulders with the helmet, forearm, hand, fist, elbow or shoulders (2-20-2).

Targeting: Penalty

15 yards. Signal 38, 24.

Targeting: Case Play

9.4.3 SITUATION V: Defensive back B1 sees receiver A1 running a crossing route while A2 is taking the under route. As they near each other, B1 takes aim at A1 and: (a) makes contact to A1 above the shoulders with the shoulder pads of B1; (b) makes contact to A1 above the shoulders with the helmet of B1; (c) misses A1 but makes contact with A2 above the shoulders with the shoulder pads of B1; or (d) misses A1 but makes contact with A2 above the shoulders with the helmet of B1. **RULING:** In (a) and (c), B1 has committed a foul for targeting; in (b) and (d), B1 has committed both a targeting foul and a foul for illegal helmet contact. In (b) and (d), the targeting foul should be reported and enforced.

 9.4.3 COMMENT: It is critical that all game officials in a contest be aware of the actions of the players who may not be near the football. In addition to potentially being considered defenseless and needing additional protection, even those players directly involved in the play may not be targeted for contact above the shoulders (2-20-2; 9-4-3m).

◪ Rationale

Continuing with the focus on risk minimization, the committee determined that taking aim at an opponent with the helmet, forearm, hand, fist, elbow or shoulder, to initiate contact above the shoulders with an intent that goes beyond making a legal tackle, a legal block or playing the ball is prohibited. Furthermore, the committee feels it is important to separate and draw specific attention to this illegal act.

Initiating Contact with a Helmet-less Opponent

No player or nonplayer shall initiate contact with an opposing player whose helmet has come completely off (9-4-3l).

Initiating Contact with a Helmet-less Opponent: Penalty

15 yards. Signal 38.

Topic 5

Substitutions and Participation

PlayPic®

Key Terms

A player is one of the 22 team members who is designated to start either half of the game or who subsequently replaces another player. A player continues to be a player until a substitute enters the field and indicates to the player that he is replaced, or when the substitute otherwise becomes a player (2-32-1).

A nonplayer is a coach, athletic trainer, other attendant, a substitute or a replaced player who does not participate by touching the ball, hindering an opponent or influencing the play (2-32-10).

Participation is any act or action by a player or nonplayer that has an influence on the play (2-30). Participation by a replaced player, substitute, coach, athletic trainer or other team personnel is illegal participation (3-7-4 NOTE, 9-6).

Each team shall designate a player as field captain and only he may communicate with game officials. His first choice of any offered decision is final, except as in 6-5-4. Decisions involving penalties shall be made before any charged time-out is granted either team (1-4-1).

For convenience, a player is designated by his position on offense during the snap (1-4-2).

Topic:
Substitution

Each team shall begin the game with 11 players, but if it has no substitutes to replace injured or disqualified players, it may continue with fewer (1-1-3). A substitute is a team member who may replace a player or fill a player vacancy. A substitute becomes a player when he enters the field and communicates with a teammate or a game official, enters the huddle, is positioned in a formation or participates in the play. An entering substitute is not considered to be a player for encroachment restrictions until he is on his team's side of the neutral zone (2-8; 2-32-15).

A team member entering the field to fill a player vacancy remains a substitute until he is on his team's side of the neutral zone (2-32-15).

A replaced player is one who has been notified by a substitute that he is to leave the field. A player is also replaced when the entering substitute becomes a player (2-32-12).

Between downs any number of eligible substitutes may replace players. Upon meeting the criteria of 2-32-12, replaced players shall begin to leave the field within three seconds (3-7-1). During the same dead-ball interval, no substitute shall become a player and then withdraw and no player shall withdraw and re-enter as a substitute unless a penalty is accepted, a dead-ball foul occurs, there is a charged time-out or the period ends (3-7-3).

Substitution: Case Plays

1.1.3 SITUATION: During the waning moments of the game, a fight erupts and several players from each team are disqualified. When order is restored, it is discovered Team A has 11 players available and B has only nine. There are no other team members eligible for participation following the mass disqualification. **RULING:** Each team must have at least 11 players in order for the game to start. The game may continue even though one team does not have 11 players. There is no penalty for a team having fewer than 11 players, except when that team is on offense, there must be at least seven players on the line of scrimmage. If a team has fewer than seven players on the field when it is on offense, it may not put the ball in play and, therefore, must forfeit the game (2-14-1; 7-2-5a).

3.7.3 SITUATION A: B11 mistakenly believes he is his team's 12th player and leaves the field before the snap on his sideline and enters his team box. B11 then discovers his error and returns to field on his team's side of the neutral zone before the snap. **RULING:** There is no foul as long as B11 remains a player (2-32-1).

3.7.3 SITUATION D: It is third and 3 on A's 30 and A1 is downed short of the line to gain on his 28. Specialized kicker A12 immediately enters the field to replace A3 when the whistle is sounded, but prior to the referee signaling a time-out, because he had detected holding by B1. The captain of A accepts the penalty which results in first and 10 for A from its 38. Realizing the change of status: (a) A12 returns to his team box and is replaced by A3; or (b) A4 requests and is granted a charged time-out during which A12 returns to the team box. **RULING:** In (a), A12 may return as a penalty has been accepted for a foul which occurred during the down. In (b), A12 may be replaced without penalty because the substitution was made during a charged time-out.

3.7.5 SITUATION A: Substitute (a) A1, or (b) B1, noticing his team has only 10 players on the field, comes onto the field just as the ball is about to be snapped. **RULING:** In (a), A1 must be on the field on A's side of the neutral zone, inside the 9-yard marks, and not violate the shift or motion provisions. Furthermore, the act of his coming onto the field must not deceive the defensive team. In (b), the substitution is legal as long as B1 is on the field on B's side of the neutral zone prior to the snap (3-7-6; 7-2-1,6,7; 9-6-4).

Dead-Ball Illegal Substitution

A player, replaced player or a substitute who has been unable to complete the substitution, is required to leave the field at the side on which his team box is located and go directly to his team box (3-7-2).

During the same dead-ball interval, no substitute shall become a player and then withdraw and no player shall withdraw and re-enter as a substitute unless a penalty is accepted, a dead-ball foul occurs, there is a charged time-out or the period ends (3-7-3).

Dead-Ball Illegal Substitution: Penalty

5 yards. Signals 7 and 22.

Dead-Ball Illegal Substitution: Case Plays

3.7.1 SITUATION A: Substitutes A12 and B12 properly enter the game between downs. The replaced player of A remains in the team huddle while the replaced B player leaves the field within three seconds. **RULING:** In this situation, A is charged with a 5-yard penalty (dead ball) for an illegal substitution because the replaced player of A did not leave within three seconds as required.

3.7.3 SITUATION A: B11 mistakenly believes he is his team's 12th player and leaves the field before the snap on his opponent's sideline. **RULING:** B11 has committed illegal substitution by leaving on the opponent's sideline (3-7-2).

3.7.3 SITUATION B: It is first and 10 on B's 12-yard line and substitute B12 comes onto the field to replace B2 and communicates with him. Prior to the ball becoming live: (a) B2 leaves the field of play through the end zone and across B's sideline without crossing the end line and continues toward his team box; or (b) B12, seeing that he will be unable to replace B2 before the ball is snapped, returns to his team box; or (c) B2, seeing that he will not be able to reach the sideline before the ball is snapped, leaves the field through the end zone and remains to observe the play; or (d) B12 becomes confused and withdraws through the end zone across the end line and goes around the field to return to B's team box. **RULING:** In (a), the act is legal. In (b), (c) and (d), it is a nonplayer foul for illegal substitution. A player, replaced player or substitute is required to go directly to his team box. A substitute may not enter and withdraw in the same dead ball interval.

3.7.3 SITUATION C: With fourth and 5 from B's 40, B12 enters and takes a position as a punt-returner and the replaced player leaves the field. B12 then realizes A is not going to punt and he returns to his team box. **RULING:** Illegal substitution. B12 became a player when he positioned in the formation and he must remain in the game for at least one down unless a penalty is accepted, a dead-ball foul occurs, there is a charged time-out or the period ends (2-32).

Live-Ball Illegal Substitution

During a down a replaced player or substitute who attempts unsuccessfully to leave the field and who does not participate in or affect the play, constitutes an illegal substitution (3-7-4).

An entering substitute shall be on his team's side of the neutral zone when the ball is snapped or free kicked (3-7-5).

During a down a replaced player or substitute who enters but does not participate constitutes illegal substitution (3-7-6).

Live-Ball Illegal Substitution: Penalty

5 yards. Signal 22.

Live-Ball Illegal Substitution: Case Plays

3.7 COMMENT: A procedure has been adopted to provide an equitable penalty as it relates to illegal substitution. The following are examples of the most common situations and rulings:

1. If a replaced player or substitute attempts to leave the field, but does not get off prior to the snap, the foul is considered as having occurred simultaneously with the snap and the penalty is enforced from the previous spot (3-7-4; 10-4-2a).
2. If a replaced player does not leave the field within three-seconds, it is a dead-ball, illegal-substitution foul (3-7-1).
3. If a replaced player or substitute goes off the field on the wrong side of the field during the down, it is an illegal substitution (live-ball foul at snap) (10-4-4).
4. If an entering substitute is not on his team's side of the neutral zone at the snap, illegal substitution is considered to have

occurred simultaneously with the snap. If he then participates, it becomes a live-ball foul, illegal participation (3-7-5; 9-6-4a).

5. When a replaced player or substitute leaves on the wrong side of the field or goes across the end line prior to the snap, it is a dead-ball foul for illegal substitution (3-7-2; 10-4-4).

6. If a replaced player or substitute enters the field during the down, but does not participate, it is a foul for illegal substitution by a nonplayer, a 5-yard penalty from the succeeding spot (3-7-5; 9-6-4a). In addition, the following chart should help game officials distinguish the actions of various individuals who enter the field, during the down, but do not participate.

Nonplayer enters during down.	5 yards	Succeeding spot (non player)
Substitute enters during down.	5 yards	Succeeding spot (non player)
Player re-enters during down after being on field of play for previous down then leaves the field.	5 yards	Nonplayer foul
Player who should be on field of play enters during down (11th or fewer player).	5 yards	Succeeding spot (non player)

3.7.1 SITUATION B: A number of team substitutes enter the field between downs. The game officials do not recognize that one replaced player does not leave the field within three seconds. When the ball is snapped: (a) B12 is attempting to get off the field, or (b) A12 is in the formation as an extra lineman. **RULING:** In (a), it is an illegal substitution foul and in (b) it is illegal participation.

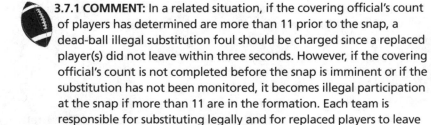 **3.7.1 COMMENT:** In a related situation, if the covering official's count of players has determined are more than 11 prior to the snap, a dead-ball illegal substitution foul should be charged since a replaced player(s) did not leave within three seconds. However, if the covering official's count is not completed before the snap is imminent or if the substitution has not been monitored, it becomes illegal participation at the snap if more than 11 are in the formation. Each team is responsible for substituting legally and for replaced players to leave within three seconds as required (3-7-4; 9-6-4c).

3.7.5 SITUATION B: Prior to the snap, B11 recognizes he is to be in the game and he enters on A's side of the neutral zone. The ball is snapped before B11 gets to his team side. **RULING:** Illegal substitution at the snap. If the 5-yard penalty is accepted, it is enforced from the previous spot (10-4-2).

In Simple Terms

From 1926 to 1936, substitutes could not verbally communicate with teammates until after one play had been run.

5.1.2 SITUATION B: During A1's run for a first down to B's 20-yard line, B12 commits a nonplayer foul for a substitute entering the field during the down, but not participating. Immediately following the down, A1 taunts an opponent. **RULING:** If accepted, the penalty for B entering during the down is enforced from the succeeding spot. After the decision on this penalty, A will be penalized 15 yards for unsportsmanlike conduct and A will have the ball for a new series, first and 10 (3-7-6; 9-5-1a).

Topic:
Illegal Participation

Prior to a change of possession, or when there is no change of possession, no player of A or K shall go out of bounds and return to the field during the down unless blocked out of bounds by an opponent. If a player is blocked out of bounds by an opponent and returns to the field during the down, he shall return at the first opportunity (9-6-1).

No player shall intentionally go out of bounds during the down and return to the field, intentionally touch the ball, influence the play or otherwise participate (9-6-2a-d).

No replaced player, substitute, coach, athletic trainer or other team personnel shall hinder an opponent, touch the ball, influence the play or otherwise participate (9-6-3).

It is illegal participation when any player, replaced player, substitute coach, athletic trainer or other team personnel enters and participates during a down (9-6-4a).

It is illegal participation if an injured player is not replaced for at least one down, unless the halftime or intermission occurs; to have 12 or more players participating at the snap or free kick; to use a player, replaced player or substitute in a substitution or pretended substitution to deceive opponents at or immediately before the snap or free kick; for a player to be lying on the ground to deceive opponents at or immediately before the snap or free kick; for a disqualified player to re-enter the game; or for a player whose helmet comes completely off during a down to continue to participate beyond the immediate action in which the player is engaged (9-6-4b-g). A disqualified player is a player barred from further participation in a game (2-32-6). A disqualified player shall be removed (10-5-6).

Illegal Participation: Penalty

15 yards, previous spot. Signal 28.

Illegal Participation: Case Plays

3.7.1 SITUATION B: A number of team substitutes enter the field between downs. The game officials do not recognize that one replaced player does not leave the field within three seconds. When the ball is snapped: (a) B12 is attempting to get off the field, or (b) A12 is in the formation as an extra lineman. **RULING:** In (a), it is an illegal substitution foul and in (b) it is illegal participation.

3.7.1 COMMENT: In a related situation, if the covering official's count of players has determined there are more than 11 prior to the snap, a dead-ball illegal substitution foul should be charged since a replaced player(s) did not leave within three seconds. However, if the game official's count is not completed before the snap is imminent or if the substitution has not been monitored, it becomes illegal participation at the snap if more than 11 are in the formation. Each team is responsible for substituting legally and for replaced players to leave within three seconds as required (3-7-4; 9-6-4c).

> **Did You Know?** In the 1950s, the foul for a player who attempted the hide-out play was known as "lingering."

3.7.3 SITUATION A: B11 mistakenly believes he is his team's 12th player and leaves the field before the snap (a) on his opponent's sideline, or (b) on his sideline and enters his team box. B11 then discovers his error and returns to field on his team's side of the neutral zone before the snap. **RULING:** In (a) B11 has committed illegal substitutions by leaving on the opponent's sideline (3-7-2). In (b), there is no foul as long as B11 remains a player (2-32-1). If done intentionally to gain an advantage, it is illegal participation foul or it could be an unsportsmanlike foul. If B11 returns to the field after the snap in either (a) or (b) and participates, it is a live-ball foul for illegal participation (9-5-1f; 9-6-4 a and d).

9.6 COMMENT: A procedure has been adopted to provide an equitable penalty as it relates to illegal participation. The following are examples of the most common situations and rulings:

1. If there are more than 11 players in the formation at the snap, either offensively or defensively, the foul is considered as having occurred simultaneously with the snap and is illegal participation. The 15-yard penalty is enforced from the previous spot (9-6-4c).

2. If a substitute enters the field during the down and participates, it is illegal participation and enforced from the basic spot using the all-but-one principle. The spot of the foul is where the substitute participated, not necessarily where he entered the field (9-6-4a).

3. If a nonplayer hinders an opponent outside the field of play, it constitutes illegal participation. The spot of the foul is on the yard line directly inbounds (9-6-3).

4. Prior to a change of possession or when there is no change of possession, a player of A or K who goes out of bounds and then comes back in during the down commits illegal participation (9-6-1). In addition, the following chart should help game officials distinguish the actions of various team members who enter the field during the down and participate.

Play situation (violator does not participate)

Nonplayer enters during down.	5 yards	Succeeding spot (nonplayer)
Substitute enters during down.	5 yards	Succeeding spot (nonplayer)
Player re-enters during down after being on field of play for previous down then leaves the field.	5 yards	Nonplayer foul
Player who should be on field of play enters during down (11th or fewer player).	5 yards	Succeeding spot (nonplayer)

9.6.1 SITUATION A: With third down and 20 from B's 40-yard line, A1 accidentally steps out of bounds at B's 30 while running a sideline pattern. A1 returns inbounds at the 28. Quarterback A2's forward pass is: (a) overthrown and incomplete; or (b) caught by A1 at B's 25; or (c) in flight to A1 when B1 contacts him and it falls incomplete. **RULING:** In (a) and (b), it is illegal participation by A1. In (c), A1's illegal participation and B1's pass interference result in a double foul and replay of the down.

 9.6.1 COMMENT: When A1 goes out of bounds voluntarily or by accident, or delays his return after being blocked out by an opponent, he commits an illegal participation foul when he returns inbounds. The spot of the foul is where he returns inbounds (10-2-1).

9.6.1 SITUATION B: Third and 10 from B's 40-yard line. A1's forward pass is intercepted by B1 on B's 20 and returned to midfield. End A2 accidentally steps on the sideline at B's 30: (a) before, or (b) after the interception. In both cases A2 returns inbounds at B's 25, but does not make any attempt to catch the ball or tackle B1. **RULING:** In (a), it is an illegal participation foul at B's 25 because A2 returned after being out of bounds prior to the interception. No foul in (b) because A2 did not go out of bounds until after the change of possession with the interception by B1.

9.6.1 SITUATION C: Fourth and 15 on K's 30-yard line. K1 accidentally steps on the sideline while K2's punt is in the air. K1 returns inbounds at midfield: (a) before, or (b) after R1 catches the ball and makes the tackle on R's 40. **RULING:** Since K1 went out of bounds before the change of possession, it is an illegal participation foul in both (a) and (b) when he returns inbounds. In (a), if accepted, the penalty is enforced from the previous spot as the foul occurred during a loose ball play. In (b), since the foul occurred during R1's run, the 15-yard penalty is enforced from the end of R1's run.

9.6.1 SITUATION D: Between second and third downs, Team A's head coach sends several substitutes into the game. A11, believing that he has been replaced, leaves the field and goes directly to his team's box. Realizing that his position has not been substituted for, A11 enters the field as the ball is being snapped, runs a pass pattern, and catches the ball for a first down. **RULING:** This is illegal participation and is marked off 15 yards from the basic spot.

9.6.2 SITUATION A: Eligible receiver A1 runs beyond Team B's end line. Quarterback A2 throws a legal forward pass in A1's direction. A1 leaps and, while airborne, bats the ball to eligible teammate A3, who is in Team B's end zone. **RULING:** Illegal participation on A1. Because A1 went out of bounds intentionally and influenced the play, he has gained an advantage and illegal participation.

9.6.2 SITUATION B: Linebacker B1 runs out of bounds while the ball is live. As runner A2 advances past B1, B1 reaches inbounds and tackles A2. **RULING:** Illegal participation.

9.6.2 SITUATION C: K1 free-kicks the ball toward the sideline. R1 runs to a sideline and intentionally steps out of bounds. While R1 is still out of bounds, he intentionally touches the ball as it nears the sideline. The ball is declared dead by the covering official. **RULING:** Illegal participation by R1 (4-3-1; 6-1-9).

9.6.4 SITUATION A: Several A substitutes enter the field between downs and go to the team's huddle, but one replaced player does not leave within three seconds and is not detected. However, when they break the huddle the replaced player runs toward his sideline and leaves the field just before the ball is snapped. **RULING:** An illegal participation foul if the game official judges that A was using a replaced player or substitute in a substitution or pretended substitution to deceive the opponents. If not, it is illegal substitution.

 9.6.4 COMMENT: It is becoming prevalent to see more than 11 players/replaced players in a team's huddle or in the defensive formation between downs. The replaced player is to leave the field within three seconds and in such a manner that it does not confuse or deceive the opponents (3-7-1).

◪ Rationale

It is becoming prevalent to see more than 11 players/replaced players in a team's huddle or in the defensive formation between downs. The rule prevents a replaced player from failing to leave the field immediately and in such a manner that it does not confuse or deceive the opponents.

*9.6.4 SITUATION B: Following a kickoff return, A1 and A2 enter the field while A3, A4 and A5 move toward the sideline. A5 stops within the 9-yard marks while A3 and A4 continue toward the team box. The ball is blown ready for play with A3 and A4 outside the 9-yard marks and is snapped without a huddle and the quarterback throws a forward pass to A4, who has gone downfield as a wide receiver. **RULING:** This play is illegal because a pretended substitution is used to deceive the opponents. The penalty of 15 yards for the illegal participation foul will be administered from the previous spot since the foul occurred at the snap (9-6-4d).

9.6.4 SITUATION C: With third and 10 from B's 30-yard line, A1 runs to B's 18-yard line where he is tackled. During the down: substitute A12 comes onto the field and blocks B1. **RULING:** A12 is guilty of illegal participation (2-16-2; 2-32; 2-41-8).

9.6.4 SITUATION D: A1 is injured and is treated on the field. A subsequently requests a time-out. During the next down, A1 runs 20 yards for the go-ahead score. Following the score, B requests a time-out so the coach may discuss A1's participation with the referee. **RULING:** A rule obviously has not been correctly applied as A1 must leave the game for at least one down following his injury. The touchdown is canceled and a penalty for illegal participation is enforced. A1 must leave the game for at least one down (3-5-10).

9.6.4 SITUATION E: With third down and 12 yards to go from A's 45-yard line, quarterback A1 throws a pass to A2 at B's 45-yard line. Teammate A12 moves to get a better view of the play and enters the field of play at B's 40-yard line. During the run after the reception, (a) A2 collides with A12 and is thereafter tackled by B1; or (b) B1 slows to avoid A12 as A1 runs for a touchdown. **RULING:** Illegal participation in (a) and (b). The penalty of 15 yards is enforced using the "all-but-one" principle. Illegal participation occurs since substitute A12 hindered a teammate or an opponent and participated in the play. The spot of the foul is where the participation occurred, not where A12 entered the field (2-30; 9-6-4a).

9.6.4 SITUATION F: A1 is engaged with B1 in close line play. A1's helmet comes completely off as the play goes downfield without being caused by a foul by any member of B. A1, without his helmet, pursues the play downfield and (a) does or (b) doesn't make contact with a blocker. **RULING:** Illegal participation in both (a) and (b). Once the player's helmet comes completely off, he is to cease involvement with the play. He must also be removed for the next play if the helmet coming off was not caused by an opponent's foul (9-6-4, 3-5-10d).

9.6.4 SITUATION G: B54's helmet comes completely off during an attempt to tackle A32. Without losing contact, A32 drags B54 for a few yards before finally going down to the ground. **RULING:** Legal play by B54 because he is still engaged in the "immediate action" of attempting to tackle A32. After the play is over, B54 must leave the field for at least one play (3-5-10d; 9-6-4g).

9.6.4 SITUATION H: B54's helmet comes completely off during an attempt to tackle A32. A32 fumbles the ball, and B54: (a) without disengaging, completes his tackle of A32 who recovers the fumble; (b) without disengaging, completes his tackle of A32, and upon contacting the ground, recovers the ball that has fallen directly below him; (c) disengages immediately from A32 and tries to recover the fumble that has rolled away from the two players; or (d) after tackling A32, then attempts to recover the fumble. **RULING:** Legal in (a). In (b), recovery is legal provided all contact was in the immediate area. In (c) and (d), it is illegal participation. In all cases, B54 must leave the field for at least one play (3-5-10d; 9-6-4g).

Topic 6

Enforcements

PlayPic®

Key Terms

A rule is one of the groups of regulations which govern the game. A rule sometimes states what a player may do, but if there is no such statement for a given act (such as faking a kick), it is assumed that he may do what is not prohibited. In like manner, a rule sometimes states or implies that the ball is dead or that a foul is involved. If it does not, it is assumed that the ball is live and that no foul has occurred. If a foul is mentioned, it is assumed that it is not part of a double or multiple foul unless so stated or implied (2-37).

A penalty is a result imposed by rule against a team or team member that has committed a foul (2-16-5). A foul is a rule infraction for which a penalty is prescribed (2-16-1). No foul causes loss of the ball (2-16-3). No foul causes a live ball to become dead (2-16-4).

A player is one of the 22 team members who is designated to start either half of the game or who subsequently replaces another player. A player continues to be a player until a substitute enters the field and indicates to the player that he is replaced, or when the substitute otherwise becomes a player (2-32-1).

Fundamental X-2
Penalties are either 5, 10 or 15 yards.

A nonplayer is a coach, athletic trainer, other attendant, a substitute or a replaced player who does not participate by touching the ball, hindering an opponent or influencing the play (2-32-10).

A runner is a player who is in possession of a live ball or is simulating possession of a live ball (2-32-13).

The spot where a run ends is where the ball becomes dead in the runner's possession, but the related run (related running play) continues until the ball becomes dead or any player gains possession, where the runner loses player possession if his run is followed by a loose ball, or the spot of the catch or recovery when the momentum rule is in effect (2-41-9a-c; 10-3-3 a-c).

Enforcement of a penalty cannot take the ball more than half the distance from the enforcement spot to the offending team's goal line. If the prescribed penalty is greater than this, the ball is placed halfway from the spot of enforcement to the goal line (10-1-5).

Game situations which produce results somewhat similar to penalties, but which are not classified as fouls are: disqualification of a player, first touching of a kick by K and forfeiture of a game (2-16-6).

A captain represents his team to make penalty decisions following a foul (2-32-5b).

◪ Rationale

Acceptance of a penalty should not place a team at a disadvantage. Declining the distance portion of a penalty eliminates that potential in kicking situations.

Topic:
Types of Fouls

Before or After Change of Possession

If each team fouls during a down in which there is a change of team possession and the play does not have a post-scrimmage kick foul, the team last gaining possession may retain the ball, provided the foul by the team last gaining possession is not prior to the final change of possession and the team last gaining possession declines the penalty for its opponent's foul(s), other than a nonplayer or unsportsmanlike foul. In this case, the team that was not last in possession has no penalty options until the team last in possession has made its penalty decision on the fouls prior to the change of possession. After that decision by the team last in possession, the team not last in possession may decline or accept the penalty by the team last in possession or choose which foul to have enforced in the case that the team last in possession committed more than one foul following the change (10-2-2).

If each team fouls during a down in which there is a change of possession and all R fouls are post-scrimmage kick fouls, then R may retain the ball, provided R declines the penalty for K's foul(s), other than a nonplayer or unsportsmanlike foul. In this case, the team that was not last in possession has no penalty options until the team last in possession has made its penalty decision. After that decision by the team last in possession, the team not last in possession may decline or accept the penalty by the team last in possession or choose which foul to have enforced in the case that the team last in possession committed more than one foul following the change (10-2-3).

A foul during a try is not paired with a dead-ball foul to create a double or multiple foul (10-2-6).

Rationale

The "clean hands" rule prevents an inequity that once appeared in the rules. If A2 were illegally in motion and B1 intercepted a pass, a foul by B2 during the runback would have constituted a double foul and caused the down to be replayed. The current rule allows team B the option of accepting the penalty for the foul by A2 or declining it and retaining the ball. If the penalty for A's foul were declined in order to keep the ball, the penalty for the foul by B2 would then be administered. The rule separates the two fouls and removes them from the double foul category. A foul by the team after it has gained possession is penalized.

Before or After Change of Possession: Case Plays

10.1.3 SITUATION: With fourth and 10 at the 50-yard line, K2 illegally uses his hands during a scrimmage kick by K1. R1 signals for a fair catch. The ball is caught by R2, who advances following the whistle. **RULING:** R may decline the penalty for the illegal use of hands by K2 and retain possession. If this choice is made, R will put the ball in play first and 10 following the penalty for the dead-ball, delay-of-game foul by R2. If R decides to accept the penalty for the foul by K2, the result will be fourth and 15 for K following the enforcement of penalties for both fouls and the down will be replayed (3-6-2b; 10-2-2).

10.2.2 SITUATION A: During a legal forward pass which crosses the neutral zone, A1 is illegally in motion at the snap. B1 intercepts and during his return, B2 clips A2. **RULING:** The illegal motion by A1 and the clipping by B2 are both live-ball fouls, but because the foul by B2 followed a change of team possession, they do not automatically constitute a double foul. The captain of B (last team in possession) may accept or decline the penalty for A's foul. If accepted, this creates a double foul and the down is replayed. If declined, then the penalty for B's foul is enforced if accepted by A (10-1-3; 10-2-1b).

10.2.2 SITUATION B: A1's pass is intercepted by B1 at B's 40-yard line. During B1's return, A1 and B2 begin fighting at A's 40-yard line. B1 returns the ball to A's 2-yard line. **RULING:** The captain of B (last team in possession) may accept or decline the penalty for A's foul. If B accepts the penalty for A1's foul, it creates a double foul. B may retain possession by declining the penalty for A1's foul, in which case, it would be B's ball at its own 45-yard line following enforcement of B's penalty (if accepted by A). Both A1 and B2 will be disqualified for fighting.

10.2.2 COMMENT: Whenever both teams foul during a change of possession down and the team in final possession gets the ball free of a foul (with "CLEAN HANDS") they have the opportunity to retain possession. The fact that their opponent's foul occurred after the change of possession has no bearing on the enforcement. However, when B, the "clean hands" team, retains possession by declining the opponent's foul, the penalty for B's foul may be enforced (9-4-1 Penalty; 10-2-1b).

10.2.2 SITUATION C: A leads 21-20 with three seconds remaining in the fourth quarter. It is A's ball fourth and 1 yard to go on A's 45-yard line. A1 muffs the snap, and A2 holds while the ball is loose. B1 recovers and advances to A's 1-yard line where he is downed. During B1's advance, B2 clips at A's 10-yard line and time expires during the down. In an effort to prevent a double foul, Team B declines the penalty for A2's foul. The captain of A then wishes to decline the penalty for B2's foul. **RULING:** The game is over as there is no accepted penalty on the play (3-3-3a).

10.2.3 SITUATION: A scrimmage kick by K1 is caught by R1, who advances to K's 10. During the run by R1, there is clipping by R2 at K's 30 and K2 trips R2. **RULING:** Because there was a change of team possession during the down and R2's foul followed the change, R may decline the penalty for the tripping foul by K2 and retain possession. If R chooses to do this, it will be first and 10 for R from K's 45-yard line. If R accepts the penalty for tripping by K2, it automatically results in a double foul and a replay of the down.

10.4.4 SITUATION A: Fourth and 5 for K from R's 49-yard line. R9 catches the kick on the 15-yard line and returns the ball to R's 40-yard line, where he is downed. During the return, R3 holds K7 at R's 30-yard line. **RULING:** Following enforcement of R's holding penalty, it would R's ball, first and 10 from R's 20-yard line. This is not a post-scrimmage kick enforcement, but a post-possession foul (2-41-6).

10.4.4 SITUATION B: A1 throws a pass from B's 22-yard line. B1 intercepts the pass in his own end zone and is tackled prior to leaving the end zone. During the run, B2 holds A2 at B's 10-yard line. **RULING:** The basic enforcement spot is the 20-yard line. If the penalty is accepted, it will be enforced from the spot of the foul. B will have a first and 10 from its own 5-yard line. If the penalty is declined, it will be B's first and 10 from B's 20-yard line.

10.4.6 SITUATION B: B1 intercepts A's pass in B's end zone, B2 clips A9 at B's 10-yard line after the change of possession. B1 then fumbles in B's end zone and the ball rolls out of the end zone and out of bounds at B's 2-yard line. **RULING:** The penalty is enforced under the all-but-one principle. The basic spot is the 20-yard line. The penalty would be enforced half the distance, first and 10 for B on the 5-yard line (10-4-6).

Dead-Ball Fouls

A dead-ball foul occurs in the time interval after a down has ended and before the ball is next snapped or free kicked (2-16-2a).

Penalties for dead-ball fouls, other than when both teams commit unsportsmanlike, nonplayer or dead-ball personal fouls prior to the completion of penalty administration for those fouls, are administered separately and in the order of occurrence. A dead-ball foul is not coupled with a live-ball foul or another dead-ball foul to create a double or multiple foul (10-2-5a).

If both teams commit unsportsmanlike, nonplayer or dead-ball personal fouls prior to the completion of penalty administration for those fouls, the distance penalty for an equal number of 15-yard unsportsmanlike, nonplayer or dead-ball personal fouls will offset. Any remaining penalties will be enforced separately and in the order of occurrence (10-2-5b).

A foul during a try is not paired with a dead-ball foul to create a double or multiple foul (10-2-6).

Dead-Ball Fouls: Case Plays

10.2.5 SITUATION B: In a state where tie games are resolved by the 10-Yard Line Procedure, the game ends in a tie. Immediately following the final whistle, there is a fight between A1 and B1 and: (a) none of the game officials observed which player actually struck the first blow; or (b) A1 struck B1 who retaliated; or (c) B1 first struck A1 who retaliated. In (a), (b) and (c), A wins the toss and elects to go on defense first. **RULING:** In (a), (b) and (c), A1 and B1 will be disqualified for fighting and they may not participate in the overtime. In (a), (b) and (c), the distance penalties cancel and the overtime will begin with B putting the ball in play, first and goal, from the 10-yard line (2-11; 10-2-5b, c).

*10.2.5 SITUATION C: On third and 8 from B's 45-yard line, runner A1 falls to the ground as he goes out of bounds at B's 40. B1 piles on. A2 then punches B2. The covering official indicates the fouls by both B1 and A2. The coach of B then insults the game official for calling the foul on B1.

RULING: The distance penalties for B1's dead-ball personal foul and A2's punch cancel. The unsportsmanlike foul against the coach of B will be enforced with a 15-yard penalty, giving A a first and 10 from B's 25. A2 shall be disqualified for fighting (9-4-1; 9-4-3c; 9-8-1c; 10-2-5b, c; 10-4-4).

10.2.5 SITUATION D: A has the ball, third and 7 from A's 20-yard line and runner A1 is driven out of bounds at the A25. Following the play, a fight breaks out involving A1, A2, B1, B2, B3 and B4. All six players are flagged for their involvement in the fight. **RULING:** The distance penalties for the two fouls against Team A, and two of the fouls against Team B cancel. The remaining two fouls against Team B are enforced separately and in order, resulting in a first and 10 for A at B's 45-yard line. A1, A2, B1, B2, B3 and B4 are disqualified for fighting (9-4-1; 10-2-5b, c; 10-4-4).

10.2.5 SITUATION E: A has the ball, third and 6 from B's 45-yard line and runner A1 is driven out of bounds at B's 35-yard line. Following the play, a fight breaks out involving A1, A2, A3, A4, B1 and B2. All six players are flagged for their involvement in the fight. **RULING:** The distance penalties for two fouls against Team A, and the two fouls against Team B cancel. The remaining two distance penalties against Team A are enforced separately and in order. Since the live-ball action gave A a new series, the line to gain shall be established after A is penalized for the two remaining fouls. This results in a first and 10 for A at A's 35-yard line. A1, A2, A3, A4, B1 and B2 are disqualified for fighting (5-1-2a; 9-4-1; 10-2-5b, c; 10-4-4).

*10.2.5 SITUATION F: On third and 10 from B's 40-yard line, A1 runs out of bounds at B's 35-yard line. After A1 is out of bounds, B1 charges into A1, knocking him to the ground. A2 retaliates by shoving B1. B1 then swears at A2. A's coach swears at the wing official: (a) before the referee has determined the appropriate enforcement of the penalties; or (b) after the referee is giving his signals and the umpire begins marking off the enforcement. **RULING:** In (a), since penalty enforcement had not yet been determined, the penalties for A's two fouls will offset the penalties for B's two fouls, resulting in fourth and 5 from B's 35-yard line. In (b), because the foul on Team A's coach occurred after determination of penalty enforcement, that penalty will be enforced separately. Since there were initially two fouls by Team B and one foul by Team A, the referee would have already determined that the penalty for only one of B's fouls would be enforced 15 yards to B's 20-yard line, giving Team A a first down. Team A will then be penalized 15 yards for the last foul from B's 20-yard line to B's 35-yard line, where it will be first and 10 for Team A.

Double Fouls

It is a double foul if both teams commit fouls, other than nonplayer or unsportsmanlike, during the same live-ball period in which there is no change of team possession, unless all fouls committed by R are post-scrimmage kick fouls; there is a change of team possession, and the team in possession at the end of the down fouls prior to final change of possession unless all fouls committed by R are post-scrimmage kick fouls; or there is a change of possession and the team in final possession accepts the penalty for its opponent's foul. In the event of a double foul, the penalties cancel and the down is replayed (2-16-2b, 10-2-1a-c).

Fundamental IX-4
A foul during a try is not paired with a dead-ball foul to make a double or multiple foul.

Double Fouls: Case Plays

7.5.10 SITUATION A: During a forward-pass play in which the ball crosses the neutral zone, A1, an ineligible receiver, is illegally downfield and: (a) B1 illegally contacts him with an elbow; or (b) A1 blocks B1. **RULING:** In (a), the personal foul by B1 and A1's foul for being downfield combine to make a double foul and the down will be replayed. The contact by B1 is not defensive pass interference because A1 was an ineligible receiver. Defensive pass interference may occur only against eligible receivers. Had there been no contact and had ineligible A1 touched such a pass, the result would have been illegal touching. In (b), it is a multiple foul for an ineligible illegally downfield and also offensive pass interference (7-5-6a; 7-5-13; 10-2-1, 10-2-3).

10.2.1 SITUATION A: During a run by A1, A2 is holding B1. Thereafter, a fumble by A1 is recovered by B2 who advances for a touchdown. While the ball was loose during the fumble, B3 clipped A3. **RULING:** Double foul. Both fouls occurred before the change of team possession and the action thus constitutes a double foul. The penalties cancel and the down shall be replayed (10-2-2).

10.2.1 SITUATION B: K1 is in an illegal position and the scrimmage kick by K2 is caught by R1. During the return by R1, there is clipping by R2 and a subsequent fumble by R1 is recovered by K3. **RULING:** Double foul. Even though there was a change of team possession during the down, the team gaining final possession had fouled before gaining possession. Both fouls occurred during the live-ball period and the result is a double foul. The penalties cancel and the down shall be replayed (10-2-2).

10.2.1 SITUATION C: With fourth and 15 from midfield, K is called for illegal formation. R1 catches K1's punt, but is tackled by the face mask/helmet opening by K2. R2 strikes K3 prior to the end of the run. **RULING:** If R accepts the penalty for either foul by K, it is a double foul. R may decline the penalties and retain possession following enforcement of the penalty for R2's foul. In either case, R2 shall be disqualified (9-4-3h; 10-2-3).

Flagrant Fouls

A flagrant foul is a foul that results in disqualification that may or may not involve physical contact and may include but is not limited to fighting, intentionally contacting an official, a foul so severe or extreme that it places an opponent in danger of serious injury, a foul that involves vulgar language or gestures, or a foul that involves persistent or extreme abusive conduct (2-16-2c). Acts that may be judged to be flagrant include, but are not limited to illegal helmet contact against an opponent lying on the ground, illegal helmet contact against an opponent being held up by other players, and/or illegal helmet to helmet contact against a defenseless opponent (9-4-3i NOTE).

Flagrant Fouls: Penalty

15 yards and disqualification. Signal 47.

Live-Ball Fouls

A live-ball foul occurs during a down (2-16-2d).

Multiple Fouls

Multiple fouls are two or more live-ball fouls (other than nonplayer or unsportsmanlike) committed during the same down by the same team at such a time that the offended team is permitted a choice of penalties. When two or more live-ball fouls (other than nonplayer or unsportsmanlike) are committed during the same down by the same team (multiple fouls), only one penalty may be enforced. The offended captain may choose which one shall be administered, or the captain may decline all penalties. When a team commits a nonplayer or unsportsmanlike foul during that same down, it is administered from the succeeding spot as established by the acceptance or declination of the penalty for the other foul (2-16-2e, 10-2-4).

A foul during a try is not paired with a dead-ball foul to create a double or multiple foul (10-2-6).

Multiple Fouls: Case Plays

7.5.10 SITUATION A: During a forward-pass play in which the ball crosses the neutral zone, A1, an ineligible receiver, is illegally downfield and: (a) B1 illegally contacts him with an elbow; or (b) A1 blocks B1. **RULING:** In (a), the personal foul by B1 and A1's foul for being downfield combine to make a double foul and the down will be replayed. The contact by B1 is not defensive pass interference because A1 was an ineligible receiver. Defensive pass interference may occur only against eligible receivers. Had there been no contact and had ineligible A1 touched such a pass, the result would have been illegal touching. In (b), it is a multiple foul for an ineligible illegally downfield and also offensive pass interference (7-5-6a; 7-5-13; 10-2-1, 10-2-3).

8.2.2 SITUATION E: Prior to the ball being thrown during a play in which A1 catches a touchdown pass and advances for a touchdown, B1 holds A2 to prevent him from going out for a pass on the side away from the play. When given options, A elects to enforce the penalty for the defensive holding foul on the subsequent kickoff. During the successful two-point try, B1 is guilty of holding A1. Does A have the option of having the 10-yard penalty added on to the previous 10-yard penalty on the subsequent kickoff? **RULING:** Yes. The fouls did not occur during the same down, so these are not multiple fouls and, therefore, they may both be enforced on the subsequent kickoff (8-3-5b; 10-2-4).

10.2.4 SITUATION: With first and 10 from A's 30, A1 advances to B's 40, where he fumbles. A2 recovers and advances to B's 10, where he is downed. While the ball was loose following A1's fumble, B1 held A1, and during the advance by A2, B2 grabbed A2's face mask/helmet opening. **RULING:** This is a multiple foul and the captain of Team A may accept either penalty or decline both and take the results of the play. If the penalty is accepted for B1's foul it will be enforced from the end of A1's run where he fumbled. It would be first and 10 from B's 30. If the penalty for B2's foul is accepted, it will be enforced from the end of A2's run. In this case it would be first and goal for A from B's 5-yard line (10-3-3a).

Noncontact Fouls by Players

No player shall act in an unsportsmanlike manner once the game officials assume authority for the contest. Examples are, but not limited to baiting or taunting acts or words or insignia worn which engenders ill will; using profanity, insulting or vulgar language or gestures; any delayed, excessive or prolonged act by which a player attempts to focus attention upon himself; using disconcerting acts or words prior to the snap in an attempt to interfere with A's signals or movements; intentionally kicking at the ball, other than during a legal kick; leaving the field between downs to gain an advantage unless replaced or unless with permission of a game official; refusing to comply with a game official's request; or using tobacco or smokeless tobacco (9-5-1a through h).

The NFHS disapproves of any form of taunting which is intended or designed to embarrass, ridicule or demean others under any circumstances (9-5-1a NOTE).

When the ball becomes dead in possession of a player, he shall not intentionally kick the ball, spike the ball into the ground, throw the ball high into the air or from the field of play or intentionally fail to place the ball on the ground or immediately return it to a nearby game official (9-5-2a through d).

Noncontact Fouls by Players: Penalty

15 yards. Signal 27. Disqualification if flagrant, or if a player or nonplayer accumulates two unsportsmanlike fouls. Signal 47.

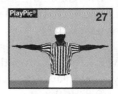

Noncontact Fouls by Players: Case Play

7.1.7 SITUATION C: On third and 10 from A's 40-yard line, all team A players are set. While quarterback A1 is calling signals, defensive back B1, starting from a position eight yards behind his line of scrimmage, runs toward the neutral zone. B1 stops directly in front of tackle A4 but does not enter the neutral zone. In response to B1's charge, A4 (a) does not move, or (b) flinches. **RULING:** No foul in (a). In (b), A4 is guilty of a dead-ball foul for false start. If in the game official's judgment the action by B1 was for the purpose of disconcerting or hindering A, it is an unsportsmanlike conduct foul. In this case, the game official should sound the whistle before the snap (7-1-7; 9-5-1d).

Noncontact Fouls by Nonplayers

No coach, substitute, athletic trainer or other team attendant shall act in an unsportsmanlike manner once the game officials assume authority for the contest. Examples are, but not limited to using profanity, insulting or vulgar language or gestures; attempting to influence a decision by a game official; disrespectfully addressing a game official; indicating objections to a game official's decision; using any illegal communication equipment as outlined in 1-5-3c(2) and 1-6; holding an unauthorized conference; failure of a team to comply with the restrictions regarding the coin toss or simulated coin toss, to be ready to start the first half, to be on the field following the conclusion of the halftime intermission or be ready to start the second half at the conclusion of the mandatory warm-up period, or failure of the head coach, following verification, to have his/her player(s) wear or use legal and/or required equipment, including 1-5-2, 1-5-3 and 1-5-5; being on the field except as a substitute or replaced player; using tobacco or smokeless tobacco; or a substitute leaving the team box during a fight (9-8-1a through l).

The NFHS disapproves of any form of taunting which is intended or designed to embarrass, ridicule or demean others under any circumstances (9-5-1a NOTE).

Between downs, communications between players and coaches near the sideline are not considered conferences, as defined in 2-6 (9-8-1f NOTE).

A nonplayer shall not be outside the team box, but not on the field; nor be outside his team box unless to become a player or to return as a replaced player. A maximum of three coaches may be in the restricted area. No player, nonplayer or coach shall be in the restricted area when the ball is live (9-8-1k, 9-8-3).

Nonplayer and Unsportsmanlike Fouls

A nonplayer or unsportsmanlike foul is a noncontact foul (other than unintentional contact as specified in 9-4-8) while the ball is dead or during the down which is not illegal participation and does not influence the play in progress (2-16-2f; 9-5; 9-8).

Unintentional contact between a nonplayer and a game official in the restricted area while the ball is live is a foul (9-4-8).

Nonplayer and Unsportmanlike Fouls: Penalty

15 yards. Signal 27. A single flagrant act may result in disqualification. Two unsportsmanlike fouls by the same player or nonplayer results in disqualification. Signal 47. Failure of a team to comply with the restrictions regarding the coin toss or simulated coin toss, to be ready to start the first half, to be on the field following the conclusion of the halftime intermission or be ready to start the second half at the conclusion of the mandatory warm-up period, or failure of the head coach, following verification, to have his/ her player(s) wear or use legal and/or required equipment, including 1-5-2, 1-5-3 and 1-5-5 are 15-yard penalties charged to the head coach.

For nonplayers illegally outside the team box: First offense — warning. Signal 15. Second offense — 5 yards. Signals 7 and 29. Each subsequent offense — 15 yards. Signals 7, 29 and 27. Nonplayer foul (Art. 1m). Signals 27, 23 — 5 yards.

Nonplayer Foul: Case Plays

9.4.8 SITUATION A: Third and five for A on B's 30-yard line when B1 intercepts A1's pass at B's 15-yard line. B1 returns the interception along A's sideline and is downed on A's 40-yard line. During B1's run the Head Linesman unintentionally runs into: (a) a cameraman between the restraining line and sideline at B's 20-yard line; (b) A's assistant coach in the restricted area at B's 45-yard line; or (c) A's head coach on the field of play at the 50-yard line. **RULING:** No foul in (a), but the game administrator must ensure the area between the playing field and the restraining line is clear of all non-authorized personnel. In (b) and (c) A's head coach is assessed a 15-yard non-player, illegal personal contact penalty at the succeeding spot. A second offense would result in a disqualification of the head coach.

9.4.8 SITUATION B: A1 throws a forward pass that is intercepted by B1 on B's 30-yard line and returned 70 yards along the B sideline for a B touchdown. During B1's run, the covering official is forced to change his course to run around an assistant team B coach who is in B's restricted area. The covering official drops his flag near B's restricted area. Later during the return, B12, a nonplayer, leaves the team box and runs alongside (yet out of bounds) B1 all the way to the goal line. B12 never enters the field of play during the down. The referee flags B12 for a nonplayer foul. **RULING:** Team B has committed two separate nonplayer fouls during this play, which cannot be combined to create a multiple foul. Team B's assistant coach has committed a violation of 9-8-3 for being in the restricted area while the ball is live while B12 has violated 9-8-1k and 9-8-3 by being outside his team box. Both fouls are administered. The first foul results in a sideline warning. The second violation is a 5-yard sideline interference foul for which the offended team may take the penalty on the try or the subsequent kickoff (8-2-4; 9-8-1k; 9-8-3; 10-2-4; 10-2-5).

9.4.8 SITUATION D: A1 is illegally in motion at the snap. The play goes to the sideline where one of B's coaches makes unintentional contact with a game official (9-4-8). **RULING:** Both fouls will be penalized, first the live-ball foul for A's illegal motion, then the 15 yards for unintentional contact in the restricted area. The 9-4-8 foul is a nonplayer foul and is therefore penalized as a dead-ball foul, even though the contact occurred during a live ball (2-16-2f; 10-4-5c).

9.5.1 SITUATION A: In the process of scoring a touchdown, A1: (a) holds and waves the ball overhead the last 10 yards; or (b) after crossing the goal line, he momentarily raises the ball overhead, but then quickly drops it to the ground. **RULING:** Unsportsmanlike conduct in (a), but no foul in (b).

9.5.1 SITUATION B: B1 calls defensive signals loudly: (a) before A takes its set position; or (b) during the time A1 is giving his cadence count; or (c) while A1 is using audibles. **RULING:** Legal in (a). In (b) and (c), if in the covering official's judgment the action by B1 was for the purpose of disconcerting or hindering A, it is an unsportsmanlike-conduct foul. In this case, the covering official should sound his whistle before the snap (9-5-1d).

9.5.1 SITUATION C: B1 intercepts A1's pass and returns it 95 yards for the go-ahead score. After entering the end zone, B1 (a) does a series of back flips, or (b) runs toward his team box, then stops and struts back and forth in front of this team's fans. **RULING:** An unsportsmanlike foul in both (a) and (b), penalized from the succeeding spot. The touchdown stands.

9.5.2 SITUATION: After A1 carries the ball into B's end zone, he: (a) throws the ball into the bleachers; or (b) kicks the ball from the field; or (c) spikes the ball to the ground with force; or (d) is knocked down by B1 clearly after the ball is dead. **RULING:** Unsportsmanlike conduct foul in (a), (b) and (c), the touchdown counts and A will be penalized 15 yards on the try or on the subsequent kickoff. In (d), B1's contact foul will be penalized on the try to the 1½-yard line or on the subsequent kickoff. If judged by the game official to be flagrant, B1 could be disqualified (9-4-2b; 9-5-2a, b, c; 10-4-4b).

*9.8.1 SITUATION D: In the first quarter, the coach for Team A commits an illegal contact foul by accidentally bumping a game official while the coach was out of the team box. Team A is penalized 15 yards. In the second quarter, the coach of Team A is penalized 15 yards for an unsportsmanlike conduct foul for disagreeing with a foul called by one of the game officials. **RULING:** The first foul is for illegal personal contact and the second foul is for unsportsmanlike conduct. The penalties are not combined to force ejection of the head coach (9-4-8).

9.8.1 SITUATION E: Following the second 15-yard penalty for an unsportsmanlike foul by the coach of B, the referee notifies him that he may no longer remain in the vicinity of the playing field and that he may not have any contact with his players, either direct or indirect, throughout the remainder of the game including halftime. The coach departs to the: (a) stands; or (b) press box; or (c) the team locker room. **RULING:** Illegal in (a) and (b). Legal in (c). In (c), if the coach has been disqualified in the first half and has gone to the locker room, he must leave the locker room if the team comes to the locker room. He may not have contact with the team at halftime (9-8 Penalty).

9.8.1 SITUATION F: In the first half, the head coach of A has been penalized: (a) 5 yards and then 15 yards for being outside the team box, but not on the field of play; or (b) 15 yards for being outside the team box and on the field of play. In the third period the coach is again in violation as in (a) and (b). What is the penalty and procedure? **RULING:** In both (a) and (b), another 15-yard unsportsmanlike penalty is assessed and the coach must be disqualified since he has now committed his second 15-yard unsportsmanlike foul. The initial 5-yard penalty in (a) for sideline interference is not counted as one of the two fouls leading to disqualification (9-8 Penalty).

9.8.1 SITUATION L: During an official's time-out for injury, may a player(s) of either team go near the sideline to communicate with the coach? **RULING:** Yes. This is a period between downs. If a coach enters the field to attend the injured player, he may not confer with players (9-8-1f Note).

9.8.3 SITUATION A: In the first period, Team A is warned and then later penalized 5 yards for sideline interference for having more than three coaches or for having noncoaches in the restricted area between the sideline and the team box. The same infraction occurs again in the third period and again in the fourth period. How are these situations penalized? **RULING:** The third and fourth infractions are both 15-yard penalties. Since the head coach is responsible for the team box, the fouls are all charged to the head coach. The second penalty for a 15-yard unsportsmanlike foul results in the disqualification of the head coach.

 9.8.3 COMMENT: The 2-yard belt becomes a restricted area when the ball becomes live (1-2-3g).

9.8.3 SITUATION B: Team A has a player who is deaf. A's coach requests the referee to (a) permit a signer to go to the team huddle while they are on offense to relay the play-call to the deaf player, (b) permit the signer to move up and down the sideline inside the restricted area without penalty. **RULING:** Not permitted in (a) or (b).

10.4.5 SITUATION C: With fourth and 40 from A's 10-yard line, A1 runs to A's 44 where he is downed. During the down, substitute B1 enters the field, but does not participate. **RULING:** B1's foul is a nonplayer foul penalized from the succeeding spot. It is B's ball first and 10 from A's 49-yard line (2-16-2f; 3-7-6).

10.5.3 SITUATION B: Third down and 12 on A's 40-yard line. A1 drops back to throw a pass. The pass is completed to A2 who scores on the run following the reception. During the down, (a) A3 holds B1 on A's 37-yard line or (b) A's coach is observed standing inbounds on B's 20-yard line. **RULING:** (a) If B accepts the penalty for holding by A3, the score is nullified and following enforcement, it will be A's ball, third down and 25 to go on A's 27. In (b), the score stands. Following enforcement, the try will be from A's 18-yard line or the foul may be enforced on the subsequent kickoff (8-2-4; 9-2-1c, 9-8-1k, 10-5-3).

Player Foul

A player foul is a foul (other than nonplayer or unsportsmanlike) by a player in the game (2-16-2g).

PSK Fouls

Post-scrimmage kick penalty enforcement is used after a foul by R (other than illegal substitution or participation) when the foul occurs during scrimmage kick plays other than a try or successful field goal; during a scrimmage kick play in which the ball crosses the expanded neutral zone; beyond the expanded neutral zone; before the end of a kick; and K will not be next to put the ball in play (2-16-2h 1-5).

Post-scrimmage kick fouls are enforced from the basic spot. The basic spot is a point of reference for penalty enforcement. It is the previous spot for a loose-ball play unless the only accepted fouls meet the requirements of a post-scrimmage kick foul (2-16-2h; 10-4).

The post-scrimmage spot is the spot where the kick ends. R retains the ball after penalty enforcement from the post-scrimmage spot when a post-scrimmage foul occurs. Fouls by R behind the post-scrimmage spot are spot fouls (2-41-6).

◤ Rationale

By punting the ball, K has indicated it has ended its series. PSK allows R to keep the ball after enforcement of a penalty for a foul committed under the correct circumstances.

PSK Fouls: Case Plays

10.2.1 SITUATION D: Fourth and five from K's 20-yard line, K is in an illegal formation at the snap. While K1's punt is in flight, beyond the expanded neutral zone, R2 blocks K8 in the back at the 50-yard line. R4 catches the kick at R's 36-yard line and returns it for a touchdown. **RULING:** This is a post-scrimmage kick foul by R. Therefore, R may decline the penalty for K's foul and keep the ball after enforcement of the 10-yard penalty for the block in the back, or it may accept the penalty against K, thereby creating a double foul in which case the down shall be replayed (10-2-1b).

10.4.3 SITUATION A: Fourth and 8 for K from its own 45-yard line. Prior to R2 catching the kick, R7 clips K5 at the 50-yard line and R2 catches the kick at his 20-yard line and is immediately tackled. **RULING:** The ball will belong to R, first and 10 at its 10-yard line. The basic spot is the 20-yard line as post-scrimmage kick enforcement applies (2-41-6).

10.4.3 SITUATION B: Fourth and 9 for K from its own 40-yard line. R10 holds K11 at K's 42-yard line. R11 catches the kick at R's 25-yard line and is tackled at R's 29-yard line. **RULING:** If K accepts the penalty for holding, it will be K's ball, first and 10 from the 50-yard line. Post-scrimmage kick enforcement applies only to R fouls committed beyond the expanded neutral zone (2-41-6).

10.4.3 SITUATION C: Fourth and 11 from K's 36-yard line. While the ball was in flight, beyond the expanded neutral zone, R6 was guilty of holding K3 at R's 32-yard line. The kick goes into the end zone. **RULING:** Since the kick ended in R's end zone, the post-scrimmage kick enforcement spot is the 20-yard line. It will be R's ball, first and 10 from R's 10-yard line after the half-the-distance enforcement (2-41-6).

10.4.3 SITUATION D: K is in punt formation from the 50-yard line. Following the snap, but prior to the ball being kicked, R6 holds K4 at R's 46-yard line. The punt crosses the neutral zone, bounces at R's 25, and rolls to R's 18 where R4 recovers. **RULING:** This foul satisfies all the conditions for post-scrimmage kick enforcement as the foul occurred during the down and on R's side of the expanded neutral zone, so the basic spot is R's 18-yard line. Since R6's foul occurs beyond the basic spot, the penalty is enforced from the basic spot. R is penalized half the distance to the goal, making it R's ball first and 10 at R's 9-yard line (2-16-2h).

10.4.3 SITUATION E: K2 punts from the 50-yard line. The punt crosses the neutral zone, bounces at the R45 and then rebounds back to K's 48-yard line where R4 recovers. Prior to the end of the kick, R6 clips K11 at R's 40-yard line. **RULING:** This foul satisfies all the conditions for post-scrimmage kick enforcement, so the basic spot is K's 48-yard line. Since R6's foul occurs behind the basic spot, the penalty is enforced from the spot of the foul. R is penalized 15 yards, making it R's ball first and 10 at R's 25-yard line (2-16-2h).

10.4.4 SITUATION A: Fourth and 5 for K from R's 49-yard line. R9 catches the kick on the 15-yard line and returns the ball to R's 40-yard line, where he is downed. During the return, R3 holds K7 at R's 30-yard line. **RULING:** Following enforcement of R's holding penalty, it would be R's ball, first and 10 from R's 20-yard line. This is not a post-scrimmage kick enforcement, but a post-possession foul (2-41-6).

Simultaneous With the Snap

A foul simultaneous with the snap is an act which becomes a foul when the ball is snapped or free kicked (2-16-2i).

Topic:
Types of Plays

If a foul does occur, the game officials must know whether it was during a loose-ball play or during a running play, because this immediately determines the basic spot of enforcement (Football Penalty Enforcement).

Loose-Ball Play

A loose-ball play is action during a free kick or scrimmage kick other than post-scrimmage kick fouls; a legal forward pass; during a backward pass (including the snap), an illegal kick or fumble made by A from in or behind the neutral zone prior to a change of team possession; and the run or runs which precedes a legal or illegal kick, legal forward pass, backward pass or fumble (2-33-1a-d, 10-3-1a-c). A loose ball may be part of a running play and should not be confused with a loose-ball play. If a foul were to occur during a running play while the ball was loose, the basic enforcement spot is the spot where the run ended, as for any running play (Football Penalty Enforcement).

While it is possible to have several running plays during a down, with each one having its own basic spot for penalty enforcement (where the related run ended), there can only be one loose ball play during a down. Rule 10-3-1d states in part "also includes the run (or runs) which precedes such legal pass, legal or illegal kick or fumble" (from in or behind the neutral zone). This means it includes all action from the time of the snap to the end of the "loose-ball play." When any foul occurs during a free kick, scrimmage kick, legal forward pass, backward pass (including the snap) or fumble made by A from in or behind the neutral zone — even if several of these actions happen during the same down — the basic spot remains the same: the previous spot, which is the spot of the snap or free kick (Football Fundamental IX-6; 10.4.2 SITUATION B COMMENT).

Running Play

Any play that is not a loose-ball play is a running play, including the related run as in 2-41-9a (2-33-2). In or behind the neutral zone, a running play includes a run not followed by a loose ball and a run followed by an illegal forward pass. Beyond the neutral zone, a running play includes a run and the run followed by a loose ball, including an illegal forward pass or illegal kick. A run ends when a runner loses possession but the related run continues until the ball becomes dead or some player again gets possession (Football Penalty Enforcement).

Topic:
Spots

Basic Spot

The basic spot is a point of reference for penalty enforcement (2-41-1).

Basic Spot is the Goal Line

The basic spot is the goal line for fouls, which are committed during running plays by the opponent of the team in possession at the time of the foul when the team in possession is responsible for forcing the ball across its own goal line, and the related run ends in the end zone and is followed by a loose ball, regardless of where the loose ball becomes dead (10-4-7).

Basic Spot is the Goal Line: Case Play

10.4.7 SITUATION: B1 intercepts A1's pass at B's 6-yard line and retreats to B's end zone where B1 is grabbed by the face mask by A2 who twists the mask. B1 then fumbles while in the end zone and (a) the ball rolls back into the field of play and then goes out of bounds at B's 2-yard line; (b) the ball rolls back into the field of play where B7 recovers the ball at B's 5-yard line. **RULING:** In both (a) and (b), the basic spot is the goal line and the accepted penalty will result in a first down for Team B at its 15-yard line.

Basic Spot is the 20-Yard Line

The basic spot is the 20-yard line for fouls by either team when the opponent of the team in possession at the time of the foul is responsible for forcing the ball across the goal line of the team in possession, and the related run ends in the end zone and is followed by a loose ball, regardless of where the loose ball becomes dead (10-4-6).

Basic Spot is the 20-Yard Line: Case Play

10.4.6 SITUATION A: B1 intercepts A1's pass in B's end zone where B1 is grabbed by the face mask by A2 who twists the mask. B1 then fumbles while in the end zone and (a) the ball rolls back into the field of play and then goes out of bounds at B's 2-yard line; (b) the ball rolls back into the field of play where B7 recovers the ball at B's 5-yard line. **RULING:** In both (a) and (b), the basic spot is the 20-yard line and the accepted penalty will result in a first down for Team B at its 35-yard line.

Enforcement Spot

The enforcement spot is the point from which a penalty is enforced (2-41-2).

Dead-Ball Spot

The dead-ball spot is the spot under the foremost point of the ball when it becomes dead by rule (2-41-3). A ball touching the goal-line plane when it becomes dead is in the end zone, even though it is moving away from the nearer end line and has its foremost point in the field of play (5-3-4).

Previous Spot

The previous spot is where the ball was last snapped or free kicked (2-41-7).

Spot of the Foul

The spot of a foul is where the foul occurs. If a foul occurs out of bounds, the spot of the foul is at the intersection of the nearer inbounds line and the yard line extended on which the foul occurs (2-41-8).

Spot Where the Run Ends

The spot where a run ends is where the ball becomes dead in the runner's possession but the related run (related running play) continues until the ball becomes dead or any player gains possession (2-41-9a), where the runner loses player possession (2-41-9b), or the spot of the catch or recovery when the momentum rule is in effect (2-41-9c).

Succeeding Spot

The succeeding spot is where the ball would next be snapped or free kicked if a foul had not occurred. When a foul occurs during a down in which a touchdown is scored, as in Rules 8-2-2, 8-2-3, 8-2-4 and 8-2-5, the succeeding spot may, at the option of the offended team, be the subsequent kickoff (2-41-10). The basic spot is the succeeding spot for an unsportsmanlike foul; a dead-ball foul; a nonplayer foul; or when the final result is a touchback (10-4-5 a-d).

The succeeding spot may, at the option of the offended team, be the subsequent kickoff as in 8-2-2, 8-2-3, 8-2-4 and 8-2-5 (10-4-5 NOTE).

Spots: Case Plays

5.1.3 SITUATION B: During a fourth-down scrimmage kick by K1 from K's 40, R1 is first to touch the kick beyond the neutral zone where he muffs it at R's 30-yard line. The kick is recovered by R2 at R's 10-yard line. Following the muff by R1, while the ball is loose, there is holding by K2. **RULING:** If the penalty is accepted by R, the down would be replayed from K's 30-yard line. If the penalty is declined, R will put the ball in play first and 10 from its 10-yard line, the spot of recovery (5-1-3d).

5.1.3 SITUATION C: Fourth and 10 on K's 45-yard line. K1 punts the ball beyond the neutral zone. R1 muffs the ball back behind the neutral zone where K1 recovers and: (a) falls on the ball at K's 40-yard line; or (b) throws a forward pass to K3 which is complete at the 50-yard line and R1 interferes with K3; or (c) K1 punts the ball and R1 fair catches at his 30-yard line. **RULING:** Since R1 touched the kick beyond the neutral zone, it will be first down for the team in possession in (a), (b) and (c). In (a), it is a first down for K at K's 40-yard line. In (b), the pass is legal as there had been no change of team possession. If K accepts the penalty for pass interference, it will be K's ball at R's 40-yard line. In (c), the second punt is legal as there had been no change of team possession. The ball belongs to R first and 10 on its own 30-yard line (5-1-3f; 6-2-1; 7-5-1).

> ## In Simple Terms
>
> If a foul occurs during a down, the basic spot is determined by the action that occurs during the down.

5.2.2 SITUATION B: With fourth down and 4 from the 50, A1 runs to B's 40 and then throws an incomplete forward pass. **RULING:** If B declines the penalty, it will be A's ball first and 10 from B's 40-yard line. If B accepts the 5-yard penalty for the illegal forward pass, it will still be a first down for A from B's 45-yard line. The loss of down part of the penalty has no significance since the succeeding spot is beyond the line to gain and a new series is awarded.

8.3.2 SITUATION A: Following a penalty, the try is from B's 8. A1 advances to B's 4 and fumbles. The fumble rolls into the end zone where B1 intentionally bats or kicks the ball across the end line. **RULING:** The measurement for the penalty for B1's foul is from B's 4 where A1's run ended. The new try is from the 2-yard line anywhere between the hash marks (9-7-1, 2; 10-3-2, 3; 10-4-3).

8.5.1 SITUATION D: It is first down and 10 on A's 3. Runner A1 fumbles on his 2-yard line. B1 intentionally kicks the loose ball which is: (a) on A's 2; or (b) in the end zone. The ball then goes out of bounds behind the goal line. **RULING:** Undoubtedly, Team A will decline the penalty for the illegal kick in (a) and take the touchback. A will accept the penalty for the illegal kick in (b), because declining it would give B a safety (8-5-2b, 3c; 9-7-1).

8.5.1 SITUATION E: A1's forward pass is intercepted in B's end zone by B1 who attempts to advance, but is downed there. B2 clips at B's 3: (a) during B1's run, or (b) after B1 is downed. **RULING:** It is a touchback in both (a) and (b) and the basic spot is the succeeding spot. In (a), it is first and 10 for B from B's 1½ yard line. In (b), the dead-ball foul will be penalized from B's 20 resulting in first and 10 from B's 10-yard line (8-5-3d; 10-4-4d).

9.4.3 SITUATION K: With first and 10 from A's 5-yard line, A1 drops back into his end zone, where he is tackled by the face mask/helmet opening and fumbles. The ball rolls out of bounds at A's 3-yard line. **RULING:** The fumble by A is a loose-ball play behind the neutral zone which would be enforced from the previous spot. Following penalty administration, it will be A's ball, first and 10, at A's 20-yard line.

10.1.1 SITUATION A: Where is the ball spotted following penalty acceptance when it is snapped from the right-side hash mark and the run ends in the left-side zone and the foul is: (a) illegal motion by A1; or (b) holding by A1 in the middle of the field behind the end of the run; or (c) grasping the face mask/helmet opening by B1 in making the tackle? **RULING:** In (a), it is spotted at the right-side hash mark. In (b), it is spotted in the middle of the field since the enforcement spot was the spot of the foul. In (c), it is spotted at the left hash mark.

10.1.1 SITUATION B: B1 holds A1 during an unsuccessful try. A's captain wants to accept the penalty and replay of the down, but wishes to decline the distance penalty because A's kicker is more comfortable kicking from the previous distance. **RULING:** This is a legal request. The distance penalty for any foul may be declined.

10.3.1 SITUATION A: With third and 10 from B's 40, A1 takes the snap and runs wide and pitches back to A2. A2 catches the ball behind the neutral zone and runs to B's 10 where he is downed (a) During the pitch, there is holding by B1; or (b) B2 grasps A2 by the face mask/helmet opening during the tackle. **RULING:** In (a), the holding by B1 occurred during a loose-ball play. The basic spot is the previous spot. If A accepts the penalty it will be A's ball first and 10 at B's 30-yard line. In (b), the face-mask/helmet opening penalty occurred during a running play. The basic spot is the end of the run. If A accepts the penalty, it will be A's ball first and goal at B's 5 (10-4-2b, 10-4-3).

10.3.1 SITUATION B: A1 receives the snap and begins a run behind the neutral zone. A1 fumbles the ball and then kicks it while it is rolling on the ground. **RULING:** It is a foul during a loose-ball play and will be penalized from the spot of the illegal kick because it is a foul by A1 behind the basic spot (10-3-1c, 10-3-3b).

10.3.3 SITUATION B: K1 kicks off from K's 40. The kick is caught by R1 at R's 5-yard line. R2 then clips at the 50-yard line. After the clip, R1 fumbles at R's 20-yard line, where R3 picks up fumble and advances for touchdown. **RULING:** The basic spot is where the run ended, which was the fumble at R's 20. After penalty enforcement, it would be R's ball, first and 10, at R's 10-yard line.

10.4.2 SITUATION A: Quarterback A1 receives the snap and while in or behind the neutral zone, throws a backward pass to A2. During his advance, but while still in or behind the neutral zone, A2 fumbles. While the ball is loose, there is a foul by B1. The fumble is recovered by A3. **RULING:** This is a foul during a loose-ball play. The penalty, if accepted, will be administered from the basic spot, which is the previous spot. A loose-ball play includes the run or runs which preceded the loose ball. A fumble by A2 in or behind the neutral zone constitutes a loose-ball play (10-3-1c; 10-3-1 NOTE).

10.4.2 SITUATION B: During a scrimmage down, quarterback A1 throws a backward pass to A2 who runs about 30 yards behind the neutral zone and toward the sideline before throwing a forward pass downfield. There is holding by A3: (a) during the backward pass; or (b) during the run which preceded the forward pass; or (c) during the forward pass at the line of scrimmage. **RULING:** It is a loose-ball play in (a), (b) and (c). The basic spot in all three cases is the previous spot.

 10.4.2 COMMENT: All the action which preceded A2's forward pass is included in this single loose-ball play. While it is possible to have several running plays during a down, with each one having its own basic spot of enforcement (where the related run ended), there can only be one loose ball play during a down. Rule 10-3-1 NOTE states: "The run(s) which precedes such legal or illegal kick, legal forward pass, backward pass or fumble is (are) considered part of the action during a loose-ball play." This means it includes all action from the time of the snap to the end of the "loose-ball play." When any foul occurs during a free kick, scrimmage kick, legal forward pass, backward pass (including the snap) or fumble made by A from in or behind the neutral zone...even if several of these actions happen during the same down ... the basic spot remains the same, the previous spot which is the spot of the snap or free kick (10-3-1 NOTE).

10.4.2 SITUATION C: On third and 20 from his own 35-yard line, A1 throws a forward pass to A2. Prior to the catch, B1 is detected holding. A2 advances to B's 45 following the catch. **RULING:** B1's foul occurred during a loose-ball play and if the penalty is accepted it will be enforced from the previous spot. A obviously will decline the penalty since it has gained 10 yards more and has a first down. The holding penalty cannot be added to the end of the run because the foul was committed during the loose-ball play (10-3-1b; 10-4-2b).

10.4.2 SITUATION D: A1 behind the neutral zone has the ball batted from his possession by B1. While the ball is loose: (a) A2 holds B1, or (b) B2 grasps A2's face mask/helmet opening. **RULING:** Since A1 lost possession, the status of the ball is the same as if it had been fumbled by A1, therefore fouls during this interval are fouls during a loose-ball play. In (a), the penalty is enforced from the previous spot if A1's foul was beyond the previous spot or from the spot of the foul if A1's foul was committed behind the previous spot. In (b), the penalty is enforced from the previous spot, regardless of where B1's foul occurred or where the down ends.

10.4.4 SITUATION C: With third and 7 from A's 25-yard line, A1 advances to A's 35-yard line where he fumbles the ball. Before A1 fumbled the ball, A2 held B3 at A's 40-yard line. A3 recovers the fumble at A's 30-yard line. If B accepts the penalty for holding, where will the basic spot for penalty enforcement be? **RULING:** The basic spot is the spot where the run ended, which is A's 35-yard line. A would still have third and 7 from its own 25-yard line (2-41-8).

10.4.4 SITUATION D: It is third and 6 from B's 40-yard line. A1 advances to B's 30 where B1 grabs his face mask/helmet opening in attempting the tackle. (a) A1 fumbles and B1 recovers and advances to B's 40; or (b) A1 hands off to A2 who is subsequently tackled on the 20; or (c) A1 pitches back to A2 who advances to B's 18-yard line. Where is the basic spot of enforcement if A accepts the penalty for B1's foul? **RULING:** In (a) and (c), the basic spot is where A1 lost possession by his fumble or pass and this is the end of the run. In both cases the penalty will be administered from B's 30 and put the ball on the 15-yard line. In (a), A retains possession since it had possession when the foul occurred. In (b), the handoff to A2 did not end the run. A1's run does not end unless possession is lost by the runner either fumbling or passing. The end of the run is where A2 was tackled. The penalty enforcement will result in the ball being placed on B's 10-yard line.

10.4.4 SITUATION E: R1 catches a punt on his 4-yard line and his momentum carries him behind his goal line where he is downed in the end zone. After the kick has ended, but before the ball becomes dead: (a) K1 holds in R's end zone; or (b) K1 holds at R's 5-yard line; or (c) R2 holds in the end zone. **RULING:** If R accepts the penalty in either (a) or (b), it will be R's ball first and 10 from its 14-yard line. R will put the ball in play by a snap. If R declines the penalty in either (a) or (b), the ball will be put in play by R at the 4-yard line since the kick was caught there. In (c), it is a safety since the foul occurred in the end zone.

 10.4.4 COMMENT: When the "momentum" exception applies and the ball becomes dead behind the goal line, if the penalty for a foul by either team is accepted, the end of the run is the spot where the kick, fumble or pass was caught or recovered. The penalty is enforced under the all-but-one principle. If "momentum" is not involved, the end of the run is the goal line (8-5-2a Exception; 10-3-3c).

Topic:
Enforcement

All-But-One Principle

Enforcement philosophy is based on the fact that a team is given the advantage of the distance which is gained without assistance of a foul. It is assumed that the only foul which would give this aid is a foul by the offense behind the basic spot. Therefore, all fouls but this one, that is a foul by the offense behind the basic spot, are penalized from the basic spot. This one foul is penalized from the spot of the foul (10-6; Football Penalty Enforcement).

All-But-One Principle: Case Plays

9.6.4 SITUATION E: With third down and 12 yards to go from A's 45-yard line, quarterback A1 throws a pass to A2 at B's 45-yard line. Teammate A12 moves to get a better view of the play and enters the field of play at B's 40-yard line. During the run after the reception, (a) A2 collides with A12 and is thereafter tackled by B1; or (b) B1 slows to avoid A12 as A1 runs for a touchdown. **RULING:** Illegal participation in (a) and (b). The penalty of 15 yards is enforced using the "all-but-one" principle. Illegal participation occurs since substitute A12 hindered a teammate or an opponent and participated in the play. The spot of the foul is where the participation occurred, not where A12 entered the field (2-30; 9-6-4a).

10.4.5 SITUATION H: B1 intercepts a pass in his own end zone and is tackled there after attempting to advance. During B1's run, B2 clips A1 at B's 4-yard line. **RULING:** The basic spot is the 20-yard line. If the penalty is accepted it will be enforced from the spot of the foul, B's ball first and 10 from B's 2-yard line. If the penalty is declined, it is B's ball first and 10 from B's 20-yard line.

Dead-Ball Fouls

When a foul occurs during a dead ball between downs or prior to a free kick or snap, the covering official shall not permit the ball to become alive. The referee shall notify the captains, and the captain of the offended team will be presented with the options and the effect of acceptance or declination on the down and distance to be gained. The captain may accept or decline the penalty (10-1-2). The distance penalty for any foul may be declined (10-1-1).

Penalties for dead-ball fouls, other than when both teams commit unsportsmanlike, nonplayer or dead-ball personal fouls prior to the completion of penalty administration for those fouls, are administered separately and in the order of occurrence. A dead-ball foul is not coupled with a live-ball foul or another dead-ball foul to create a double or multiple foul (10-2-5a).

If both teams commit unsportsmanlike, nonplayer or dead-ball personal fouls prior to the completion of penalty administration for those fouls, the distance penalty for an equal number of 15-yard unsportsmanlike, nonplayer or dead-ball personal fouls will offset. Any remaining penalties will be enforced separately and in the order of occurrence (10-2-5b).

Dead-Ball Fouls: Case Plays

9.4.1 SITUATION A: With the ball on B's 2-yard line and between downs, a fight starts between A1 and B1. The game officials do not know which player struck the first blow. **RULING:** Disqualify both A1 and B1 and signal personal fouls against each team, but the penalties cancel (2-11; 10-2-4).

*9.4.1 SITUATION B: It is A's ball, third down and 1, on A's 10-yard line. B1 tackles A1 with a hard legal tackle at the line of scrimmage. A1, feeling the tackle was unjustly harsh, jumps to his feet and attacks B1, delivering blows with his fist. In response, B1 directs a profanity toward A1. **RULING:** The penalties for A1's dead-ball personal foul and B1's unsportsmanlike conduct foul would cancel. A1 shall be disqualified for fighting; B1 would remain in the game unless the game officials judged that his reaction was flagrant or it was his second unsportsmanlike conduct foul. It's A's ball fourth down and on its own 10-yard line (2-11; 9-8-1 Penalty; 10-2-5b, c).

Foul During a Loose-Ball Play

If a foul occurs during a loose-ball play, the basic spot is the previous spot unless post-scrimmage kick enforcement applies (10-4-2b; Football Penalty Enforcement).

Foul During a Loose-Ball Play: Case Play

10.5.4 SITUATION A: A's ball second and 5 from its own 9-yard line. A2 fumbles the ball on his own 5-yard line and the ball rolls into the end zone. A1 recovers the ball in the end zone and is downed in the end zone, but B3 held A3 while the ball was loose. **RULING:** A undoubtedly will accept the penalty, because to decline would result in a safety. The foul occurred during a loose-ball play, therefore, the previous spot will be the enforcement spot, making it first and 10 for A from its own 19-yard line.

Foul During a Running Play

If a foul occurs during a running play, the basic spot is the spot where the run ended (2-41-1; 10-4). If the runner does not lose possession, the ball becomes dead when the run ends (Football Penalty Enforcement).

Last Timed Down of a Period

A period shall be extended by an untimed down if one of the following occurred during a down in which time expires: there was a foul, other than unsportsmanlike or nonplayer, or fouls that specify loss of down by either team and the penalty is accepted; there was a double foul; there was an inadvertent whistle; or a touchdown was scored. If a touchdown was scored, the try is attempted unless the touchdown is scored during the last down of the fourth period and the point(s) would not affect the outcome of the game or playoff qualifying.

If any of the above occurs during the untimed down, the procedure is repeated (3-3-3a-d).

A period shall not be extended by an untimed down if one of the following occurred during a down in which time expires: the defense fouls during a successful try/field goal and the offended team accepts the results of the play with enforcement of the penalty from the succeeding spot; there is a foul that specifies loss of down and the penalty is accepted. The score is cancelled in the event of an accepted penalty that specifies a loss of down; or there was a foul by either team and the penalty is accepted for unsportsmanlike fouls, non-player fouls, fouls that specify a loss of down and penalties that are enforced on the subsequent kickoff as in Rule 8-2-2 or 8-2-3; or fouls for which enforcement, by rule, result in a safety (3-3-4a-c).

◪ Rationale

The rule prevents a team from gaining an advantage by committing a "loss of down" foul and having the period extended by an untimed down. If not for the rule, a team could retain possession of the ball and repeat the down when it is the last timed down of a period.

Last Timed Down of a Period: Case Plays

3.3.3 SITUATION A: With the score B-7 and A-6, it is second and goal from B's 9-yard line. The clock is stopped due to an incomplete pass with four seconds remaining in the game. A1's pass into the end zone is intercepted by B1 who runs to his 30-yard line where he is downed. Following the interception and during the run by B1, there is clipping in the end zone by B2. Time expires during the run. **RULING:** If the penalty for the foul by B2 is declined, the period is over. If the penalty is accepted, it results in a safety (two points) for A; however, the period is not extended. If this occurs at the end of period one or three, the teams will change ends of the field and B will kick from B's 20-yard line (3-3-4b(5)).

3.3.3 SITUATION B: Near the end of the third period, it is third and 4 for A from B's 48-yard line. A1 advances to B's 45 and during the run there is holding by B1. The penalty is accepted. At the end of the down there are three seconds remaining in the period. Because the penalty was the only reason for the clock to be stopped, it is started with the ready-for-play signal and the period ends before A snaps the ball. **RULING:** A is not entitled to an untimed down as time did not expire during the down.

*3.3.3 SITUATION D: With the ball at B's 1-yard line and 12 seconds remaining in the game, A1 advances to the ½-yard line. After the ball is dead, B1 fouls. The clock is stopped with five seconds remaining in the game. The clock is restarted when the ball is marked ready for play. Before A can snap the ball, time expires. **RULING:** The game is ended. There is no extension of the period for an untimed down, unless there is acceptance of the penalty for a foul that occurs during a down in which time expires. B1's foul did not occur during the down. However, if the referee judges B1 committed the foul to consume time, he shall delay starting the clock until the snap.

 3.3.3 COMMENT: When either team attempts to conserve or consume time illegally, the referee shall invoke Rule 3-4-6 and start or delay the start of the clock as authorized (3-4-6; 3-6-2f; 9-10-2)

3.3.3 SITUATION E: A1 breaks free on B's 20-yard line and is near the goal line on a run which will score the go-ahead touchdown. Just before entering the end zone, A1 turns and taunts B1. Time in the fourth period expires during the run. **RULING:** The touchdown is scored and the unsportsmanlike foul by A1 cannot be penalized. While such situations do not occur frequently, it must be recognized that at some point penalty enforcement is ended. If the try is required for playoff qualification, the penalty is enforced on the try (10-4-5a).

3.3.3 SITUATION F: With the score A-14, B-23, A scores a touchdown: (a) as time expires in the fourth period; or (b) as time expires in the third period; or (c) as time expires in the fourth period in a state in which a tie-breaking procedure for playoff qualification is based on points scored. **RULING:** In (a), the try will not be permitted – the game is over and the final score is A-20, B-23. In (b), the try is attempted as part of the third period. The try in (c) is permissible if the potential point(s) is needed in a tie-breaker system for playoff qualification. Each state must interpret this provision as it applies to its particular qualifying plan (8-3-1 Exception).

3.3.3 SITUATION G: K1 punts on fourth and 15 from his own 20-yard line. R1 signals for a fair catch at R's 30. K2 commits kick-catching interference at R's 35 and time for the second period expires during the down. R2 recovers the kick at R's 28. **RULING:** If R declines the penalty, the period is over. If R accepts an awarded catch or has the penalty otherwise enforced, the period will be extended by an untimed down (6-1-9b; 6-5-6 Penalty).

*3.3.5 SITUATION A: A trails by three points in the fourth period with the ball on B's 20, fourth and 10 and two seconds on the clock. A1 throws an incomplete pass into B's end zone with time expired. The referee quickly glances to each sideline and then begins to leave the field. After the referee crosses the sideline, the referee hears the line judge blowing his whistle. The line judge explains that B1 committed pass interference during the down in which time expired. **RULING:** The game is not officially over even though the referee left the field. Since a foul had been called, the referee will give A a chance to accept the penalty and extend the period with an untimed down from B's 10-yard line.

3.3.5 COMMENT: The game is officially over when the referee holds the ball overhead and leaves the field. Before doing this however, he should pause briefly and glance to both sidelines and make sure there are no fouls, no obvious timing error, no request for a coach-referee conference, etc.

3.3.5 SITUATION B: Time expires at the end of the second period during a scrimmage kick. After the down, K1 piles on and R1 strikes K2. **RULING:** The penalties for these dead-ball fouls cancel. R1 will be disqualified for fighting (9-4-1; 10-2-5b, c; 10-4-5b).

8.2.2 SITUATION C: During the down in which time expires for the fourth period, the opponents of Team A foul on a play where Team A: (a) scores a touchdown that leaves Team A trailing by one point, (b) scores a field goal which ties the game, or (c) scores a touchdown that leaves team A trailing by one point and the opponents also foul on the try. **RULING:** In (a), Team A has the option to keep the score, with the penalty assessed on the try. The penalty cannot be assessed on the first play of overtime as there is no subsequent kickoff. In (b), Team A has the option to keep the score, with penalty assessment on the first play of overtime as the first play of overtime is the succeeding spot. In (c), Team A may only have the penalty for the opponent foul on the scoring play enforced on the try but cannot carry over the penalty to overtime; however, the foul by the opponent during the try could be enforced on the first play of overtime at Team A's choice.

10.4.5 SITUATION D: With the score, B-14 and A-8, a pass from A1 is complete in the end zone to A2 during the down in which time expires for the fourth period. During the down, there is holding by B1 and after the down, B2 is charged with an unsportsmanlike foul. **RULING:** A will undoubtedly accept the result of the play and enforce the holding penalty from the 3-yard line and enforce the penalty for the unsportsmanlike foul. The ball would then be snapped for the try from the 3/4-yard line (3-3-3a; 10-5-1f).

10.4.5 SITUATION E: A scores on the last play of the second period to make the score, B-21 and A-19. During A's successful 2-point try, B1 commits an unsportsmanlike foul. **RULING:** The penalty is enforced from the succeeding spot on the kickoff to start the third period (2-41-9; 3-3-3d).

10.5.4 SITUATION B: During the last timed down of the first half, A1 retreats into his own end zone to attempt a pass, but he is downed there. During the down there is holding in the end zone by: (a) A2, or (b) by B1. **RULING:** In (a), it is a safety and B would score 2 points whether the penalty is accepted or declined since the run ended in the end zone and the foul was in the end zone. If B accepts the penalty, the period is not extended with an untimed down. In (b), if the penalty is accepted it will be enforced from the goal line and the period is extended.

Live-Ball Fouls

When a foul occurs during a live ball, the referee shall, at the end of the down, notify both captains. He shall inform the captain of the offended team regarding the rights of penalty acceptance or declination and shall indicate to him the number of the ensuing down, distance to be gained, and status of the ball for each available choice. The distance penalty for any foul may be declined. If the penalty is declined or if there is a double foul, there is no loss of distance. In case of a double foul, the captains are not consulted since the penalties offset. The captain's choice of options may not be revoked. Decisions involving penalties shall be made before any charged time-out is granted either team (10-1-1).

Fundamental IX-1

No live-ball foul causes the game official to sound his whistle immediately.

Live-Ball Fouls: Case Plays

9.4.3 SITUATION Q: A has possession, 3rd and 10 from the A10. A25 is running in the open field and B1 uses an illegal horse collar to bring him down (a) at the 50 after he was grabbed by the collar at the A45; or (b) at the A25 after he was initially grabbed by the collar at the A30 but the runner had retreated on his own to the A25; or (c) on B's 4 yard line and A25 drags B1 into B's end zone. **RULING:** Each of these plays are running plays, so the foul is enforced from the end of the run. In (a) it will be enforced from the 50, making it first and 10 for A at the B35; in (b) the foul is enforced from the A25, making it first and 10 for A at the A40; in (c) the touchdown is scored and A has the option of enforcing the foul on the try or the subsequent kickoff.

9.4.3 SITUATION R: A has possession 4th and 8 from the B40. A1 advances 7 yards where B1 grabs him and commits an illegal horse collar foul. The jersey/collar is grabbed one yard inbounds and B1 pulls him down a) inbounds at the B33 or 2) just out of bounds with A1 crossing the sideline at the B33. **RULING:** In both (a) and (b), the penalty for illegal horse collar is penalized from the end of the run and A is award a new series as the horse collar foul is to be enforced as a live ball foul, it will be first and 10 for A at the B18.

Live-Ball Foul Followed by a Dead-Ball Foul

When a live-ball foul by one team is followed by a dead-ball foul by the opponent, the penalties are administered separately and in the order of occurrence (10-1-3).

When the same team commits a live-ball foul followed by one or more dead-ball fouls, all fouls may be penalized (10-1-4).

Live-Ball Foul Followed by a Dead-Ball Foul: Case Plays

5.1.2 SITUATION B: During A1's run for a first down to B's 20-yard line, B12 commits a nonplayer foul for a substitute entering the field during the down, but not participating. Immediately following the down, A1 taunts an opponent. **RULING:** If accepted, the penalty for B entering during the down is enforced from the succeeding spot. After the decision on this penalty, A will be penalized 15 yards for unsportsmanlike conduct and A will have the ball for a new series, first and 10 (3-7-6; 9-5-1a).

5.2.5 SITUATION: K1 punts the ball to R1. R1 catches the punt on his own 10-yard line and begins to advance. During the run, K1 grabs R1's face mask/helmet opening at R's 20-yard line. R1 continues to advance, but is hit and fumbles the ball on K's 10-yard line. K2 recovers the fumble on K's 5-yard line and K commits a dead-ball foul. **RULING:** If R accepts the penalty for the face mask/helmet opening foul, it will be enforced from the end of R1's run (the spot of the fumble), thus making it first and goal for R from K's 5-yard line. The dead-ball foul would be administered from that point making it first and goal for R from K's 2½-yard line. If R refuses the face mask/helmet opening penalty, the ball would belong to K on K's 5-yard line. R then may accept the penalty for the dead-ball foul by K3, making it K's ball first and 10 from K's 2½-yard line. The box and chain are set following enforcement of the dead-ball foul (5-2-1; 5-2-5e).

7.2.1 SITUATION B: With fourth down and 8 from K's 20-yard line and K in scrimmage kick formation, K1 kicks the ball, but at the snap, K had only six players on the line of scrimmage. After the play is over, R1 throws K2 to the ground and swings at him. **RULING:** These fouls would be enforced separately and in order. R will likely decline the penalty for the K foul so that R will get the football, and then R's dead-ball personal foul is then enforced (and R1 is disqualified) with the ball being placed 15 yards behind the end of the run.

8.3.5 SITUATION C: During a successful two-point try, B1 is flagged for pass interference against A1. After the untimed down is over, A1 taunts B1. **RULING:** Team A may accept the score and have the penalty enforced at the succeeding spot. However, B may accept the penalty for the dead ball foul by A, and have 15 yards marked off from the spot where the ball is placed after enforcement of B's penalty. The ball would then be free-kicked from K's 40-yard line.

10.4.5 SITUATION F: After A1 scores a touchdown, he is struck by B1. The coach of A then insults a game official before the penalty for the personal foul by B1 is administered. **RULING:** The penalties for both the dead-ball personal foul by B1 and the unsportsmanlike foul by the coach of A will cancel. If B1's act was judged by the game official to be fighting, he shall be ejected (2-41-10; 8-2-5; 8-3-2; 9-4-3b, g, j; 9-8-1c; 10-2-5b, c).

Nonplayer and Unsportsmanlike Fouls

Nonplayer and unsportsmanlike fouls are treated as dead-ball fouls regardless if they are committed while the ball is live or dead (2-16-2f).

If an unsportsmanlike or nonplayer foul occurs during a down resulting in a change of possession or a first down, the line-to-gain equipment is set following enforcement of the penalty. Penalizing unsportsmanlike-player fouls from the succeeding spot provides consistent enforcement for all unsportsmanlike-conduct fouls. It also supports the philosophy that no unsportsmanlike-conduct foul should go unpenalized. A team does not have to decline an unsportsmanlike-conduct penalty in order to retain possession of the ball (10-4-5a-d; 10.4.5 SITUATION B COMMENT).

Nonplayer and Unsportsmanlike Fouls: Case Plays

10.4.5 SITUATION A: With third and goal from B's 2-yard line, A1's forward pass is intercepted by B1 in the end zone and returned for an apparent touchdown. During B1's run, B2 clips at the 50, after which the coach of B comes on the field at A's 40 to criticize the covering official's call. **RULING:** First and 10 for B on its 20-yard line. Since the foul by B's coach is an unsportsmanlike foul, it is enforced from the succeeding spot after the penalty for B2's live-ball foul is enforced. The line-to-gain equipment is not set until all penalties have been administered. This is not a multiple-foul situation.

10.4.5 SITUATION B: During a run by A1 on first down from A's 10 to midfield, A2 clips B1 at A's 20 (a) B1 swears at A2; or (b) A3 taunts B2. **RULING:** The unsportsmanlike foul in (a) or (b) is not paired with any other foul to create a double or multiple foul. Following the acceptance of the penalty for the clip by A2, the unsportsmanlike fouls will be administered from A's 10 which is the succeeding spot. In (a), it will be A's ball first down and 10 from its own 25-yard line. In (b), it will be A's ball first and 15 from A's 5-yard line.

 10.4.5 COMMENT: If a nonplayer or unsportsmanlike foul occurs during a down resulting in a change of possession or a first down, the line-to-gain equipment is set following enforcement of the penalty. Penalizing unsportsmanlike-player fouls from the succeeding spot provides consistent enforcement for all unsportsmanlike-conduct fouls. It also supports the philosophy that no unsportsmanlike-conduct foul should go unpenalized. A team does not have to decline an unsportsmanlike-conduct penalty in order to retain possession of the ball (2-16-2f).

10.4.5 SITUATION D: With the score, B-14 and A-8, a pass from A1 is complete in the end zone to A2 during the down in which time expires for the fourth period. During the down, there is holding by B1 and after the down, B2 is charged with an unsportsmanlike foul. **RULING:** A will undoubtedly accept the result of the play and enforce the holding penalty from the 3-yard line and enforce the penalty for the unsportsmanlike foul. The ball would then be snapped for the try from the 3/4-yard line (3-3-3a; 10-5-1f).

PSK Fouls

If a post-scrimmage kick foul occurs, the basic spot is the post-scrimmage kick spot (2-41-6; 10-4-2b; Football Penalty Enforcement).

PSK Fouls: Case Plays

10.2.1 SITUATION D: Fourth and five from K's 20-yard line, K is in an illegal formation at the snap. While K1's punt is in flight, beyond the expanded neutral zone, R2 blocks K8 in the back at the 50-yard line. R4 catches the kick at R's 36-yard line and returns it for a touchdown. **RULING:** This is a post-scrimmage kick foul by R. Therefore, R may decline the penalty for K's foul and keep the ball after enforcement of the 10-yard penalty for the block in the back, or it may accept the penalty against K, thereby creating a double foul in which case the down shall be replayed (10-2-1b).

10.4.3 SITUATION A: Fourth and 8 for K from its own 45-yard line. Prior to R2 catching the kick, R7 clips K5 at the 50-yard line and R2 catches the kick at his 20-yard line and is immediately tackled. **RULING:** The ball will belong to R, first and 10 at its 10-yard line. The basic spot is the 20-yard line as post-scrimmage kick enforcement applies (2-41-6).

10.4.3 SITUATION B: Fourth and 9 for K from its own 40-yard line. R10 holds K11 at K's 42-yard line. R11 catches the kick at R's 25-yard line and is tackled at R's 29-yard line. **RULING:** If K accepts the penalty for holding, it will be K's ball, first and 10 from the 50-yard line. Post-scrimmage kick enforcement applies only to R fouls committed beyond the expanded neutral zone (2-41-6).

10.4.3 SITUATION C: Fourth and 11 from K's 36-yard line. While the ball was in flight, beyond the expanded neutral zone, R6 was guilty of holding K3 at R's 32-yard line. The kick goes into the end zone. **RULING:** Since the kick ended in R's end zone, the post-scrimmage kick enforcement spot is the 20-yard line. It will be R's ball, first and 10 from R's 10-yard line after the half-the-distance enforcement (2-41-6).

10.4.3 SITUATION D: K is in punt formation from the 50-yard line. Following the snap, but prior to the ball being kicked, R6 holds K4 at R's 46-yard line. The punt crosses the neutral zone, bounces at R's 25, and rolls to R's 18 where R4 recovers. **RULING:** This foul satisfies all the conditions for post-scrimmage kick enforcement as the foul occurred during the down and on R's side of the expanded neutral zone, so the basic spot is R's 18-yard line. Since R6's foul occurs beyond the basic spot, the penalty is enforced from the basic spot. R is penalized half the distance to the goal, making it R's ball first and 10 at R's 9-yard line (2-16-2h).

10.4.3 SITUATION E: K2 punts from the 50-yard line. The punt crosses the neutral zone, bounces at the R45 and then rebounds back to K's 48-yard line where R4 recovers. Prior to the end of the kick, R6 clips K11 at R's 40-yard line. **RULING:** This foul satisfies all the conditions for post-scrimmage kick enforcement, so the basic spot is K's 48-yard line. Since R6's foul occurs behind the basic spot, the penalty is enforced from the spot of the foul. R is penalized 15 yards, making it R's ball first and 10 at R's 25-yard line (2-16-2h).

10.4.4 SITUATION A: Fourth and 5 for K from R's 49-yard line. R9 catches the kick on the 15-yard line and returns the ball to R's 40-yard line, where he is downed. During the return, R3 holds K7 at R's 30-yard line. **RULING:** Following enforcement of R's holding penalty, it would R's ball, first and 10 from R's 20-yard line. This is not a post-scrimmage kick enforcement, but a post-possession foul (2-41-6).

Topic:
Additional Penalties

Awarded First Down
Fouls by B that give A an automatic first down are roughing the kicker or holder; roughing the passer; and roughing the snapper (10-1-7a-c).

Disqualification
A disqualified player is a player barred from further participation in a game (2-32-6). A disqualified player or nonplayer shall be removed (10-2-5c, 10-5-6). It is illegal participation for a disqualified player to re-enter the game (9-6-4f).

Any single flagrant foul is disqualification. A second unsportsmanlike foul with a 15-yard penalty results in disqualification (9-5). A disqualified member of the coaching staff shall be ejected from the stadium area and be prohibited from any further contact, direct or indirect, with his team during the remainder of the game. For failure to comply, the referee may forfeit the game (9-8).

Fighting, intentionally contacting an official, striking, kicking or kneeing result in a 15-yard penalty and disqualification (9-4).

Disqualification: Case Plays
*9.4.3 SITUATION A:** As A1 is advancing for a touchdown from B's 10-yard line, B1 blindsides A2 at B's 15-yard line. The covering official rules that not only was the contact unnecessarily rough, it was judged by the game official to be flagrant. **RULING:** The penalty for the foul may be enforced from the succeeding spot or the succeeding kickoff and A's touchdown stands. B1 is disqualified because the foul was judged by the game official to be flagrant.

 9.4.3 COMMENT: It has been reported that plays like this have occurred and game officials have simply ruled touchdown. Game officials must be alert for flagrant fouls and enforce the disqualification portion of the penalty if necessary (9-4-3g Penalty; 10-5-1).

9.5 SITUATION: During the first period, A1 is penalized 15 yards for an unsportsmanlike foul. In the third period, A1 is in the restricted area on the sideline and receives another 15-yard penalty for an unsportsmanlike foul. **RULING:** A1 is disqualified. A second unsportsmanlike foul results in disqualification. The rule requires disqualification on the second unsportsmanlike foul regardless of whether it occurs when A1 is a player or a nonplayer.

Loss of Down

Fouls by A that include loss of the right to replay a down are illegally handing the ball forward; illegal forward pass; and illegal touching of forward pass by an ineligible (10-1-6a-c).

Loss of Down: Case Plays

*3.3.4 SITUATION C: On a down in which time expires for the period, Team A throws a pass which is intercepted by B1. B1 advances to the 3-yard line where he: (a) throws an incomplete pass; (b) throws a pass to B2 in the end zone for an apparent touchdown; or (c) hands the ball forward to B2 who runs for an apparent touchdown. **RULING:** In (a) and (b), B has thrown an illegal forward pass. In (c), B is guilty of illegal handing the ball forward. In (a), A will accept the penalty. In (b) and (c), A will accept the penalty to negate the score. If this occurs at the end of the first or third period, B will have the ball first and 10 to start the subsequent period following enforcement of the penalty. If this occurs at the end of the half, the half is over. In (a), (b) and (c), the period will not be extended as Team B has committed a foul for which the loss-of-down aspect does not apply to the penalty when enforced (5-2-2).

3.3.4 SITUATION D: In the middle of a period, Team A throws a pass which is intercepted by B1. B1 advances to the 8-yard line where he: (a) throws an incomplete pass; (b) throws a pass to B2 in the end zone for an apparent touchdown; or (c) hands the ball forward to B2 who runs for apparent touchdown. **RULING:** In (a), (b) and (c), the accepted foul will result in B having the ball, first and 10 after enforcement of the distance penalty, as the loss-of-down aspect of the penalty would not apply (5-2-2).

Topic:
___ Special Enforcements _____

Free Kick Out of Bounds

If a free kick is kicked out of bounds between the goal lines untouched inbounds by R, R may accept a 5-yard penalty from the previous spot and have K rekick; put the ball in play at the inbounds spot 25 yards beyond the previous spot at the inbounds spot; or decline the penalty and put the ball in play at the inbounds spot (6-1-8a-c; 10-5-1a).

◩ Rationale

Offering choices other than a re-kick to begin a new series speeds up the game.

Free Kick Out of Bounds: Case Plays

2.29.3 SITUATION: A free kick by K1 is touched by R1 on his 15-yard line and then it: (a) rolls out of bounds at R's 5-yard line; or (b) contacts a game official in the field of play and thereafter rolls out of bounds at the 5-yard line; or (c) contacts a game official who is straddling the sideline at the 5-yard line; or (d) contacts a game official in the end zone. **RULING:** The ball will be put in play by R from its 5-yard line in (a), (b) and (c). In (a), R1 was the last to touch the kick before it went out of bounds. In (b), the fact that the ball touched a game official who was inbounds does not change its status. In fact, this touching is ignored and therefore R1, in effect, was the last to touch the ball before it went out of bounds. In (c), when the loose ball touches a game official who is straddling the sideline, it causes the ball to be out of bounds and R1 was the last to touch it. In (d), the ball is dead when it breaks the goal-line plane and a touchback results (6-1-9; 8-5-3a).

6.1.8 SITUATION B: The free kick by K1 from K's 40-yard line: (a) is touched by R1 at R's 5 and goes out of bounds at the 8-yard line; or (b) is muffed by R1 at his 15 and then touched by K2 before it rolls out of bounds at R's 10-yard line; or (c) bounces out of bounds on R's 30-yard line untouched by R or K. **RULING:** In (a) and (b) the ball belongs to R at the inbounds spot. In (c), it is a foul by K. The receivers may take the ball at the inbounds spot, take the ball at the inbounds spot at R's 35 which is 25 yards beyond the previous spot, or accept the 5-yard penalty and have K free kick from K's 35-yard line (6-1-9; 2-41-4).

6.1.8 SITUATION C: R1 is running near a sideline as he attempts to catch a free kick in flight. R1 has: (a) both feet inbounds; or (b) one foot on the sideline, when he reaches through the plane of the sideline. The ball bounces off his hands and lands out of bounds. **RULING:** In (a), the ball is not yet out of bounds until it hit the ground there. Since R1 touched it, he caused it to go out of bounds and R will have the ball at the inbounds spot. In (b), since R1 is out of bounds when the ball is touched, the kicker has caused the ball to be out of bounds.

6.1.8 SITUATION D: K1 tries an onside kick from K's 40, as the ball bounces near the sideline the ball is muffed out-of-bounds by K2 at R's 49. **RULING:** R could have K rekick after a five yard penalty, or take the ball 1st and 10 at the inbounds spot at R's 49, or take the ball 1st and 10 at the inbounds spot at R's 35.

6.1.8 SITUATION G: Team K free kicks from its own 40-yard line. K1's onside kick is rolling at K's 46-yard line, when K2 muffs the ball, which then touches R3's leg and goes out of bounds at K's 48-yard line. **RULING:** Since R's touching is now ignored, this is a free kick that went out of bounds. R has the option of accepting the ball at the spot of first touching by K or having the penalty enforced for the free kick out of bounds with all these options: (a) re-kick following a 5-yard penalty; (b) awarded the ball at the inbounds spot at the yard line where the ball went out of bounds; or (c) accept the ball at the inbounds spot 25 yards from the yard line of the free kick (10-5-1a).

6.1.8 SITUATION H: Team K, after accepting the penalties for multiple R fouls, is now free kicking from R's 20-yard line. In attempting to onside kick, the ball goes out bounds untouched in the field of play. **RULING:** R may take the ball at the inbounds spot, or accept the 5-yard penalty and have K re-kick from R's 25-yard line. Fouls During or After

Fouls During or After Scoring Plays

If during a successful try, a foul by B occurs, A is given the choice of accepting the penalty and replaying the down following enforcement; or accepting the result of the play and enforcement of the penalty from the succeeding spot (8-3-5a, b; 10-5-1d).

If an opponent of the scoring team commits a foul (other than unsportsmanlike conduct or a nonplayer foul) during a down in which a touchdown is scored and there was not a change in possession during the down, A may accept the results of the play and choose enforcement of the penalty on the try or on the subsequent kickoff (8-2-2a, b; 10-5-1f).

If an opponent of the scoring team commits a foul (other than unsportsmanlike conduct or a nonplayer foul) during a down in which a touchdown is scored and there was a change of possession during the down, and such foul occurs after the change of possession, the scoring team may accept the results of the play and choose enforcement of the penalty on the try or on the subsequent kickoff (8-2-3a, b; 10-5-1f).

If either team commits an unsportsmanlike conduct or a nonplayer foul during a down in which a touchdown is scored, the opponent may accept the results of the play and choose enforcement of the penalty on the try or on the subsequent kickoff (8-2-4a, b, 10-5-1f).

If after a down in which a touchdown is scored, and prior to the initial ready-for-play signal for the try, either team commits any foul for which the basic spot is the succeeding spot, the offended team may accept the penalty and choose enforcement of the penalty on the try or on the subsequent kickoff (8-2-5a, b; 10-5-1f).

The score is nullified if the penalty is accepted for a foul, other than nonplayer or unsportsmanlike, by A which occurs during a down resulting in a successful try, field goal or touchdown (10-5-3).

Fouls During or After Scoring Plays: Case Plays

8.2.2 SITUATION A: During (a) A9's run for a touchdown, B2 holds A1, or (b) K1's field goal, R2 holds K1. **RULING:** In (a), A will likely keep the score and may choose to enforce the penalty on the try or enforce the penalty on the subsequent kickoff. In (b), K may keep the points and have the penalty enforced from the succeeding spot, or have the penalty enforced from the previous spot and replay the down (8-4-3).

8.2.2 SITUATION B: On the down in which time expired for the second period, Team A: (a) scores a field goal or (b) scores a touchdown. In both cases, the opponents of the scoring team commit a live-ball foul. **RULING:** In (a), the offended team has the option to keep the score, with the penalty assessed on the second half kickoff as this is the succeeding spot. In (b), the offended team has the option to keep the score, with penalty assessment on either the try or on the second half kickoff as this would be the subsequent kickoff.

8.2.2 SITUATION C: During the down in which time expires for the fourth period, the opponents of Team A foul on a play where Team A: (a) scores a touchdown that leaves Team A trailing by one point, (b) scores a field goal which ties the game, or (c) scores a touchdown that leaves team A trailing by one point and the opponents also foul on the try. **RULING:** In (a), Team A has the option to keep the score, with the penalty assessed on the try. The penalty cannot be assessed on the first play of overtime as there is no subsequent kickoff. In (b), Team A has the option to keep the score, with penalty assessment on the first play of overtime as the first play of overtime is the succeeding spot. In (c), Team A may only have the penalty for the opponent foul on the scoring play enforced on the try but cannot carry over the penalty to overtime; however, the foul by the opponent during the try could be enforced on the first play of overtime at Team A's choice.

8.2.2 SITUATION D: A1 scores a touchdown. After the score, B commits a (a) dead-ball, (b) unsportsmanlike or (c) nonplayer foul prior to the initial ready for play on the try. **RULING:** In (a), (b) or (c), Team A may elect to enforce the foul at the succeeding spot or on the subsequent kickoff.

8.2.2 SITUATION E: Prior to the ball being thrown during a play in which A1 catches a touchdown pass and advances for a touchdown, B1 holds A2 to prevent him from going out for a pass on the side away from the play. When given options, A elects to enforce the penalty for the defensive holding foul on the subsequent kickoff. During the successful two-point try, B1 is guilty of holding A1. Does A have the option of having the 10-yard penalty added on to the previous 10-yard penalty on the subsequent kickoff? **RULING:** Yes. The fouls did not occur during the same down, so these are not multiple fouls and, therefore, they may both be enforced on the subsequent kickoff (8-3-5b; 10-2-4).

8.2.2 SITUATION F: During a touchdown run by A1, B1 holds. During the successful kick try, there is a foul by B2. **RULING:** If A accepts the penalty for B's holding foul, A may accept the score and attempt the try from the 1 1/2-yard line or accept the score and have the penalty enforced on the subsequent kickoff. For a foul on the try, A may accept and replay the try from the 3/4-yard line or accept the 1-point try and enforce the penalty for B's try foul on the subsequent kickoff. The captain of A may choose to have both penalties enforced on the subsequent kickoff.

8.2.2 SITUATION G: A1 scores a touchdown. During the scoring play, (a) A commits an unsportsmanlike foul or (b) B commits an unsportsmanlike foul. **RULING:** In (a) and (b), the touchdown will be scored. The offended team will have the option to enforce the penalty on the try or carry it to the subsequent kickoff.

8.3.2 SITUATION C: During a try, A1 completes a pass to A2 in the end zone and B2 interfered with A2. **RULING:** A undoubtedly will accept the result of the play and enforce the penalty from the succeeding spot (7-5-10 Penalty; 7-5-12 Penalty; 8-3-5).

8.3.5 SITUATION A: During a kick try: (a) B1 holds and the try is successful; or (b) A1 holds and the try is successful; or (c) B1 roughs the kicker/holder and the try is unsuccessful. **RULING:** In (a), A may accept the score and have the penalty enforced from the succeeding spot or enforce it from the previous spot and replay the down. In (b), B undoubtedly will accept the penalty and replay. In (c), A obviously would accept the penalty and replay (8-3-7; 10-5-2).

8.3.5 SITUATION B: During a successful two-point try: (a) B1 roughs the passer; or (b) B2 holds tight end A8. **RULING:** In both (a) and (b), Team A may accept the score and have the penalty assessed from the succeeding spot.

8.4.3 SITUATION: With fourth and 5 from B's 18, K1's field-goal attempt is successful. B1 roughs the kicker/holder. **RULING:** K may accept the result of the play (3 points) and have the penalty enforced from the succeeding spot, or accept the penalty. If the penalty is accepted and K retains possession, it will be first and goal from R's 9-yard line (9-4-5; 10-5-1f).

8.5.2 SITUATION D: Fourth and 15 for A from its own 8-yard line. A1 is in punt formation and receives the snap in his end zone, but fumbles the ball. A1 quickly recovers and throws a forward pass to ineligible A2, who is also in the end zone. A2 muffs the ball and it falls incomplete. **RULING:** If B accepts the penalty for A2's illegal touching, it results in a safety. If B declines the penalty for the foul by A2, the result is B's ball first and goal from A's 8-yard line (5-1-3c; 7-5-13 Penalty; 8-5-2c; 10-5-5).

9.4.3 SITUATION Q: A has possession, 3rd and 10 from the A10. A25 is running in the open field and B1 uses an illegal horse collar to bring him down (a) at the 50 after he was grabbed by the collar at the A45; or (b) at the A25 after he was initially grabbed by the collar at the A30 but the runner had retreated on his own to the A25; or (c) on B's 4 yard line and A25 drags B1 into B's end zone. **RULING:** Each of these plays are running plays, so the foul is enforced from the end of the run. In (a) it will be enforced from the 50, making it first and 10 for A at the B35; in (b) the foul is enforced from the A25, making it first and 10 for A at the A40; in (c) the touchdown is scored and A has the option of enforcing the foul on the try or the subsequent kickoff.

10.4.5 SITUATION G: A2 commits an unsportsmanlike dead-ball foul: (a) following a touchdown by A1; or (b) following a successful try. **RULING:** In (a), B is given the option of accepting the penalty enforcement on the try or the subsequent kick. In (b), the succeeding spot is the kickoff (2-15; 2-41; 8-2-4).

10.4.5 COMMENT: If the try had been the last play of the game and the score was tied, the succeeding spot for enforcement of the penalty for the foul by A2 would be the start of the overtime procedure. If an overtime is not authorized, the foul cannot be penalized because there would be no succeeding spot.

10.5.3 SITUATION A: With third and 6 from B's 35-yard line, a pass from A1 is intercepted at B's 25 by B1 who advances for an apparent touchdown. During the run by B1, A1 kicks B2. **RULING:** B may (a) accept the touchdown and enforce the penalty on the try or on the subsequent kickoff; (b) decline the penalty. In either case, A1 is disqualified for fighting (8-2-3; 9-4-1).

10.5.3 SITUATION B: Third down and 12 on A's 40-yard line. A1 drops back to throw a pass. The pass is completed to A2 who scores on the run following the reception. During the down, (a) A3 holds B1 on A's 37-yard line or (b) A's coach is observed standing inbounds on B's 20-yard line. **RULING:** (a) If B accepts the penalty for holding by A3, the score is nullified and following enforcement, it will be A's ball, third down and 25 to go on A's 27. In (b), the score stands. Following enforcement, the try will be from A's 18-yard line or the foul may be enforced on the subsequent kickoff (8-2-4; 9-2-1c, 9-8-1k, 10-5-3).

10.5.3 SITUATION C: Late in the game R is trailing by 9 points as K prepares to punt from its 4-yard line. During the kick, K2 holds R4 in the end zone. R5 returns the punt for a touchdown. **RULING:** R may (a) accept the penalty, score the safety and have K free-kick from its 20-yard line; or (b) decline the penalty and accept the results of the play, which would be a touchdown (8-2-3).

10.5.4 SITUATION B: During the last timed down of the first half, A1 retreats into his own end zone to attempt a pass, but he is downed there. During the down there is holding in the end zone by: (a) A2, or (b) by B1. **RULING:** In (a), it is a safety and B would score 2 points whether the penalty is accepted or declined since the run ended in the end zone and the foul was in the end zone. If B accepts the penalty, the period is not extended with an untimed down. In (b), if the penalty is accepted it will be enforced from the goal line and the period is extended.

Fouls Before or After a New Series Awarded

The team in possession has a series of four downs numbered 1, 2, 3 and 4 to advance the ball to the line to gain, which is usually 10 yards in advance of the spot where the series begins (1-1-2). After a first, second or third down, a new series of downs shall be awarded only after considering the effect of any act during the down other than non-player and unsportsmanlike conduct fouls by A, and any dead-ball foul by B (5-1-2a). After a fourth down, a new series of downs shall be awarded only after considering the effect of any act during the down, except for nonplayer or unsportsmanlike fouls (5-1-2b).

On fourth-down plays, A must get a first down by virtue of the yardage gained, including any yardage or an automatic first down from penalties for player fouls during the down, or it is a new series for B automatically when the down ends unless the down is to be repeated. The penalties for all unsportsmanlike and nonplayer fouls which occur during the down in which a new series is awarded, and dead-ball fouls prior to the subsequent ready-for-play signal, will be administered before the new line to gain is established and the chain and box are set. In all cases it will be first and 10 for A unless it is inside the opponent's 10-yard line. On plays other than on fourth down, Team A may gain a first down by virtue of the yards gained or from penalty enforcement (5.1.2 SITUATION E COMMENT).

Fouls Before or After a New Series Awarded: Case Plays

5.1.2 SITUATION C: Third and 10 for A from B's 40-yard line. A1 gains 10 yards and is downed on B's 30. A2 taunts B1 during the run. **RULING:** Since the live-ball action gave A a new series, the line to gain shall be established after A is penalized for A2's unsportsmanlike act. It will be first and 10 for A from B's 45-yard line.

*5.1.2 SITUATION D: With fourth and 5 on B's 20, A1 is downed on B's 16-yard line. During the down, the coach of B is on the field arguing with a game official. Following the down, A1 uses profanity. **RULING:** Since A did not gain a first down on the fourth-down run by A1, B has a new series. Enforcement of the penalties for the foul on the coach of B and for the foul on A1 offset. B will have the ball first and 10 at B's 16-yard line.

5.1.2 SITUATION E: Fourth and 2 on B's 25-yard line. A1 is tackled at the 26, short of the line to gain, and B2 then piles on. **RULING:** The referee shall signal a change of possession by signaling first down toward A's goal. The penalty for B2's dead-ball foul is administered and the line-to-gain equipment then set, making it first and 10 for B from its own 13-yard line.

5.1.2 SITUATION F: With second and 5 at B's 40, A1 advances to B's 30. Following the down, A2 illegally contacts B1. **RULING:** The 15-yard penalty is enforced and then the chain is set. It will be first and 10 for A at B's 45.

5.1.2 SITUATION G: With fourth and 40 from A's 10-yard line, A1 runs to A's 44 where he is downed. During the down, B1 commits a personal foul against A2. **RULING:** B1's foul is penalized from the end of the run. It is A's ball first and 10 from B's 41-yard line (2-16-2f; 5-1-2b).

10.2.2 SITUATION D: B's coach is on the field during a forward-pass play. B1 intercepts and A1 grabs B1's face mask/helmet opening during the return. **RULING:** B's ball following enforcement of the penalty for A1's foul. The unsportsmanlike foul on the coach cannot be paired with A1's foul to create a double foul. The unsportsmanlike foul is enforced from the succeeding spot, and then the line-to-gain equipment is set (9-8-2; 10-4-5a).

10.2.5 SITUATION A: With third and 8 on B's 40, A1 advances to B's 35 where he is downed. B1 piles on and, almost immediately thereafter, A2 spears B1. **RULING:** The distance penalties for the dead fouls cancel. The down counts; it will now be fourth and 3 from B's 35. If A2's spearing is judged by the game official to be flagrant, he shall be disqualified (9-4-3i; 10-2-5b, c).

Goal Line is the Basic Spot

The basic spot is the goal line for fouls which are committed during running plays by the opponent of the team in possession at the time of the foul when the team in possession is responsible for forcing the ball across its own goal line, and the related run ends in the end zone and is followed by a loose ball, regardless of where the loose ball becomes dead (10-4-7). The enforcement spot for any foul by the defense is the goal line when the run ends in the end zone and would result in a safety (10-5-2).

Goal Line Is the Basic Spot: Case Plays

10.3.3 SITUATION A: B1 intercepts A's pass at the A10 and returns for a touchdown. B2 clips in A's end zone after the interception, but before the score. **RULING:** The basic spot is end of run which is the goal line. After penalty enforcement, it would be B's ball, first and 10, at A's 15-yard line.

10.5.2 SITUATION: A's ball second and 5 from its own 9-yard line. A2 muffs the handoff and the ball rolls into A's end zone. A1 picks up the ball and is immediately tackled by B3 in the end zone. B3 grasped A1 by the face mask/helmet opening in making the tackle. **RULING:** If A declines the penalty, this play would result in a safety. If the penalty is accepted, it will be enforced from the goal line, making it first and 10 for A from its 15-yard line (8-5-2b).

Kick-Catching Interference

While any free kick is in flight in or beyond the neutral zone to the receiver's goal line or any scrimmage kick is in flight beyond the neutral zone to the receiver's goal line, K shall not touch the ball or R, unless blocked into the ball or R or to ward off a blocker, nor obstruct R's path to the ball. This prohibition applies even when no fair-catch signal is given, but it does not apply after a free kick has been touched by a receiver, or after a scrimmage kick has been touched by a receiver who was clearly beyond the neutral zone at the time of touching (6-5-6b, 10-5-1b). The captain may choose to free kick or snap anywhere between the inbounds lines on the yard line through the spot of the catch when a fair catch is made or through the spot of interference, when a fair catch is awarded. These choices remain if a dead-ball foul occurs prior to the down, or a foul or an inadvertent whistle occurs during the down and the down is replayed (6-5-6 Penalty).

Kick-Catching Interference: Penalty

R may accept the results of the play, an awarded fair catch after enforcement of a 15-yard penalty from the spot of the foul, or a 15-yard penalty from the previous spot and a replay of the down. Signal 33.

Kick-Catching Interference: Case Plays

6.1.7 SITUATION A: A free kick from K's 40 is high and comes down over K's 45 where it is muffed in flight by K2 after which it is recovered by K3 on R's 40. **RULING:** This is first touching and also kick-catching interference by K2. R may choose to take the ball at the spot of first touching, take the results of the play or accept the 15-yard penalty for kick-catching interference. If the distance penalty is accepted, it is R's choice to have the penalty enforced from the spot of the foul or to have it enforced from the previous spot and require K to rekick.

6.1.7 COMMENT: The clock will not be started when there is first touching of a free kick. The purpose is to prevent the kickers from taking advantage by touching the ball to start the clock and thereby deny the receivers the opportunity of putting the ball in play. The exception "the clock not starting with first touching," is protection for the receiving team and is consistent with the philosophy that the receiving team be given an opportunity of putting the ball in play following a free kick (3-4-1; 6-5-4, 6).

6.1.7 SITUATION B: The ball is free kicked from K's 40-yard line and in flight, it crosses the 50-yard line before a strong wind blows it back to K's 45 where it is touched in flight by K1. **RULING:** Kick-catching interference.

6.5.6 SITUATION A: K2's punt is partially blocked by R1 in or behind the neutral zone and it then travels beyond the neutral zone. R2 is in position to catch the ball, but it first touches K2's shoulder before hitting the ground, where it is recovered by R2. **RULING:** Since R1's touching is ignored, it is kick-catching interference by K2, because R2 was in position to catch the ball.

6.5.6 SITUATION B: K1's punt is coming down over R's 15-yard line and (a) R2 is in position to catch the ball, or (b) all R players have moved away from where the ball will land. In both (a) and (b), K3 catches the ball. **RULING:** In (a), it is kick-catching interference and R has the option to take the results of the play, or accept the 15-yard penalty for kick-catching interference. If the distance penalty is accepted, it is R's choice to have the penalty enforced from the spot of the foul or to have it enforced from the previous spot and require K to rekick. In (b), the play is legal and the ball is dead as soon as K3 catches it. The spot of the catch is also a spot of first touching and R will put the ball in play on that yard line, first and 10.

6.5.6 SITUATION C: K5, running down field under a punt, has the kick strike him on his helmet: (a) R1 is in a position to catch the kick if he so chooses; or (b) no R player is in position to be able to get to the ball and catch it. **RULING:** In (a), K5 has committed kick-catching interference. In (b), there is no foul.

6.5.6 SITUATION D: K1's punt is high but short. R2, from well down field, runs toward the ball to get in position to attempt to catch it. K2 is also moving toward the ball or just standing there when: (a) K2 is contacted by R2; or (b) K2 causes R2 to veer away from the ball but there is no contact by K2. The ball strikes the ground and is recovered by R3. **RULING:** K2 has committed kick-catching interference in both (a) and (b) since K2 did not provide R2 an unobstructed opportunity to catch the ball. R may choose to take the results of the play, or accept the 15-yard penalty for kick-catching interference. If the distance penalty is accepted, it is R's choice to have the penalty enforced from the spot of the foul or to have it enforced from the previous spot and require K to replay the down.

6.5.6 SITUATION E: While K1's punt is in flight beyond the neutral zone, R2 (a) gives a valid fair catch signal, or (b) does not give a signal. The ball strikes R2 on the shoulder and bounces high into the air. While the loose ball is still airborne, K4 pushes R2 in the chest and K4 catches the ball at that spot. **RULING:** In both cases, the ball is dead when K4 catches it. There is no foul for kick-catching interference since R2's protection ended when the kick was touched.

9.7.2 SITUATION A: With fourth and 4 from R's 40-yard line, K1 punts. The kick is bounding near R's goal line and K2, in an attempt to keep it from penetrating the plane of the goal line, bats the ball at the 2-yard line back toward his own goal line. **RULING:** The bat by K2 is legal because it occurred beyond the neutral zone.

*9.7.2 SITUATION B: K1's punt is coming down over R's 10-yard line and: (a) R3 is in position to catch the ball; or (b) no R player is in position to catch the ball, when K2 bats the ball toward his own goal line while it is in flight, but the batted ball subsequently goes into R's end zone. **RULING:** In (a), it is a foul for kick-catching interference by K2 as well as first touching, and R may choose to take the result of the play, which is a touchback, or take an awarded fair catch at R's 25-yard line (15 yards in advance of the spot of interference after enforcement of the penalty) or the ball at the spot of first touching at the 10-yard line, or penalize K 15 yards from the previous spot and replay the down. In (b), there is no foul and the result of the play is a touchback. R will put the ball in play first and 10 from its own 20-yard line (6-5-6 Exception; 8-5-3; 9-7-2 Exception).

Roughing the Passer

The enforcement spot is the dead ball spot when the dead ball spot is beyond the neutral zone and A has possession of the ball at the end of the down, and there has been no change of team possession. Otherwise, the penalty is 15 yards and an automatic first down from the previous spot (9-4 PENALTY, 10-5-5g).

Unfair Acts

If a player or nonplayer or person(s) not subject to the rules hinders play by an unfair act which has no specific rule coverage; either team repeatedly commits fouls which halve the distance to the goal line; or either team commits any act which, in the opinion of the referee, tends to make a travesty of the game, the referee enforces any penalty he considers equitable, including the award of a score (9-10 Penalty, 10-5-1c).

No team shall repeatedly commit fouls which halve the distance to the goal line (9-10-2).

No player shall hide the ball under a jersey. No player shall use a kicking tee in violation of Rule 1-3-4. The penalties for an illegal tee and hiding a ball under a jersey are not charged to the coach or player for the purpose of unsportsmanlike conduct disqualifications (9-10 NOTE).

Unfair Acts: Penalty

15 yards, basic spot. Signal 27.

Unfair Acts: Case Play

*9.10.1 SITUATION A: A is trailing by five points near the end of the fourth quarter and has no time outs left when the play ends on B's 3. The referee does not feel there is any illegal delay in unpiling and that time will definitely expire before the ball is ready and A gets in position to snap. Quarterback A1 reaches into the pile of players and grabs the ball. He then throws the ball to midfield. **RULING:** Even if the referee imposes a 15-yard penalty for an unsportsmanlike act, A has accomplished its goal — the clock is stopped and it can get in position and be ready to run a play even though the clock will start on the ready-for-play signal. This situation illustrates when it is appropriate for the referee to invoke the unfair-act rule and handle the situation in any way that the referee feels is equitable. In this specific situation the referee should wind the clock and end the game without giving A an opportunity to put the ball in play.

 9.10.1 COMMENT: The rule also gives the referee authority to take appropriate action whenever someone not subject to the rules hinders play (3-4-6).

9.10.1 SITUATION B: From a field goal formation, potential kicker A1 yells, "Where's the tee?" A2 replies, "I'll go get it" and goes legally in motion toward his team's sideline. Ball is snapped to A1 who throws a touchdown pass to A2. **RULING:** Unsportsmanlike conduct prior to snap. The ball should be declared dead and the foul enforced as a dead-ball foul.

Topic 7

Time-Outs and Other Play Stoppages

PlayPic®

Key Terms

The clock running time for a game shall be 48 minutes for high schools with periods and intermissions (3-1-1).

The clock shall be stopped when the down ends following a foul; an official's time-out is taken; a charged or TV/radio time-out is granted; the period ends; the ball is out of bounds; a score or touchback occurs; a fair catch is made; an inadvertent whistle is sounded; or an airborne receiver is carried out of bounds, unless the receiver is carried backwards and his forward progress was stopped inbounds (3-4-4a-j).

By state association adoption, if, at the end of the fourth period, the teams have identical scores, the tie may be resolved if a method has been approved by the state high school association. This may include extending playing time. The overtime is considered part of the fourth period (3-1-1 NOTE).

Topic:
Conserving/Consuming Time

When a team attempts to conserve or consume time illegally, the referee shall order the clock started or stopped (3-6-3; 9-10-5).

Conserving/Consuming Time: Case Plays

3.4.6 SITUATION A: With time expiring in the second or fourth period and A behind in the score, A1 intentionally throws the ball forward to the ground in order to stop the clock. A1's action took place immediately after receiving a direct hand-to-hand snap. **RULING:** The grounding is legal and the clock remains stopped until the subsequent snap.

 3.4.6 COMMENT: Is there suggested guidance in determining situations where a team may be conserving or consuming time illegally and the referee should consider starting/stopping the clock as in 3-4-6? Yes. In general, the referee must be aware of game situations where A could manipulate the clock by repeatedly committing dead-ball fouls, or in other ways, intentionally try to restart the play clock in a situation when it would normally start on the ready in order to manipulate the remaining time.

The following represent examples of plays where the referee may need to start or stop the clock to ensure competitive fairness to both teams: a) With 19 seconds remaining on the game clock but only 5 seconds remaining on the play clock, the game clock is running in the first quarter. Team K is in punt formation on fourth down. K will apparently be kicking into a strong wind. Lineman K62 commits a 'false start' just before the snap. If this occurs, K should be penalized 5 yards if accepted. The referee will invoke 3-4-6 and start the clock on the snap. b) Team K is in field-goal formation with 5 seconds remaining in the half and the clock running. Team R encroaches. After the penalty administration, the referee should invoke Rule 3-4-6 and start the clock on the snap in order to allow K a field-goal attempt since R fouled with insufficient time to guarantee K a play which it otherwise would have had. c) With the game clock running, A2 does not have his chinstrap snapped as the ball is about to become "live." In this case, if the delay foul is accepted, the clock will start on the snap, unless the referee invokes Rule 3-4-6 if he felt an advantage was intentionally gained. d) With only seconds remaining in the game and the clock running, Team A is trailing by two points and wants to 'spike' the ball to stop the clock. Quarterback A12 "muffs" the hand-to-hand snap which rolls up his arm. He gains control of the ball, then throws it immediately to the ground in front of him. In this case, A should be penalized 5 yards from the spot of the foul and loss of down for the illegal attempt to conserve time. Since this was an illegal attempt to conserve time, the referee should invoke 3-4-6 and start the clock on the ready-for-play signal. e) A is ahead near the end of a half with the game clock under 25 seconds and the play clock set to expire before the game clock and A commits a dead-ball or intentional live-ball foul. The referee should not allow this type of action to end the half and may order the clock started on the snap. This list is not intended to be exhaustive but only to offer guidance to referees.

3.4.6 SITUATION B: With less than a minute remaining in the game, the score is 21-20 in favor of B. The clock is running and the ball is on B's 10-yard line. An option play on third down gains 5 yards, but is short of a first down. Following the tackle, the tackler B1 holds A1 down for a few moments, but the covering official does not judge the action to be illegal. **RULING:** Even though B1 held A1 down momentarily, the clock will continue to run because no foul was called (3-4-3h).

3.4.6 COMMENT: In some situations there is a delay in unpiling and no individual player or team is to blame. In such situations the referee is authorized to stop the clock momentarily so no more clock time than normal is used in getting the ball ready for play (3-4-3h).

6.1.7 SITUATION A: A free kick from K's 40 is high and comes down over K's 45 where it is muffed in flight by K2 after which it is recovered by K3 on R's 40. **RULING:** This is first touching and also kick-catching interference by K2. R may choose to take the ball at the spot of first touching, take the results of the play or accept the 15-yard penalty for kick-catching interference. If the distance penalty is accepted, it is R's choice to have the penalty enforced from the spot of the foul or to have it enforced from the previous spot and require K to rekick.

6.1.7 COMMENT: The clock will not be started when there is first touching of a free kick. The purpose is to prevent the kickers from taking advantage by touching the ball to start the clock and thereby deny the receivers the opportunity of putting the ball in play. The exception "the clock not starting with first touching," is protection for the receiving team and is consistent with the philosophy that the receiving team be given an opportunity of putting the ball in play following a free kick (3-4-1; 6-5-4, 6).

*9.10.1 SITUATION A: A is trailing by five points near the end of the fourth quarter and has no time outs left when the play ends on B's 3. The referee does not feel there is any illegal delay in unpiling and that time will definitely expire before the ball is ready and A gets in position to snap. Quarterback A1 reaches into the pile of players and grabs the ball. He then throws the ball to midfield. **RULING:** Even if the referee imposes a 15-yard penalty for an unsportsmanlike act, A has accomplished its goal — the clock is stopped and it can get in position and be ready to run a play even though the clock will start on the ready-for-play signal. This situation illustrates when it is appropriate for the referee to invoke the unfair-act rule and handle the situation in any way that the referee feels is equitable. In this specific situation the referee should wind the clock and end the game without giving A an opportunity to put the ball in play.

9.10.1 COMMENT: The rule also gives the referee authority to take appropriate action whenever someone not subject to the rules hinders play (3-4-6).

Topic:
Ending/Extending/Shortening a Period

Approximately four minutes before the end of each half, the referee shall notify the field captains and their coaches of the time remaining. If time is not out, the referee shall order the clock stopped while he does this. If an electric field clock is the official timepiece, no notification nor stoppage of the clock is required (3-3-1).

If time for any period expires during a down (clock indicates 0:00), play shall continue until the down ends, even though a mechanical signal is allowed to sound (3-3-2).

At the end of each period the referee shall hold the ball in one hand overhead to indicate the period has officially ended, after delaying momentarily to ensure that no foul has occurred, no obvious timing error has occurred, no request for a coach-referee conference has occurred and no other irregularity has occurred (3-3-5a-d).

If a dead-ball foul occurs after time expires for any period, the penalty shall be measured from the succeeding spot unless 8-2-5 applies (3-3-6, 8-2-5).

A period or periods may be shortened in any emergency by agreement of the opposing coaches and the referee. By mutual agreement of the opposing coaches and the referee, any remaining period may be shortened at any time or the game terminated (3-1-3).

By state association adoption, a point differential may be established whereby if one team has gained the established point differential, the game shall be terminated. A state association may also establish guidelines to use a running clock when the point differential is reached (3-1-2).

Period Extended or Not Extended

A period shall be extended by an untimed down if one of the following occurred during a down in which time expires: there was a foul, other than unsportsmanlike or nonplayer, or fouls that specify loss of down by either team and the penalty is accepted; there was a double foul; there was an inadvertent whistle; or a touchdown was scored. If a touchdown was scored, the try is attempted unless the touchdown is scored during the last down of the fourth period and the point(s) would not affect the outcome of the game or playoff qualifying.

If any of the above occurs during the untimed down, the procedure is repeated (3-3-3a-d).

A period shall not be extended by an untimed down if one of the following occurred during a down in which time expires: the defense fouls during a successful try/field goal and the offended team accepts the results of the play with enforcement of the penalty from the succeeding spot; there is a foul that specifies loss of down and the penalty is accepted. The score is cancelled in the event of an accepted penalty that specifies a loss of down; or there was a foul by either team and the penalty is accepted for unsportsmanlike fouls, non-player fouls, fouls that specify a loss of down and penalties that are enforced on the subsequent kickoff as in Rule 8-2-2 or 8-2-3; or fouls for which enforcement, by rule, result in a safety (3-3-4a-c).

Period Extended or Not Extended: Case Plays

3.3.3 SITUATION A: With the score B-7 and A-6, it is second and goal from B's 9-yard line. The clock is stopped due to an incomplete pass with four seconds remaining in the game. A1's pass into the end zone is intercepted by B1 who runs to his 30-yard line where he is downed. Following the interception and during the run by B1, there is clipping in the end zone by B2. Time expires during the run. **RULING:** If the penalty for the foul by B2 is declined, the period is over. If the penalty is accepted, it results in a safety (two points) for A; however, the period is not extended. If this occurs at the end of period one or three, the teams will change ends of the field and B will kick from B's 20-yard line (3-3-4b(5)).

*3.3.4 SITUATION C:** On a down in which time expires for the period, Team A throws a pass which is intercepted by B1. B1 advances to the 3-yard line where he: (a) throws an incomplete pass; (b) throws a pass to B2 in the end zone for an apparent touchdown; or (c) hands the ball forward to B2 who runs for an apparent touchdown. **RULING:** In (a) and (b), B has thrown an illegal forward pass. In (c), B is guilty of illegal handing the ball forward. In (a), A will accept the penalty. In (b) and (c), A will accept the penalty to negate the score. If this occurs at the end of the first or third period, B will have the ball first and 10 to start the subsequent period following enforcement of the penalty. If this occurs at the end of the half, the half is over. In (a), (b) and (c), the period will not be extended as Team B has committed a foul for which the loss-of-down aspect does not apply to the penalty when enforced (5-2-2).

3.3.4 SITUATION D: In the middle of a period, Team A throws a pass which is intercepted by B1. B1 advances to the 8-yard line where he: (a) throws an incomplete pass; (b) throws a pass to B2 in the end zone for an apparent touchdown; or (c) hands the ball forward to B2 who runs for apparent touchdown. **RULING:** In (a), (b) and (c), the accepted foul will result in B having the ball, first and 10 after enforcement of the distance penalty, as the loss-of-down aspect of the penalty would not apply (5-2-2).

◪ Rationale

Giving A an untimed down in that situation prevents B from benefiting from a foul that could shorten or end the quarter or game. Similarly, if B were trailing and A fouled, extending the period would prevent A from the same unfair advantage.

3.3.3 SITUATION B: Near the end of the third period, it is third and 4 for A from B's 48-yard line. A1 advances to B's 45 and during the run there is holding by B1. The penalty is accepted. At the end of the down there are three seconds remaining in the period. Because the penalty was the only reason for the clock to be stopped, it is started with the ready-for-play signal and the period ends before A snaps the ball. **RULING:** A is not entitled to an untimed down as time did not expire during the down.

3.3.3 SITUATION C: During a down when time expires, A1 gains 10 yards and fumbles. The covering official inadvertently sounds his whistle while the ball is loose. **RULING:** The period shall be extended for an untimed down and A may put the ball in play where it lost possession or it may choose to replay the down from the previous spot (3-3-3c).

***3.3.3 SITUATION D:** With the ball at B's 1-yard line and 12 seconds remaining in the game, A1 advances to the ½-yard line. After the ball is dead, B1 fouls. The clock is stopped with five seconds remaining in the game. The clock is restarted when the ball is marked ready for play. Before A can snap the ball, time expires. **RULING:** The game is ended. There is no extension of the period for an untimed down, unless there is acceptance of the penalty for a foul that occurs during a down in which time expires. B1's foul did not occur during the down. However, if the referee judges B1 committed the foul to consume time, he shall delay starting the clock until the snap.

3.3.3 COMMENT: When either team attempts to conserve or consume time illegally, the referee shall invoke Rule 3-4-6 and start or delay the start of the clock as authorized (3-4-6; 3-6-2f; 9-10-2)

3.3.3 SITUATION E: A1 breaks free on B's 20-yard line and is near the goal line on a run which will score the go-ahead touchdown. Just before entering the end zone, A1 turns and taunts B1. Time in the fourth period expires during the run. **RULING:** The touchdown is scored and the unsportsmanlike foul by A1 cannot be penalized. While such situations do not occur frequently, it must be recognized that at some point penalty enforcement is ended. If the try is required for playoff qualification, the penalty is enforced on the try (10-4-5a).

3.3.3 SITUATION F: With the score A-14, B-23, A scores a touchdown: (a) as time expires in the fourth period; or (b) as time expires in the third period; or (c) as time expires in the fourth period in a state in which a tie-breaking procedure for playoff qualification is based on points scored. **RULING:** In (a), the try will not be permitted – the game is over and the final score is A-20, B-23. In (b), the try is attempted as part of the third period. The try in (c) is permissible if the potential point(s) is needed in a tie-breaker system for playoff qualification. Each state must interpret this provision as it applies to its particular qualifying plan (8-3-1 Exception).

3.3.3 SITUATION G: K1 punts on fourth and 15 from his own 20-yard line. R1 signals for a fair catch at R's 30. K2 commits kick-catching interference at R's 35 and time for the second period expires during the down. R2 recovers the kick at R's 28. **RULING:** If R declines the penalty, the period is over. If R accepts an awarded catch or has the penalty otherwise enforced, the period will be extended by an untimed down (6-1-9b; 6-5-6 Penalty).

3.3.4 SITUATION B: The clock is running with 10 seconds remaining in the fourth period as A1 drops back about 4 yards and intentionally grounds a forward pass to stop the clock. The penalty is accepted. The referee starts the clock on the ready following penalty enforcement and time expires before A can snap the ball. **RULING:** If B accepted the penalty for A's foul, the game is over and there is no untimed down as the foul specified a loss of down and the clock did not expire during the down in which A1 committed the foul (3-4-6).

*3.3.5 SITUATION A: A trails by three points in the fourth period with the ball on B's 20, fourth and 10 and two seconds on the clock. A1 throws an incomplete pass into B's end zone with time expired. The referee quickly glances to each sideline and then begins to leave the field. After the referee crosses the sideline, the referee hears the line judge blowing his whistle. The line judge explains that B1 committed pass interference during the down in which time expired. **RULING:** The game is not officially over even though the referee left the field. Since a foul had been called, the referee will give A a chance to accept the penalty and extend the period with an untimed down from B's 10-yard line.

3.3.5 COMMENT: The game is officially over when the referee holds the ball overhead and leaves the field. Before doing this however, he should pause briefly and glance to both sidelines and make sure there are no fouls, no obvious timing error, no request for a coach-referee conference, etc.

3.3.5 SITUATION B: Time expires at the end of the second period during a scrimmage kick. After the down, K1 piles on and R1 strikes K2. **RULING:** The penalties for these dead-ball fouls cancel. R1 will be disqualified for fighting (9-4-1; 10-2-5b, c; 10-4-5b).

3.4.2 SITUATION C: Near the end of a period with 28 seconds left, K1 punts on fourth down. During the kick the covering official inadvertently sounds his whistle. The clock is stopped with 23 seconds remaining. **RULING:** The clock will be started with the ready-for-play signal. The down must be replayed.

8.2.2 SITUATION B: On the down in which time expired for the second period, Team A: (a) scores a field goal or (b) scores a touchdown. In both cases, the opponents of the scoring team commit a live-ball foul. **RULING:** In (a), the offended team has the option to keep the score, with the penalty assessed on the second half kickoff as this is the succeeding spot. In (b), the offended team has the option to keep the score, with penalty assessment on either the try or on the second half kickoff as this would be the subsequent kickoff.

8.2.2 SITUATION C: During the down in which time expires for the fourth period, the opponents of Team A foul on a play where Team A: (a) scores a touchdown that leaves Team A trailing by one point, (b) scores a field goal which ties the game, or (c) scores a touchdown that leaves team A trailing by one point and the opponents also foul on the try. **RULING:** In (a), Team A has the option to keep the score, with the penalty assessed on the try. The penalty cannot be assessed on the first play of overtime as there is no subsequent kickoff. In (b), Team A has the option to keep the score, with penalty assessment on the first play of overtime as the first play of overtime is the succeeding spot. In (c), Team A may only have the penalty for the opponent foul on the scoring play enforced on the try but cannot carry over the penalty to overtime;

however, the foul by the opponent during the try could be enforced on the first play of overtime at Team A's choice.

10.4.5 SITUATION D: With the score, B-14 and A-8, a pass from A1 is complete in the end zone to A2 during the down in which time expires for the fourth period. During the down, there is holding by B1 and after the down, B2 is charged with an unsportsmanlike foul. **RULING:** A will undoubtedly accept the result of the play and enforce the holding penalty from the 3-yard line and enforce the penalty for the unsportsmanlike foul. The ball would then be snapped for the try from the 3/4-yard line (3-3-3a; 10-5-1f).

10.4.5 SITUATION E: A scores on the last play of the: (a) second period; or (b) fourth period, to make the score, B-21 and A-19. During A's successful 2-point try, B1 commits an unsportsmanlike foul. **RULING:** In (a), the penalty is enforced from the succeeding spot on the kickoff to start the third period. In (b), the penalty for B1's foul will be administered from the succeeding spot if an overtime is played (2-41-9; 3-3-3d).

10.5.4 SITUATION B: During the last timed down of the first half, A1 retreats into his own end zone to attempt a pass, but he is downed there. During the down there is holding in the end zone by: (a) A2, or (b) by B1. **RULING:** In (a), it is a safety and B would score 2 points whether the penalty is accepted or declined since the run ended in the end zone and the foul was in the end zone. If B accepts the penalty, the period is not extended with an untimed down. In (b), if the penalty is accepted it will be enforced from the goal line and the period is extended.

Topic:
Time-Outs

Authorized Conference

Coach-Referee Conference – The referee confers with the coach at the sideline in front of his team box in the field of play (2-6-1). Authorized Team Conference – There are two types of authorized team conferences: Outside 9-Yard Mark Conference – One or more team members and one or more coaches directly in front of the team box within 9 yards of the sideline (2-6-2a), or Between 9-Yard Mark Conference – One coach on the field to confer with no more than 11 players at his team's huddle between the hash marks (2-6-2b).

An authorized conference may be held during a charged time-out; for an official's time-out for unusual heat or humidity which may create a health risk to players; for a TV/radio time-out that is permitted and granted as authorized by state association policy; the one-minute intermission between the first and second and the third and fourth periods; and during the one-minute intermission following a try, successful field goal or safety and prior to the succeeding free kick (3-5-8a(1) through (3)).

LAN phones and/or headsets may be used by coaches, other non players and players; however, players may use LAN phones and/or headsets only during authorized outside 9-yard mark sideline conferences (1-6-2).

Authorized Conference: Case Plays

1.4.1 SITUATION: Team A's captain requests a time-out prior to: (a) making a penalty decision; or (b) deciding whether A will snap or free kick following a fair catch; or (c) designating where the ball is to be spotted on the 3-yard line for a try. **RULING:** Not allowed in (a), but permissible in (b) and (c).

1.4.1 COMMENT: In the case of considering an awarded fair catch, the captain would have to make his decision on the penalty prior to requesting a time-out. After accepting the penalty via an awarded catch, a time-out can be taken to consider whether to snap or free kick (2-32-5; 6-5-4; 10-1-1).

3.5.8 SITUATION A: During a charged time-out, an official's time-out for heat/humidity, a TV/radio time-out, or the intermission between the first and second or the third and fourth periods, or following a try: (a)

team members of A confer with their head coach in front of the team box near the sideline; or (b) the coach of B goes to the huddle of B between the 9-yard marks, and talks to an assistant via a headset he brought to the huddle; or (c) the coach of B goes on the field and uses the time to berate and loudly question the referee regarding a previous play; or (d) the coach wishes to discuss the previous play with the referee; or (e) the head coach of A goes to the team huddle on the field for 30 seconds and then comes out and another coach takes his place for the rest of the time-out. **RULING:** It is a legal conference in (a) and (b). In (a), the players may use the headsets. In (b), the players may not use the headsets. In (c) and (e), it is illegal. In (d), this conference must be held at the sideline in front of the team box regardless of which authorized conference procedure is used (2-6-2; 9-8-1c; 9-8-1i).

Did You Know? Before 1975, teams were allowed a maximum of four charged time-outs per half.

9.8.1 SITUATION A: During the course of the game, quarterback A1 runs to the vicinity of his team-box area for the purpose of receiving instructions from his coach. No time-out is requested, there is no delay in declaring the ball ready for play, and the coach does not leave the team-box. **RULING:** This type of communication is legal (9-8-1f Note).

9.8.1 SITUATION B: During a charged time-out: (a) A1 goes to the sideline to talk to his head coach. Thereafter, A2, A3 and A4 go to the sideline, but other team members remain between the 9-yard marks; or (b) while A1 is near the sideline talking to one coach, another coach of A goes between the 9-yard marks to the huddle on the field. **RULING:** Legal in (a), but an unauthorized conference in (b). In (b), only one type conference can be used during a given time-out (2-6-2).

9.8.1 SITUATION C: During a charged time-out or a time-out for heat/humidity the coach of A confers with A1 near the sideline and in front of his team box. The conference continues for 30 seconds. A1 then returns to the huddle and A2 comes to the sideline to confer with the coach for the remainder of the charged time-out. **RULING:** This is a legal conference (2-6-2).

In Simple Terms

Successive time-outs are allowed — thus, each team may be granted more than one charged time-out during a given dead-ball period, provided it has time-outs remaining.

Charged Team Time-Outs

Each team is entitled to three charged team time-outs each half. Unused first-half time-outs cannot be used in the second half. Unused second-half time-outs cannot be used in overtime (3-5-1).

A charged team time-out occurs when the ball is dead and the request of either a player or the head coach (or head coach's designee) is legally granted (3-5-2a). The head coach's designee shall remain place for the entire game except in case of emergency (3-5-2a NOTE); the repair of faulty player equipment requires the assistance of a team attendant or attendants, or which, without the assistance of a team attendant delays the ready-for-play signal for more than 25 seconds (3-5-2b); or a time-out is requested and granted for the purpose of reviewing a game official's application of a rule which may have been misapplied or misinterpreted. The time-out remains charged to the requesting team, if no change in the ruling results (3-5-2c).

A single charged time-out shall not exceed one minute. The referee shall notify the teams within five seconds after the time-out expires and shall declare the ball ready for play. Charged time-outs shall be reduced in length only if both teams are ready to play prior to the 25-second ready-for-play signal by the referee (3-5-3). Successive charged time-outs may be granted during the same dead-ball period (3-5-4).

After a team has used its permissible charged time-outs for the half, any subsequent request shall be denied unless it is for an apparently injured player who is so designated when the request is made; necessary repair to player equipment; or the review of a possible misapplication or misinterpretation of a rule (3-5-5). If repair of equipment without the assistance of a team attendant delays the ready-for-play signal for more than 25 seconds, or requires the assistance of a team attendant(s) and the player's team has used all permissible time-outs, the player shall be replaced for at least one down (3-5-6).

An official's time-out may follow a charged time-out if it is for the continuance of a coach-referee conference, or if safety is involved (3-5-4). Three attendants, none of whom is a coach, may enter the field to attend their team during a charged time-out or a TV/radio time-out;

during the one-minute following a try, a successful field goal or safety; and prior to the succeeding free kick, between periods and during an official's time-out for unusual heat and humidity (9-8-2).

Rationale

Heat and humidity time-outs reduce risk by ensuring that participants replace fluids lost through perspiration.

Charged Team Time-Outs: Case Plays

3.5.1 SITUATION A: Team A and Team B are tied at the conclusion of the fourth period. Team A has utilized one time-out in the second half and Team B has used three. State association overtime guidelines grant one time-out to each team in each overtime period. The coach of Team A asks the Referee if his team will now have three time outs in overtime (the two unused plus the one for the first overtime). **RULING:** The Referee must rule that the team has only one time-out per period, and that the unused second half time-outs did not carry over to overtime. Both teams will have one time-out per overtime period as per State Association guidelines.

3.5.1 SITUATION B: Team A and Team B are in the third overtime series attempting to resolve a tied game using the NFHS-recommended Resolving Tied Games procedure. Team A has not utilized any time-outs during overtime. As Team B sets up for a field goal attempt in the third overtime, Team A calls time-out. Following the time-out, the head coach requests another time-out due to the fact that he has not yet utilized a time-out during overtime. **RULING:** The request is denied as unless otherwise altered by the state association, the NFHS-recommended Resolving Tied Games procedure limits time-outs to one per overtime period.

3.5.2 SITUATION B: Team A wishes to call a time-out: (a) a player requests a time-out (b) the head coach on the field requests a time-out (c) an assistant coach on the field requests a time-out (d) the head coach is in the press box and an assistant coach on the field requests a time-out or (e) the head coach has been disqualified and an assistant coach on the field requests a time-out. **RULING:** In (a) and (b), upon visual contact, the time-out is granted. In (c), (d) and (e), the time-out is granted only if the coach is the head coach's designee. NOTE: The designee shall remain in place for the entire game except in case of emergency.

3.5.4 SITUATION: Near the end of the second period, A requests and is granted a charged time-out. After both teams are ready to play, A comes to the line of scrimmage in an unusual formation. The captain of B immediately requests a time-out which is granted. At the end of this time-out period, when A comes to the line of scrimmage again, A1 notices B has adjusted its defense. A1 then requests a second charged time-out during the same dead-ball period. **RULING:** If A has time-outs remaining, the referee will grant the request for the charged time-out. Successive time-outs by the same team, or by one team followed by the other team, are permissible.

In Simple Terms
A coach is not permitted to question any judgment decisions by the game officials during a coach-referee conference.

Coach-Referee Conferences

A player, directed by his coach or the head coach, may request and be granted a time-out for the purpose of the coach and the referee reviewing a decision which may have resulted from misapplication or misinterpretation of a rule, provided the request is made prior to the time the ball becomes live following the play to be reviewed, unless the period has officially ended (3-5-11). The referee will confer with the coach at the sideline in front of his team box in the field of play. If the conference results in the referee altering his ruling, the opposing coach will be notified, the revision made, and the time-out shall be an official's time-out (3-5-11). If the referee's ruling prevails, the time-out remains charged to the team requesting the time-out for the conference (3-5-2c). If all the permissible charged time-outs for the coach's team have been used, and there is no change in the ruling, the coach's team is penalized for delay of game (3-6-2c Penalty).

An official's time-out may follow a charged time-out if it is for the continuance of a coach-official conference (3-5-4).

Coach-Referee Conferences: Case Plays

*3.5.2 SITUATION A: The captain of A requests a time-out and informs the referee that the coach wishes to have a conference concerning the previous play. During the conference: (a) the captain or all A players go near the sideline to confer with their coaches, or (b) the coach of B goes on the field to the team's huddle to confer. **RULING:** Permissible in both (a) and (b). The time-out, when granted, is charged to A, thus legalizing the conferences. If a game official has erred and a correction is made, the conference in both (a) and (b) is terminated. In that case, the time-out is not charged to A, but is an official's time-out. If the coach is in error, the time-out remains charged to A (2-6; 3-5-2c).

3.5.2 SITUATION B: Team A wishes to call a time-out: (a) a player requests a time-out; (b) the head coach on the field requests a time-out; (c) an assistant coach on the field requests a time-out; (d) the head coach is in the press box and an assistant coach on the field requests a time-out; or (e) the head coach has been disqualified and an assistant coach on the field requests a time-out. **RULING:** In (a) and (b), upon visual contact, the time-out is granted. In (c), (d) and (e), the time-out is granted only if the coach is the head coach's designee. NOTE: The designee shall remain in place for the entire game except in case of emergency.

3.5.8 SITUATION A: During a charged time-out, an official's time-out for heat/humidity, a TV/radio time-out, or the intermission between the first and second or the third and fourth periods, or following a try: (a) team members of A confer with their head coach in front of the team box near the sideline; or (b) the coach of B goes to the huddle of B between the 9-yard marks, and talks to an assistant via a headset he brought to the huddle; or (c) the coach of B goes on the field and uses the time to berate and loudly question the referee regarding a previous play; or (d) the coach wishes to discuss the previous play with the referee; or (e) the head coach of A goes to the team huddle on the field for 30 seconds and then comes out and another coach takes his place for the rest of the time-out. **RULING:** It is a legal conference in (a) and (b). In (a), the players may use the headsets. In (b), the players may not use the headsets. In (c) and (e), it is illegal. In (d), this conference must be held at the sideline in front of the team box regardless of which authorized conference procedure is used (2-6-2; 9-8-1c; 9-8-1i).

3.5.11 SITUATION B: Following a fourth-down incomplete forward pass late in the fourth period, a time-out is properly requested for a coach-referee conference regarding possible misapplication of a rule. (a) The coach of B questions a pass interference call on B1 during a second forward pass by A1; or (b) the coach of A questions why no pass interference by the defense was called and why the covering official inappropriately signaled that the pass was not catchable. In either case the referee determines the coach was correct and an incorrect ruling and inappropriate signal had been applied. **RULING:** In (a), the penalty marker is picked up. In (b), a penalty marker may be dropped and the pass interference penalized. Misapplication of a rule or an incorrect signal may result in picking up a flag or dropping a marker to indicate a foul did occur and giving the appropriate signal.

3.6.2 SITUATION A: During the down, there is a foul by A1 and the penalty is enforced. The captain of A requests a time-out for a coach-referee conference regarding misapplication, even though A has no time-outs remaining. The referee confers with the coach and there is no change of decision. **RULING:** A will be penalized for delay of game and the clock will be started with the snap unless Rule 3-4-6 applies.

9.6.4 SITUATION D: A1 is injured and is treated on the field. A subsequently requests a time-out. During the next down, A1 runs 20 yards for the go-ahead score. Following the score, B requests a time-out so the coach may discuss A1's participation with the referee. **RULING:** A rule obviously has not been correctly applied as A1 must leave the game for at least one down following his injury. The touchdown is canceled and a penalty for illegal participation is enforced. A1 must leave the game for at least one down (3-5-10).

Illegal/Unauthorized Conference

Holding an unauthorized conference is a foul. Unauthorized conferences include using more than one type of conference during any one time-out; a player using headphones during a conference in the middle of the field; having more than 11 players in the huddle for a conference in the middle of the field; holding a conference when there is no charged time-out or if an official's time-out is not for unusual heat or humidity which may create a health risk to the players for a TV/radio time-out that is permitted and granted as authorized by state association policy or for a one-minute intermission between the first and second and the third and fourth periods and following a try, successful field goal or safety and prior to the succeeding free kick (3-5-7, 8).

Between downs, communications between players and coaches near the sideline are not an unauthorized conference (9-8-1f NOTE).

Illegal/Unauthorized Conference: Penalty

15 yards. Signal 27.

Illegal/Unauthorized Conference: Case Plays

3.5.8 SITUATION A: During a charged time-out, an official's time-out for heat/humidity, a TV/radio time-out, or the intermission between the first and second or the third and fourth periods, or following a try: (a) team members of A confer with their head coach in front of the team box near the sideline; or (b) the coach of B goes to the huddle of B between the 9-yard marks, and talks to an assistant via a headset he brought to the huddle; or (c) the coach of B goes on the field and uses the time to berate and loudly question the referee regarding a previous play; or (d) the coach wishes to discuss the previous play with the referee; or (e) the head coach of A goes to the team huddle on the field for 30 seconds and then comes out and another coach takes his place for the rest of the time-out. **RULING:** It is a legal conference in (a) and (b). In (a), the players may use the headsets. In (b), the players may not use the headsets. In (c) and (e), it is illegal. In (d), this conference must be held at the sideline in front of the team box regardless of which authorized conference procedure is used (2-6-2; 9-8-1c; 9-8-1i).

9.8.1 SITUATION B: During a charged time-out: (a) A1 goes to the sideline to talk to his head coach. Thereafter, A2, A3 and A4 go to the sideline, but other team members remain between the 9 yard marks; or (b) while A1 is near the sideline talking to one coach, another coach of A goes between the 9-yard marks to the huddle on the field. **RULING:** Legal in (a), but an unauthorized conference in (b). In (b), only one type conference can be used during a given time-out (2-6-2).

9.8.1 SITUATION C: During a charged time-out or a time-out for heat/humidity the coach of A confers with A1 near the sideline and in front of his team box. The conference continues for 30 seconds. A1 then returns to the huddle and A2 comes to the sideline to confer with the coach for the remainder of the charged time-out. **RULING:** This is a legal conference (2-6-2).

Injury Time-Out

An official's time-out (which is not charged to either team) occurs, and the player shall be replaced for at least one down, unless halftime or an overtime intermission occurs when:

• An apparently injured player is discovered by a game official while the ball is dead and the clock is stopped and for whom the ready-for-play signal is delayed, or for whom the clock is stopped (3-5-10a).

• Any player who exhibits signs, symptoms or behaviors consistent with a concussion (such as loss of consciousness, headache, dizziness, confusion or balance problems) shall be immediately removed from the game and shall not return to play until cleared by an appropriate health-care professional (3-5-10b). (See NFHS Suggested Guidelines for Management of Concussion, in Appendix B in the NFHS Football Rules Book.)

• A game official discovers any player who is bleeding, has an open wound, has any amount of blood on his/her uniform, or has blood on his/her person. The player shall be directed to leave the game until the bleeding is stopped, the wound is covered, the uniform and/or body is appropriately cleaned, and/or the uniform is changed before returning to competition (3-5-10c). (See NFHS Communicable Disease Procedures, in Appendix D in the NFHS Football Rules Book.)

• The helmet comes completely off during the down or subsequent dead-ball action related to the down without being directly attributable to a foul by an opponent (3-5-10d).

During a time-out for injury, the coach and/or such attendants as may be deemed necessary by the referee may, with permission, enter to attend the injured player(s) (9-8-2).

When an official's time-out is granted due to an injury, only an Outside 9-Yard Mark Conference (one or more team members and one or more coaches directly in front of the team box within 9 yards of the sideline) may be used (2-6-2a, 3-5-8c).

◪ Rationale

Mandating that a bleeding player be removed until the wound is covered reduces the risk of spreading blood-borne pathogens.

Injury Time-Out: Case Plays

3.5.8 SITUATION B: A game official stops the clock for an injury to player A1. While the injured played is being attended to, the coach of Team B attempts to hold a conference (a) between the 9-yard marks; or (b) in front of the team box outside the 9-yard marks. **RULING:** In (a) the conference must move outside the 9-yard marks; in (b), legal conference.

3.5.8 COMMENT: If the injured player is being attended in the area outside the 9-yard marks, the game officials should relocate the conference outside the 9-yard marks to an area that allowed for uninhibited access to the injured player by all appropriate health-care professionals.

3.5.10 SITUATION A: A game official stops the clock when he notices quarterback A1 has a bloody nose. A1 is directed to go to his team box. The coach of A then requests a time-out and A1's bleeding is stopped during the time-out. A1 re-enters with other teammates following the time-out. **RULING:** A1 must remain in the team box for at least one down. A time-out called after a game official has stopped the clock for an injured player does not allow the injured player to remain in the game. Any conference during the official's time-out must be held outside the 9-yard marks. If the coach's request for a charged time-out is granted, either type of conference may be used, but A1 may not re-enter the game until one play has elapsed and cannot participate in an on-field conference (3-5-8a(3); 3-5-8c; 3-5-10).

3.5.10 SITUATION B: A1 has an open wound or scratch on his arm. In (a) Team A takes a charged team time-out before the wound is noticed by a game official; or (b) the covering official calls an official's time-out for the player's injury to be evaluated. **RULING:** In (a), if A1's wound is properly treated before the time-out ends, he may return to the game immediately; in (b), because the covering official's time-out was taken, A1 must leave the game for at least one down and may not return until the wound is properly treated. In (b), any conference must be held outside the 9-yard marks (3-5-8a(3), 3-5-8c).

3.5.10 SITUATION C: Midway through the second period, the clock is stopped for: (a) an incomplete forward pass; or (b) a measurement; or (c) an out-of-bounds play, when a game official notices that A1 appears to be injured. **RULING:** A1 must be replaced for at least one down in (a), (b) and (c). As it is an official's time-out. If A1 is injured during the last down of either half, he may return for the first play or down of the second half or overtime period.

3.5.10 SITUATION D: What guidelines should the game officials follow in determining if a player may have a concussion? **RULING:** Game officials should observe players. If any player who exhibits signs, symptoms or behaviors consistent with a concussion (such as loss of consciousness, headache, dizziness, confusion or balance problems), the game officials shall ensure that the player is immediately removed from the game. All game officials should review the NFHS Suggested Guidelines for Management of Concussion in Sports in the back of the NFHS Football Rules Book.

9.6.4 SITUATION D: A1 is injured and is treated on the field. A subsequently requests a time-out. During the next down, A1 runs 20 yards for the go-ahead score. Following the score, B requests a time-out so the coach may discuss A1's participation with the referee. **RULING:** A rule obviously has not been correctly applied as A1 must leave the game for at least one down following his injury. The touchdown is canceled and a penalty for illegal participation is enforced. A1 must leave the game for at least one down (3-5-10).

Helmet Coming Off: Case Plays

3.5.10 SITUATION E: During a down, the helmet of A1 or B1 comes off: (a) after an opponent grasps the face mask, chin strap or tooth and mouth protector; (b) after a legal block to the opponent; (c) after a legal block by an opponent; or (d) after either falls to the ground without contact; (e) after either falls to the ground immediately following the ball becoming dead. **RULING:** In (a), the player does not have to be replaced for one down. In (b), (c), (d) and (e), the player must be replaced for one down unless halftime or an overtime intermission occurs. When in doubt, and particularly when no foul is called, the player must be replaced for one down unless halftime or an overtime intermission occurs. An officials or charged team time-out does not exempt the player from being replaced for one down.

3.5.10 SITUATION F: While tackling runner A1, B1's helmet comes off as a result of the legal tackle. **RULING:** B1 must be replaced for one down unless halftime or an overtime intermission occurs.

3.5.10 SITUATION G: Runner A1 is tackled legally by B1 and B2. A1's helmet comes off during the tackle. **RULING:** A1 must be replaced for one down unless halftime or an overtime intermission occurs. The ball becomes dead when A1's helmet comes off (4-2-2k).

Length of Time-outs

A single charged time-out shall not exceed one minute. The referee shall notify the teams within five seconds after the time-out expires and shall declare the ball ready for play. Charged time-outs shall be reduced in length only if both teams are ready to play prior to the 25-second ready-for-play signal by the referee (3-5-3).

Official's Time-Out

Unless the clock is already stopped, an official's time-out shall be taken as soon as the ball becomes dead following a change of team possession or whenever the covering official declares the ball dead, and it appears to him the ball has reached the line to gain (3-5-9).

An official's time-out (which is not charged to either team) occurs during a dead ball without a time-out being charged to either team for measurement of a possible first down; when a first down is declared; following a change of team possession; when captains and coaches are notified of the time remaining; for a player in need of equipment repair; to dry or change the game ball; for unusual heat or humidity which may create a health risk to the players; when a coach-referee conference concerning the misapplication of a rule results in the referee altering his ruling (see 3-5-11); after a foul, to administer the penalty; for any unusual delay in getting the ball ready for play; for a TV/radio time-out that is permitted and granted as authorized by state association policy; and for a one-minute intermission between the first and second and the third and fourth periods and following a try, successful field goal or safety and prior to the succeeding free kick (3-5-7a-l).

An official's time-out may follow a charged time-out if safety is involved (3-5-4).

Three attendants, none of whom is a coach, may enter the field to attend their team during an official's time-out for unusual heat and humidity (9-8-2).

Request Denied

A time-out request from a player, head coach or head coach's designee shall not be granted when a decision on a penalty is pending until the captain makes his choice (3-5-2a), or when a team's permissible charged time-outs for the half have been used. In the latter case, that team's captain and coach should be notified (3-5-4).

After a team has used its permissible charged time-outs for the half, any subsequent request shall be denied unless it is for an apparently injured player who is so designated when the request is made, necessary repair to player equipment, or the review of a possible misapplication or misinterpretation of a rule (3-5-5a-c).

If repair of equipment without the assistance of a team attendant delays the ready-for-play signal for more than 25 seconds, or requires the assistance of a team attendant(s) and the player's team has used all permissible time-outs, the player shall be replaced for at least one down (3-5-6).

Request Denied: Case Play

3.5.2 SITUATION B: Team A wishes to call a time-out: (a) a player requests a time-out; (b) the head coach on the field requests a time-out; (c) an assistant coach on the field requests a time-out; (d) the head coach is in the press box and an assistant coach on the field requests a time-out; or (e) the head coach has been disqualified and an assistant coach on the field requests a time-out. **RULING:** In (a) and (b), upon visual contact, the time-out is granted. In (c), (d) and (e), the time-out is granted only if the coach is the head coach's designee. NOTE: The designee shall remain in place for the entire game except in case of emergency.

In Simple Terms

There is no penalty for requesting a time-out when a team has none remaining. The request is simply denied.

Topic:
Interrupted Games

Games interrupted because of events beyond the control of the responsible administrative authority shall be continued from the point of interruption, unless the teams agree to terminate the game with the existing score, or as otherwise provided for by state association adoption (3-1-4).

When weather conditions are construed to be hazardous to life or limb of the participants, the crew of game officials is authorized to delay or suspend the game (3-1-5).

Interrupted Games: Case Plays

*3.1.5 SITUATION A: During the second period, a cloudburst brings a torrent of rain onto a grass field. The game officials suspend play and after a 20-minute delay determine the field is no longer playable. **RULING:** While the game officials are authorized to delay or suspend a game when weather conditions are construed to be hazardous to life or limb, such as lightning, tornado alert, etc., a heavy shower which only affects the playing conditions, may or may not be judged by the game officials to be hazardous to life or limb. While the game officials are the final authority on suspending play, it is a good practice for the game officials to discuss the alternatives with game management and representatives of both teams before suspending the game.

3.1.5 SITUATION B: During the second period, a cloudburst brings a torrent of rain onto a grass field. The game officials suspend play and after a 20-minute delay determine the field is no longer playable. **RULING:** While the game officials are authorized to delay or suspend a game when weather conditions are construed to be hazardous to life or limb, such as lightning, tornado alert, etc., a heavy shower which only affects the playing conditions, should not be construed as hazardous to life or limb. While the game officials are the final authority on suspending play, it is a good practice for the game officials to discuss the alternatives with game management and representatives of both teams before suspending the game.

Topic:
Timing Errors

The referee shall have authority to correct obvious errors in timing if discovery is prior to the second live ball following the error, unless the period has officially ended per rule 3-3-5 (3-4-7).

▰ Rationale

The correction procedure applies to obvious errors. The coverage does not authorize attempting to correct trivial or incidental lag in starting or stopping the clock. The error must result in an acknowledged discrepancy in the time and does include a slight lag due to human reaction. Correctable errors will have resulted for a failure to apply the provision of the timing rule on the part of the game official or failure of the clock operator to follow the directions of the field official, or from a mechanic failure of the clock. The error to be corrected must not involve judgment. In a situation in which the clock was not stopped after the score or during the administration of a penalty, the referee is permitted to put time back on the clock. If there had been a failure to start the clock with the snap following an incompleted forward pass, or with the legal touching of the free kick following a touchdown, the referee would be permitted to compensate by taking time off the clock.

Timing Errors: Case Play

3.4.7: During the second down of a series, the field clock goes directly from 1:45 to :45 and is not detected. Following third down, time expires for either the first or second period: (a) before, or (b) after the referee has indicated the period has officially ended, the error is discovered.

RULING: In (a), the timing error is correctable because it was discovered prior to the second live ball and before the period officially had ended. However, in (b), the timing error cannot be corrected whether it is the first or second period (3-3-5).

Topic:
Intermissions

A one-minute intermission, charged as an official's time-out, occurs between the first and second and between the third and fourth periods (3-5-7m). During that intermission, the teams shall change goals. Team possession, number of the next down, the relative position of the ball and the line to gain remain unchanged (3-2-4).

An intermission ("halftime") follows the second period. When teams leave the field, the intermission is 10 to 20 minutes (15 minutes is normal). It may be increased to a maximum of 20 minutes, provided opponents have been notified no later than five minutes prior to the game. By mutual agreement of the opposing coaches, the intermission may be reduced to a minimum of 10 minutes (not including the mandatory warm-up period) (3-1 Table).

A mandatory 3-minute warm-up activity follows intermission. The game officials are responsible for ensuring that there is a 3-minute warm-up period posted on the clock and the clock immediately started for use by the coaches immediately after the halftime intermission expires. The head coach is responsible for his team being on the field for mandatory warm-up time at the end of the scheduled halftime intermission (3-1 Table).

State high school associations may determine the length of halftimes, provided it is not less than 10 minutes and not more than 20 minutes (1-7).

Intermissions: Case Plays
3.1.1 SITUATION A: The home management notifies the game officials and the visiting-team coach 30 minutes prior to the scheduled kickoff that the halftime intermission will be extended for homecoming activities. **RULING:** The maximum length of the halftime intermission is 20 minutes. Any greater extension is not permitted either by mutual agreement or prior notification.

3.1.1 COMMENT: By agreement of the opposing coaches, the halftime intermission may be reduced to a minimum of 10 minutes.

3.1.1 SITUATION B: Prior to the game, the participating schools have agreed to a 20-minute halftime: (a) After 20 minutes have been placed on the clock, planned band performances are canceled because of cold weather. Both teams arrive on the field with six minutes remaining on the clock. Both coaches tell the game officials they have agreed to shorten the halftime and want the game to start as soon as they have both had three minutes to warm up; or (b) As the teams leave the field, the timer places 20 minutes on the clock and upon reaching 0:00, places three additional minutes on the clock. **RULING:** In (a), mutual agreement of coaches to shorten the halftime is permitted. They may not, however, shorten it to less than 10 minutes. Regardless of what it is shortened to, the three-minute warm-up time always must be added to whatever is agreed to for the halftime intermission. In (b), the time has been posted properly.

*3.1.1 SITUATION C: Upon returning to the field near the end of the normal 15-minute halftime intermission, the game officials notice one team standing quietly in front of its bench during the entire three minutes posted for warm-up. The game officials: (a) start the game as soon as the three minutes have elapsed, or (b) inform the coach of that team that the team must actively warm up by running or doing some kind of exercises. **RULING:** The game officials are correct in (a), but in error in (b). The rules book contains no definition of what constitutes a warm-up. It simply requires that an opportunity to warm up be made available.

3.1.1 SITUATION D: Both teams are informed of a 15-minute halftime intermission. The game officials remind the teams that the halftime intermission period is nearing an end, and that the three-minute warm-up period will begin immediately. Team A returns to the field prior to the end of the intermission, however Team B is not on the field when the intermission ends and the timer immediately and appropriately starts the three-minute warm-up period. Team B does not arrive on the field until the three-minute warm-up period has expired. **RULING:** The head coach of Team B is charged with unsportsmanlike conduct and B is penalized 15-yards to start the second half. Though Team B has violated the rule by not being on the field at the end of the intermission, and by not being on the field at the end of the three-minute warm-up period, only one unsportsmanlike conduct foul is penalized.

Topic:
Inadvertent Whistle

The ball becomes dead and the down is ended when a game official sounds his whistle inadvertently (4-2-2j, 4-2-3a).

The down shall be replayed, if during a down, or during a down in which the penalty for a foul is declined, an inadvertent whistle is sounded while a legal forward pass or snap is in flight, or during a legal kick (4-2-3a).

The team last in possession may choose to either put the ball in play where possession was lost or replay the down, if during a down, or during a down in which the penalty for a foul is declined, an inadvertent whistle is sounded while the ball is loose following a backward pass, fumble, illegal forward pass or illegal kick (4-2-3b).

The team in possession may choose to either accept the results of the play at the dead-ball spot or replay the down, if during a down, or during a down in which the penalty for a foul is declined, an inadvertent whistle is sounded while the ball is in player possession (4-2-3c).

The penalty shall be administered as determined by the basic spot, and takes precedence over inadvertent whistle administration, if during a down, a live-ball foul occurs prior to the inadvertent whistle and the penalty is accepted (4-2-3d).

Whenever an inadvertent whistle sounds while the ball is loose following a fumble, the ball is returned to the spot of the fumble or spot of last possession. Theoretically, this is where the ball becomes dead. Regardless of where the ball is fumbled, the team last in possession may choose to have the ball put in play where possession was lost and count the down or choose to replay the down (4.2.3 SITUATION C COMMENT).

The basic spot is the previous spot for a foul which occurs during a down in which a legal kick occurs and an inadvertent whistle ends the down prior to possession by either team (10-4-2c).

The game clock shall be stopped when an inadvertent whistle is sounded (3-4-4i). The clock shall start with the ready-for-play signal on a down beginning with a snap if the clock was stopped because of an inadvertent whistle (3-4-2c).

Inadvertent Whistle: Case Plays
3.3.3 SITUATION C: During a down when time expires, A1 gains 10 yards and fumbles. The covering official inadvertently sounds his

whistle while the ball is loose. **RULING:** The period shall be extended for an untimed down and A may put the ball in play where it lost possession or it may choose to replay the down from the previous spot (3-3-3c).

3.4.2 SITUATION C: Near the end of a period with 28 seconds left, K1 punts on fourth down. During the kick the covering official inadvertently sounds his whistle. The clock is stopped with 23 seconds remaining. **RULING:** The clock will be started with the ready-for-play signal. The down must be replayed.

4.2.3 SITUATION A: With fourth and 2 from K's 38-yard line, a scrimmage kick by K1 is muffed beyond the neutral zone by R1 following his signal for a fair catch. While the ball is loose following the muff, the covering official sounds his whistle inadvertently. **RULING:** Because the whistle was inadvertently sounded during a kick, the down will be replayed even though R1 was first to touch the scrimmage kick beyond the neutral zone. The clock will start on the ready-for-play signal (3-4-2c).

4.2.3 SITUATION B: While a legal forward pass is in flight: (a) B1 interferes with eligible A1 and then there is an inadvertent whistle; or (b) a whistle is inadvertently sounded after which B2 contacts A2 while the ball is still in flight. **Ruling:** In (a), if the captain accepts the penalty for a foul which occurred prior to the inadvertent whistle, the penalty takes precedence. It will be a new series for A, 15 yards in advance of the previous spot. In (b), the contact by B2 occurred during a dead-ball period and unless it is a personal foul, will be ignored. Because the whistle was inadvertently sounded while a legal forward pass was in flight, the down shall be replayed (7-5-10a).

4.2.3 SITUATION C: With fourth and goal on B's 4-yard line, A1 is hit and fumbles, and as the ball rolls into the end zone, an inadvertent whistle is sounded. The fumble occurs: (a) at the 5-yard line, or (b) at the 3-yard line. **RULING:** In (a) and (b), A will have a choice of taking the play at the spot of the fumble or replaying the down. If A takes the play, it is B's ball at the 5 in (a), and at the 3 in (b) (4-2-3b).

4.2.3 SITUATION D: A1 throws a forward pass from his own 40-yard line. B1 intercepts on his 2-yard line and circles back into his end zone. While B1 is in the end zone, the covering official inadvertently sounds his whistle. **RULING:** Since B1 is in possession, B has the option of accepting the results of the play at the time of the whistle or asking for a replay of the down. Since the result of the play would be a safety, B would normally chose to replay the down (4-2-3c; 8-5-2a).

4.2.3 SITUATION E: K's ball, fourth and 12, on R's 45-yard line. K8's punt is rolling on R's 16 when an inadvertent whistle sounds. R76 blocks K84 in the back on R's 22-yard line during the down prior to the whistle. **RULING:** By rule, an inadvertent whistle during the kick (loose-ball play) and declination of all fouls, stipulates a replay of the down. However, if the penalty for R's illegal block is accepted, the penalty is enforced from the previous spot and K will replay fourth down, fourth and 2 from R's 35-yard line (2-16-2h; 4-2-2j; 4-2-3a; 4-2-3d; 6-2-7; 10-4-3).

4.2.3 SITUATION F: A1 is in scrimmage kick formation with his back heel near the end line in the end zone. On a high snap, the potential kicker jumps and is able to keep the ball from going out of the end zone. It falls to the ground and is rolling around 5 yards into the end zone. In a panic, A1 then kicks the ball off the ground and it rolls to the A25 and is bounding around when there is an inadvertent whistle. The ball rolls dead at the A27. **RULING:** B has a choice of accepting the penalty for an illegal kick, which if accepted, results in a safety against A. If the penalty is declined, the inadvertent whistle rule allows for A to ask for a replay of the down since the ball was not in player possession at the time of the whistle.

4.2.3 SITUATION G: A's ball, third and 8 on A's 30-yard line. A1's pass is intercepted by B2. Prior to the interception, B1 is flagged for defensive pass interference. After the ball is intercepted by B2, the covering official blows an inadvertent whistle with B2 in possession at the B40. **RULING:** If A accepts B's penalty for pass interference, it is A's ball, first and 10 at A's 45-yard line as the inadvertent whistle aspect is ignored. If A declines B's penalty for pass interference, B will accept the ball at B's 40-yard line (4-2-3c).

6.5.4 SITUATION: R1 signals for a fair catch beyond the neutral zone on K's 40. K2 interferes with R1's opportunity to make the catch. R chooses an awarded catch and to put the ball in play with a snap. During the next down an inadvertent whistle sounds during A1's forward pass. **RULING:** The down is replayed and A has the option to snap or free kick (10-4-5a).

NFHS-Recommended Resolving Tied Games Procedure

Each state association, in accordance with Rules 1-7 (7) and 3-1-1, may adopt a procedure by which it allows games tied after the fourth quarter to be resolved. The following is one possible procedure which would allow for ties to be broken. This procedure may be accepted as written, amended, or rejected, in whole or part, by each member state association.

An overtime period is untimed play after a regulation game has ended with the score tied. During an overtime period each team has an opportunity for an offensive series of downs. However, an overtime period may include only one offensive series of downs if the defensive team scores a safety or touchdown (Resolving Tied Games Procedure).

When the score is tied at the end of the fourth period, the referee will instruct both teams to return to their respective team boxes. There will be a three-minute intermission during which both teams may confer with their coaches. All game officials will assemble at the 50-yard line, review the Resolving Tied Games procedure, determine the number of the second half time-outs remaining for each team, and discuss how penalties, if any, including any carry-over penalties from the regulation contest will be assessed to start the Resolving Tied Games procedure. At the end of the intermission, the head linesman will go to the team on the side of the field where the line to gain equipment is located and the line judge will go to the other team. They will inform the coaches of the number of time-outs each team has remaining and any special penalty enforcements that apply (Resolving Tied Games Procedure 3-1).

At the coin toss in the center of the field the visiting-team's captain shall be given the privilege of choosing "heads" or "tails" before the coin is tossed. The winner of the toss shall be given his choice of defense or offense first, or of designating the end of the field at which the ball will be put in play for this set of downs. The loser will have his choice of the other options. The referee will indicate the winner of the toss by placing a hand on his shoulder. To indicate which team will go on offense, the referee will have that captain face the goal toward which his team will advance and indicate this with the first-down signal. The other team captain will face the offensive captain with his back toward the goal he will defend (Resolving Tied Games Procedure 3-2-1).

Each team shall be permitted one time-out during each Resolving Tied Games period (a series for A and a series for B). The team scoring the greater number of points in the Resolving Tied Games Procedure shall be declared the winner. The final score shall be determined by totaling all points scored by each team during both regulation time and overtime periods (Resolving Tied Games Procedure 3-5-1).

To start the Resolving Tied Games Procedure, the offensive team shall put the ball in play, first and goal, on the defensive team's 10-yard line or succeeding spot if carry-over penalty has been administered (15-yard line for six-player football) anywhere between the hash marks (4-3-6g). The first offensive team shall have a series of four downs. That series shall be terminated by any score by the offensive team or if the defensive team has possession of the ball. If the team on offense scores a touchdown, it is entitled to the opportunity for a try unless the points would not affect the outcome of the game or playoff qualifying. A field-goal attempt is permitted during any down. If the defensive team gains possession, the ball becomes dead immediately and the offensive team's series of downs is ended. After the first team on offense has completed its series of downs, the first team on defense will become the offensive team with the ball in its possession at the same 10-yard line anywhere between the hash marks. The same end of the field will be used for possessions by both teams during the two sets of downs to ensure equal game conditions and conserve time. If the score remains tied after each team has been given one series of downs in a Resolving Tied Games period, then the procedure shall be repeated with other Resolving Tied Games Procedure periods until a game winner is determined. In this case, there shall be an intermission of two minutes. At the subsequent meeting of team captains, the loser of the Resolving Tied Games Procedure coin toss will be given first choice of the options. If additional Resolving Tied Games Procedure periods are required, then first options will be alternated with no coin toss (Resolving Tied Games Procedure 5-1-1).

If a safety is scored by the offensive team, the succeeding spot will be the 10-yard line in possession of the team that was on defense, provided the defensive team has not had its series of downs (the temporary Resolving Tied Games Procedure score is: Team A-2; Team B-0). When the defensive team gains possession of the ball, the down and series immediately end for the offensive team (Resolving Tied Games Procedure 5-1-2).

The offensive team shall be awarded a new series of downs when the offensive team recovers a scrimmage kick (field-goal attempt) between the goal lines after it has been touched first by the defensive team beyond the neutral zone, or the defensive team is guilty of roughing the kicker, place-kick holder, snapper or passer (Resolving Tied Games Procedure 5-2-1a through b).

The line to gain is always the goal line regardless of whether or not a penalty enforcement places the ball more than 10 yards from the goal line to start the new series (Resolving Tied Games Procedure 5-3-1).

If the defensive team scores a safety or touchdown, the game is ended (Resolving Tied Games Procedure 8-1).

No try will be attempted if the winner of the game has been determined (Resolving Tied Games Procedure 8-3).

For those state associations utilizing the procedure as written, post scrimmage kick enforcement is not applicable in this procedure (Resolving Tied Games Procedure 10-4-3).

Resolving Tied Games Procedure: Interpretations

(Editor's note: Interpretations 3.1.1 Situation A through 3.1.1 Situation J in this section are taken from the Resolving Tied Games portion of the NFHS Football Rules Book. The reference numbers are not to be confused with those from the NFHS Football Case Book.)

3.1.1 SITUATION A: On fourth down in Resolving Tied Games Procedure play, A scores a touchdown. After the score, but before the try, B1 commits an unsportsmanlike foul. **RULING:** The penalty is enforced from the succeeding spot on the try. Nonplayer fouls, nonplayer unsportsmanlike fouls and dead-ball fouls are penalized on the succeeding spot.

3.1.1 SITUATION B: During the down in which time expires for the fourth period, A1 advances for a touchdown making the score B-22 and A-20. On the try A2 passes complete to A3 in the end zone. Following the try B1 commits an unsportsmanlike foul. **RULING:** The penalty for the foul by B1 after the successful try will be administered from the succeeding spot to begin Resolving Tied Games Procedure play.

 3.1.1 COMMENT: In this situation the referee should explain to the captains at the time of the coin toss the fact the penalty will be administered on the first series of downs in the Resolving Tied Games Procedure. The place from which the ball will be put in play for each team could have an effect on the choice made by the winner of the toss.

*3.1.1 SITUATION C: Upon returning to the field near the end of the normal 15-minute halftime intermission, the game officials notice one team standing quietly in front of its bench during the entire three minutes posted for warm-up. The game officials: (a) start the game as soon as the three minutes have elapsed, or (b) inform the coach of that team that the team must actively warm up by running or doing some kind of exercises. **RULING:** The game officials are correct in (a), but in error in (b). The rules book contains no definition of what constitutes a warm-up. It simply requires that an opportunity to warm up be made available.

3.1.1 SITUATION D: On third and 4 in Resolving Tied Games Procedure play, B recovers a fumble or intercepts a pass. **RULING:** The down ends as soon as B1 recovers or intercepts. In both cases the series of downs is ended for A.

3.1.1 SITUATION E: On third and 6 in Resolving Tied Games Procedure play Team A attempts a field goal. The attempt is not successful and B recovers on the 1-yard line. **RULING:** The down ends when B1 recovers. The series is ended for A.

3.1.1 SITUATION F: The fourth quarter ends during a scoring play. During the successful 2-point try, B9 is called for pass interference. A accepts the result of the play, which ties the score and chooses to have the penalty assessed at the succeeding spot. **RULING:** This is correct. Since A, by rule, can choose succeeding spot enforcement, and the try was successful, A will likely take enforcement at the succeeding spot to begin the Resolving Tied Games Procedure. Game officials must be certain to explain the options clearly, not only during penalty administration, but also during the Resolving Tied Games Procedure coin toss.

3.1.1 SITUATION G: In Resolving Tied Games Procedure play with third and goal from B's 4-yard line, B1 interferes during a forward pass. **RULING:** If the penalty is accepted it will be third and goal for A on B's 2-yard line.

3.1.1 SITUATION H: In Resolving Tied Games Procedure play on second down from the 8-yard line, B1 commits pass interference. **RULING:** Second down for A on the 4-yard line if the penalty is accepted.

3.1.1 SITUATION I: In overtime play, (a) on second; or (b) fourth down from the 9-yard line, A1 interferes on an incomplete forward pass. **RULING:** In (a) it is A's ball second down from its 24-yard line. In (b) B will decline the penalty and take the ball on the 10-yard line.

3.1.1 SITUATION J: At the end of the regulation game the score is tied, 7-7. It was previously announced that the recommended tie-breaking procedure would be followed. Immediately after the last down of the fourth period A1 strikes B1. **RULING:** A1 will be disqualified and may not participate during the Resolving Tied Games Procedure period. The penalty for A1 's foul will be administered from the succeeding spot. If B is the first to put the ball in play it will be from the 5-yard line. If A is the first to put the ball in play it will be from the 25-yard line.

3.1.1 SITUATION K: At the beginning of the Resolving Tied Games Procedure, A wins the toss and elects to go on offense. On first down, B1 intercepts a pass, but then fumbles and A1 recovers. **RULING:** The ball became dead and A's series ended immediately when B1 intercepted. A1 recovered a dead ball. B will put the ball in play to start its series of four downs, first and goal from anywhere between the inbound lines on the 10-yard line.

3.1.1 SITUATION L: During the down in which time expires for the fourth period, A scores a touchdown to make the score 14-13. During the successful kick try, B1 roughs the kicker/holder. **RULING:** If A accepts the score, the penalty is enforced to start the Resolving Tied Games Procedure, if it is played. If A accepts the penalty, the try will be replayed from the 1 1⁄2-yard line (2-41-10; 8-3-5).

3.1.1 SITUATION M: During a Resolving Tied Games Procedure period, it is fourth and goal from the 6-yard line. During A's unsuccessful field-goal attempt, B1 charges into the place-kick holder. **RULING:** It will be first and goal for A at the 3-yard line following enforcement of the roughing penalty which also includes an automatic first down.

3.1.1 SITUATION N: Following a scoreless first Resolving Tied Games Procedure period, the captain of B chooses to play the second Resolving Tied Games Procedure period at the opposite end of the field. **RULING:** This is permissible, as it is one of the options to begin each Resolving Tied Games Procedure period.

3.1.1 SITUATION O: During the first Resolving Tied Games Procedure period, A chooses to go on offense first and scores a touchdown on the third play of the series. During the successful kick try, the holder is roughed by B1. A accepts the successful kick try. **RULING:** Since A accepted the result of the play, B will be penalized from the succeeding spot. B will start its Resolving Tied Games Procedure series from the 25-yard line after the penalty for roughing the holder is enforced (10-5-2).

3.1.1 SITUATION P: In Resolving Tied Games Procedure play with fourth and goal from B's 24-yard line, B1 interferes during a legal forward pass. **RULING:** Fourth down and goal for A on the 12-yard line if the penalty is accepted.

3.1.1 SITUATION Q: During the first overtime period, Team A: (a) scores on its first series; or (b) is stopped short of the goal line on its first series. Following the first series, Team A huddles near its sideline with all players from the previous play remaining inbounds. Team B reports to the 10-yard line of scrimmage ready to begin its series. Team A remains at the sideline when the ready for play is blown by the referee. **RULING:** In (a), because there was a score, there is a one-minute intermission after the try. In (b), the series begins immediately following the change of A and B to respective sides of the line of scrimmage without a break. The covering official should not allow the ball to be put in play, and should assess a delay of game foul on Team A to prevent a travesty (3-5-7l, 3-6-2f).

3.5.1 SITUATION A: Team A and Team B are tied at the conclusion of the fourth period. Team A has utilized one time-out in the second half and Team B has used three. State association Resolving Tied Games Procedure guidelines grant one time-out to each team in each Resolving Tied Games Procedure period. The coach of Team A asks the referee if his team will now have three time outs in Resolving Tied Games Procedure (the two unused plus the one for the first Resolving Tied Games Procedure). **RULING:** The referee must rule that the team has only one time-out per period, and that the unused second half time-outs did not carry over to Resolving Tied Games Procedure. Both teams will have one time-out per Resolving Tied Games Procedure period as per State Association guidelines.

Topic 8

Game Officials and Their Duties

PlayPic®

Topic:
Game Officials and Their Duties

The game is administered by game officials whose title and duties are stated in the NFHS Game Officials' Manual (1-1-4). Each state association has the authority to make decisions and provide coverage regarding the number of game officials to be used in the game (1-1-4 NOTE, 1-1-7).

Protests of NFHS rules are not recognized (1-1-11).

The game officials are responsible for ensuring that there is a three-minute warm-up period posted on the clock and the clock immediately started for use by the coaches immediately after the halftime intermission expires. The head coach is responsible for his team being on the field for mandatory warm-up time at the end of the scheduled halftime intermission (3-1 Table).

Authority and Duties of the Referee

Prior to the game, the referee shall meet with the head coach(es) and captain(s) and explain that everyone is expected to exhibit good sportsmanship throughout the game (1-1-5).

The referee has authority to rule promptly, and in the spirit of good sportsmanship, on any situation not specifically covered in the rules. The referee's decisions are final in all matters pertaining to the game (1-1-6).

The referee shall decide whether the ball meets specifications. If the field is wet, the referee may order the ball changed between downs (1-3-3).

Players of the home team shall wear dark jerseys and players of the visiting team shall wear white jerseys. The visiting team is responsible for avoidance of similarity of colors, but if there is doubt, the referee may require players of the home team to change jerseys (1-5-1b(6)e, 1-5-1b(7)e, 1-5-1b(2)e, 1-5-1b(3)e).

Prior to the start of the game, the head coach shall be responsible for verifying to the referee and umpire that all of his players are legally equipped and in compliance with the rules (1-5-4).

The referee's decision to forfeit a game is final (1-1-10).

A period or periods may be shortened in any emergency by agreement of the opposing coaches and the referee. By mutual agreement of the opposing coaches and the referee, any remaining period may be shortened at any time or the game terminated (3-1-3).

Before the scheduled game starting time, the referee, in the presence of the field captains, shall instruct the visiting captain to give a "heads" or "tails" choice before the coin toss (3-2-1).

Unless an electric field clock is the official timepiece, approximately four minutes before the end of each half, the referee shall notify the field captains and their coaches of the time remaining. If time is not out, the referee shall order the clock stopped while he does this (3-3-1).

When a team attempts to conserve or consume time illegally, the referee shall order the clock to be started or stopped (3-4-6).

The referee shall notify the teams within five seconds after the time-out expires and shall mark the ball ready for play (3-5-3).

The referee shall correct the number of the next down prior to the ball becoming live after a new series of downs is awarded and prior to the declaration of the end of any period (5-1-1b).

The referee shall have authority to correct obvious errors in timing if discovery is prior to the second live ball following the error, unless the period has officially ended per rule 3-3-5 (3-4-7). The referee may call for the head linesman to bring the official line-to-gain equipment on the field for a measurement (5-3-2). A measurement may be requested by the captain prior to the ball being marked ready for play, but it may be denied if, in the referee's opinion, it is obvious the line to gain has or has not been reached (5-3-2 NOTE).

In an emergency, such as a pool of water on K's free-kick line, the referee has authority to move the ball to a playable line (6-1-2).

A player or nonplayer or person(s) not subject to the rules shall not hinder play by an unfair act which has no specific rule coverage (9-10-1). Neither team shall commit any act which, in the opinion of the referee, tends to make a travesty of the game (9-10-5). For violations, the referee has authority to enforce any penalty he considers equitable, including the award of a score.

When the score is tied at the end of the fourth period and the NFHS-Recommended Resolving Tied Games Procedure is to be used, the referee will instruct both teams to return to their respective team boxes. There will be a three-minute intermission during which both teams may confer with their coaches. All game officials will assemble at the 50-yard line, review the NFHS-Recommended Resolving Tied Games Procedure and discuss how penalties, if any, including any carry-over penalties from the regulation contest will be assessed to start the Resolving Tied Games Procedure (Resolving Tied Games Procedure 3-1).

Authority and Duties of the Referee: Case Plays

1.1.6 SITUATION: Prior to the game, both teams wait for the other team to go on the field first. **RULING:** The referee shall direct the home-team coach to have his team enter first. The referee has authority to rule on any situation not specifically covered in the rules.

> # Did You Know ?
>
> In 1974, the rules specified the referee was responsible for tracking the official score.

1.3.2 SITUATION C: Prior to the start of the game, A has provided two balls for the referee's examination, but B has not provided a ball. **RULING:** There is no penalty if a team does not provide a ball; however, in this case, B will have to use the ball(s) provided by A until such time B offers a legal ball for the referee's approval.

1.3.2 SITUATION D: The referee has examined and verified the legality of a number of balls provided by each team prior to the game. However, during the course of the game, the weather conditions change dramatically and the teams wish to have additional balls approved for use. **RULING:** This is permissible and is within the intent of the rule.

1.5.3 SITUATION A: During the pregame visits with both teams, the referee notices that Team B's jerseys have a series of symbols representing a company or the jersey has both a logo and a company reference, but it is not the company's logo/reference or trademark. The referee indicates that the jersey is illegal and that the symbols must be removed. **RULING:** The referee is correct. Jersey and pants may not have anything representing the manufacturer except for one logo/reference or trademark, and that mark must meet the size restrictions (1-5-3a(1)).

3.1.5 SITUATION B: During the second period, a cloudburst brings a torrent of rain onto a grass field. The game officials suspend play and after a 20-minute delay determine the field is no longer playable. **RULING:** While the game officials are authorized to delay or suspend a game when weather conditions are construed to be hazardous to life or limb, such as lightning, tornado alert, etc., a heavy shower which only affects the playing conditions, should not be construed as hazardous to life or limb. While the game officials are the final authority on suspending play, it is a good practice for the game officials to discuss the alternatives with game management and representatives of both teams before suspending the game.

*3.3.3 SITUATION D: With the ball at B's 1-yard line and 12 seconds remaining in the game, A1 advances to the ½-yard line. After the ball is dead, B1 fouls. The clock is stopped with five seconds remaining in the game. The clock is restarted when the ball is marked ready for play. Before A can snap the ball, time expires. **RULING:** The game is ended. There is no extension of the period for an untimed down, unless there is acceptance of the penalty for a foul that occurs during a down in which time expires. B1's foul did not occur during the down. However, if the referee judges B1 committed the foul to consume time, he shall delay starting the clock until the snap.

 3.3.3 COMMENT: When either team attempts to conserve or consume time illegally, the referee shall invoke Rule 3-4-6 and start or delay the start of the clock as authorized (3-4-6; 3-6-2f; 9-10-2).

*9.10.1 SITUATION A: A is trailing by five points near the end of the fourth quarter and has no time outs left when the play ends on B's 3. The referee does not feel there is any illegal delay in unpiling and that time will definitely expire before the ball is ready and A gets in position to snap. Quarterback A1 reaches into the pile of players and grabs the ball. He then throws the ball to midfield. **RULING:** Even if the referee imposes a 15-yard penalty for an unsportsmanlike act, A has accomplished its goal — the clock is stopped and it can get in position and be ready to run a play even though the clock will start on the ready-for-play signal. This situation illustrates when it is appropriate for the referee to invoke the unfair-act rule and handle the situation in any way that the referee feels is equitable. In this specific situation the referee should wind the clock and end the game without giving A an opportunity to put the ball in play.

 9.10.1 COMMENT: The rule also gives the referee authority to take appropriate action whenever someone not subject to the rules hinders play (3-4-6).

9.10.1 SITUATION B: From a field goal formation, potential kicker A1 yells, "Where's the tee?" A2 replies, "I'll go get it" and goes legally in motion toward his team's sideline. Ball is snapped to A1 who throws a touchdown pass to A2. **RULING:** Unsportsmanlike conduct prior to snap. The ball should be declared dead and the foul enforced as a dead-ball foul.

 9.10.1 COMMENT: Football has been and always will be a game of deception and trickery involving multiple shifts, unusual formations and creative plays. However, actions or verbiage designed to confuse the defense into believing there is problem and a snap isn't imminent is beyond the scope of sportsmanship and is illegal.

Coin Toss

A captain of a team is a player designated to represent his team during the pregame and overtime coin toss (Limit of four captains in game uniform) (2-32-5a); the selection of second half options (2-32-5b), penalty decisions following a foul (2-32-5b) and ball placement on a try, a kickoff, after a safety, after a fair catch or awarded fair catch, after a touchback and to start an overtime (2-32-5c). Each team shall designate a player as field captain and only he may communicate with game officials (1-4-1). At the coin toss or simulated coin toss conducted three minutes prior to the scheduled starting time on the field of play as in 3-2-1, not more than four team members in game uniform (captains) from each team may be present at the coin toss and only one from each team shall be designated as its spokesperson. All other team members in game uniform must remain outside the field of play unless required to be present at the coin toss per state association policies (3-2-2).

Before the scheduled game starting time, the referee, in the presence of the field captains, shall instruct the visiting captain to give a "heads" or "tails" choice before the coin toss. If the coin toss, or simulated coin toss, is held on the playing field, it shall be held three minutes prior to the scheduled game starting time, or as otherwise specified by individual state associations (3-2-1).

The winner of the toss shall have first choice of options for the first half or to defer and have first choice for the second half. The loser shall have the first choice of options for the half the winner of the toss did not select. The options for each half shall be to choose whether his team will kick or receive or to choose the goal his team will defend. The team not having the first choice of options for a half shall exercise the remaining option (3-2-3).

When the score is tied at the end of the fourth period and the NFHS-Recommended Resolving Tied Games Procedure is to be used, the referee will conduct the coin toss in the center of the field. the visiting-team's captain shall be given the privilege of choosing "heads" or "tails" before the coin is tossed. The winner of the toss shall be given his choice of defense or offense first, or of designating the end of the field at which the ball will be put in play for this set of downs. The loser will have his choice of the other options. The referee will indicate the winner of the toss by placing a hand on his shoulder. To indicate which team will go on offense, the referee will have that captain face the goal toward which his team will advance and indicate this with the first-down signal. The other team captain will face the offensive captain with his back toward the goal he will defend (Resolving Tied Games Procedure 3-2-1).

Duties of the Umpire

Prior to the start of the game, the head coach shall be responsible for verifying to the umpire and referee that all of his players are legally equipped and in compliance with the rules. Any questions regarding legality of a player's equipment shall be resolved by the umpire (1-5-4).

The following auxiliary equipment may be worn if sanctioned by the umpire as being made of soft, nonabrasive, nonhardening material:

• Forearm pads, which may be anchored on each end with athletic tape (1-5-2a).

• Gloves, which may be anchored with athletic tape, and even though modified, must meet the NOCSAE test standard at the time of manufacture, unless made of unaltered plain cloth. Gloves, unless made of unaltered plain cloth, must have a permanent, exact replica of the NOCSAE glove seal (Meets NOCSAE Standard), that must be visible and appear legibly on the exterior wrist opening of the glove (1-5-2b).

• Tape, bandage or support wrap on the hand or forearm to protect an existing injury (1-5-2c).

No player shall participate while wearing illegal equipment. This applies to any equipment, which in the opinion of the umpire is dangerous, confusing or inappropriate (1-5-3).

If the score is tied at the end of the fourth period and the NFHS-Recommended Resolving Tied Games Procedure is to be used, there will be a three-minute intermission during which both teams may confer with their coaches. All game officials will assemble at the 50-yard line, review the Resolving Tied Games Procedure, determine the number of the second half time-outs remaining for each team, and discuss how penalties, if any, including any carry-over penalties from the regulation contest will be assessed to start the Resolving Tied Games Procedure Resolving Tied Games Procedure 3-1, 8-3-5, 6).

Duties of the Umpire: Case Plays

*1.5.2 SITUATION A: During the pregame conference, the home team's coach informs the umpire that all players' football gloves are new but none of the gloves have the required NOCSAE or SFIA label/stamp indicating compliance with the NOCSAE test standard or the SFIA Specification. **RULING:** The gloves may not be worn; all gloves must have the required NOCSAE or SFIA label/stamp.

*1.5.3 SITUATION C: Prior to the game, the coach of B requests the umpire to examine a cast/splint on the forearm of a player. The protective item has "hard" material, but is padded with at least ½-inchthick, closed-cell, slow-recovery foam padding. The coach: (a) provides; or (b) does not provide to the umpire prior to the start of the game, a written author ization from a licensed medical physician directing the use of the cast/splint as necessary to protect an injury. **RULING:** In (a) and (b), the cast/splint may be worn during the game. Written authorization is no longer required but the umpire must ensure the cast/split is properly padded (1-5-3b(1)).

1.5.3 SITUATION D: During the pregame visit with the head coach of A, the umpire notices that some squad members have eyeshields which are: (a) dark, or (b) clear with no tint. The head coach of A has a letter from a physician indicating that the dark shield is a necessity for the player. **RULING:** In (a), the umpire indicates to the head coach only eyeshields which are clear without the presence of any tint may be worn, a physician's statement cannot supersede this rule without expressed written consent of the state association. In (b), the eyeshield is legal if, in addition to being clear, it is also molded and rigid, and securely attached to the helmet (1-5-3c(4)).

Duties of the Head Linesman and Line Judge

If the score is tied at the end of the fourth period and the NFHS-Recommended Resolving Tied Games Procedure is to be used, there will be a three-minute intermission during which both teams may confer with their coaches. All game officials will assemble at the 50-yard line, review the Resolving Tied Games Procedure, determine the number of the second half time-outs remaining for each team, and discuss how penalties, if any, including any carry-over penalties from the regulation contest will be assessed to start the Resolving Tied Games Procedure. At the end of the intermission, the head linesman will go to the team on the side of the field where the line to gain equipment is located and the line judge will go to the other team. They will inform the coaches of the number of time-outs each team has remaining and any special penalty enforcements that apply (Resolving Tied Games Procedure 3-1, 8-3-5, 6).

Topic:
Game Officials' Authority

The game officials shall have the authority to make decisions for infractions of the rules (1-1-9). The game officials shall assume authority for the contest, including penalizing unsportsmanlike acts, 30 minutes prior to the scheduled game time — an earlier time if requried by the state association — or as soon thereafter as they are able to be present (1-1-7).

The game officials' authority extends through the referee's declaration of the end of the fourth period or overtime. The game officials retain clerical authority over the game through the completion of any reports, including those imposing disqualifications, that are responsive to actions occurring while the game officials had authority. State Associations may intercede in the event of unusual incidents that occur before, during or after the game officials' authority has ended or in the event that a game is terminated prior to the conclusion of regulation play (1-1-8).

◪ Rationale

By specifying a time for the start of game officials' authority, the NFHS empowers game officials to penalize unsportsmanlike acts that occur before the game.

Game Officials' Authority: Case Plays

1.1.7 SITUATION: With 35:00 on the countdown clock, individuals on the field for pregame warm-up engage in unsportsmanlike behavior. The state association rule is that game officials: (a) assume authority 30 minutes before the game; (b) assume authority 45 minutes before the game; or (c) authority prior to the game is not addressed in state association rules. **RULING:** In (a) and (c), there is no foul as this is a game administration issue and not one under authority of the game officials. In (b), the unsportsmanlike conduct fouls would be assessed prior to the kickoff, and should be explained thoroughly by the referee prior to the coin toss options being given.

1.1.8 SITUATION A: A fight occurs toward the end of a game and the game has been terminated early. In (a) game officials identify the players in the altercation on the field immediately and report the numbers to head coaches of both teams; in (b) game officials meet in the locker room to reconcile and agree on information and record the player numbers who were involved in the altercation. **RULING:** In (a) and (b), this is correct procedure. Game officials must then adhere to state association policy with regard to the filing of post-game reports.

1.1.8 SITUATION B: A fight occurs during or at the immediate end of the game and game officials record the known player numbers who were involved in the altercation. After the game, the state association requests a copy of the game film and in accordance with adopted state association procedures, determines addi tional players were involved and revises the numbers and names of the players involved and issues final rulings. **RULING:** This is correct procedure.

1.1.8 SITUATION C: Immediately following the contest, the coach of Team A curses the game officials as they are leaving the field and prior to their return to their dressing room. This occurs: (a) before; or (b) after the referee has declared the end of the contest with the proper signal. **RULING:** In either situation, this is an unsportsmanlike act. Fouls such as this foul will not involve a distance penalty as the game has ended for the purpose of on-field play, but unsportsmanlike acts such as this remain under the authority of the game officials for the purpose of filing necessary reports regarding unsporting acts. Incidents such as this shall be reported to the home school state association in accordance with adopted procedures.

1.2.3 SITUATION: The game officials inspect the playing field as a part of their pregame routine and determine that (a) the game field does not have the required markings such as a restraining line marked at all on the field from the sidelines and end lines or contains commercial logo art that obstructs the yard lines; or (b) the 3-yard line that is marked on the game field for the try is only 12 inches in length. **RULING:** In both (a) and (b), the field markings are not legal by rule, but the game will be played. In (a), a 4-inch-wide restraining line shall be placed around the outside of the field, at least 2 yards from the sidelines and end lines, as an extension of the line limiting the team box area, except in stadiums where the total playing enclosure does not permit. In (b), a line 4 inches wide and a minimum of 24 inches in length shall be centered in the field of play, 3 yards from each goal line.

1.2.3 COMMENT: The game officials shall notify game management and the football administrator in their respective state association office to let them know that the football game field at this school was not properly marked as stated by NFHS football rules (1-2-3d; 1-2-3k; 1-2-3l).

*3.1.1 SITUATION C: Upon returning to the field near the end of the normal 15-minute halftime intermission, the game officials notice one team standing quietly in front of its bench during the entire three minutes posted for warm-up. The game officials: (a) start the game as soon as the three minutes have elapsed, or (b) inform the coach of that team that the team must actively warm up by running or doing some kind of exercises. **RULING:** The game officials are correct in (a), but in error in (b). The rules book contains no definition of what constitutes a warm-up. It simply requires that an opportunity to warm up be made available.

*3.3.5 SITUATION A: A trails by three points in the fourth period with the ball on B's 20, fourth and 10 and two seconds on the clock. A1 throws an incomplete pass into B's end zone with time expired. The referee quickly glances to each sideline and then begins to leave the field. After the referee crosses the sideline, the referee hears the line judge blowing his whistle. The line judge explains that B1 committed pass interference during the down in which time expired. **RULING:** The game is not officially over even though the referee left the field. Since a foul had been called, the referee will give A a chance to accept the penalty and extend the period with an untimed down from B's 10-yard line.

3.3.5 COMMENT: The game is officially over when the referee holds the ball overhead and leaves the field. Before doing this however, he should pause briefly and glance to both sidelines and make sure there are no fouls, no obvious timing error, no request for a coach-referee conference, etc.

Supplementary Equipment

The use of any replay or television monitoring equipment by the game officials in making any decision relating to the game is prohibited (1-1-9).

Supplementary equipment to aid in game administration may be used if authorized by the state association (1-3-7).

Supplementary Equipment: Case Plays

1.1.8 SITUATION: A1 advances the ball to near B's goal line where several B players try to prevent the score. The covering official rules a touchdown. Sideline replay equipment clearly shows: (a) A1 fumbled the ball at B's 1-yard line; or (b) A1 stepped out of bounds on B's 2-yard line; or (c) A2 was illegally in motion at the snap. **RULING:** The touchdown is scored in all cases. Video monitoring or replay equipment shall not be used by game officials to make any decision relating to the game.

1.3.7 SITUATION: The game officials are advised by the home-team management that supplementary equipment such as: (a) a ball-spotting device; (b) a ball-tracking device; or (c) a 25-second clock will be used during the game. **RULING:** None of the supplementary devices as described may be used unless the state association has given specific authorization.

1.3.7 COMMENT: If responsibility for such supplementary equipment (such as the 25-second clock) is given to a non-official, the operator must be capable and approved.

Topic:
Officials' Time-Out

An official's time-out shall be declared to permit prompt repair of equipment which becomes illegal or defective through use (1-5-5, 3-5-7f).

An official's time-out occurs during a dead ball without a time-out being charged to either team for measurement of a possible first down; when a first down is declared; following a change of team possession; when captains and coaches are notified of the time remaining; for a player who appears to be injured; for a player in need of equipment repair; to dry or change the game ball; for unusual heat or humidity which may create a health risk to the players; when a coach-referee conference concerning the misapplication of a rule results in the referee altering his ruling; after a foul, to administer the penalty; for any unusual delay in getting the ball marked ready for play; for a TV/radio time-out that is permitted and granted as authorized by state association policy; for a one-minute intermission between the first and second and the third and fourth periods and following a try, successful field goal or safety and prior to the succeeding free kick (1-5-5, 3-5-7).

An authorized conference may be held during a charged time-out (3-5-8a 1); an official's time-out for unusual heat or humidity (3-5-8a 2, 3-5-7g); for a TV/radio time-out (3-5-8a 3, 3-5-7k); for the one-minute intermission between quarters or after a score and preceding the free kick (3-5-8a 2, 3-5-7l); or if granted by the referee when a player must be replaced due to injury (3-5-8a 3, 3-5-10).

Unless the clock is already stopped, an official's time-out shall be taken as soon as the ball becomes dead following a change of team possession or whenever the covering official declares the ball dead, and it appears to him the ball has reached the line to gain (3-5-9).

Officials' Time-Out: Case Plays

*3.5.2 SITUATION A: The captain of A requests a time-out and informs the referee that the coach wishes to have a conference concerning the previous play. During the conference: (a) the captain or all A players go near the sideline to confer with their coaches, or (b) the coach of B goes on the field to the team's huddle to confer. **RULING:** Permissible in both (a) and (b). The time-out, when granted, is charged to A, thus legalizing the conferences. If a game official has erred and a correction is made, the conference in both (a) and (b) is terminated. In that case, the time-out is not charged to A, but is an official's time-out. If the coach is in error, the time-out remains charged to A (2-6; 3-5-2c).

3.5.8 SITUATION A: During a charged time-out, an official's time-out for heat/humidity, a TV/radio time-out, or the intermission between the first and second or the third and fourth periods, or following a try: (a) team members of A confer with their head coach in front of the team box near the sideline; or (b) the coach of B goes to the huddle of B between the 9-yard marks, and talks to an assistant via a headset he brought to the huddle; or (c) the coach of B goes on the field and uses the time to berate and loudly question the referee regarding a previous play; or (d) the coach wishes to discuss the previous play with the referee; or (e) the head coach of A goes to the team huddle on the field for 30 seconds and then comes out and another coach takes his place for the rest of the time-out. **RULING:** It is a legal conference in (a) and (b). In (a), the players may use the headsets. In (b), the players may not use the headsets. In (c) and (e), it is illegal. In (d), this conference must be held at the sideline in front of the team box regardless of which authorized conference procedure is used (2-6-2; 9-8-1c; 9-8-1i).

3.5.11 SITUATION B: Following a fourth-down incomplete forward pass late in the fourth period, a time-out is properly requested for a coach-referee conference regarding possible misapplication of a rule. (a) The coach of B questions a pass interference call on B1 during a second forward pass by A1; or (b) the coach of A questions why no pass interference by the defense was called and why the covering official inappropriately signaled that the pass was not catchable. In either case the referee determines the coach was correct and an incorrect ruling and inappropriate signal had been applied. **RULING:** In (a), the penalty marker is picked up. In (b), a penalty marker may be dropped and the pass interference penalized. Misapplication of a rule or an incorrect signal may result in picking up a flag or dropping a marker to indicate a foul did occur and giving the appropriate signal.

9.6.4 SITUATION D: A1 is injured and is treated on the field. A subsequently requests a time-out. During the next down, A1 runs 20 yards for the go-ahead score. Following the score, B requests a time-out so the coach may discuss A1's participation with the referee. **RULING:** A rule obviously has not been correctly applied as A1 must leave the game for at least one down following his injury. The touchdown is canceled and a penalty for illegal participation is enforced. A1 must leave the game for at least one down (3-5-10).

Topic 9

Nine-, Eight-, and Six- Player Rule Differences

PlayPic®

Preface

When "11 players" is used in the NFHS football rules book it should be understood 11 would be replaced with the number of players participating (nine, eight, six).

Topic:
Nine-Player

RULE 1: Each team has nine players. The field is 80 yards between goal lines and 40 yards wide with 48 feet 4 inches side zones. 7-yard marks, 12 inches in length and 4 inches in width, shall be located 7 yards from each sideline. The 7-yard marks shall be marked so that at least each 10-yard line bisects the 7-yard marks. These marks shall not be required if the field is visibly numbered. If on-the-field numbers are used, the tops of those numbers shall be 7 yards from the sideline. By state association adoption, the 11- player field may be designated as official, and the dimensions of the field may be altered.

RULE 2: The free-blocking zone is a square area extending laterally 3 yards either side of the spot of the snap and 3 yards behind each line of scrimmage.

RULE 2: The Outside 9-Yard Mark and Between 9-Yard Mark Conferences shall be held outside or between the 7-yard marks, respectively.

RULE 6: K's free-kick line is its 30-yard line and R's free-kick line is the 40. K is required to have at least three players on each side of the kicker.

RULE 7: a. At least five A players shall be on the line at the snap and may have any legal jersey number. b. After the ball is marked ready for play, each player of A who participated in the previous down, and each substitute for A must have been, momentarily, between the 7-yard marks, before the snap. c. Each A player (regardless of jersey number) who at the snap was on the end of the scrimmage line (total of two) and each A player who was at the snap was legally behind the scrimmage line (possible total of four) is eligible. There are no numbering requirements.

RULE 10: The basic spot for a foul as in 10-4-6 shall be the 15-yard line.

Topic:
Eight-Player

GENERAL: Eleven-player rules are used for eight-player football with the following modifications.

RULE 1: Each team has 8 players. The field is 80 yards between goal lines and 40 yards wide with 15-yard side zones. 7-yard marks, 12 inches in length and 4 inches in width, shall be located 7 yards from each sideline. The 7-yard marks shall be marked so that at least each 10-yard line bisects the 7-yard marks. These marks shall not be required if the field is visibly numbered. If on-the-field numbers are used, the tops of those numbers shall be 7 yards from the sideline. By state association adoption, the 11-player field may be designated as official, and the dimensions of the field may be altered.

RULE 2: The free-blocking zone is a square area extending laterally 3 yards either side of the spot of the snap and 3 yards behind each line of scrimmage.

RULE 2: The Outside 9-Yard Mark and Between 9-Yard Mark Conferences shall be held outside or between the 7-yard marks, respectively.

RULE 6: K's free-kick line is its 30-yard line and R's free-kick line is the 40. K is required to have at least three players on each side of the kicker.

RULE 7: b. After the ball is marked ready for play, each player of A who participated in the previous down, and each substitute for A must have been, momentarily, between the 7-yard marks, before the snap. c. Each A player (regardless of jersey number) who at the snap was on an end of the scrimmage line (total of two) and each A player who at the snap was legally behind the scrimmage line (possible total of three) is eligible.

RULE 8: On the eight-player field, the ball is snapped after a touchback and is free kicked after a safety from the 15-yard line.

RULE 10: The basic spot for a foul as in 10-4-6 shall be the 15-yard line.

Topic:
Six-Player

GENERAL: Most six-player football rules are the same as for the 11-player game.

RULES 1 and 2: Offense must advance 15 yards instead of 10 in four downs.

RULE 1: Each team has 6 players. The field is 80 yards between goal lines and 40 yards wide with 15- yard side zones. 7-yard marks, 12 inches in length and 4 inches in width, shall be located 7 yards from each sideline. The 7-yard marks shall be marked so that at least each 10-yard line bisects the 7-yard marks. These marks shall not be required if the field is visibly numbered. If on-the-field numbers are used, the tops of those numbers shall be 7 yards from the sideline. By state association adoption, the 11-player field may be designated as official, and the dimensions of the field may be altered.

RULE 2: The free-blocking zone is a square area extending laterally 3 yards either side of the spot of the snap and 3 yards behind each line of scrimmage.

RULE 2: The Outside 9-Yard Mark and Between 9-Yard Mark Conferences shall be held outside or between the 7-yard marks, respectively.

RULES 2 and 7: Unless the ball is kicked or forward passed, it may not be advanced across the line of scrimmage until after a direct handoff or clear pass has been made by the snap receiver (If a violation occurs, ball is returned to previous spot and the down counts). If a forward pass is thrown to the snapper, it must travel at least 1 yard in flight.

RULE 3: Length of quarters —10 minutes; between quarters —2 minutes; between halves —15 minutes.

RULE 6: K's free-kick line is its 30-yard line and R's free-kick line is the 40. K is required to have at least two players on each side of the kicker.

RULE 7: At least three A players shall be on their line of scrimmage at the snap and may have any legal jersey number.

RULE 7: a. After the ball is marked ready for play, each player of A who participated in the previous
down, and each substitute for A must have been, momentarily, between the 7-yard marks, before the snap. b. Ball may be handed in any direction during a kickoff down and during a scrimmage down after a direct handoff, clear pass, a legal forward pass or kick has been made.

c. If a fumble occurs before there has been a direct handoff or clear pass and if a player of A recovers it, he may not carry it beyond the line. d. When a passer catches his own pass it is ruled as incomplete unless it was touched by any B player. e. All players are eligible to catch a forward pass, except that a pass is ruled incomplete when caught by the passer (7-5-4).

RULE 8: a. Field goal counts 4 points. Try for point 2 points if successful through place or drop kick and 1 point if successful by pass or scrimmage. b. On the six-player field, the ball is snapped after a touchback and is free kicked after a safety from the 15-yard line.

RULE 10: a. If B fouls during a successful kick try, the penalty is automatically enforced from the succeeding spot. b. The basic spot for a foul as in 10-4-6 shall be the 15-yard line.

Nine-, Eight-, and Six-Player: Case Play

10.4.6 SITUATION A: B1 intercepts A1's pass in B's end zone where B1 is grabbed by the face mask by A2 who twists the mask. B1 then fumbles while in the end zone and (a) the ball rolls back into the field of play and then goes out of bounds at B's 2-yard line; (b) the ball rolls back into the field of play where B7 recovers the ball at B's 5-yard line. **RULING:** In both (a) and (b), the basic spot is the 20-yard line (15-yard line in 6, 8 and 9 player) and the accepted penalty will result in a first down for Team B at its 35-yard line.

OFFICIAL FOOTBALL SIGNALS

1 Ball ready for play *Untimed down	2 Start clock	3 Time-out Discretionary or injury time-out (followed by tapping hands on chest)
4 TV/radio time-out	5 Touchdown, Field goal, Point(s) after touchdown	6 Safety	7 Dead ball foul, Touchback (move side to side)
8 First down	9 Loss of down	10 Incomplete forward pass Penalty declined No play, no score Toss option deferred	11 Legal touching of forward pass or scrimmage kick	12 Inadvertent whistle
13 Disregard flag	14 End of period	15 Sideline warning	16 First touching Illegal touching
18 Encroachment	19 False start Illegal formation	20 Illegal shift (2 hands) Illegal motion (1 hand)	21 Delay of game	22 Substitution infraction

23 Failure to wear required equipment

24 Illegal helmet contact Targeting

25 Illegal horse-collar tackle

27 Unsportsmanlike conduct Noncontact foul

28 Illegal participation

29 Sideline interference (Face press box)

30 Running into or Roughing kicker or holder

31 Illegal batting/kicking (Followed by pointing toward toe for kicking)

32 Invalid fair catch Illegal fair catch signal

33 Forward pass interference Kick catching interference

34 Roughing passer

35 Illegal pass/forward handing (Face press box)

36 Intentional grounding

37 Ineligible downfield on pass

38 Personal foul

39 Clipping

40 Blocking below waist

41 Chop block

42 Holding/obstruction Illegal use of hands/arms

43 Illegal block

44 Helping runner Interlocked blocking

45 Grasping face mask or helmet opening

46 Tripping

47 Disqualification

 PlayPic® PlayPics courtesy of **REFEREE** Note: Signal numbers 17 and 26 is for future expansion.

RECOMMENDED CREW COMMUNICATION SIGNALS

PlayPic®

Double stakes	11 players	Snapper protection	Unbalanced line
	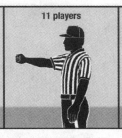		
Indicates that more than ten yards to go before first down, to prevent accidental stopping of clock.	Fist extended straight out with elbow not bent and the thumb up in fist, indication of 11 players in game when counting complete.	Indicates to each other (R and U) that this play requires protection for snapper in accordance with rules.	Hand on cheek, indicating unbalanced line to trigger all to look for ineligibles and umpire to check numbering. Also used for indicating two or more players or no players outside the tackle on the line of scrimmage.

PlayPic®

Last play was out of bounds	Backward pass	Play ends inbounds	Five second count

Start clock on snap.	Given by R unless immediately thrown after snap in which case wing has crew option to signal. NO signal if forward. Also, same signal by wing officials to indicate player nearest wing official is off the line of scrimmage.	Start clock on ready.	Visible count by R (Four-Game Officials Crew) and BJ (Five-Game Officials Crew), of the last five seconds when on-field 25-second clocks are not utilized.

Penalty Summary

LOSS OF 5 YARDS   SIGNAL

Failure to properly wear mandatory player equipment
during down 27-23
Delay of game 7-21
Failure to properly wear mandatory player equipment
just before snap 7-21-23
Illegal substitution 22
Free-kick infraction 7-19
Encroachment 7-18
Free kick out of bounds 19
Invalid or illegal fair-catch signal 32
Snap infraction 7-19
False start 7-19
Illegal formation 19
Less than seven players on A's line or numbering violation 19
Illegal shift or illegal motion 20
Planned loose-ball infraction 19
Illegally handing ball forward (also loss of down) 35-9
Illegal forward pass (by A) (also loss of down) 35-9
Illegal forward pass (by B) 35
Intentional grounding (also loss of down) 36-9
Ineligible receiver illegally downfield 37
Illegal touching (also loss of down) 16
Helping runner 44
Incidental grasping of face mask (or any helmet opening, chin strap, or
attached tooth and mouth protector) 45
Running into kicker/holder 30
Sideline interference 7-29
Attendant illegally on field 19
Nonplayer outside of the team box, but not on field 7-29

LOSS OF 10 YARDS   SIGNAL

Illegal blocking technique 42
Interlocked blocking 44
Holding 42
Runner grasping a teammate 42
Illegal use of hands or arms 42
Illegal block in the back 43
Illegal block on free kick 43

LOSS OF 15 YARDS SIGNAL

Unsportsmanlike conduct by player or nonplayer................. 27
Illegally kicking or batting ball 31
Illegal block after valid or invalid fair-catch signal 40
Kick-catching interference 33
Forward-pass interference 33
　If intentional an additional 15 yards 27
Illegal block below waist or on free-kicker or holder............... 40
Clipping.. 39
Chop block 41
Tripping.. 46
Illegal personal contact outside restricted area 38
Charging into an opponent obviously out of the play.............. 38
Grasping opponent's face mask (or any helmet opening,
or chin strap, or attached tooth and mouth protector)............38-45
Butt block, face tackle or spear (illegal helmet contact) 24
Horse-collar...38-25
Roughing passer (also first down)...........................34-8
Roughing kicker or holder (also first down) 38-30-8
Roughing snapper (also first down) 38-8
Slapping blocker's head 38
Illegal participation 28
Sideline interference (third and subsequent)................... 7-29-27
Nonplayer illegally on field 27
Unfair acts... 27
Illegal personal contact in restricted area.......................38-29
Initiate contact with a helmet-less opponent...................... 38
Participation without a helmet beyond immediate action........... 28
Contact against a defenseless player............................. 24
Targeting an opponent 38-24

DISQUALIFICATION ASSOCIATED WITH CERTAIN
15-YARD PENALTIES SIGNAL

Fighting by player or nonplayer 38-47
Intentionally contacting a game official 38-47
Striking, kicking, kneeing....................................38-47
Any act if unduly rough or flagrant
(give proper signal and follow with 47)......................... 47
A second unsportsmanlike foul by player or nonplayer 27-47
A substitute leaving team box during a fight 27-47

NFHS PUBLICATIONS
Prices effective April 1, 2016 — March 31, 2017

RULES PUBLICATIONS

Baseball Rules Book $8.20
Baseball Case Book....................................$8.20
Baseball Umpires Manual (2017 & 2018)...$8.20
Baseball Simplified & Illustrated Rules $8.95
Baseball Rules by Topic $8.95
Basketball Rules Book $8.20
Basketball Case Book.................................$8.20
Basketball Simplified & Illustrated Rules $8.95
Basketball Officials Manual (2015-17) $8.20
Basketball Handbook (2016-18) $8.20
Basketball Rules by Topic $8.95
Field Hockey Rules Book............................$8.20
Football Rules Book...................................$8.20
Football Case Book $8.20
Football Simplified & Illustrated Rules.......$8.95
Football Handbook (2015 & 2016).............$8.20
Football Game Officials Manual
  (2016 & 2017) $8.20
Football Rules by Topic..............................$8.95

Girls Gymnastics Rules Book & Manual
  (2016-18) $8.20
Ice Hockey Rules Book $8.20
Boys Lacrosse Rules Book $8.20
Girls Lacrosse Rules Book..........................$8.20
Soccer Rules Book.....................................$8.20
Softball Rules Book $8.20
Softball Case Book.....................................$8.20
Softball Umpires Manual (2016 & 2017) $8.20
Spirit Rules Book $8.20
Swimming & Diving Rules Book.................$8.20
Track & Field Rules Book $8.20
Track & Field Case Book $8.20
Track & Field Manual (2017 & 2018) $8.20
Volleyball Rules Book $8.20
Volleyball Case Book & Manual $8.20
Water Polo Rules Book $8.20
Wrestling Rules Book $8.20
Wrestling Case Book & Manual $8.20

MISCELLANEOUS ITEMS

NFHS Statisticians' Manual...$7.00
Scorebooks: Baseball-Softball, Basketball, Swimming & Diving, Cross Country, Soccer,
  Track & Field, Gymnastics, Volleyball, Wrestling and Field Hockey $11.50
Diving Scoresheets (pad of 100) $7.25
Volleyball Team Rosters & Lineup Sheets (pads of 100) $7.25
Libero Tracking Sheet (pads of 50) $7.25
Baseball/Softball Lineup Sheets – 3-Part NCR (sets/100) $8.75
Wrestling Tournament Match Cards (sets/100)..$7.25
Flipping Coin $6.00
NFHS Pin...$4.00
Competitors Numbers (Track and Gymnastics – Waterproof, nontearable, black numbers
  and six colors of backgrounds Numbers are 1-1000 sold in sets of 100.........................$15.00/set
Lane Numbers (1-8), size 4" x 2 1/2" $7.25/set

MISCELLANEOUS SPORTS ITEMS

Court and Field Diagram Guide $21.50
NFHS Handbook (2016-17)..................$10.00
Let's Make It Official..............................$5.00
Sports Medicine Handbook.................$19.95

Sportsmanship. It's Up to You. Toolkit .$19.95
High School Activities – A Community
  Investment in America $39.95

2016-17 NFHS ORDER BLANK

Name: _____ Phone: _____

School and/or Organization: _____

Address: _____

_____
City   State   Zip

(No PO Boxes. If charging order to a credit card please use address on card.)
If address has changed in the last year please fill in old address.

_____
Street   City   State   Zip

Check one of the following: ☐ Visa   ☐ MasterCard

Account No. _____-_____-_____-_____ Exp. Date: _____

Signature: _____

P.O. # _____ (Order totals $25 or more)
             (attach P.O.)

Item#	Description	Unit Quantity	Price	Total

Subtotal: _____

SHIPPING & HANDLING CHARGES: If your subtotal is:

$0.00 to $25.00 ....add **$8.35**	$135.01 to $175.00 ....add **$24.10**
$25.01 to $40.00 ....add **$10.45**	$175.01 to $250.00 ....add **$27.25**
$40.01 to $55.00 ....add **$12.55**	$250.01 to $500.00 ....add **$30.40**
$55.01 to $75.00 ....add **$17.80**	$500.01 – UP, add **6%** of
$75.01 to $95.00 ....add **$19.90**	merchandise total
$95.01 to $135.00 ....add **$22.00**	

Second Day = Standard shipping charges plus **$15.00**
Overnight = Standard shipping charges plus **$25.00**
All shipments to Alaska, Hawaii, Virgin Islands and Canada add **$10.00**
Call for charges outside continental U.S. Payment must be in U.S. dollars.

Shipping & Handling Charge: _____

TOTAL _____

Send to: NFHS Customer Service
PO Box 361246,
Indianapolis, IN 46236-5324
Phone 800-776-3462,
Fax 317.899.7496 or
online at www.nfhs.com

ORDERING INFORMATION

PURCHASE ORDERS are welcomed but all orders under $25 must be prepaid. Purchase orders may be **either faxed or mailed** to our Customer Service office. If you mail a purchase order after it has been faxed to our Customer Service office, please show it as a **confirming order**. Terms net 30 days per invoice. All delinquent accounts are charged 1.5% finance charges. **PREPAID ORDERS** will be shipped upon receipt of completed order form accompanied by a check or money order. **All orders must include the proper amount for shipping and handling.**

*****SHIPMENTS OUTSIDE UNITED STATES OR CANADA:** Please write to NFHS headquarters for a quotation of total charges which will include a $2.00 surcharge and actual shipping charges. **Payment must be in U.S. dollars.** Please refer to www.nfhs.com to view our Return Policy.

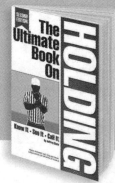
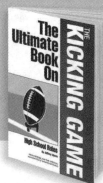